LATIN FOR THE 21ST CENTURY

From Concept to Classroom

Richard A. LaFleur
The University of Georgia

Scott Foresman - Addison W

D1637115

Editorial Offices: Glenview, Illinois • Menlo Park, California
Sales Offices: Reading, Massachusetts • Atlanta, Georgia • Glenview, Illinois
Carrollton, Texas • Menlo Park, California

http://www.sf.aw.com

ISBN: 0–673–57608–6

http://www.sf.aw.com

5 6 7 3 9 10-EB-06 05 04

Contents

APPROACHES TO HIGH-SCHOOL LATIN

ARTICULATION AND APPROACHES TO COLLEGE LATIN

GRADUATE EDUCATION AND TEACHER TRAINING

SPECIAL ISSUES, SPECIAL RESPONSES

CORNUCOPIA: RESOURCES FOR TEACHING LATIN

"A teacher affects eternity; he can never tell where his influence stops."

Henry Brooks Adams, *The Education of Henry Adams*

Preface

This book is addressed to a wide audience of people who have ties to Latin: teachers of Latin at all levels from elementary school through graduate programs, prospective teachers of Latin, trainers of teachers—both pre-service and in-service, language curriculum specialists at state and local levels, and many other administrators who need information found in this volume in order to make more informed decisions about Latin in their schools. Most of these people will undoubtedly say "finally!" when they get their hands on the book, since no single resource of this kind has been available to our profession for many years.

Seldom, in fact, has a professional field had a greater need for such a text. We have over 10,000 people already teaching Latin in our schools and colleges, and each year many others begin their teaching, but we have had no common textbook on the *ars docendi*. We have a vast array of recent and new teaching and resource materials, but some of these remain unknown or underutilized, or possibly even misunderstood, by many teachers and professors. We have information on new methods and new applications of technology but have not gotten the word to a wide enough audience. *Latin for the 21st Century* will help thousands of teachers respond even more successfully to the needs and interests of the hundreds of thousands of Latin students in our schools and colleges and will provide valuable information to parents, administrators, and other friends of Latin in our educational system.

I personally am especially grateful for the timing of this book: I announced at the beginning of my second term as President of the American Classical League that of all the needs in the profession, I saw none greater than to improve both the quantity and the quality of Latin teacher training in North America. *Latin for the 21st Century* will contribute greatly to this effort, for it will be the primary resource book for every college professor in North America, whether in Classics or Education, who has any role whatsoever in recruiting, counseling, or training Latin teachers for the schools. It will also be the primary textbook for the teaching candidates for the schools. And it will be invaluable for teachers already in the field, both neophytes and veterans, who are striving to become even more effective in the classroom.

The contributors to this book are a true all-star team: they know well the history as well as the current opportunities of the profession as a whole; they understand the pressures and needs and opportunities of individual Latin teachers at all levels; they know materials and methods and technologies, and can skillfully apply what they know; and, most important, they understand the wide range of student needs and interests that we must learn to respond to with greater effectiveness. Moreover, after we have read what is in this book and have looked at the references each contributor has provided, we have a bonus awaiting us: we also can contact them personally to learn even more (via the addresses provided in the Author Biographies at the end of the book). Thank you, contributors, for what you have already done, and for the further services you will render as we continue to draw upon your expertise.

Finally, it is to Prof. Richard LaFleur, the editor of *Latin for the 21st Century*, that the profession is especially indebted. We are fortunate that it is he who has brought this book to reality, for he brings to the volume all the right insights and expertise: he has a long and distinguished record of working to improve teacher training through national and University of Georgia-based projects; he served as President of the American Classical League 1984–86 and has been chair of one of the nation's leading Classics departments since 1980; he is an outstanding educator with numerous state, regional, and national teaching and service awards; he has provided us with a number of valuable books for use in our Latin classes; he has carefully monitored the needs and interests of the profession in his role as editor of the *Classical Outlook* since 1979; and he has always been a good listener. He knows what the profession needs, both conceptually and practically, and has provided it in *Latin for the 21st Century: From Concept to Classroom*.

GLENN M. KNUDSVIG
The University of Michigan

Introduction

RICHARD A. LAFLEUR
University of Georgia

"We teach as we were taught"—and the rest we learn the hard way. Certainly that's how a great deal of my own early teaching developed. And of course that's not all bad: I had some wonderful instruction along the way (may I mention my high-school Latin teacher Gladys Giddens and my dear mentor and professor Arthur Stocker at the University of Virginia?), else I would most likely not have chosen the profession myself. And I learned much from my teachers, not only about Latin and Classics, but about how to present those subjects to students and, in the process, how (on the good days, at least) to inspire their interest. But two points are irrefutable: first, if we teach only as we were taught, we are certain both to be perpetuating old methods and to be shortchanging our students. There are countless new ideas and new resources available for the 21st-century Latin class, and we need to explore and exploit them. Second, we surely do learn both matter and manner by teaching—*discimus docendo*—and a certain amount of that trial-and-error, on-the-job training comes at a cost to ourselves and our students. How many of us *veterani veteranaeque*, in reflecting on our first years as teachers, have thought to ourselves, "If only I knew then what I know now, how much more effective might my teaching have been—and how much happier my students!"

PROFESSORS AND TEACHING ASSISTANTS

Teachers in the schools, of course, are generally better off in this regard than university professors. Most of them at least have had some training along the way in educational psychology and learning styles, classroom management, how to construct a proper test, and the uses of an overhead projector or the latest high-tech computer resources; moreover, schools tend to be far less conservative than colleges, and thus more willing to experiment with new ideas and methods (occasionally to their detriment, but more often, in the case of Latin teaching, to their credit). Lamentably, on the other hand, far too little has been done by way of preparing doctoral students formally for the responsibilities of teaching at the college level—almost nothing, in fact, until the late 1970s and the advent of "offices of instructional development" on university campuses.

Going, going, but not quite gone is the mistaken assumption that, if you know the subject, you know how to teach it. Even today the experience of my son at a "prestigious" state university is still too often repeated in academic departments across the country: having been appointed a graduate teaching assistant during the first semester of his M.A. work and given full responsibility for his own class of undergraduates (not in Classics, but *mutato nomine* . . .), his preparation consisted quite literally of his being handed the book and shown the classroom door. Though I expect he did a darned good job anyway, under the circumstances, there is no doubt that both my son and his students learned less than they might have, had his department, and the college of arts and sciences, taken an aggressive, or at least a reasonably responsible, role in training TAs and classroom instructors in general. In preparing teachers, universities must "see to the matter," to be sure, but they cannot assume that "the manner" will see to itself.

Fortunately, in Classics and in higher education generally, the situation is gradually improving, as can be seen from the chapters in this book by Mark Morford, Cynthia White, and Gilbert Lawall. Certainly the American Philological Association (APA), particularly via its Committee on Education and through greater collaboration with the American Classical League (ACL), has demonstrated since the 1980s an increasing interest in pedagogical matters—though far more can be done, and ought to be, to prepare graduate students and mentor new assistant professors for careers as effective college teachers. The imperative for action is all the more vital in light of growing public concern over the quality of undergraduate education in America and public, even legislative challenges to the priority given during the past generation to research and publication at the expense of teaching (I cringe at one of the most patent manifestations of this trend, the proliferation of mammoth freshman/sophomore humanities courses, with 100, 200, 300 or more students herded into cavernous lecture halls to be "told" what a poem means, rather than being asked). Research is indeed a crucial part of the professor's mission, and scholarly publication an obligation (even, on good days, a joy!)—but as in all else we need to heed Horace's call for keeping to "the golden mean."

PREPARING TEACHERS FOR K–12

By and large we have done a better job of training teachers for careers in K–12 schools than we have of preparing young professors. But even here our shortcomings have been considerable and our needs great. Most public-school English and math teachers are trained in departments of English education or mathematics education, generally with the collaboration of at least some of the faculty in the English and math departments in the college's or university's arts and sciences division. But how are we preparing our Latin teachers? Rare are the programs as comprehensive and discipline-based as that at the University of Massachusetts (described below in Chapter 19). Instead, teachers trained in a college or department of education often enroll in generic methodology courses (this is very often the case with K–8 teachers) or at best in foreign language methods courses that are focused primarily or exclusively on modern languages. While this latter scenario is not nearly as unfortunate as is sometimes assumed—we have much to learn from our modern language colleagues, not least the importance of a "four-skills" approach to language teaching—methods and materials specific to the Latin classroom are too often given little or no attention by the instructor in such a course, who rarely has any Latin background.

Frequently the Latin teacher's only training in the subject, and only discipline-specific preparation for teaching, takes place in the Classics department, in the college of arts and sciences rather than in the college of education. Well and good, many might say, especially arts and sciences faculty inclined to underrate colleagues in professional education with whom they rarely if ever have any discourse and of whose competencies they are often all but entirely unaware. Again the situation is not quite so desperate as that provocative remark might suggest: but the simple fact is that all of us interested in the quality of Latin instruction would benefit from greater dialogue between education and arts and sciences, between schools and colleges, and between classical and modern languages, a point further elaborated below in Sheila Dickison's chapter on articulation. In fact, classicists have generally proven to be a more collaborative lot than their counterparts in many other arts and sciences disciplines; like that other rental-car company, we are smaller and frequently do try harder, and we often work together, especially Classics professors and Latin teachers, remarkably well. Nevertheless, it is essential that faculty in Classics departments assume an even more active role in preparing effective teachers for the schools, not only by setting examples of good teaching, but also by keeping themselves current on pedagogical matters, providing classes and workshops for their students who are interested in teaching, maintaining textbook and instructional resource centers, and cooperating as fully as possible both with teachers in the schools and with colleagues in the modern languages and language education.

LATINA RESURGENS: THE RENAISSANCE OF LATIN

Since the late 1970s we have been enjoying a steady resurgence of interest and enrollments in Latin throughout the United States. After declining abruptly between the mid-60s and mid-70s, college Latin has grown and stabilized; high-school enrollments have increased nearly 25% over the past two decades; middle-school enrollments have tripled since the early 1980s; and the growth of interest in Latin in the elementary grades has been remarkable (see LaFleur

1997). There are now as many as half a million students enrolled in Latin classes at all levels in the United States, and at least 10,000 teachers, professors, and graduate assistants are teaching the language, while many others are preparing for new Latin teaching assignments in the schools and colleges. Both a cause and an effect of this renaissance has been the development of a rich array of lively and effective new basal textbooks, supplementary readers, audiovisuals, computer software programs, and other resources for the Latin classroom, much of it surveyed in this book. Traditional texts have been revised and improved; newer methodologies have been elaborated and refined. A variety of curriculum recommendations and guidelines for all levels have been formulated (notably in Sally Davis' *Latin in American Schools*), and most recently we have welcomed publication of the first national *Standards for Classical Language Learning*, a collaborative project of ACL, APA, and the major regional classical associations (detailed below in the chapter by Abbott, Davis, and Gascoyne). Special programs and scholarships for teachers of Latin and Classics abound, sponsored not only by these professional organizations but also by a host of colleges and universities and such groups and agencies as the National Endowment for the Humanities, the Council for Basic Education, the Fulbright Program, the American Academy in Rome, the American School of Classical Studies at Athens, the Vergilian Society, the Center for Hellenic Studies, and many others, all of them regularly announced in ACL's journal, the *Classical Outlook*, the *ACL Newsletter*, and the ACL Web site (umich.edu/ ~ acleague).

Thus, these are some of the best of times. Perhaps the worst predicament we face as a consequence is not so much a crisis as a challenge. The rise in Latin enrollments has not been matched by a proportionate increase in the number of certified Latin teachers for grades K-12. While the teacher shortage, alluded to earlier, is not as serious today as it was in the mid-1980s, when the renaissance of Latin was just gaining momentum, we clearly still do not have the number of well qualified teachers needed to meet the demand (LeaAnn Osburn's chapter demonstrates that this is particularly true of the middle schools, where interest in Latin is skyrocketing). Addressing the teacher shortage was the principal thrust of my ACL presidency during the mid-80s and of the book *The Teaching of Latin in American Schools: A Profession in Crisis*, and it has again been declared, here at the turn of the century and the millennium, a major objective of the League, as noted by Glenn Knudsvig (ACL President 1994–98) in his preface to this volume.

LATIN FOR THE 21ST CENTURY

As Prof. Knudsvig remarks in his preface, *Latin for the 21st Century: From Concept to Classroom*, the first comprehensive Latin methods and resource text to appear since the 1960s, is a book for everyone interested in the quality of Latin instruction in this country—whether teachers-in-training, neophytes, or veterans, foreign language coordinators or curriculum specialists, high-school principals or college Classics department heads, Classics graduate advisors, trainers of teaching assistants, elementary-school language arts specialists and FLES program directors, or middle-school foreign language exploratory program coordinators. For the administrators in this group, I would hope the volume contains a range of ideas helpful to program initiatives and curriculum and resource development.

But in particular this is a book for teachers, and for those who teach teachers, at all levels, from grade school to graduate seminar. My hope is that it will enable them to teach not solely as they were taught, and to learn new lessons not only "the hard way." If you are a teacher, make this little book your *vade mecum*: it will not tell you everything you need to know, but it will tell you a great deal and, via its bibliography and the various discussions and resource lists, it will point you in most of the right directions. And I hope, though the temptation may be to select one chapter or another in accordance with your specific interests or level of teaching, that you will read the volume *in toto*, for the global view of Latin pedagogy that it will provide. I myself have learned so much about the total range of methods and resources available to Latin teachers by observing and listening to my colleagues who instruct at different levels, and even those who teach other languages, that I can do nothing less than urge you to network, communicate, collaborate—and to use this book, for whatever help it may provide in establishing the common ground between your own teaching and that of your many colleagues throughout the profession.

Just as most of the individual chapters move from concept and context to detailed, hands-on classroom issues, the volume itself proceeds from the general to the specific. The initial chapters set the context for Latin teaching in the 21st century, tracing the development of pedagogical theory and practice from antiquity into the present (Kitchell), surveying the theoretical underpinnings of the methodologies most commonly employed over the past 30 years, the "grammar-translation" and "reading" approaches in particular (Sebesta), examining what we have learned, and need to learn, both from modern linguistics (Knudsvig and Ross) and from current educational trends (Abbott), and discussing the design and intent of the new *Standards for Classical Language Learning* (Abbott, Davis, and Gascoyne). Two chapters explore the latest in methods and materials for introducing Latin to youngsters in the elementary and middle grades (Polsky and Osburn); four chapters examine approaches to high-school Latin, offering a detailed look at the grammar-translation and reading methods (Singh, Perry), Advanced Placement courses (Brucia), and a wealth of extra-curricular and enrichment activities available to secondary-school programs (Hall).

Dickison's discussion of the importance of school-college articulation, at both the personal and curricular levels, is followed by four chapters on college Latin, detailing the use of grammar-translation and reading approaches in beginning classes (May, Gruber-Miller) and discussing the successful design and dynamics of recruitment, curriculum development, and a junior-senior seminar for undergraduate Latin majors (Platter, Smith). Three chapters look both philosophically and practically at graduate education, TA training, and teacher preparation in American universities (Morford, White, Lawall); three look at successful responses to three special challenges, including making the Latin-Spanish connection (George), designing a Latin curriculum for learning-disabled students (Ashe), and distance learning via correspondence and the electronic classroom (Daugherty). While nearly all these discussions examine texts and materials appropriate to their specific focus, the book's last two chapters survey the veritable cornucopia of classroom resources available to Latin teachers at all levels, including instructional and tutorial software, textual and visual databases, simulations, E-mail and and Internet facilities, visuals for bulletin boards, maps, reference books and periodicals, pleasure reading, realia and reproductions, videotapes, filmstrips, slide sets, and a host of others (Latousek, Kitchell).

Each of the contributors I have been fortunate to recruit for this project is a distinguished professional, highly experienced in the subject assigned. Each could have told us far more, but for the limitations of space by which we were constrained. Still, I think each of them has rendered us a splendid service, economically providing us with context, concept, and details of classroom applications appropriate to the topic at hand. In general, the "how-to" sections found in most of the chapters are written in an informal style, and in editing I have tried to allow each contributor his or her own "voice." Nevertheless, readers will find an evenness in the book's collective voice: the how-to discussions are consistently descriptive, rather than prescriptive. Readers will feel comfortable, I think, agreeing or disagreeing with a particular point of theory or practice presented in the book; they will find much that is familiar, but even more that is new. Since some readers, despite the appeal made earlier in this introduction, will read selectively, I have allowed (and in some instances encouraged and even designed) a degree of overlap between individual chapters. Both the teacher in the elementary grades and the high-school teacher need to know about the ACL's Teaching Materials and Resource Center, for example; and the separate discussions of employing the reading approach in high school and in college, while repeating certain crucial points, nevertheless give us, when read together, a whole perspective that is greater than the sum of its parts.

In the case of the bibliography, however, I have decided to avoid duplication, for reasons of economy, by collecting all the works cited into a single bibliography at the end of the book, subdivided into a few broad categories, including textbooks, articles and books specific to Latin teaching and curriculum, and general studies. Though I had initially hoped for an even more comprehensive bibliography, considerations of economy again prohibited (the list of works cited alone comes to nearly 20 pages in as minute a font as my middle-aged eyes will tolerate). The only partial list of textbooks is also perhaps excused by the fact that complete textbook surveys are published on a quite regular basis, by Judith Sebesta (one of our contributors), in the *Classical World*; for pedagogical articles and textbook reviews that are not cited, readers are referred to the indexes of five journals in which well over 90% of such publications have appeared over the past 20 or more years, *Classical Journal, Classical Outlook, Classical World,* the *New England Classical Journal (and Newsletter)*, and *Foreign Language Annals*. As the bibliography contains only articles and books, readers are referred, for computer programs and Web sites, to the *Software Directory for Classics* together with other materials cited in Chapter 23, and, for maps, games, audiovisuals, and similar classroom resources, to the extensive listings in the book's several chapters (especially Chapters 6–8 and 24) and the audiovisual surveys appearing regularly in the *Classical World*.

CARPE LIBRUM!

Good teaching, like good poetry, requires both passion and planning, a touch of madness as well as a good bit of method. "All the best teachers are thieves," I tell the students in my Latin Teaching Apprenticeship at the University of Georgia: keep your eyes and ears open, and if you come upon an idea that will work in your classes, steal it and make it your own! In my own elementary Latin courses, I use a traditional grammar-translation text. But, thanks to the many victims of my mercurial thefts over the years, I have lots more in my bag of tricks. One I cannot resist promoting is the "four-skills," or rather multiple-skills, approach described in one way or another in several of this book's chapters. "When in Rome, remember your SANDALS," I urge all teachers-in-training: *Spectate, Audite—Nunc Dicite, Agite, Legite, Scribite!* Though I too "like grammar" (just as John Gruber-Miller confesses at the outset of his chapter on using the reading approach in college), my students learn a great deal of their Latin by Looking, Listening, Speaking, and Doing, as well as via the traditionally more emphasized skills of Reading and Writing. Thanks to my willingness to purloin good teaching ideas and run with them, I always (like Mercury) remember my SANDALS! And you, gentle reader, are hereby invited to do likewise: seize the day, seize this book, and make any of its ideas that appeal to you your own.

For the publication of this modest *libellus,* my deepest gratitude is due to a great many people: to the teachers and colleagues from whom I have learned; to my editor Bill Fleig and foreign language product manager Cathy Wilson, of

Scott Foresman-Addison Wesley, for their steadfast confidence in the merits of this book; to Wyatt W. Anderson, Dean of the Franklin College of Arts and Sciences, for his constant support of our Classics programs here at the University of Georgia; to the volume's several contributors, who have generously shared their considerable expertise and never once complained of my editorial quirks; to friend and assistant editor Mary Wells Ricks, who has worked at my side for nearly 20 years on the *Classical Outlook* and on countless other scholarly and pedagogical "adventures," not only for her professionalism in handling every aspect of the manuscript's preparation but also for her profound dedication to the importance of the Classics in American education; and, of course, to my dear wife Laura, our children Jean-Paul, Caroline, and Kimberley, and Mom and Dad Lenox, all of whom lovingly tolerate the "passion and planning," and the excesses of time, that seem always to go into my little projects. *Omnibus vobis carissimis maximas gratias ago!*

ATHENS, GEORGIA
Summer, 1997

"GLADLY WOLDE HE LERNE, AND GLADLY TECHE."
Chaucer, *Canterbury Tales*, Prol. 308

1

The Great Latin Debate:
The Futility of Utility?

KENNETH F. KITCHELL, JR.
Louisiana State University

The impetus for this chapter arises squarely from personal experience, for the timing of my career is such that I have seen both a heyday (early in the 1960s) and the nadir (in the late 1960s and 1970s) of Latin enrollments in this country. The causes of the decline are painfully remembered by anyone who lived through them. Latin was, to put it mildly, condemned as irrelevant. It was attacked forcefully as a throwback to medieval education, good perhaps for nostalgia but of no pragmatic use in today's world. Moreover, in the 1960s and 1970s, marked by strong anti-establishment sentiment, Latin was twice doomed, since, as a requirement in many curricula, it both stood for and was enforced by the establishment. Colleges and high schools alike began a flight from tradition and Latin was among the major casualties.

Yet this disastrous plunge brought with it a unique opportunity as well. I have been fortunate to have participated in what might be called the Great Counter-Offensive—the mobilization of the Latin profession to counteract the decline in Latin enrollments. The ways in which this counter-offensive affected the debate over pedagogical methodology will be examined further by Prof. Sebesta in the next chapter; here I would like to concentrate on the arguments that were used to justify Latin's existence in the curriculum. During these busy years, classicists at all levels rallied to defend the study of the language that is our common bond. We produced brochures and pamphlets extolling the virtues of studying Latin, showing that Latin students had better vocabularies, could think better, developed better study skills, and had contact with the finest literary and civic minds of all time. We cited statistics which showed that Latin would help the college-bound student, quoting studies indicating they did better on the SAT scores, stood out favorably among college applicants, and, once admitted, did quite well in their studies. While we debated forcefully that Latin was not just for the elite, stunningly successful programs arose in several inner-city venues, mostly aimed at improving language arts skills. This movement, built with the toil of countless proponents, did its work, for Latin enrollments leveled off, grew, and are continuing to climb (LaFleur 1997). While false security is not called for, it is admittedly pleasant to realize that the cleverness of our arguments won the day.

It thus came as something of a blow, when researching another piece (Kitchell 1995), to find that the same arguments had already been raised in an influential book (West) which I will discuss below. As I read its theses, penned some 80 years ago, I realized I had forgotten one of the great lessons from antiquity—that there are cycles in human events and that, as *Ecclesiastes* put it so well, *Nihil sub sole novum,* "There is nothing new under the sun." I set out, therefore, to research the history of the teaching of Latin. What methods had been used before our day? What arguments had been raised by proponents and opponents alike over the teaching of Latin? Finally, what might we learn from what has gone before? More reading has led me to the knowledge that there is a vast literature on the subject and an interesting monograph remains to be written on the history of Latin's place in the curriculum. There is neither time nor space here to raise all the issues at stake or to present a full version of my thesis. Nevertheless, as we begin a book devoted to how Latin is to be taught today, it is well to stop a moment and look back over our collective shoulders at how Latin has been taught, attacked, and defended at various crucial points in its history. History may not precisely repeat itself, but Cicero himself understood the principle when he wrote (*Orator* 34.120): *Nescire autem quid ante quam natus sis acciderit, id est semper esse puerum,* "Not to know what happened before you were born is to remain always a child." It behooves us, then, to look backward before progressing forward, and to choose wisely from those arguments which seem soundest (or recur most frequently). In our quick survey we will look to antiquity, the Middle Ages (Aelfric and Aelfric of Bata), the 16th century, colonial America, the Civil War period, and the great period of educational reform that spanned the late 19th and early 20th centuries—the age of committee reports. Further, this study will concentrate on the argument of utility, for it seems that Latin has risen and fallen over the years mostly on the basis of how useful or useless it has seemed to the current generation. Teaching methods and advocacy movements have, predictably, reacted to these perceptions.

THE ROMAN WAY

It is commonly, if tacitly, accepted that the Romans, at least, were spared the tedious acquisition of their language. They were, after all, native speakers. Such an argument is both intuitively and factually incorrect. Anyone who has had the misfortune to listen to a call-in sports show or to overhear a heated debate in a tavern knows instinctively that being born into a language does nothing to insure its proper usage. Quintilian himself complains (1.6.45) about the Latin spoken by the crowds at the theater or the circus, and McCartney has shown through numerous examples that correct Latin was indeed difficult even for native Romans to master. How they taught it should, therefore, be very enlightening. Although much remains to be learned about schooling in Rome, and while some of the older views of Marrou have been challenged (Harris 1989: 233–48), the basic outlines are fairly secure (Kennedy 1987).

It is important to stress that utility for a Roman education first demanded *recte loquendi scientiam et poetarum enarrationem* (Quintilian 1.9.1)—"the ability to speak Latin properly and to elucidate the poets" (Marrou, 274f). In its higher forms, of course, it aimed at the proper use of the language in the fine art of rhetoric, for the way to success in the Roman world was through the effective use of oratory. This surely is the height of the utilitarian argument—the effective use of one's native tongue—and the methodology used was quite pragmatic. In primary school (Little, vol. 2, 80–82, 122–25), for example, the children acquired the rudiments of their language in a sequence which sounds rather modern. First they learned the alphabet by rote, forward and backward, and, through the use of letters carved out of ivory and by tracing the letters as they had been carved into their wax tablets, they learned to write them. They then moved on to pronouncing syllables made up of these letters, often reciting long lists of such syllables, even when they were jumbled into nonsense combinations. After this they graduated to short sentences, often concentrating on those with decidedly moral value, a trait that we will see repeated in later ages. Most of the work in Roman schools was done aloud, and we hear from Martial (9.68) that to live near a school was to be drowned in noise (Kennedy 1984: 9).

Once the students had the rudiments down, they moved on to the grammar school (Little, vol. 2, 82f, 125–29) where, from roughly ages 6 or 7 until 11 or 12, they began the acquisition of Latin grammar under the tutelage of the appropriately named *grammaticus*. Marrou (275) carefully defines the subject matter, based as it was on Greek educational models:

> Grammar still meant essentially the same abstract analysis of the elements of language—letters, syllables, words, and parts of speech—and the same meticulous distinctions and classifications: 'nouns'— which were still not separate from what we call 'adjectives'—were studied according to the six accidents—quality, degree of comparison, gender, number, figure, and case; and common nouns were separated into twenty-seven classes—corporeal, incorporeal, primitive, derived, diminutive, etc.

But remember that another main goal of Roman education was the *enarratio poetarum*, in order to acquire a proper appreciation of the Latin classics. Students were expected to be able to read, aloud and with expression, a given passage from a poet. Then they were grilled, line by line, word by word, on the many intricacies of the grammar, rhetorical figures, and mythological allusions.

Read the following excerpt from Priscian, who, though late, depicts well enough the classical procedures. This is his account of a question and answer session on *Aeneid* 1.1 (Marrou, 279–80):

> **Q.** Scan the line. **A.** *Arma vi/rumque ca/no Tro/iae qui / primus ab / oris.* **Q.** How many caesuras are there? **A.** Two **Q.** What are they? **A.** The penthemimera and the hephthemimera. **Q.** Which is which? **A.** The penthemimera is *Arma virumque cano* and the hephthemimera *Arma virumque cano Troiae.* **Q.** How many "figures" has it? **A.** Ten. **Q.** Why has it got ten? **A.** Because it is made up of three dactyls and two spondees. [sic] **Q.** How many words ["parts of speech"] are there? **A.** Nine. **Q.** How many nouns? **A.** Six—*Arma, Virum, Troiae, qui* [sic] *primus, oris.* **Q.** How many verbs? **A.** One—*cano.* **Q.** How many prepositions? **A.** One—*ab.* **Q.** How many conjunctions? **A.** One—*que.* **Q.** Study each word in turn. Let us begin with *arma.* What part of speech is it? **A.** A noun. **Q.** What is its quality? **A.** Appellative. **Q.** What kind is it? **A.** General. **Q.** What gender? **A.** Neuter. **Q.** How do you know? **A.** All nouns ending in *-a* in the plural are neuter.

The rapid fire drill, coupled with the fact that corporal punishment was fairly common in Roman schools (Little, 136–38) must have caused more than one student to have weak knees. If truth be told, each of us remembers a class, either from our own student days or from observations of others, which was not terribly different from this: "What is the mood of *cano?* The voice? The person? To what does *qui* refer? What is its function in the clause?"

In addition to this negative parallel with our times (see Kennedy 1987: 13), we also see the first examples of some themes that will recur throughout the history of teaching Latin. The utility presupposed in this sort of teaching is the reading of great literature, specifically poetry (Mayer). Later, in the rhetor's school, the active creation and utilization of the skills acquired in earlier years will take precedence, but many an argument has been raised in modern times that the sole reason to study Latin is to read the great authors from Roman antiquity. Further, the method is unremittingly oral. The student is learning about the language while using the language, a goal espoused by many oral-aural, "direct," methodological approaches to learning Latin today (Ganss, 219; cf. Nutting; Distler, 1–9). It is interesting to note that this approach was also used by the Romans who wanted their children to acquire Greek, often beginning this study before the study of Latin (Marrou, 262–64). The Romans also saw utility in the choice of literature studied, for this imparted proper moral values, another outlook which long remained in place. Finally, the ultimate utility was the fact that being able to speak properly and forcefully led to a successful career in the far flung Roman world. Kaster (11) prints a baptismal prayer from Eustratius which, though in Greek, preserves the sentiment perfectly: "Lord, give me the grace of good understanding, that I might learn letters and gain the upper hand over my fellows."

THE MIDDLE AGES

This attitude was not to go away. Although the methods were modified to fit contemporary requirements, not the least of which was the need to teach people to read sacred manuscripts (Sheerin, 56–58), the basic Roman grammatical texts continued to play a large part in the teaching of the rudiments of Latin well into the Middle Ages (Law). As had been the case in antiquity, in elementary school "the chief objective and emphasis of teachers and pupils was the ability to speak Latin with ease. Success in this almost automatically entailed ability to read and write it as well" (Ganss, 122). Proper forms and whole sentences, often of a highly moral nature, were memorized as they had been in antiquity. As students moved up to the secondary level and beyond, the skills of reading and writing Latin were given equal emphasis. Ganss (124) stresses that the language was taught by the direct method—teaching Latin in Latin. Much memorization was required and the hours were long, but the students acquired a spoken familiarity with the language long before they attempted any serious study of formal literature. Indeed this is one of the reasons that they began their Latin at such a young age, and it is curious to note that throughout subsequent ages, in the face of many a challenge, educators and reformers alike would recommend that the study of Latin be commenced at a younger age and that the reading of the great authors only be gradually undertaken after the student was thoroughly at ease with the language (Eliot 1894: 74; American Philological Association 1899).

While much of the elementary Latin education seems to have been stilted, there is one educator who seems to have been literally centuries ahead of his time. Aelfric was a British monk who wrote (ca. 993) the first vernacular grammar of the Latin language. In it are all the subtle niceties that Latin grammarians thrive on, and each major part of speech is meticulously treated. We might, therefore, expect his teaching to be dull and crabbed. Yet, when we come to his colloquy, we find it delightful. Aelfric of Bata, his student, adapted Aelfric's work and expanded it, mixing in his own colloquies with those of his master.

In these colloquies—conversational texts that teach Latin (Porter, 463)—the students, who are oblates in a monastery, entreat their teacher to instruct them in the language (*Nos pueri rogamus te, magister, ut doceas nos loqui latialiter recte*). The request was a vital one, for members of the monastery were supposed to avoid the vernacular in daily life, and their study of scripture was, of course, completely in Latin. The goal of their study is, therefore, highly utilitarian, and it is instructive to examine how Aelfric and his student Aelfric Bata sought to achieve this most pragmatic end.

The colloquies aim first at teaching the new members of the monastic community the words and phrases they will need as they go through their days. Bata's finished collection of colloquies is arranged "roughly in the chronology of several monastic days" (Porter, 465). The students are presented throughout with scenes of starting the day, dressing, performing common chores around the monastery, journeys, play, and virtually any situation in which the young oblates would find themselves. The exercises thus resemble a well-constructed modern textbook, such as *Ecce Romani* or the Oxford or Cambridge series (see Chapters 2, 9, and 14, below), in that these textbooks also make a conscious effort to incorporate as many day-to-day situations into the narrative as they can.

The most striking thing about the colloquies, however, is that they anticipate by centuries the advent of the direct, communicative method. In an excellent article, David Porter has analyzed several of the ways in which Aelfric and Aelfric Bata alike used an intuitive sense of fine teaching to get their method across. Porter stresses (466–67) that in the colloquies, as in the communicative method, fluency is preferred over total grammatical correctness. That is, the method implies that the most important priority is that the student speak rather than memorize endings. He also stresses correctly that Bata is very interested in teaching vocabulary through the use of equivalents put directly into the sentence. Consider this sentence which offers a wide variety of weather terms: *En tetrica aura est et lurida aura et procellosa aura et rigida aura et nivosa aura et algida aura, et non est squalida aura vel suda aura*[1] (Stevenson, 70.1–4; Porter, 473). In response to the simple question, *Et quid bibis?*, the hypothetical postulants of colloquy 6 respond *Cervissam vel medonem, quod est mulsum, seu lac si non habeo cervisam* (Stevenson, 98.25; Porter, 473). Porter tends to the belief that this is done simply to enlarge vocabulary by putting them into meaningful contexts. This is, of course, true. Here beer is followed by mead and then a synonym, *mulsum*, is provided. In colloquy 6, a hypothetical fowler lists almost 20 birds when simply asked *Quales aves sepissime capis?* (Stevenson, 85). I would like to take this idea further, for I think these colloquies also anticipate the use of substitution drills.

Colloquy 1 has the dramatic setting of a monk beginning his day (*Surge, amice, de tuo lecto; tempus est tibi si hodie surgis*). The boy is given a command: *Audi puer! Vade et custodi equos meos vel tuos . . . vel in campo, vel in prato . . . ne fures venient et deripiant vel furentur eos diligenter* (Stevenson, 1.12f) A bit later the boy begins an exchange: *"Audi, princeps, vel episcope, vel doctor aeclesiae!" "Audio te. Quid tu vis hodie? Quae est tua necesitas? Pro qua causa huc venisti?" "Haec est necesitas mea; cupio librum legere tecum." "Quem librum vis legere?" "Volo legere canonicum librum, vel evangelium vel librum gramaticum id est Donaticum"* (Stevenson, 3.11f). To give further quick examples: *Venite nunc et salutate episcopum vel abbatem sive seniorem nostrum* (Stevenson, 25.36); *Audi tu, puer, et veni huc ad me cito, et perge ad amnem sive ad fontem, et deporta nobis . . . huc limpidam aquam cum aliquo scipho vel urceo ut manus nostras et oculos nostros et totas facies nostras possimus lavare* (27.12f); *O nostri scolastici! venite huc . . . Legite fortiter aut cantate, aut alias docete quicquid boni scitis, aut sumite pennas vestras et scedulas et scribite pulchre in eis cum atramento vestro aut in tabulis vestris cum vestris graphiis seu artavis, aut imagines pingite aliquas aut sculpite, aut aliquam artem bonam discite et exercete!* (42.9f).

Each of the extended sentences cited above is clearly too long and has too many variables to make it easily memorized. But these sentences bear a striking resemblance to a substitution or pattern drill where a basic sentence can be endlessly modified by insertion of new vocabulary. Note this example, translated, from a modern Greek book patterned on the Rassias method. The basic sentence is first given "The bee entered the church." Then the following subjects are to be substituted for "The bee" and the verb adjusted accordingly: "we, I, the bees, you (pl.), you (s.)." On the same page is another version which, if printed in the manner of these colloquies, would read "Listen to me or him, or her, or us, or them, or it, or those things, or those ladies" (Bien, 39). The authors even tell us how to do such a drill, and in their instructions we can hear what lies behind some of Aelfric's methods: "First, the teacher recites the opening sentence and elicits two choral responses from the class. The teacher gives the first cue, which is the underlined word in the next sentence. At the same time, the teacher points to a student. This student then repeats the original sentence, but substitutes in the proper place the cue word or words" (Bien, 6). If we simply read "the word preceded by 'sive'" for "the underlined word" we might be hearing Aelfric's own directions for how to use his text when conducting a class.

There is much more work to be done on Aelfric, but enough has been demonstrated to show that, in order to arrive at the utilitarian aim for Latin necessitated by his day and age, he found a methodology which ranks him among the premier innovators in Latin pedagogy. Aelfric's contribution was not universally embraced, however. For the most part, medieval elementary Latin instruction was modeled on Roman schools, and the classes were surely not as entertaining as those of Aelfric, though Ganss has argued most persuasively that the classrooms of the Middle Ages were doing many things correctly. Up until the beginning of the Renaissance, as he remarks (220):

> the chief objective of teachers and pupils alike continued to be the simple one of earlier centuries: the threefold art of speaking, reading, and writing the language with fluency. Latin was regarded as a medium of communication rather than as a field for mental gymnastics. In a word, Latin then served approximately all the functions or purposes which the vernacular does today in elementary, secondary, and lower college education. The study of it, like that of the vernacular today, was simultaneously utilitarian and cultural.

"The threefold art of speaking, reading, and writing" was to be stressed frequently in the centuries to follow, but the success achieved in producing these skills was rarely matched after the medieval period.

In his excellent essay, "A Historical Sketch of the Teaching of Latin," Ganss (218–58) outlines many of the techniques used during the Middle Ages, such as the direct method, starting Latin at a very early age, and not introducing canonical authors until the students had a colloquial written and spoken familiarity with the language. These too would be frequently, if sporadically touted by later reformers. Why, then, did they fall away? Ganss convincingly argues (146f) that it was the Renaissance, with its insistence on resurrecting the style of Cicero, that put an end to this method of teaching Latin, which, as was true for Aelfric, stressed fluency over correct style. According to this view, the movement toward the stilted and contrived language of Cicero did as much as the rise of the vernaculars to make Latin an artificial thing and in no way a living language. Even the papacy joined men such as Scaliger and Valla in encouraging the Ciceronian style (Ganss, 151f; Grendler, 156–202). The utility of communication had passed over to the utility of being stylish, and Latin suffered as a result.

AMERICA: THE COLONIAL PERIOD

What, then, of our own country? The early years of the American republic are often thought of as a period ruled by a devotion to the Classics, and to a large degree this is so. Yet the picture was not totally rosy and for the purposes of this essay we will concentrate on the attacks that were raised against a classical education. Such was the early republic's stress on pragmatism, that Reinhold entitled the second chapter of his book *Classica Americana* (1984) "The Quest for Useful Knowledge in Eighteenth-Century America." As early as 1711, at a town meeting in Boston, a group of parents rose to their feet to petition the townsmen to change the curriculum at the now hallowed Boston Latin School. Their argument? Why, practicality, of course: "very many hundreds of boys in this town, who by their parents were never designed for a more liberal education, have spent two, three, and four years or more of their early days at the Latin School, which hath proved of very little or no benefit to their after accomplishment" (Reinhold 1984: 118). Subsequent critics, such as Ben Franklin and Cadwallader Colden (a lieutenant governor of New York), wrote pointed essays stressing the need for practical knowledge in the schools—that English should be studied instead of Latin and that mathematics and geography were of more use to a future merchant than a study of Greek poetry. In 1768 one William Livingston summed up the general opinion well: "We want hands, my lord, more than heads. The most intimate acquaintance with the classics, will not remove our oaks; nor a taste for the *Georgics* cultivate our lands. Many of our young people are knocking their heads against the *Iliad*, who should employ their hands in clearing our swamps and draining our marshes" (Reinhold 1984: 63). Such were the very arguments used against Latin in the dark years of the 1960s and 1970s when computer skills were more highly praised than parsing skills.

The attacks by Benjamin Rush were even more vicious. Once a defender of the Classics, Rush said in 1810–11: "Were every Greek and Latin book (the New Testament excepted) consumed in a bonfire, the world would be the wiser and better for it . . .. *Delenda, delenda est lingua Romana* should be the voice of reason and liberty and humanity in every part of the world" (Reinhold 1984: 74–75). In 1789, the year Rush began his attack, he even went so far as to claim that Latin and Greek caused juvenile delinquency (Reinhold 1984: 129): "Many sprightly young boys of excellent capacities for useful knowledge, have been so disgusted with the dead languages as to retreat from the drudgery of schools, to low company, whereby they have become bad members of society, and entailed misery upon all who have been connected with them." It is no small irony that Rush's monument in Washington D.C. bears an inscription in Latin.

The attacks multiplied. Whereas many of the founders believed that a study of the Classics would inculcate morals and civic values (Reinhold 1984: 142–73), the view was not universal. Quakers argued that many of the Classics contained stories which were too lascivious and immoral for young minds, and many charged that benefit to be derived from works written in Latin and Greek could now be taken from the English translations which were beginning to proliferate. There was also a fairly loud outcry against the archaic and sometimes barbaric teaching methods. Whipping was a universally accepted part of the Latin classroom (Richard, 14–17) and one is reminded of the grilling of the student reported above in a text of Priscian and of Quintilian's pleas for teachers not to use corporal punishment (1.3.8f). Despite the attacks, the Classics remained at the center of the educational curriculum for years to come. One utilitarian counter argument for the Classics pointed out that they had long been required for entry into college (Fromm, 186–88; cf. LaFleur 1991). Richard (196–231) has recently addressed what he sees as Reinhold's overstatements concerning the perceived "classical decline," but it remains true that these early attacks, mostly in the form of charges of utilitarianism, paved the way for what was to be the basis of the war against Latin in America. In 1828 an attempt was made to remove the Classics as an entry requirement for Yale, to "drop the dead languages and introduce something more up-to-date" (Reinhold 1987: 128–29; Kennedy 1984: 327–28). The resultant "Yale Report" defended the Classics vehemently, but the groundwork had been laid.

THE 19TH CENTURY

Although there is much more to be said, let us move on in time to the last period we will study closely. The period just prior to the Civil War had seen several attacks on the traditional curriculum and the period after the war caused the nation to re-evaluate many of its previously accepted values. The 1768 statement of Livingstone quoted above could be equally applied to the Industrial Revolution and to Reconstruction—technological creativity and know-how were simply more in demand (and need) than were Cicero and Homer. More "practical" courses were called for in the schools and, as the university system opened up, much as it would after World War II, students entering were not all equally equipped to tackle the rigors of the pre-war curriculum.

In 1856, David Cole, principal of Trenton Academy, addressed the major issues confronting the classical curriculum in an essay of astonishing prescience. He begins by asking "whether the system of study pursued in our Colleges, Academies, and High Schools is adapted to the wants of the age or whether any modification or material improvement of it is called for by the progressive spirit of the times" (Cole, 67). He further admits that modern languages were making inroads into the curriculum and that "it is asserted that good Classical scholars are never good for anything else" (84). But Cole then cleverly goes on to claim that, once we understand the true aims of education, then only the classical curriculum will do, for "the importance of a full, comprehensive course [of study] will be generally acknowledged as soon as it is admitted that the object of study is, not to fill a cavity in the head, but to discipline and strengthen the mind" (85). This argument, based on mental discipline, would often be raised in years to come, most commonly joined with the idea of transference, which claimed that the skills gained from learning a structured language such as Latin could be transferred over to the learning of other subjects. This is, of course, a prime example of an argument from utility.

During this time, teaching methods were frequently condemned as woefully out of date—as they would be by critics from my generation. James Russell Lowell (208), speaking in 1886, summed it up rather well: "Many a boy has hated, and rightly hated, Homer and Horace the pedagogues and grammarians, who would have loved Homer and Horace the poets, had he been allowed to make their acquaintance." Tayler Lewis, in an 1855 speech, shows astonishingly modern ideas about the teaching of the languages.[2] His basic premise is that an overly narrow stress on grammar prevents students from reading adequate amounts of the ancient authors, which, he claims, is the aim of the discipline. His suggestion is simply that teachers should abandon overly literal translations because they do not produce English, but rather "the barbarous dialect of the school room" (289). Using a Greek example, he recommends "he has a headache," as opposed to "he is in pain as to the head" (293), and stresses that good, flowing English is always the goal. He recommends oral work, thereby making us think both of Aelfric and of modern exhortations (Davis, 50; and see Chapter 5 below on the new National Standards), and he recommends practices which today would be called pre-reading (481–85). He ends with an appeal to the utility to be gained from Latin's mental discipline (491).

Lewis was many years ahead of his day, but he could not blunt the attacks begun by people such as Franklin and Rush. Likewise, the administrators who wrote the "Yale Report" in 1828 were no longer around to stem the tide, and the curriculum was soon to change. One of the main figures behind this change was Charles W. Eliot, president of Harvard and perhaps the major voice in educational theory of the day.

In certain respects Eliot was a moderate. In his inaugural address as Harvard president in 1869 (Thomas, 25; Eliot 1898: 1), he stated clearly that there was no "real antagonism between literature and science." But in the long run he championed an elective system which severely damaged the position Latin held in the American curriculum. The apologia by Hale in 1887 shows that there were further attacks underway, and in 1890–91 the National Education Association (NEA) commissioned the "Committee of Ten" to study the concept of uniformity of curricula in secondary-school programs and in college admissions policies. Eliot and the committee did not so much wish to downgrade the Classics as to elevate other disciplines to an equal rank of study. History, English and its literature, French, German, and natural science were specifically mentioned as important areas of study. As in the 1960s, the problem then was that there was too much in the curriculum and too little time to teach it all.

Moreover, the student body had changed (Eliot 1894: 51):

> The secondary schools of the United States, taken as a whole, do not exist for the purpose of preparing boys and girls for colleges . . . their main function is to prepare for the duties of life . . .. A secondary school programme intended for national use must therefore be made for those children whose education is not to be pursued beyond the secondary school.

This curriculum did not necessarily include the Classics. Four separate and distinct secondary-school curricula were devised but only one kept Greek and only two Latin (Kitchell 1995). The sub-committee on Latin (Eliot 1894: 60f) recommended moving the study of Latin back to about age 12, an interesting evocation of medieval practice. They attacked the standard authors as too hard and far too uninteresting. The *Gallic Wars,* long in the curriculum (Owen), were declared: "altogether too difficult for beginners; it is too exclusively military in contents to be generally interesting . . . its vocabulary is too largely restricted . . . to afford the best introduction to subsequent reading; and, finally, it touches human life at too few points to be morally helpful and significant" (63–64). The sub-committee went further, warning against "an undue prominence of rules and the treatment of syntax as an end in itself" (Owen, 65), condemning the use of "translation English" (cf. Lewis' "barbarous dialect of the school room") and, remarkably, even suggesting that, if a sentence was easy, the class could simply read it without stopping to translate it (72). Finally, they recommended the introduction of easier authors for beginning students (74), a cry that will be heard many times throughout the years (American Philological Association 1899: 26f; Ramey).

The very next year, the Commission on the Reorganization of the Secondary Education (CRSE) of the NEA published its *Cardinal Principles of Secondary Education*. Its very first sentence (7) reads: "Secondary education should be determined by the needs of the society to be served, the character of the individuals to be educated, and the knowledge of educational theory and practice available," and it clearly states throughout that the goals of education should aim mostly at producing a nation filled with dutiful citizens prepared to participate in the governing and productivity of the country. The age of progressive education represented by this particular version of utility would be in place for 50 years (Ravitch, 43f).

INTO THE 20TH CENTURY

Space does not allow a full study of subsequent events, and there is is a definite need for research in this period, for Latin often lay at the heart of the controversies. The early decades of the 20th century saw many books and articles produced which studied how Latin was taught, recommending many changes in the process (D'Ooge; Kirsch; Paxson; White 1936, 1941). Predictably, the earlier committees produced many offspring and gave rise to conferences called specifically to help address the questions of Latin's potential for survival in the contemporary curriculum (Kelsey; Froula; Fromm). Andrew West called such a conference and the report on the conference reads like a summation of all the arguments which have been raised through the centuries both for and against Latin (West). When he stresses the fact (364f) that Classics students score better on the "College Entrance Examination Board," modern teachers are put in mind of the work done by Rick LaFleur (1981, 1982) in demonstrating the relationship between the study of Latin and enhanced SAT scores. West's lengthy claims (379f) that students who studied the Classics do better once they reach college reappeared in 1924 (Advisory Committee, 236f) and again in 1984 (Wiley).

In 1924 the American Classical League weighed into the fray with *The Classical Investigation*, the first comprehensive self-study on the teaching of Classics in America (Advisory Committee). Faced with changing definitions of utility and a very serious threat to Latin's position in the curriculum, the committee struck back, producing a list of objectives to be achieved through the study of Latin. Note the first three (78): "Increased ability to read and understand Latin"; "Increased understanding of those elements in English which are related to Latin"; "Increased ability to read, speak and write English." Once more the utility of Latin had been redefined to fit current needs and to blunt current attacks. The committee even added two further objectives, clearly aimed at finding a niche in the contemporary jargon, viz., "Development of an historical and cultural background," and "Development of right attitudes toward social stituations." I do not mean to accuse the committee or the study of educational pandering. They were merely doing what defenders of the classical curriculum have done for centuries. In fact the committee made many sound suggestions aimed 'at revivifying the curriculum and the classroom teaching of Latin. A current teacher could do worse than read this study for its pragmatic recommendations, many of which are in place today.

CONCLUSIONS

In the end, what has this all too swift survey demonstrated? A cynic might try to claim that it merely shows that Latin educators will grasp at any straw to keep their embattled discipline afloat. There is some truth to this. Recently former Senator Paul Simon, a long-time supporter of foreign language study, wrote a persuasive article (1991) on the need for language study in America, basing a large part of his argument on the pragmatic necessity of "international economic competitiveness" (13). In a thoughtful reply, Mary Futrell (23) said: "There is nothing wrong, if, for a time, foreign languages attain prestige because of their utilitarian value . . .. But pragmatism has never been able to ensure permanent support for the primacy of foreign language study."

So it has been for Latin. At one point in its history, Latin was the ultimate prerequisite course, serving as a *sine qua non* for entry into useful careers, university study, and the upper levels of society. So strong was this tradition that even the early attacks of the colonials were generally powerless to lessen Latin's hold on the curriculum. Yet each attack brought on a new challenge to Latin's "utility." As a profession we have fought back masterfully over the years. At various times we have claimed that Latin builds good citizens (Mackail, 6; Christophelsmeier), improves basic skills (Sussman; Read), raises scores on standardized tests (LaFleur 1981, 1982), promotes mental discipline and transfer (Advisory Committee, 55f; Kelsey, 344f), is suited for pre-professional training (West, 131f; Kelsey, 83–259; Perkins; Sage), may be of use in teaching students with learning disabilities (Sparks, et al., 1992, 1995, and Chapter 21 below by Ashe), and the profession has attempted to show that Latin study is, indeed, ultimately useful (Masciantonio 1977; Mavrogenes 1977, 1979, 1989). But at the same time, our reform movements and self studies have regularly returned to one basic fact—that how the language is taught will do far more to insure its survival than any study based on utility. It is to this end that a book such as this is dedicated.

NOTES

[1]The editions of Aelfric's Colloquies (Stevenson; Garmonsway) are filled with editorial conventions to help indicate the true state of the manuscripts; these are not

reproduced here, and most medieval spellings have been retained.

[2]The notes to the original article indicate clearly that the speech was published some years after it was initially given. My thanks to Prof. Paul Paskoff of Louisiana State University who alerted me to this intriguing article.

2

ALIQUID SEMPER NOVI:
New Challenges, New Approaches

JUDITH LYNN SEBESTA
University of South Dakota

THE POST-WAR CHALLENGE

In the years after World War II, the number of students studying languages in secondary schools and in college began a precipitous decline. Surprised by the launching of Sputnik in the mid-1950s, and with encouragement from the federal government, educators emphasized the study of the sciences over the humanities and languages. As one result, many colleges instituted the Bachelor of Science degree, which typically did not require the study of language, as an option even for social science and humanities majors. Later, in the 1960s, the philosophy of "do your own thing" led many colleges to reduce the language requirement to a single year of language study or to eliminate entirely the traditional two-year study of languages that had long been the heart of the B.A. degree (Wolverton; LaFleur 1991).

During the 1960s and 70s, many educational, social, and government leaders began to advocate a college education because it led to careers providing higher salaries and better jobs, rather than stressing the intrinsic benefits of a liberal education—a rationale reinforced by the career goals of the changing "clientele" of college students. While in the 1950s only about 25% of high-school graduates went on to college, the percentage had more than doubled by 1980. Much of this new clientele consisted of non-traditional students, who attended college to improve their work skills and gain promotion at their place of employment or qualify for better-paying jobs. Working full- or part-time, raising children, with educational debts growing steadily, such students focused on courses that had a clear relationship to their employment goals. Career education became a strong competitor with liberal education (Magnan, 325). Even those students who wanted to obtain a traditional liberal arts education found it increasingly difficult to accommodate this desire to the demands of their work-oriented or pre-professional curricula.

The marginalization of language study on the college level also affected language study in the secondary schools. In the 60s and 70s many principals and school boards saw no need to prepare students for college foreign language study, and enrollments on the secondary level steadily declined. Especially severe was the decline of Latin, which was typically characterized as a "dead language" and of less practical use by far than the modern languages (LaFleur 1987a: 2–3, 15).

There were, of course, principals, teachers, parents, and students who continued to value the study of Latin and the Classics because of their significance to western culture. If Latin could no longer be offered as a standard course in the curriculum, the classical heritage could be and, increasingly, was taught through courses in English, such as ancient history, literature in translation, and classical mythology (Reilly). For example, between 1968 and 1971, college Latin enrollments dropped 21% (LaFleur 1997: 126, Table 1), but in the same period there was a 43% increase in the number of classical civilization courses taught in English (Connor, 25). In some schools the offering of such well-enrolled courses made it possible for teachers to continue to offer Latin, but often as an "overload."

SO MUCH TO DO AND SO LITTLE TIME

All these developments caused a radical rethinking of the aims and methods of teaching Latin. While the influence of Roman culture could certainly be communicated to students in classical civilization courses, teachers of Latin remained firmly convinced that such knowledge could best be imparted through the study of the language itself. The amount of time available to teach culture through Latin, however, was diminished, because students were enrolling in the language for one or, at most, two years instead of what had been a traditional four-year curriculum. Teachers were faced with dilemmas of both content and method. What information was most important to impart to students in the reduced amount of time now allotted to Latin? And—the eternal question—how should Latin be taught to enable students to read with any fluency in so short a time? However the answers to these questions were formulated, new textbooks needed to be designed.

At the beginning of the post-war period, the teaching of Latin—and other foreign languages—was still influenced by the Coleman Report. Issued in 1929, this report argued that the most reasonable goal for foreign language study was the acquisition of reading skills. In order for a student to gain facility in reading as quickly as possible, the report advocated a gradual introduction of words and grammatical structures in textbooks through simple reading selections (Richards and Rodgers, 11).

Some of the new textbooks produced in the post-war period blended, in varying degrees, the suggestions of the Coleman Report with the traditional,

19th-century grammar-translation method of teaching Latin. Other new books, however, were based on new psychological and linguistic theories of language acquisition.

GRAMMAR-TRANSLATION:
SOMETHING OLD, SOMETHING NEW

Like 19th-century textbooks, the new breed of "traditional" textbooks first published in the 1950s and 60s utilizes the grammar-translation approach, a method that involves the student in extensive analysis of Latin grammar and in translation from Latin to English and English to Latin (see further Chapters 8 and 13 below). Each chapter of these texts typically concentrates on a new grammatical structure or paradigm. After the teacher explains the structure or paradigm, students then practice the new material first by translating short Latin sentences into English, and then by translating into Latin short English sentences that require them to utilize this new grammatical information. While older grammar-translation textbooks often required students to translate sentences that were devoid of any meaningful cultural content (e.g., "Two horses are in the field"), the newer texts use readings that present aspects of Roman culture to the student.

One of the most influential grammar-translation textbooks of the past 40 years has been *Latin: An Introductory Course Based on Ancient Authors*, by Frederic M. Wheelock, first published in 1956 and revised several times, most recently in 1995 under the title *Wheelock's Latin*. Wheelock's explanation for developing this college text reflects the changing clientele of college students, the decline in secondary-school Latin programs, and the marginalization of language study in the liberal arts degrees:

> It is notorious that every year increasing numbers of students enter college without Latin; and consequently they have to begin the language in college, usually as an elective, if they are to have any Latin at all. Though some college beginners do manage to continue their study of Latin for two or three years, a surprising number have to be satisfied with only one year of the subject. (Wheelock, xvii)

Wheelock's Latin, designed for a one-year course, was original in its employment of *sententiae antiquae* and *loci antiqui*, authentic Latin sentences and short passages selected from Roman authors not only for their utility in illustrating forms or syntax, but, even more importantly, for their intrinsic interest. Ideally the 40 chapters of syntax and forms were to be covered, as Wheelock first intended, in about three-fourths of an academic year; the remaining weeks would be spent reading the lengthier Latin passages in the second part of the textbook, prose and verse excerpts selected to "cover a wide range of interesting topics such as love, anecdotes, wit, biography, philosophy, religion, morality, friendship, philanthropy, games, laws of war, satirical comment" (Wheelock, xviii). Some passages of late and medieval Latin are also included to illustrate the continuance of Latin's influence beyond the end of the Roman Empire. Also innovative was Wheelock's use of a running vocabulary that allowed students to read passages without the drudgery of looking up words in a dictionary (which task, not infrequently, made students "lose" their place in a sentence).

Wheelock's innovative idea of having a student read real Latin sentences, rather than made-up ones (an aim enhanced in the 1995 revision through the addition of continuous reading passages to the *sententiae antiquae* in each chapter), strongly influenced subsequent textbook design. Two other grammar-translation texts widely used today are *Latin via Ovid: A First Course*, by Norma Goldman and Jacob E. Nyenhuis (first published in 1972 and revised in 1982), and *Traditio: An Introduction to the Latin Language and Its Influence*, by Patricia A. Johnston (1988). Like Wheelock, Johnston designed her college textbook for a one-year course in the language. Each chapter begins with new grammatical structures and forms, which are then practiced in a section called *Ante legenda*; a reading passage, more extensive than those in Wheelock, completes the chapter. The reading selections range from Plautus to Copernicus and are based on themes such as Roman comedy, education at Rome, mythology and astronomy, and the "Roman Experience," i.e., poets and patrons, freedmen and social mobility, the deaths of Lucretia and Julius Caesar (the beginning and end of the Republic), Romulus and Remus, and life in the city.

Latin via Ovid is used in secondary schools as well as colleges. The chapters (40 altogether) begin at first with short readings recounting some of Ovid's myths and then continue in later chapters with prose adaptations of Ovid's verse; then, beginning with Chapter 33, students are reading actual Ovidian verse with generous annotations. While *Traditio* aims to give students an overview of Roman culture, *Latin via Ovid* presents them with one specific, and important, contribution of ancient culture that has influenced modern literature, film, drama, and art.

One of the most widely adopted secondary-school textbook series, Jenney's *First Year Latin* and *Second Year Latin* by Charles Jenney, Jr., et al. (first published in 1954 and most recently revised in 1990), prepares students to begin reading in the middle of their second year excerpts from Julius Caesar's *Gallic War*, Nepos' life of Alcibiades, Plautus' *Aulularia*, Livy's history of Rome, some myths from Ovid, and epigrams of Martial. Besides introducing students to several major Roman authors, "Jenney," as it is commonly known, also emphasizes the building of English vocabulary—always an important objective of Latin study. The readings for the first year and half of the second year re-tell, in made-up Latin, Roman history from the voyages of Aeneas through the Punic Wars. Additional cultural information is presented in the numerous color illustrations of Roman art, monuments, and archaeological artifacts, and in the thematic essays, "If You Lived in Ancient Rome." These essays discuss a wide variety of cultural topics from the Forum to camps, from cooking to the role of women, from religion to health, presenting students with an extensive and comprehensive picture of Roman life.

Each of these four grammar-translation texts approaches in its own way the "new clientele" of the Latin class and the limited amount of time students are most likely to devote to their study of the language. As early as seems possible to their authors, *Wheelock's Latin*, *Traditio*, and *Latin via Ovid* give students authentic Latin excerpts to read. Designed for completion in a single year, none of these texts provide an extensive survey of Roman culture, but they do quite thoroughly cover all the basics of Latin grammar and introduce students to a range of significant readings from Roman literature. Envisioning a basic two-year course of study in the secondary school, "Jenney" extends the learning of Latin grammar over a longer period, before introducing these younger students to Latin literature, and provides a helpful survey of various aspects of Roman culture, the daily lives of the Romans, and their influence on western civilization.

BEHAVIORISM AND THE STRUCTURAL APPROACH

New psychological and linguistic theories about how the mind learns language and how language is structured revolutionized the teaching of foreign languages beginning in the 1960s. Language teachers debated the theories of behavioral psychology vs. cognitive psychology and of structural linguistics vs. transformation-generative linguistics. One result has been a variety of textbooks implementing very different methodologies.

Behaviorism, simply stated, sees a similarity between how the human mind learns and how the animal mind learns. Behavioral psychologists train animals to perform basic, non-instinctive tasks by providing immediate feedback: if the animal performs the task correctly, it gets a reward, usually food; if it does not perform correctly, it receives no reward (or a negative response, such as an unpleasant stimulus). Because behaviorists are able to train animals and birds to perform a series of tasks, they conclude that even complex actions are only a set of conditioned learning responses. As Chastain remarks (104), "Since all learning is conditioned and since human learning is similar to learning in animals, the next step was to conclude that human learning could be, and is, conditioned in the same way." "This characterization of learning," Larsen-Freeman adds (260–61), "contributed to the perception of language as verbal behavior and to language acquisition as habit formation, involving the shaping of new verbal behavior through repetition and differential reinforcement." In order to learn a language, therefore, a student needs to develop a habitual response to a given linguistic stimulus, for in normal conversation there is no time to think of a grammatical rule and apply it. Textbooks implementing behaviorism aim to implant grammar in students through manipulative drills and practice of pattern sentences. Fluency is measured by one's ability to utter without reflection patterned responses that have been drilled into the memory.

The behaviorist theory of learning resonates with the principles of structural linguistics, a field that arose out of the study of languages which have no writing system. Structural linguists argue that language is primarily oral; written language is secondary. They concentrate on studying recurring patterns, especially on the level of phonology and morphology. Because a small child learns its native language through listening, speaking, reading, and writing, in that order, they argue that language students need to learn the target language using a "four-skills approach" and to keep that natural ordering of skills in mind. Structuralism conceives of language as a collection of organized "patterns" of sounds, signs, and constructions. As languages are different in sounds and signs, and constructions, a student must "forget" the patterns of his/her native language and acquire those of the target language through extensive practice. Moreover, a language student needs not only to learn the new patterns of the target language, but to *overlearn* them until they can be uttered habitually and unconsciously. Such pattern learning involves mimicry and memory rather than deductive learning of grammatical rules (Omaggio, 94–99; Diller, 10–21).

The theories of behaviorism and structural linguistics influenced Waldo Sweet to develop a unique textbook, *Artes Latinae* (first published in 1966, the text is still available from Bolchazy-Carducci Publishers in book and CD-ROM formats). The text presents Latin forms and structures in a series of "frames," which are discrete, short paragraphs arranged in long columns on the page. A student places a masking square at the top of each column and gradually "unmasks" the frame. Each frame ends by asking a student to give a response; after responding, the student then unmasks the correct answer that follows the frame. In this way, students proceed at their own pace, frame by frame, with immediate feedback. Sweet field-tested this method extensively and found that the immediate feedback enabled students giving correct answers to proceed confidently and prompted students giving incorrect answers to review the misunderstood material immediately. A number of frames require the use of audio-lingual tapes through which the student practices pronunciation of Latin words, forms, and sentences.

Sweet also favored this methodology, which is called "programmed instruction," because it allowed him to present Latin forms and structures in a very gradual way. Traditional textbooks, he thought, presented too many forms or structures at a single time, and many students were unable to handle such a dense load of information. The frame method enabled him to present new material incrementally.

Sweet determined the order of presentation by the principle of structural linguistics that attention should focus initially on forms that are most unlike those of the student's native language. Among the most distinctive differences between Latin and English, Sweet observed, were the ways the two languages distinguished between subject and direct object, and the way adjectives modify nouns. Another innovative method of presentation he pioneered is the horizontal presentation of a case across several declensions, e.g., the accusative case of the first, second, and third declensions is presented simultaneously.

Like Wheelock, Sweet also employed authentic Latin *sententiae*, aphoristic in nature, for his initial readings, selecting them on the basis of both their inherent interest and their illustration of a particular grammatical pattern. With these and other virtues, Sweet's *Artes Latinae* has recently found a growing audience among home-schoolers, for whom the self-paced lessons and audio-lingual tapes are very practical.

Sweet's pioneering application of behavioral psychology and structural linguistics has influenced a number of subsequent textbooks such as *Living Latin: A Contemporary Approach*, by Clara W. Ashley and Austin M. Lashbrook (first published in 1974 and revised most recently in 1981). Though this secondary-school text does not employ Sweet's frame method, it does apply his idea of inductive and incremental presentation, extensive pattern drilling, use of audio-lingual tapes, and Latin *sententiae* to illustrate the new material. *Living Latin*, moreover, includes extensive made-up Latin passages for reading practice. These passages begin with a story about a Roman named Pudens through which the authors convey cultural information; later passages retell several fables, myths, and historical events to prepare students to read excerpts from Caesar's *Gallic War* in the last half of the series' second volume. Similarly inspired by Sweet is the college text *Latin for Reading: A Beginner's Textbook with Exercises*, by Glenn M. Knudsvig, et al., initially published in 1982 and revised in 1986. Though the authors employ a number of Sweet's *sententiae* for the basic sentences and readings, they have further developed the concepts of kernels, modifiers, and connectors as basic structural elements of Latin sentences (see further Chapter 3 below).

COGNITIVE PSYCHOLOGY AND THE READING APPROACH

Both cognitive psychology and transformational grammar have influenced the methodology called the "reading approach." Unlike behavioral psychology, which argues that even a complex act such as speaking is the result of conditioned learning responses, cognitive psychology is based on the premise that the human mind actively acquires knowledge, including knowledge of a new language. Cognitive psychologists point out that, every day, people utter phrases, expressions, and sentences that they have never heard before: no conversation consists only of a set of memorized strings of words. Therefore, cognitive psychologists argue, one's ability to utter sentences one has never before heard indicates that humans have an innate capacity to learn a specialized "cognitive code" called human language (Ellis, 3). Especially influential in education are the ideas of cognitive psychologist David Ausubel, who argues that learning most easily takes place if it is meaningful and able to be related to an individual's cognitive structure (Omaggio, 54–59). Cognitive psychology views the pattern practice drills favored by behaviorism as meaningless utterances that a student cannot relate to any conversational situation in actual daily life. Instead, cognitive psychologists maintain, language instruction must have a content that students can relate to their daily lives, e.g., textbook lessons for secondary students may introduce vocabulary or grammar in readings and dialogues about the lives of teenagers in Germany, China, or ancient Rome.

Like cognitive psychologists, Noam Chomsky (1957, 1965) was intrigued by people's ability to utter phrases, expressions, and sentences that they had never heard before. Chomsky argued that the study of language should focus on syntax, because language is rule-governed, internal behavior. One is able to speak a language not by memorizing and practicing patterns, but only by learning the language's set of rules (i.e., grammar). Only then, by applying these rules can a person produce a variety of original and unique sentences.

In applying cognitive psychology and Chomsky's theories to language teaching, cognitive theory educators argue that students should experience a rule of grammar (e.g., the accusative case indicates the direct object) before they are formally taught it, because students can apply the rules of the target language only after they have become familiar with them. Students must also be provided with activities and learning situations that allow them to use the language creatively. The cognitive approach to language teaching forms the basis of the reading-approach textbooks which have become increasingly popular in this country since the 1980s (see further Chapters 9 and 14 below). Corder explains (133):

> The teaching of grammar is intricately bound up with the teaching of meaning. It is not sufficient merely to enable the learner to produce grammatical sentences; he must know when and how to use them. The distinction between competence and performance is no longer seen as relevant. Grammatical ability is only one element contributing to communicative competence. This means that there is now an insistence on understanding the meaning of grammatical forms and that the teaching of grammar cannot be divorced from the teaching of meaning as it so clearly used to be both in the extreme deductive approach, the "grammar-translation" method, and also in the extreme inductive approach, the "structural method." What little we know about the psychological processes of second language learning, either from theory or from practical experience, suggests that a combination of induction and deduction produces the best results. We call this a "guided inductive approach."

The most popular reading-approach textbooks include: the *Cambridge Latin Course*, first published in England in 1970 and now widely used in its new North American edition (Phinney and Bell 1988–91), predominantly in middle and secondary schools; *Ecce Romani*, first developed in Scotland in 1971, edited for U.S. teachers by Gilbert Lawall (1984; revised 1994–95), and similarly used in middle and secondary schools as well as a number of colleges and universities; and the *Oxford Latin Course*, another, newer British production by Maurice Balme and James Morwood (1987; revised 1996–97), now gaining increased use in colleges and schools. All three series contextualize the grammar in culturally rich narratives. The extensive reading passages in the *Cambridge Latin Course* begin with events in the life of the family of Caecilius Jucundus, a Roman who did actually live in Pompeii and whose house has been excavated. When Vesuvius erupts, the young son of the family escapes the destruction of Pompeii, and the subsequent readings involve his experiences in Rome, Alexandria, and Britain. *Ecce Romani* re-tells the events in the life of a Roman senatorial family, the Cornelii. The main characters are the children, whose activities illustrate typical Roman amusements, education, and the ceremonies of marriage and the *toga virilis*. The *Oxford Latin Course* concentrates on the life of Horace, which allows the authors to introduce information about Augustan Rome and important literary figures such as Vergil. Additional cultural information is presented in all three textbook series via extensive essays and illustrations; the emphasis throughout is on communicating cultural information that is both interesting and historically accurate.

The method of "guided induction" (to use Corder's expression) is clearly seen in the way new forms and structures are introduced by these textbooks. A new form or structure first appears to students, without any grammatical comment or explanation, within the reading passages that are the heart of each lesson. Students' comprehension of a new grammatical structure is facilitated by the strong story line of the narratives, the accompanying illustrations, and, in the *Cambridge Latin Course* and the *Oxford Latin Course*, by the pre-reading cartoon frames and their simplified captions. Only after students have seen a number of examples of a new structure contextualized in several narratives is their understanding of it "consolidated" in a chapter's grammatical discussion.

Other features of guided induction in these reading-approach textbooks can be traced back to Sweet and his employment of structural linguistics. Characteristics of Latin that are most different from English receive special attention in each of the series' beginning texts, and Sweet's introduction of forms across declensions and conjugations is also employed.

The main goal of these textbooks, however, is to enable students to read extensively and easily in Latin. The reading passages from the first lesson on are lengthier than in other textbooks, and exercises focus on understanding what is read rather than the ability to repeat paradigms or patterns from memory.

Most often exercises are "comprehension" questions that require students to give answers in Latin and to form novel sentences rather than to practice pattern sentences and expressions.

TOWARD A PARADIGM FOR THE 21ST CENTURY

At the beginning of the post-war period, as we have seen, a paradigm shift in education occurred, from the traditional ideal of the liberally educated person that emphasized the study of the humanities and language, to the concept of utility and the practically educated person. At first this utility was linked to the scientific education deemed necessary for national strength in the ensuing cold-war period. As the cold war continued, however, the emphasis on science was expanded to include other subjects, such as business and computer science, that would enable a person to train for a particular job after graduation.

This paradigm shift at first affected adversely all foreign language enrollments and particularly Latin. Since the late 1970s, however, foreign language study has been on the rebound in this country, and there has been a remarkable resurgence of interest and enrollments in Latin (surveyed most recently by LaFleur 1997). The reasons for this renaissance are many and complex; certainly the industry and dedication of talented Latin and Classics teachers at all levels has been vitally important. But another crucial factor—both a cause and an effect of Latin's rebirth—is the development over the past 30 years of the new, livelier, and more effective texts and methodologies that have been examined in this brief survey and that will be explored in greater detail, along with a vast array of other new classroom resources and strategies, in the remaining chapters of this book.

3

The Linguistic Perspective

GLENN M. KNUDSVIG
DEBORAH PENNELL ROSS
The University of Michigan

WHAT IS A "LINGUISTIC PERSPECTIVE"?

During the last several decades, we in the profession of teaching Latin have experienced a shift in emphasis from writing to reading. Reading Latin is now a primary goal; we are concerned with teaching our students to read with increased comprehension, and to develop their sight reading skills and strategies. This new emphasis, along with a growing awareness of the various learning styles and multiple intelligences that students bring to our classrooms, has become a catalyst for changing the way in which we teach. We are finding that we need better answers to old questions, and that new issues may benefit from a fresh vantage point. In this chapter, we discuss what a linguistic perspective on Latin can offer, and how it can enable us to expand our understanding of the language itself and shape our teaching of it so that our students become more skilled and proficient readers.

In general terms, a linguistic perspective involves bringing to bear the principles and findings of linguistic science to the description and understanding of a given language—in our case Latin. It allows us to view and describe the target language as one in its own right, with the features of a language system, rather than as an encrypting of English. The linguist acknowledges and is concerned with all the systems of language—phonology, morphology, syntax, semantics (the world of meaning), pragmatics (the world of context), the lexicon—and with their interrelations.

Pedagogically, perhaps the most significant contribution linguistics offers is the notion of *categories*. Frank Smith, in his seminal work on reading theory, claims that "'teaching' is often little more than telling children that a category exists" (Smith 1988:12). If students have categories, they have a system within which to organize new information; categories allow readers to assign meaning and therefore to predict more effectively. Linguistic categories and hierarchies offer a variety of ways to organize and analyze linguistic information: clear distinctions between morphology, syntax, and semantics illuminate the relationships between form, function, and meaning; linguistic terms and concepts provide new insights and new categories to use when talking about text.

Traditionally, the structures of Latin have been described according to morphological criteria and characterized in terms of their semantics. A linguistic perspective on Latin can provide additional categories that will aid the reader: high-level syntactic ones based on or defined in terms of syntactic relationships rather than morphological information. These syntactic categories can provide a paradigm for the syntax of a language, just as declension and conjugation patterns provide a paradigm for the morphology. If students have an understanding of high-level categories, they are able to analyze even complex sentences in some meaningful way.

Syntactic categories allow the reader to interpret the information conveyed by morphology before assigning semantic roles. For instance, *case* is a syntactic device, not a semantic one. The nominative marks a word as having a subject (vs. direct object) role with respect to a finite verb, but provides the reader with no information for determining whether that nominative word represents the agent of the action or the patient. The ablative case indicates an adverbial relationship between the ablative noun and some other element of the sentence, but does not *per se* indicate whether the semantic nature of that relationship is means, time, or cause. Only consideration of the semantics of the ablative noun, coupled with the semantic information of its head (i.e., the word modified), can allow this latter discrimination.

The understanding that there are distinctions between morphological, syntactic, semantic, and pragmatic information is a valuable tool for the reader of a Latin text. The reader moves from consideration of the information presented by an individual word in isolation, to analyzing its role within the context of the sentence, and then beyond the individual sentence to the world of the text.

A HISTORICAL LOOK AT LINGUISTICS

In order to view with clearer understanding the state of the art in modern linguistics, and thus what it has to offer to Latin pedagogy, it is useful to have some historical context. In the 19th century, the greater part of linguistic scholarship was concerned with the comparative and historical study of languages. Linguists of this era were engaged primarily in detailing the phonological and morphological systems of languages, both ancient Indo-European and modern European, and with establishing the relationships between them (Lehmann). The focus of such scholarship was the phoneme, the morpheme, and the word, as these were the units of comparison between languages, and it was at these levels that a description of a common proto-language was initially formulated. Descriptions of individual languages were organized primarily on the basis of phonology, morphology, and the lexicon, and in these areas they were highly systematized and categorization was extensive. Such comprehensive work, however, extended only minimally beyond morphology and the word to syntax and the sentence, and rarely to the areas of semantics and pragmatics.

In the early part of the 20th century, American linguists such as Boas, Bloomfield, and Sapir moved their attention beyond the word to the sentence and its constituents, and from historical and comparative considerations to descriptive linguistics. Field work by linguists and anthropologists collected data from an increasingly wider variety of the world's languages. This additional linguistic data allowed linguists to see patterns and identify univerals even in unrelated languages. Structuralists such as Gleason and Hockett continued work in descriptive linguistics into the middle of this century; in 1957 Chomsky introduced his theory of transformational grammar, which ushered in several decades of work on syntactic theory and inspired spinoffs into generative phonology and generative semantics.

In the latter half of the 20th century, linguists in America and elsewhere have continued to develop and refine various theories of syntax and semantics (e.g., Dik; Givón; Lyons), and have moved to issues of language beyond the sentence encompassed in the growing field of pragmatics and discourse analysis (e.g., Brown and Yule; Halliday and Hasan 1976; Levinson). It is the application of theories arising from this work that has allowed languages, including Latin, to be described more fully in all aspects. As linguistic study is directed not only to more of the systems in language, but to more of the world's languages themselves, our understanding of the nature of human language continues to increase.

LINGUISTICS AND THE READING OF LATIN

The advancements in linguistic science over the period described above represent two major shifts in focus in studying and describing language. The shifts themselves, as well as the insights gained from them, help to provide new perspectives for understanding and describing Latin for the purpose of reading. The first shift was that of moving from a focus on the word in isolation to a focus on the sentence and on the interrelations of individual words in a sentence. The second, more recent shift has been that of moving beyond the sentence as the primary unit of analysis to a consideration of how sentences interrelate in a text and how they jointly and individually depend upon context for meaning, that is, the issues of what makes a text a text.

In the section below we introduce some new perspectives gained from these advances and examine how they can help us to refine, replace, or supplement the categories and descriptions we use in characterizing Latin for the purposes of reading it.

NEW PERSPECTIVES ON THE
WORD WITHIN THE SENTENCE

We use the following topics to illustrate how the understanding of individual words changes when viewed from the perspective of the sentence and the needs of the reader.

A Shift in Understanding Morphology

One of the significant contributions of structural linguistics was in the area of morphology:

> The concept of allomorphs and morphemes, and of other "allos" and "emes," is one of the most basic in descriptive linguistics. Its importance both as a tool and as an insight into the operation of language can hardly be overestimated. It stands behind the two basic units of linguistic description, the phoneme and the morpheme, as well as behind other lesser concepts such as the grapheme. The principle involved is largely responsible for the high development of linguistic theory and techniques (Gleason, 61).

The notion of morpheme and allomorph was a significant breakthrough for the teaching and learning of morphology. For example, paradigms of nouns are traditionally presented vertically, giving the learner an overview of all the possible forms of a word within a certain pattern. However, attention also to the system of allomorphs in Latin is useful for the reader who must respond to case in any of its variant spellings. We highlight this when we present for the learner the horizontal view of noun morphology, e.g., that across declensions the accusative singular is marked by vowel + -*m*, or that the accusative plural is marked by stem vowel (long in quantity) + *s*. When -*am*/-*um*/-*em* are learned as allomorphs of the accusative case, readers typically become more sensitive to the importance of word endings, and also to accusative as a meaningful category.

A Shift in Understanding Part of Speech

Traditionally, "part of speech" was treated in many textbooks as primarily a set of headings for organizing morphology (e.g., nouns, adjectives, and verbs each have certain forms and inflectional patterns). Definitions of parts of speech, when given, were generally semantic rather than syntactic, e.g., a noun is a person, place, or thing. Part of speech was treated as an identifying feature of a word, rather than a shorthand for its syntactic possibilities. The nature of part of speech is described by Pinker (106): "A part of speech . . . is not a kind of meaning; it is a kind of token that obeys certain formal rules, like a chess piece or a poker chip. A noun, for example, is simply a word that does nouny things."

With *noun* as a meaningful notion rather than as an empty label, thinking and analysis such as the following is possible: *This is a noun, therefore what do I expect and what is precluded?* When part of speech is understood in a broader linguistic perspective such as this, the reader is able to make observations or predictions about: *possible or obligatory syntactic functions within the sentence* (e.g., a subordinating conjunction always signals a dependent clause while a particle such as *autem* does not; a coordinating conjunction raises the expectation of two syntactically equivalent items); *possible or obligatory semantic roles within the sentence* (e.g., a noun indicates a participant role, but an adjective does not).

A Shift in Understanding Semantic Categories

The field of semantics has increased our awareness of the importance of identifying for each part of speech a wider range of semantic categories useful for the reader. Though many Latin students have learned various sense groups (e.g., rooms of the house, members of the family, occupations), the systematic study of semantics and the relationship of semantics to pragmatics has led to more categories and more useful categories.

For example, categorizing nouns as animate or non-animate enables the reader to determine whether an ambiguous noun form is more likely to be dative or ablative; these categories also heighten the reader's awareness of semantic compatibility (e.g., an animate noun is semantically compatible with only certain verbs—unless metaphor is involved). The category "verbs of motion" prevents the reader from expecting a direct object, since such verbs are very likely to be intransitive (another category of importance to the reader).

NEW PERSPECTIVES ON SYNTAX OF THE SENTENCE

New perspectives on syntax have established the high-level categories *kernel* and *modifier*. These categories provide a view of the syntax of the Latin sentence which highlights such useful notions as syntactic equivalents and noun clause. A distinction between kernel (the obligatory elements of the clause, i.e., subject, verb, object/complement) and modifier (an element that adds descriptive information to a head) facilitates a binary decision-making process for the reader whereby words or groups of words can be classified as either kernel *or* modifier, and if modifier, as either adjectival *or* adverbial. For the reader, any kernel item raises the minimal expectation of another kernel item; a modifier raises the expectation of a head. Classifying the modifier as adjectival or adverbial enables the reader to form even more specific expectations about the head that will complete the unit.

Once the categories of kernel and modifier are in place, it is possible to introduce the notion of syntactic equivalents, that is, structures which can have the same syntactic function in the sentence. Being able to place a range of structures in the same functional category enables the reader to make decisions much faster, thereby aiding the comprehension process. Consider the following English examples: He did it *carefully* [adverb as adverbial modifier]. He did it *with care* [prepositional phrase as adverbial modifier]. He did it *when he was asked* [dependent clause as adverbial modifier]. Examples of some of these high-level categories and some of the syntactically equivalent structures which are included in each category are:

> *Adverbial modifiers*: adverbs; prepositional phrases; ablative absolutes; dependent finite clauses (e.g., those signaled by *dum, cum, si, ubi,* etc.); nouns in the ablative without prepositions (except ablative "objects" or ablatives expressing description); nouns in the dative (except dative "objects")
>
> *Adjectival modifiers*: adjectives, relative clauses, participles, nouns in the genitive
>
> *Noun equivalents*: nouns; pronouns; substantives; finite noun clauses (e.g., indirect commands); non-finite noun clauses (e.g., indirect statements).

NEW PERSPECTIVES ON TEXT

Just as insights gained from linguistics have enabled us to expand our understanding of the word and the sentence, so too have they enabled us to understand more about what constitutes text, and, therefore, to learn more about how to help our students read more effectively. Pragmatics, text linguistics, and discourse analysis have provided language and categories for talking about the features of text, and theories which present those features in an organized and useful way.

When we are able to embrace this broader view of Latin as a language, with all the attendant features of language, we can learn to recognize in Latin texts those features, such as cohesive devices operating both within and beyond the sentence, which help relate one sentence to another, and thus serve to create text.

We have learned that one of the universal characteristics of text is that various types of cohesive relation are evident throughout. "Cohesion occurs where the interpretation of some element in the discourse is dependent on that of another. The one presupposes the other, in the sense that it cannot be effectively decoded except by recourse to it" (Halliday and Hasan 1976: 4). Consider the following example in English: "Maria gave some books to the little boy and girl who live next door. She could read all of the stories but he only a few." The interpretation of the pronouns *she, he,* and *few* depends on items in the previous sentence (reference); the omission of the verb in "he only a few" is an example of a cohesive device across clauses (gapping); *books* and *stories* are related by meaning (lexical chain).

According to Halliday and Hasan (1976), the reality of cohesion and the devices used can be listed finitely and compared across languages. We can now make readers more aware of the mechanisms Latin uses in order to create surface links between the clauses of a sentence as well as between the sentences of a text. Thus we can help students learn what they should expect within any text they are reading, and they can proceed to develop reading strategies built on this knowledge.

The types of cohesive devices most useful to readers of Latin (as well as English) include:

Reference

Reference is the cohesive device most familiar to students, since it is characterized by the use of pronouns, both personal and demonstrative, such as *hic* and *ille*.

Lexical Cohesion

The selection of vocabulary creates the cohesive effect of lexical cohesion, which is also referred to as the use of *lexical chains*. One type of lexical cohesion especially useful to students of Latin is *reiteration*; this has three easily identified subtypes: 1) the repetition of a word in more than one sentence; 2) the use of synonyms, or near synonyms, across sentences; and 3) the combination of lexical items and their superordinates (e.g., the use of *spear* in one sentence and *weapon* in another).

Text Connectors

A third characteristic of text is the presence of *text connectors,* conjunctions which semantically link new information to the preceding context. Examples of these text connectors in Latin include: *tamen, autem, igitur, nam.* Latin students who are aware of this cohesive device are able to form better expectations of what is to be learned from the sentence which follows, using the context of what they have just read.

Gapping

Gapping (also called ellipsis) is a phenomenon which has been observed in many languages: a word or words in common to more than one clause in a sentence may be *gapped* in one of the clauses (Ross 1970; Seligson and Knudsvig; Panhuis 1980). A word in common to more than one sentence may be gapped in one of the sentences. The specific rules and patterns of gapping vary from language to language. Unlike the previous cohesive devices, which are primarily lexical issues, this is a syntactic feature constrained by the rules of completeness of a structure. Both Latin and English utilize gapping across clauses or sentences. "She could read all the stories, but he only a few" illustrates gapping in English across clauses. English can have a gapped verb only in the second of two clauses; Latin can have gapping in either clause. Consider the following examples: 1) *Furem fur cognoscit et lupum lupus*—"A thief recognizes a thief and a wolf a wolf"; 2) *Multi famam, conscientiam pauci vererentur*—"Many respect public opinion, few respect their conscience." The reader who understands the phenomenon of gapping and the possible patterns it has in Latin will have less difficulty in processing texts such as these than a student who assumes that the gapping patterns in Latin are the same as those in English. Gapping has traditionally been taught under the term ellipsis as a rhetorical device, but it is a very pervasive feature of the language, and students will greatly benefit from learning about gapping right from the beginning.

The cohesive nature of text is, to a great extent, universal, and can be identified and practiced in English in order to acquaint students with both the concept and the reality of cohesion. Once the categories of reference, gapping, and so forth are in place, the cohesive devices used in Latin can be identified and practiced, and students can learn to analyze a word such as *hunc* not only morphologically as "demonstrative prn, acc sg m," but syntactically as "kernel item, direct object," semantically at the word level as "an entity with masculine gender, perhaps animate, mentioned most recently," and semantically at the text level as "referent = X."

NEW PERSPECTIVES ON WORD ORDER

One of the most common stumbling blocks for Latin students has been that word order in Latin differs considerably from that of English. Students have often resorted to a hunt-and-peck method of working through a Latin text, searching for subject, then verb, then object, so that they might order the information in an understandable sequence. Reading is, however, a continuous linear process, and Latin, like English, is intended to be read in a left-to-right fashion, with each segment of preceding text providing the context necessary for interpreting the text which follows. Teaching students to process text linearly ensures that they will encounter ideas and information in the sequence intended by the author.

A renewed interest in Latin word order has grown along with the development in linguistics of functional theories of grammar (Dik; Givón) which attempt to explain phenomena in language in terms of pragmatic as well as syntactic and semantic criteria. Many of the issues and problems of word order in Latin and other languages with "free" order have been illuminated by the application of theories of functional grammar and discourse analysis. This quote from Odlin (88) outlines what we now understand about these languages:

Far from being "free" or random, word order in flexible languages seems to reflect constraints imposed by the discourse needs of speakers and listeners. The constraints are complex and some seem to be language-specific, but some of the most important constraints are evident in the limited number of patterns used to signal information about *topics* in discourse.

Current research on Latin word order within the context of discourse constraints provides us with an increasingly better understanding of why the elements in a Latin sentence occur in the sequence they do. For recent work in this area, see Panhuis (1982), Pinkster (1990), and Ross (1987, 1991).

In the sections below, we discuss two ways in which attention to word order and processing text in a linear fashion can increase reading comprehension and efficiency.

Word Order and Ambiguity

Students are often frustrated by the frequent instances of morphological and syntactic ambiguity they may encounter in reading a Latin text. In a simple example, the case of a word such as *consilium* cannot be resolved out of context, but for the reader proceeding from left to right in the following sentence, the morphological ambiguity is simply not an issue: *Gladiator fortis consilium capit.* The unambiguous form *gladiator* removes for the reader the possibility that *consilium* could be nominative. A student who can use preceding information to reduce or resolve ambiguities as they are met will be a much more efficient reader, and read with a greater degree of comprehension.

Word Order and Discourse Information

Traditional descriptions of word order in Latin do not offer much practical information for the novice reader. Beyond the information that word order in Latin is not the primary carrier of syntactic information, and the (often misleading) statement that the verb comes last, the explanation most frequently given is that Latin word order is the result of "emphasis":

> That word order in Latin is in some way involved with factors outside syntactic relationships has long been recognized, although the terminology which has come to us from theories of discourse analysis and text linguistics was not incorporated into traditional descriptions. There, situations which could not be explained in syntactic terms were regarded as stylistic or rhetorical, highly marked in some sense or another. There is a long tradition among Latin grammarians of explaining various orderings in terms of "emphasis," as being deliberate attempts on the part of the author to secure a particular effect, or produce a certain emotion. The explanatory inadequacy of this approach was recognized in the nineteenth century . . .. Several early twentieth century scholars attempted to effect change in the traditional preoccupation with syntax,

but their major weakness seems to have been that they could offer no formal paradigm as a replacement (Ross 1987: 7–8).

With the work in pragmatics, discourse analysis, and text linguistics over the past 20 years, we now have theories, along with categories and terms, which can give us a better understanding of the factors governing Latin word order. Recent studies have shown that the order of words in Latin is sensitive to certain pragmatic functions in discourse; these functions are referred to by various scholars as *topic* and *focus*, *theme* and *rheme*, *given* and *new* information. Different terms and characterizations are used in the literature to refer to the relevant discourse roles, but, for our purposes, we can describe them in terms of given and new information, given information being that which has in some fashion been previously introduced into the discourse and new information being that which the speaker/writer considers to be new or hitherto unknown to the listener/reader.

In very general terms, word order in a Latin sentence is organized by presenting given (or known) information first or early in the sentence or clause and new (or unknown) information at the end. The beginning of a Latin sentence is available for those elements which refer back to previously mentioned entities, e.g., demonstrative pronouns, connecting relatives. The information coming later in the clause or sentence introduces new information which carries the discourse forward.

If students are aware, first of all, that word order in Latin is not arbitrary, but governed by specific constraints, they are more likely to be observant of word order patterns when they are reading. Once they know that factors governing word order are discourse-related, they can respond accordingly. The numerous ways that information status (given vs. new) can be marked in English can be demonstrated in order to acquaint students with basic discourse notions. With an understanding that such notions are universal in language, and an awareness of how they are expressed in English, students can learn to observe and interpret them in Latin, and thus read with more ease and comprehension.

BRINGING A LINGUISTIC
PERSPECTIVE TO THE CURRICULUM

As we strive to give our students the skills and strategies which will make them confident and competent readers of Latin, we are finding that we need to utilize ideas and categories that traditionally have not been addressed. For a variety of historical and pedagogical reasons, the language information in the majority of Latin textbooks is based primarily on the descriptions of Latin dating from the 19th century, when scholars were absorbed with the phonological and morphological systems of language (see Chapter 2 above). The focus of this work was at the word level, and the categories are morphological. The linguistic advances in syntax, semantics, and pragmatics in the latter half of this century have not yet been incorporated consistently into descriptions of Latin (except see Kroon; Pinkster 1990) and are not yet, by and large, an organizing principle for Latin textbooks. Some texts that do incorporate a linguistic perspective are Waldo E. Sweet's ground-breaking works (Sweet 1957; Sweet, et al., 1966) and textbooks which have followed and further developed this approach.

A result of having such a limited model available to us is that there are weaknesses or holes in our knowledge and understanding of language in general, the Latin language in particular, and the nature of the reading process. A linguistic perspective can strengthen many of these weak areas and provide useful information to fill the holes. For instance, once we have the notion of completeness of thought, we become more aware of the significance and the ubiquitous nature of gapping in Latin. Models of Latin which represent the language in all its aspects, rather than focusing primarily on morphology, give us a more complete picture by incorporating all the systems of language: morphology, syntax, semantics, and pragmatics. With a cleaner set of categories for syntax, distinctions such as kernel vs. modifier are possible, and our students are able to organize their decision-making processes more effectively. By better understanding the reading process, we are able to discriminate active from passive reading, and to realize the fundamental importance of word order, expectations, and the linear processing of texts. The newest Latin textbooks have already benefitted from the advances made in linguistics over the past generation; an even more deliberate application of the linguistic perspective to future textbooks is certain to make them even more useful to our goal of helping students read Latin with greater ease and understanding.

4

Trends in Language Education: Latin in the Mainstream

MARTHA G. ABBOTT
Fairfax County Public Schools, Fairfax, Virginia

THE TEACHING OF LATIN IN THE
CONTEXT OF EDUCATIONAL REFORM

As we consider the relationship between instruction in Latin and instruction in other languages, it is important to examine the context of educational reform efforts to improve student achievement that are currently underway nationwide. Educational initiatives, particularly in the area of educational reform, are having a significant impact on the language choices of our students and on the instructional delivery in our classrooms. What do teachers of Latin need to know and do in order to ensure that Latin programs remain a vital part of the curriculum in our schools? Are there strategies and techniques used by teachers of other languages that can inform and instruct us as teachers of classical languages? And finally, what impact does research in the area of language teaching and learning have on Latin instruction? These issues are vital considerations for teachers of Latin, as changes in our schools are taking place at a rapid pace.

The call has gone out nationwide for educational improvements and the race is on to improve student achievement through a variety of initiatives. From restructuring the school day to produce longer segments of instructional time to wholesale adoption of prescribed curriculum, school districts throughout our country are scrambling to change the way they do business. Most significant of these initiatives is that of the establishment of national standards, including standards for foreign language education and the subsequent adaptation of these standards for classical languages (see Chapter 5). For the first time in American history, these standards provide a national framework for student achievement in Latin and Greek. The proactive stance of the classical associations that undertook the task of establishing standards for classical languages is a clear signal that classicists do not expect to take a back seat in these times of

36

innovative reform. However, as terms such as "multiculturalism" and "technology-based" take hold in school districts, it remains the responsibility of each teacher of the Classics to ensure that the classical languages are not overlooked in these current trends. Indeed in the early 1990s, when the American Council on the Teaching of Foreign Languages (ACTFL) identified its priorities for the coming decade, "Critical Instructional Issues in the Classics for American Schools" was one of those priorities and, looking to the future, classicists wrote, "In the decade ahead, the most important issues for classicists will be to continue and expand upon the recent initiatives of the 1980s, to continue to unite the profession through communication and collaboration, and to ensure that the teaching of Latin and the classical world is reestablished in the forefront of language education in America" (Abbott 1991). The image of the lone teacher of Latin must be replaced by the Latin teacher of the 21st century who is actively involved in all aspects of educational reform and who undertakes the responsibility of applying the research in the teaching of languages to the arena of the Latin classroom.

TEACHING LATIN AS A LANGUAGE

There is a distinct dichotomy between how people say Latin should be taught and how it is usually taught in classrooms across the country. From William Riley Parker's "The Case for Latin" (an influential tract of the early 1960s) to Lorraine Strasheim's "Latin in the 1990s and Beyond," educators have called for teaching Latin as a language instead of a complex translation puzzle that students must struggle to solve. When our classes focus predominantly on teaching students *about* the language rather than *to use* the language, classrooms become stifling environments where only the most capable students can be successful. There is not an educator today who isn't aware of the research conducted on learning styles and other research that indicate that as many senses as possible and as many approaches as feasible need to be used with students in the classroom. Our goal and our focus is on teaching students to read Latin, but in the process of doing so, it is vital to use other skills, such as listening, speaking, and writing, in order to meet the learning needs of students. This does not mean developing Latin as a conversational skill, but simply using these senses in order to help students internalize the language's patterns and to understand them when they read or hear them.

An experience that I had as an adult bears testimony to the importance of these other avenues for learning Latin. As fellow Latin teacher Jane Hall and I were developing the curriculum for the first Governor's Latin Academy to be held in Virginia for talented students from around the state, we were challenged with the need to develop a curriculum that would not be duplicated by the students' own high-school Latin program (Abbott 1992). We came up with the idea of a course in oral Latin and were determined not to use English in this

45–minute class, which students would take three times a week. Needless to say, we were challenged as the instructors to conduct the class in *lingua Latina*! We progressed from simple introductions and personal questions, *Quid nomen tibi est?*, to geography questions, *Monstra nobis mare Adriaticum in tabula geographica*, to more complex structures of purpose, *Cur Marcus in culinam intravit?* The surprising result for me as a teacher is that my own reading and understanding of Latin increased after that experience. There were obviously other senses and skills that I had never used to reinforce my own comprehension of the language, skills that took me from simply *translating* to really being able to *read* Latin. If we expect our students to develop true reading ability in Latin, we must use whatever learning modes work best for them.

There are other approaches to language teaching that have taken hold in modern language classes because of the supportive research behind them and also because of the results that teachers have experienced by using them. Following are some of these methods, approaches, and emphases that characterize the language classes envisioned in the *Standards for Classical Language Learning* (American Classical League—Chapter 5 below); these, and many other modern approaches to Latin teaching, are explored in further detail in the subsequent chapters of this book.

Focus on the Learner

One striking characteristic of foreign language education for the coming century is the premise that all students in our schools should have the opportunity to learn a language other than English. Technological innovations have radically changed the way we communicate with people around the world. The old-fashioned notion that most Americans would not have the opportunity to use languages other than English has given way to a veritable crisis in the lack of bilingual employees to meet the needs of global competition. Foreign languages, moved to the core of the curriculum by the legislation enacted by Congress in 1994, entitled "Goals 2000: Educate America," is rapidly moving to the forefront of important skills that students will need in order to be competitive in the next century. In fact, not only in the philosophy statement of the *Standards for Foreign Language Learning*, but also included in many state standards frameworks, are policies for foreign language learning that include all students in our schools. Teachers of Latin must embrace this endeavor along with teachers of modern languages, so that the needs of all students are being met in the foreign language classroom.

In the last 15 years, there has been increased focus on creating an instructional environment that takes into consideration the characteristics of the learners. From "learning styles" to "cooperative learning," educational initiatives have redirected instructional delivery to an increasingly stu-dent-centered classroom. Because most of these initiatives are presented as important for all students, teachers of Latin, for the most part, have adopted and adapted them to fit their programs. Let's examine some of the educational research of the last 30 years, its potential impact on language instruction in the United States, and how this relates to the teaching of Latin.

Teacher Expectations and Student Achievement (TESA)

Significant research conducted in the 1970s and 1980s in Los Angeles County schools on the effect of teacher expectations on student achievement indicated that teachers interacted differently with students they considered high achievers vs. those they considered to be low achievers. The researchers gathered data on the number of times individual students were given an opportunity to respond to questions, teachers' willingness to provide individual help, and how frequently and with whom they delved into questioning for higher level thinking. The researchers also examined the feedback system of teachers based on high and low achievers, how frequently students were praised and how accepting the teachers were of students' feelings. Finally, data was collected concerning the personal regard teachers had for students, how close they stood to individual students, how frequently they showed a personal interest and complimented students, and how courteously they interacted with them (Kerman and Martin).

The results of the study indicated that teachers had much more positive interactions, gave more wait time when questioning, and showed more personal interest in the students they perceived to be "high achievers." The researchers then developed five training modules which were designed to raise teachers' awareness of how they interacted with students. When teachers were trained to provide equal opportunity for all students in the classroom, low achievers showed statistically significant academic gains over their counterparts in control classes.

As a teacher who participated in the TESA training, I was skeptical of the implication that I was not encouraging all of my students. From journal entries I made at the beginning of the training—"I feel that I definitely treat students differently as far as calling on them, but I feel justified"—it was evident that I was confident in my ability to "know" the needs of my students. By the end of the training, however, my consciousness had been challenged to the point that I was writing, "The TESA program has really heightened my awareness about how much influence I have on my students and how just a simple compliment or comment can really have a great effect. In general, I have tried to take a more personal interest in my students—especially the ones that don't seek my attention."

The implications of this research are significant, if we are to include all students in our programs. We need to be aware of the strong connection between our expectations and the performance of our students. We need to believe ourselves that all students can be successful in a Latin class. This is one of the most challenging issues facing all foreign language teachers in schools today.

Cooperative Learning

In addition to learning a second language, another important skill for our students is that of being able to work cooperatively with others. Employers consistently talk of the need for employees who can work together on teams to develop new products and solve problems with existing ones. The old notion of competition in the work place or the lone worker solving problems in isolation is anachronistic today. According to Johnson, et al., over 375 studies have been conducted to answer the question of how relatively successful competitive, individualistic, and cooperative efforts are in promoting productivity and achievement. The results indicate that cooperative learning resulted in higher level reasoning, more frequent generation of new ideas and solutions, and greater transfer of what is learned within one situation to another.

As the essential skills of cooperative learning are translated into the classroom setting, it is important for teachers to establish activities that promote positive interdependence, face-to-face interaction, individual accountability, and collaborative skills. This does not mean that students share a grade or simply work together, each with his own worksheet, asking each other questions. Rather, the activity is structured so that they must rely on each other for information but at the same time maintain a personal accountability for their own work within the group. For Latin teachers, remaining the "guide on the side" instead of the "sage on the stage" is often challenging. The mantra from cooperative learning that intrigues me the most is, "First ask three, then ask me." This means that students in the group must have completely exhausted their own resources before asking the teacher for help. This focus on the learner helps to make our students see themselves as responsible for their own learning. This is a critical factor in language teaching. No one learns a language by remaining passive in a classroom and just listening. There must be active cognitive engagement in order for learning to take place. It is increasingly incumbent upon the language teacher to establish a classroom setting in which students see themselves as language learners and understand the concomitant responsibilities. Students may need to be taught the skills that are involved in working cooperatively, how to resolve conflicts, how to include everyone in the decision-making, how to let everyone have a chance to provide input. A more student-centered Latin classroom can afford students the opportunity to take on this responsibility. For example, after introducing a new text, the teacher can provide background information in various categories to different members of each group. One student might have the historical background information, another the mythological references, and another a grammar reference. Only by cooperating are the students able to come up with a workable reading of the passage; and, at the same time, they are more cognitively engaged in the reading than if a teacher-led discussion had taken place.

Total Physical Response (TPR)

The TPR approach to language teaching was developed by James J. Asher in response to research that indicated that kinesthetic involvement helped improve students' retention of vocabulary and increased listening comprehension. Coupled with Stephen Krashen's research that comprehensible input must be provided before comprehensible output can be expected, this approach is at least one strategy that teachers use in working with students. The basic premise is that the teacher provides students with commands that are then carried out by the student. For example, "Stand up, touch your head, take a bow, walk to the window, and point to the clock." Students respond to the commands and in the process internalize the meanings of the words.

In Latin classrooms teachers have begun to use this strategy to stress aural comprehension of the language (see Chapter 7 below; Salerno; Strasheim 1987). Vocabulary retention in any language is a challenge and teachers who use concrete ways of helping students connect the word in Latin with a movement or concrete object see dramatic results in the way their students are able to remember words. For example, commands such as *Surge, discipule—ambula ad fenestram et eam aperi*, engage students in the activity kinesthetically and cognitively. They quickly become adept at following the commands as a group or individually. The TPR activity can be expanded to allow students to give the commands, and, thus, the oral mode is activated as well. This active involvement not only helps students learn vocabulary items but also facilitates their internalization of structures which they are later able to understand better when reading a Latin text.

THE TEACHING OF CULTURE

The focus on integrating the teaching of culture into all aspects of language learning is an important one for teachers of Latin. The national standards present an innovative way of looking at culture which is particularly suited to the teaching of Latin. Culture is divided into three components which are interrelated: perspectives, practices, and products. Most of the buzz words in education today—multiculturalism, technology-based, values education, and so forth—can be related directly to study of the daily private and public life of the Romans and Greeks. Expanding on the perspectives, practices, and products that students learn about is another important goal of the national standards, i.e., relating these to the students' own culture. Because classicists are constantly called upon to justify the relevance of their subject, teachers who connect the ideas, beliefs, and ways of behaving of the ancient Romans and Greeks to help students understand human characteristics and motivations and how we can learn from situations that challenged the ancients, are immune from having to justify their subject. Students can see an immediate relationship between the ancient texts and today's society. These comparisons and insights should not be limited to a certain day of the week nor should they be limited to the cultural aspects. Teachers of Latin make, and should encourage students to make, comparisons and contrasts between life and language then and now.

ACHIEVEMENT VS. PROFICIENCY

The current emphasis on performance assessment and student achievement parallels well with Goal Five of the *National Standards*: "Using language beyond the classroom setting." If we limit learning in the Latin classroom to knowledge about the language, then we are doomed to the response that frequently comes from people who studied Latin in their pasts. They dutifully recite a couple of lines from a grammatical paradigm, usually *hic, haec, hoc* or *amo, amas, amat*. What this indicates is that they are much more comfortable with something they memorized than in applying what they learned to new settings. Why don't people respond with, "I'm so glad I took Latin; I truly understood the vase paintings in the museum I visited last week"? I do not mean to imply that responses like that are never given, but all to often it is the former sort of response that predominates. What is happening now in modern language classes is that emphasis is being placed on what students can "do" with the language. More and more school districts are implementing performance assessments, although they may have terms such as, "portfolio assessment," "alternative assessment," and other labels. In the Latin classroom as well, we should focus on what students can "do" with their knowledge of the language. How well can they read a passage and get the message? How can they relate that message to their own language and culture? How can they use that knowledge beyond the classroom? We are just beginning to focus on this aspect of language teaching. As teachers of Classics, though, we would be remiss not to explore the parallels that exist between the applications for modern language students and those for Latin. There are already Latin chat lines for students as well as teachers and some exciting activities for students of Classics using the Internet. What better international language than Latin for students to use to communicate with others around the world? Teachers of Latin in several states have already undertaken projects such as having their students write a chapter in a historical novel, which is then continued by students in another state. The teachers say that they have never seen their students so intent on historical, geographic, and linguistic accuracy, because they know that their work is going to be read and judged by their peers. As much as we would like to think that students want to perform well for us, their teachers, the reality is that the pressure of performing for peers produces much more dramatic results. As teachers become as comfortable as students using the new technologies, there will be more opportunities for students of Latin to see the applicability of their linguistic and cultural studies beyond the classroom, just as students of other languages do.

CONCLUSION

The traditional isolation of the Latin teacher is breaking down across the country as teachers are embracing new methodologies, new approaches, and new technologies. Just as there are significant political reasons for us, as classicists, to remain united with the larger community of foreign language professionals, there are equally compelling pedagogical reasons for doing so. The ideas presented in this chapter only briefly touch upon some of the many ways we can examine, and use for our own instruction, the current research on learning and second language acquisition and teaching culture. Our close connection and collaboration with the language teaching community will ensure that our Latin classrooms are not only meeting the needs of all students, but also are providing Latin students an understanding of a vital, relevant language and culture that can help them relate to an increasingly complex world.

5

National Standards And Curriculum Guidelines

MARTHA G. ABBOTT
Fairfax County Public Schools, Fairfax, Virginia

SALLY DAVIS
H. B. Woodlawn Program, Arlington, Virginia

RICHARD C. GASCOYNE
University at Albany, SUNY

FROM LEGISLATION TO GENERIC STANDARDS

When Congress passed legislation entitled "Goals 2000: Educate America," six goals for American education were outlined, one of which called for students to show competence in challenging core subjects including foreign languages. Goals 2000, and the complementary "Improving America's Schools Act," encouraged the development of voluntary high standards in the core disciplines. The American Council on the Teaching of Foreign Languages (ACTFL), in collaboration with the American Association of Teachers of French (AATF), the American Association of Teachers of German (AATG), and the American Association of Teachers of Spanish and Portuguese (AATSP), assembled a task force of foreign language educators to develop generic standards for language learning. After three years of receiving input on various drafts of the standards, the document entitled *Standards for Foreign Language Learning: Preparing for the 21st Century* was published. From the beginning, those who formed the policy for the project and those who crafted the standards considered classical languages to be part of the effort. The following statement comes from the "Statement of Philosophy" of *Standards for Foreign Language Learning:*

> The United States must educate students who are equipped linguistically and culturally to communicate successfully in a pluralistic American society and abroad. This imperative envisions a future in which ALL students will develop

and maintain proficiency in English and at least one other language, modern or classical.

FROM FOREIGN LANGUAGES TO LATIN AND GREEK

Even before the publication of *Standards for Foreign Language Learning,* language-specific organizations were reacting to the application of the standards to the languages they teach. Sample progress indicators provided in the document did not always fit all languages represented in the schools. For example, classicists were concerned about the emphasis on communicative interaction found in Goal 1. Since *Standards for Foreign Language Learning* was always meant to be a generic framework that individual states and local districts would use to develop their own standards and curricula, language-specific organizations began adapting the progress indicators and scenarios of classroom applications of the standards to meet the specific needs of their language communities. The American Classical League (ACL) and the American Philological Association (APA), in collaboration with several regional organizations, organized a task force to look closely at the standards for foreign language learning and to compile a document that would speak to the teaching and learning of Latin and Greek in the United States. Names and affiliations of the task force members appear in an appendix at the end of this chapter.

STANDARDS FOR CLASSICAL LANGUAGE LEARNING

Standards for Classical Language Learning, on the model of *Standards for Foreign Language Learning,* sets five "goals." The five goals are divided into two content "standards." Each standard is illustrated by a number of "sample progress indicators." The standards are further illustrated by and integrated into "scenarios" (snapshots of classroom situations). Following is an outline of these goals and standards, together with a discussion of each goal.

Goal 1:   Communication—Communicate in a Classical Language

Standard 1.1:   Students read, understand, and interpret Latin or Greek.

Standard 1.2:   Students use orally, listen to, and write Latin or Greek as part of the language learning process.

Goal 1 defines communication as it applies to the learning of a classical language. The written messages from the ancient world, from epic poetry to Pompeiian graffiti, are the major source of our knowledge of, and our major line of communication to, the Greeks and Romans. Reading, then, is the first standard (standard 1.1) and the key to communicating with the ancient world. But the Forum and the Agora were alive with the sounds of commerce, the speeches of politicians, and the noise of gossip; the recitation of poetry reflected the sounds of an active literature. To hear these sounds, to imitate those cadences in the classroom, to practice writing words and ideas in the ancient language (standard 1.2) enhances the ability to read. The second standard emphasizes the importance of oral skills, listening, and writing as tools to improve students' reading ability. It is important to note that standard 1.2 is not a "conversation" standard. It does not even use the word "speak." The document's sample progress indicators for beginners state: "Students recognize and reproduce the sounds of Latin or Greek; students respond to simple questions, statements, commands, or other stimuli; students sing songs in Latin or Greek." The advanced progress indicators state: "Students read Latin or Greek prose and poetry aloud with attention to such features as metrical structure, meaningful phrase grouping, and appropriate voice inflection; students respond appropriately to more complex spoken and written Latin or Greek." This is a statement of the oral use of Latin that is truly complementary to reading. The Task Force felt that this was an appropriate representation of a good model that currently exists and a good model for the future. It establishes a firm link with the best thinking and research in foreign language pedagogy, and it affirms the special place that classical languages have in a reading, writing, listening, and speaking world.

Goal 2:   Cultures—Gain Knowledge and Understanding of Greco-Roman Culture

Standard 2.1:   *Students demonstrate an understanding of the perspectives of Greek or Roman culture as revealed in the practices of the Greeks or Romans.*

Standard 2.2:   *Students demonstrate an understanding of the perspectives of Greek or Roman culture as revealed in the products of the Greeks or Romans.*

Understanding the relationship between the practices and the perspectives (standard 2.1) and between the products and the perspectives (standard 2.2) of the Greeks or Romans is key to an understanding of their culture. The sample progress indicators for the Cultures goal approach the teaching of culture mainly through reading Latin and Greek. One progress indicator at the beginning stage of study states, "Students identify principal Greek and/or Roman deities and heroes by names, deeds, and spheres of influence, in part by reading passages of Latin or Greek." The focus is on students being able to hear (i.e., read) and see the message of the Greeks and Romans in their products, especially their literature, and in their practices, as well as through their writing. Communication and culture cannot be separated.

Goal 3:   Connections—Connect with Other Disciplines and Expand Knowledge

Standard 3.1:   Students reinforce and further their knowledge of other disciplines through their study of classical languages.

Standard 3.2:   Students expand their knowledge through the reading of Latin or Greek and the study of ancient culture.

Goal 3 focuses on connecting the knowledge and understanding gained in Goal 1 (Communication) and Goal 2 (Culture) to other subject areas of the curriculum. One sample progress indicator states, "Students recognize and make connections with Latin or Greek terminology in the sciences and technology." Standard 3.1 stresses the language connections and standard 3.2 stresses the cultural connections. Sample progress indicators state, "Students recognize plots and themes of Greco-Roman myths in the literature of other cultures." In fact, it is increasingly more important for the foreign language class, and specifically the Latin or Greek class, to be the place where students are able—and indeed encouraged—to make connections throughout the curriculum. Goal 3 makes a statement to school policy-makers, legislators, parents, and the larger community that the foreign language class plays an important role in helping students understand the "big picture" and interconnectedness of their world.

Goal 4:   Comparisons—Develop Insight into Own Language and Culture

Standard 4.1:   Students recognize and use elements of the Latin or Greek language to increase knowledge of their own language.

Standard 4.2:   Students compare and contrast their own culture with that of the Greco-Roman world.

Another vital role that languages play for native speakers of English, as well as those learning English, is that through language study, and especially through classical language study, students can reflect on their own language and culture. Teachers have long decried students' lack of grammatical understanding, and parents and employers alike bemoan the lack of facility in English they see around them. Grammar as an abstract concept can only be understood when one attempts to learn a new language and has the opportunity to compare and contrast structural and lexical elements (standard 4.1). Likewise, the study of a different culture invites students to reflect on corresponding perspectives, practices, and products from their own culture (standard 4.2). As our communities become more ethnically and linguistically diverse and worldwide communication is at our finger tips, this is a vital area for our students to develop as they approach the 21st century. As we attempt to secure the position of classical languages in the curriculum, the Comparisons goal remains a vital focus of Latin and Greek classrooms.

Goal 5:   Communities—Participate in Wider Communities of Language and Culture

> *Standard 5.1:   Students use their knowledge of Latin and Greek in a multilingual world.*

> *Standard 5.2:   Students use their knowledge of Greco-Roman culture in a world of diverse cultures.*

In Goal 5 there is an even more vital link made between the study of language and culture in the classroom and the application to the real world of our students. Is not one of the fundamental purposes of learning Latin and Greek to expand one's world and to enjoy it more fully in one's understanding of languages (standard 5.1) and civilizations (standard 5.2)? As a profession, we must be able to demonstrate to students and to the community at large this unique benefit. Part of our curriculum must focus on helping students use the language and culture in real world applications. For example, a sample progress indicator for Goal 5 states, "Students recognize the influence of Latin or Greek in the specialized language of various professional fields." As educational reform efforts focus on performance assessments and real world applications, including the workplace, Goal 5 (Communities) will take on an increased level of importance.

FROM NATIONAL STANDARDS TO LOCAL CURRICULUM

As Latin teachers look at these standards, our first thoughts are, "But how can I use this in class?" "This doesn't tell me what to teach, or when to teach it." "What do the standards have to do with *my* program?"

It is important to understand that the standards are not meant to be a classroom tool. They are intended to describe on a national level what we expect our students to know and be able to do. They are meant as a guide to state curriculum frameworks, and a guide for curriculum development in the broadest sense at the district level. They are not a curriculum guide for our course; they are not a guide to lesson planning. *Standards for Classical Language Learning* does not mandate methodology; it is not textbook-bound; it does not tell how to teach. It provides a destination, not a road map. The document will be immediately useful to the individual teacher who needs to justify the study of classical languages to the board of education, the district office, the state education department, or a state legislature. It will help us to explain to law-makers and educational policy-makers that classical languages have standards of excellence to challenge the students of today and tomorrow.

Teachers, indeed, will need to consider the overall goals they have for their own programs in light of the standards, but a careful process of curriculum development needs to fill the gap between national standards and the local classroom.

The following illustration shows the ideal progression from national standards to local classroom. Work is currently progressing at several levels simultaneously with a hope that input from all levels is available for consideration at all other levels.

(Voluntary)

National Standards

Foreign Language Standards   **Classical Language Standards**

State Framework

District Curriculum

Unit / Lesson plans

Activities / Scenarios

This ideal scheme can get lost in paperwork, delays, and bureaucracy; in addition, it rarely exists complete in the real world. Some states have no provisions for creating or updating frameworks; in many cases Latin teachers write curriculum in isolation. Curriculum development on the state, district, and local levels is important. It informs boards of education, administrators, teachers, and the community about the program. It is the basis for financial and educational decisions about instructional methods and materials, resources for learning, time allocations, grouping, staff development, and supervision. It is the basis for development of course curriculum and daily lesson plans, and provides continuity and direction for teachers at all levels. It provides a framework for systematic assessment of student achievement and also ensures that the teacher's creative efforts and unique contributions to students are part of a larger design. How do we translate our national standards into what happens in our classrooms?

Fortunately, the philosophy that underlies the current standards for classical language learning is one that the Classics profession has embraced for many years, articulated as early as the ACL's *Classical Investigation* of the 1920s (Advisory Committee; and see Chapter 1 above). Many of today's Latin classrooms already reflect much of the spirit of the current standards. The primary focus is on the reading of the classical language, from the beginning of Latin instruction (standard 1.1). Reading is supported by oral practice of many kinds (standard 1.2). Authentic cultural information about the perspectives and products of the ancient Romans and Greeks is gleaned from many sources, in readings of the original languages whenever possible (Goal 2).

Our connections to other disciplines—the sciences, the arts, and the humanities—need to be targeted in our curriculum planning (Goal 3); the enhancement of the students' own language skills has always been an important goal of Latin instruction: Latin provides a look at language and linguistic concepts that can form a basis for a lifetime of language learning. Vocabulary building, raising SAT scores, and improving language skills in English have been the basis for many students' choosing Latin as their foreign language (Goal 4). The Communities Goal (Goal 5) provides us with perhaps the most provocative challenge. Our classical language curriculum must enrich our students' lives beyond school and should produce real world applications in their communities. Inclusiveness and the global perspective require us to look at our programs very carefully and to think about them in new ways.

We already have programs that illustrate the "new" standards. Innovative middle-school Latin programs (some stressing reading ability in English, others, multi-culturalism, oral skills, or mythology) have been developed with the same philosophy that underlies the standards. Team teaching, interdisciplinary classes, cooperative learning, and new configurations in scheduling have changed the appearance of the classroom and the school day. Latin teachers continue to adapt to these innovations and, as a result, create new curriculum, new standards, and new goals.

We are fortunate to have networks in place that connect Latin and Greek scholars and teachers across the country and across levels of the curriculum. We also have the National Latin Exam, a proven instrument that helps keep us on the right track in assessing Latin programs and students' progress in Latin (see Chapter 11 below).

CURRICULUM GUIDELINES

Although there are diverse programs in Latin from pre–K through Advanced Placement, the most common program in the nation continues to be Latin I and

II in the high school. Increasingly, in some states, Latin regularly begins in grade 7.

Curriculum guidelines for Latin I and II were compiled in the 1990s based on a survey of 1,300 American Latin teachers (Davis). These guidelines may provide an important link in translating national standards to local curriculum in Latin I and II. They offer thoughts on progression, pace, and emphasis, and may help teachers plan and evaluate their programs. These guidelines are general and need to be adapted to the resources, student needs, and conditions of a particular situation, and to the textbook. As originally developed, they show a careful development of Goals 1 and 2 of the standards for classical language learning. Local guidelines need to incorporate a careful weaving of these two main goals through Goals 3, 4, and 5. In this context curriculum guidelines for Latin I and II are presented below; the recommendations preceding the presentation of the guidelines underline their connection with the national standards.

Ten Recommendations Underlying the Guidelines

1. In an age when the need to communicate effectively is critical, all students can benefit from the study of Latin. We must take them all with whatever deficiencies they may have, and try to structure programs that offer the best opportunity for some degree of success to every student. This includes many groups that have not traditionally studied Latin: "limited English proficiency" students, learning-disabled students, the economically and culturally disadvantaged, the handicapped, and students "at-risk."

2. Since teachers are dealing with a wider range of academic readiness and ability in today's Latin student, they must begin by teaching basic tasks, information, and concepts. Students need to be taught how to study; how to do homework; how to organize their work and their thinking; what nouns and verbs are; what a sentence is; where Greece and Rome are. These "basics" can be an invaluable contribution to the lives of some students who may not, alas, learn them elsewhere—and, of course, they are the *sine qua non* for further success in Latin.

3. The objectives for Latin programs should be expanded from learning grammar and translation to include a focus on lifelong educational benefits to be gained. Students of Latin should develop at least an elementary awareness of how languages work; how they are similar and how they differ; how English and the Romance languages are indebted to Latin; how our American experience was shaped and continues to be influenced by the ancient Greeks and Romans.

4. The improvement of English language skills is a major objective and result of Latin study. Our Latin courses should include a strong component of etymology and English vocabulary work. Knowledge about English grammar, sentence structure, and style should be among the outcomes of Latin study.

5. Continued forceful efforts must be made to bring about collaboration among the different levels of Latin teaching. Elementary-, middle-, and high-school teachers, teachers at community colleges, and university professors can and must work together. Collaborative efforts produce the energy, diversity, and new life of our profession.

6. The modern foreign languages have much to offer Latin teachers. Besides legislative and financial benefits from being included under the rubric of "foreign language study," Latin programs can benefit from modern language research, pedagogical programs, and advocacy power. Latin teachers should actively pursue closer connections with modern foreign language associations.

7. All teachers of Latin should feel encouraged to employ some flexibility and variety in their teaching. The traditional stereotype of the quiet, predictable, teacher-centered classroom can be expanded to include active student involvement in learning, interaction between students, oral work for every student every day, and strategies to accommodate differing learning styles. Successful programs give each student a sense of being an appreciated member of a team united by the common goal of studying the Classics.

8. All students should have instruction and practice in the pronunciation, reading aloud, and recitation of Latin. This not only facilitates comprehension and memorization, but enhances students' appreciation of Latin as a language. The prospect of studying Latin as a language that was spoken for hundreds of years is clearly more exciting than the mechanical deciphering of a mysterious code.

9. No one ever "finishes the grammar." The teaching of reading strategies and the systematic review of grammar should be continued at every level of Latin study. The overall design of the Latin program should be a spiral in which reading and consolidation of linguistic concepts reinforce each other each step of the way. The reading of meaningful and worthwhile material in Latin should begin as soon as possible, with the eventual goal of reading the Latin classics.

10. At the end of their Latin studies, even if these last only one year, students should begin to understand and appreciate the scope of classical studies: the languages and literature, the history and culture, and the substantial contributions of the ancient classical world to our own.

Curriculum Guidelines for Latin I

Reading. Students can read simple narratives and dialogues in simple (made-up/adapted) Latin and easy (and/or highly annotated) original Latin texts. They can gather information from the Latin text, answer questions (in English) about content, paraphrase and translate it, and formulate judgments about its content. Students have regular practice at sight-reading and develop strategies for understanding sight readings. The quantity of reading will vary with age of students and availability of time.

Oral/Aural Skills. Students can pronounce the sounds of Latin, and read simple sentences aloud with expression and generally correct pronunciation. Students can respond in Latin to simple Latin questions, and can comprehend and write spoken Latin words, phrases, and short sentences correctly. Teachers may wish to encourage oral skills by the use of games, skits, storytelling, and other oral classroom activities.

Grammatical Concepts. Students understand the concept of inflection and the basic uses of the six cases of Latin (nominative, vocative, genitive, dative, accusative, and ablative). They can recognize and describe the following basic grammatical concepts (those marked with an asterisk are sometimes delayed to the second year):

parts of speech	singular, plural
no article in Latin	gender
sentence	person
subject	tense
direct object	subject/verb agreement
indirect object	noun/adjective agreement
object of a preposition	infinitive vs. finite verb
direct address	auxiliary verb
predicate nominative, adjective	linking verb
possessive	principal parts as verb stems
declension	imperative
inflection	conjugation
base of Latin noun	active and passive* voice

Morphology. The forms below are usually learned during the first year of Latin study (those marked with an asterisk are sometimes taught in the second year). The inclusion or exclusion of vocabulary items marked with a double asterisk** will depend on which textbook is used.

NOUNS	PRONOUNS
six cases	*ego, tu*
first declension	*is, ea, id*
second declension	*quis, quid*
third declension	*qui, quae, quod*
*fourth declension	*hic, haec, hoc*
*fifth declension	*ille, illa, illud*
	idem, eadem, idem
	ipse, ipsa, ipsum
	sui, sibi, se, se

ADJECTIVES
first and second declension
inter-declensional adjective/noun agreement

possessives: *meus, tuus, noster, vester*
*third declension
*comparative and superlative forms

ADVERBS
interrogatives**: *ubi, cur, quando, quomodo, quo, unde*
basic vocabulary list of adverbs**: *bene, non, semper, olim, numquam, saepe, diu, valde, cras*
formation from first- and second-declension adjectives
*formation from third-declension adjectives

PREPOSITIONS
ab, de, ex, sine, sub, cum, in, pro w/abl.
in, ad, per, contra, trans, circum, ob, propter, etc.** w/acc.

CONJUNCTIONS
et, sed, aut, quod, nam, autem, ubi, -que, neque, atque, etc.**

INTERJECTIONS
O! Io! Eheu! Euge! Mehercle!, etc.**

VERBS
finite forms: first–fourth conjugations: present, imperfect, future, perfect, *past perfect, *future perfect—active and *passive voices
imperatives: regular forms, singular and plural, active voice
    duc, dic, fac, fer
infinitives: present active, *present passive
participles: perfect passive, *present active, *future active
irregular verbs: *sum, possum, *volo, *nolo, *fero, *eo*

Syntax. The following grammatical constructions are usually taught during first-year Latin:

nom. case as subject	abl. of accompaniment
nom. case with linking verbs	abl. of means
gen. case indicating possession	abl. of manner
dat. case as indirect object	abl. of time when
*dat. case w/ special adjectives	*abl. of agent
acc. case as direct object	*abl. absolute
acc. case as object of preposition	voc. case for direct address
acc. case for place to which	*appositive
abl. case as object of preposition	relative clause

Vocabulary. List depends on textbook. Students also learn Latin vocabulary through English derivatives, and vice versa.

Etymology. Students learn a brief history of the Latin language and begin to understand the linguistic and historical relationship between English and Latin. They have some practice using a Latin dictionary and a good English dictionary. Students can break down polysyllabic Latin derivatives into prefixes, roots, and suffixes. They can recognize prefixes that have undergone spelling changes as a result of assimilation. Students know the meanings of all common Latin prefixes, suffixes, and roots, and can use this knowledge to figure out the meanings of English words. They have a rudimentary understanding of the basic principles of word formation in Latin (e.g., *amo, amor, amator, amicus, amicitia, amabilis, amabilitas)* and how these correspond to parts of speech and meanings of English equivalents.

Roman Topics. Students learn about Roman family life, homes, clothing, the alphabet, schools, and the city of Rome. They are introduced to the periods of Roman history, legendary heroes, geography of the Mediterranean, and the Greek and Roman gods and mythological stories. As they learn facts concerning these topics, they can make comparisons with their own culture and draw conclusions about the Romans. They are encouraged to consider the Roman influence on American life in the areas of language, government, architecture, and ideas.

Curriculum Guidelines for Latin II

Reading. Students can read longer passages in adapted Latin and they begin regular reading of original Latin texts. They can glean information from the Latin text, answer questions (in English) about content, paraphrase and translate it, make inferences, and formulate judgments about its content. Students continue to have regular practice at sight-reading and developing strategies for understanding unseen readings.

Oral/Aural Skills.   Practice in listening and reading aloud continues. Students learn to use reading aloud to help them understand the meaning of Latin. They learn to read with expression by breaking sentences into phrases according to meaning. Students can respond in Latin to simple Latin questions and can comprehend and write spoken Latin words, phrases, and short sentences correctly. Further oral activities such as skits, storytelling, question-and-answer drills, oral games, songs, and recitation performances are employed according to the predilection of the teacher.

Grammatical Concepts. Students continue their work on the uses of the six cases of Latin and the Latin verb system They regularly review the basic grammatical concepts that they have previously learned and are introduced to the following (those marked with an asterisk may be taught in the third year):

phrase vs. clause	transitive vs. intransitive verbs
independent vs. dependent clauses	irregular and defective verbs
adverbial, adjectival, and noun clauses	deponent verbs
	participles as adjectives
infinitives as nouns	direct vs. indirect statements

direct vs. indirect questions
direct vs. indirect commands
*wish
*condition
indicative vs. subjunctive
sequence of tenses
enclitics

substantive use of adjectives
appositives
prepositional phrases modifying
    verbs in Latin
*gerund, gerundive
idioms

Morphology. The forms below are usually learned during the second year of Latin study (those marked with an asterisk may be taught in the third year):

NOUNS: locatives; irregular nouns or pronouns such as *vis, Iuppiter, nemo*

ADJECTIVES AND PRONOUNS: *uter, neuter, unus, solus, nullus, alter, ullus, totus, alius; quidam, aliquis, quisque, quisquam*

ADJECTIVES	ADVERBS	QUESTION WORDS
irregulars	irregulars	*num, nonne*
talis, qualis	*eo, tam, ita*	
tantus, quantus		

VERBS
imperatives: negatives, deponents
infinitives: perfect active and passive, future active
infinitive as verb in indirect statement
irregular/defective verbs: *fio, coepi, memini, odi, inquit*
*gerundive
deponent verbs
impersonal verbs: *licet, oportet*, etc.
subjunctive forms and uses: hortatory, jussive, purpose, result, indirect question/command, *cum*-temporal clauses—*conditions, *anticipatory, *clauses of characteristic, *wishes, *deliberative subjunctive

Syntax. The following grammatical constructions are usually taught during the second year:

gen. of the whole
*dat. of agent w/gerundive
dat. of purpose
dat. of possession
dat. w/compound verbs
acc. case as subject of indirect
    statement
acc. of extent, duration
abl. of separation

abl. of comparison
abl. as object of *utor, fruor, fungor, potior, vescor*
abl. of respect
abl. of cause
abl. of degree of difference
relative purpose clause
connecting relative

Vocabulary. List depends on texts read. Students also learn Latin vocabulary through English derivatives, and vice versa.

Etymology. Students continue to learn about the history of the Latin language and see the linguistic and historical relationship between Latin/English and Latin/Romance languages. They continue to improve dictionary skills, and they continue the study of Latin derivatives in English and Latin word formation, extending their knowledge of prefixes, roots, and suffixes.

Roman Topics. Students deepen their knowledge of Roman customs and begin to acquire an overview of the periods of Roman history and literature. They become familiar with such historical figures as Caesar, Augustus, Hannibal, Cicero, and Vergil. They are introduced to Roman government and Rome's place in European history. The study of mythology continues, embracing the Olympians, the heroes, and stories of Greek and Roman mythology. As students learn facts concerning these topics, they can make comparisons with their own culture and draw conclusions about the Romans. They are encouraged to continue and deepen their understanding of the Roman influence on American life in the areas of language, government, architecture, and ideas.

BEYOND STANDARDS AND CURRICULUM GUIDELINES

These curriculum guidelines for Latin I and II may serve to help the single Latin teacher in a lonely school. They are, however, not a prescribed answer for a comprehensive program K–12; they are not an advanced placement curriculum; they are not a specialized curriculum for students with special needs, whether those special needs be remedial reading skills in English, a higher score on the SAT, preparation for admission to a prestigious college, or language skills to help in learning Chinese, or Arabic, or Farsi, or Spanish. Curriculum must be individualized.

Standards in classical language learning affect more than teaching in K–12. They affect teaching and learning in colleges and universities. In fact, the curriculum guidelines for Latin I and II have been suggested as equally applicable to the first two semesters of a college beginning Latin course. Fundamental changes are taking place in the realms of academia. Enrollments in classical languages in colleges and universities are acutely affected by what is happening in the schools. Standards can regularize the curricular mesh between high schools and colleges and solve some of the challenges of articulation that are explored in Chapter 12 below.

It is through these standards that we can define our subject for today's world. We must periodically re-interpret the classical tradition to our current time and location. The national standards and curriculum guidelines presented here simply constitute a framework for teaching the classical languages to today's students. The beauty of our discipline is that its subject matter can be so readily accommodated to, and compel the interest of, every age; yet, just as that subject matter must be constantly re-interpreted for each new generation, so must we constantly revisit and revise the manner in which it is taught.

TASK FORCE ON STANDARDS
FOR CLASSICAL LANGUAGE LEARNING

Richard C. Gascoyne, Task Force Chair, University at Albany, SUNY, Albany, NY
Martha Abbott, Fairfax County Public Schools, Fairfax, VA
Z. Philip Ambrose, University of Vermont, Burlington, VT
Cathy Daugherty, The Electronic Classroom, Richmond, VA
Sally Davis, Arlington County Public Schools, Arlington, VA
Terry Klein, North Allegheny School District, Pittsburgh, PA
Glenn Knudsvig, President, ACL, University of Michigan, Ann Arbor, MI
Robert LaBouve, Southwest Educational Development Laboratory, Austin, TX
Nancy Lister, Vernon Public Schools, Vernon, CT
Karen Lee Singh, Florida State University School, Tallahassee, FL
Kathryn A. Thomas, Creighton University, Omaha, NE
Richard F. Thomas, Harvard University, Cambridge, MA

6

Latin in the Elementary Schools

MARION POLSKY
Scarsdale High School, Scarsdale, New York

A MOVEMENT THAT GREW

Today if we, the public, come upon a newspaper photo showing two 10-year old *togati* (children dressed in togas), we may be interested but not struck dumb in our tracks. Headlines such as "A Dead Language Lives" (or a variation of same) are not new, but have been appearing in the leading press for more than 25 years. Many print articles and television human-interest news reports have centered on Latin learning by an unexpected population: elementary school-age children, especially the urban poor. Certainly the motivation for reporting this phenomenon stemmed, at least in part, from its shock value: "What was Latin, a language of study reserved for an elite, college-bound, even old-money population, doing in inner-city Washington, D.C., Philadelphia, or Indianapolis?" the thinking may have gone. Though it would be naive to believe that this point of view about Latin has finally been buried for good, it is fair to state that major changes in Latin education, including fresh methodologies and materials aimed at making Latin a subject for everyone at all levels of study, had their roots in the egalitarian elementary school movement.

In the early 1960s, Judith LeBovit implemented a Latin FLES (Foreign Language in the Elementary School) program in Washington, D.C., to help improve the language skills of economically and culturally disadvantaged students. Other cities, encouraged by the promising results in the District of Columbia, followed suit, most notably Philadelphia, with its seminal *Language Arts through Latin* program developed by Rudolph Masciantonio. In the 1970s and 80s, studies of standardized test scores in the areas of reading comprehension, vocabulary, and total reading ability in Los Angeles, New York City, Philadelphia, and the District of Columbia, among others, have shown that thousands of students exposed to Latin instruction for as little as 20 minutes per day have had a measurable advantage over their peers who did not study Latin (Mavrogenes 1977, 1979, 1987).[1]

The pioneering programs, some funded by the federal government through various agencies, approached the study of Latin from the perspective of improving English language skills. To some hard-line classicists, this meant the watering down or elimination of real Latin. It took a while for them to see the glass as half full, that bringing Latin to an unexpected population meant introducing methodologies previously reserved for modern spoken languages, including, most significantly, an oral/aural component, and that these methodologies were quite valid for advanced Latin students, too. To cite one example: It is hard to imagine now a high-school Latin class in which students do not read aloud regularly. In my own experience, the pleasure of hearing and speaking Latin was not introduced until college, when I studied Latin lyric and elegiac poetry. But when I worked in New York City elementary and middle schools as director of the Latin Cornerstone Project (Polsky 1986), I saw, from a teaching perspective, how important the oral component is, not just for appreciating a largely oral literature, but for contemporizing the language experience (*Quid agis, magistra?*) and enabling students to remember better the vocabulary and forms. I highlight this one example of curricular change here to underline the point that the elementary-school Latin movement has been a benchmark for the entire field. Most of the powerful arguments for choosing Latin as a course of study today apply across the board, beginning with kindergarteners. The amount of Latin language learned can vary widely (see below, under Materials and Resources), but the underlying rationale is the same. If Latin did not bear a fundamental connection to English and the Western tradition, its validity in the schools, for better or worse, would be seriously compromised.

Parents and educators outside the field warrant a detailed, honest appraisal of the benefits of Latin for elementary-school children. Money is scarce, teachers who can teach Latin even scarcer. Fortunately, there are creative solutions to these problems (see below); a bigger hurdle to overcome is the poisonous notion of "relevance," a poison that has seeped into many other areas of study, including literature before the 20th century, whole chunks of history, even modern foreign language literature (as contrasted with language) classes. On the other hand, certain contemporary emphases—global studies and diversity within a culture, for instance, as well as a wake-up call for literacy in the lower grades—can help promote the study of Latin from an early age. The arguments are compelling, and they are amply supported by the funded studies:

> 1) Given the linguistic and cultural pluralism that exists in many communities, Latin is a leveler, a language with no native speakers and one that is equally unknown to all. As Latin learners, children start out more or less on an equal footing, without prejudice. Members of the class share a fascination for this new language code. One just has to witness the expressions on the students' faces when the teacher greets them, the first day, with *Salve!* and shakes their hands. This is something new, and they are all in it together. Frequently students will test out the code at home, to tantalize and amuse their parents and

siblings. Their ability to master something totally unfamiliar and communicate with it provides a sense of self-esteem and a pure delight in language itself.

2) In learning about Roman cultural institutions and customs, students develop an informed curiosity for the past. They lose their Cecil B. DeMille image of peoples from former times, as they actively compare and contrast ancient lifestyles with their own. Often, they are more surprised by the similarities, both personal and institutional, than the differences: "They were *real people!*" remarked one bemused fifth-grader. Students examine a range of socio-cultural phenomena with open-mindedness, even as they have strong reactions to some aspects, slavery and male hegemony, for example. They are given a context for major Roman spheres of influence that have had enormous impact on Western culture—linguistic, legal, governmental, architectural, artistic, literary, and religious. At the same time, stories of gods and goddesses, chariot races, and gladiators afford endless fascination and reflection.

3) Since Latin is the ultimate source of the majority of English words (60% of all English words, 90% of those over two syllables), students measurably expand their vocabularies. They do not memorize by rote a list of derivatives, but learn the Latin root-words in context—Latin sentences and stories—just as older students do, and are taught to look for the same roots in English words. They also see how words are put together from roots, prefixes, and suffixes in both languages. Through this process, which cannot begin too early, students forever after pay attention to words in a new way.

4) Latin in the elementary school provides a practical basis for continued foreign language study at higher educational levels, whether or not the student has the opportunity to continue in Latin as well. Some 750 million people speak the Romance languages, those derived essentially from Latin, including Spanish, French, and Italian. In addition, Latin is structurally comparable to modern inflected languages such as Russian and German.

In sum, Latin gives speakers of English (both native speakers and newcomers to the United States) a solid framework for understanding how language works. Latin is particularly suitable because it is very different from English in its structure and, at the same time, intricately bound to it through both vocabulary and cultural features. The foundation laid by visionary language educators of the past three decades has surely born fruit. Despite severe budgetary cutbacks in many places, Latin in the elementary school is here to stay; materials and programs continue to proliferate. As one of my former students put it, "My opinion on Latin is: if you learn it, you will love it."

MATERIALS AND RESOURCES

The elementary-school years, K–6, cover a period of tremendous cognitive development and represent a greater diversity in school settings than in any other period of schooling. Thus, the choice of Latin program will depend on a number of variables: age and grade level of students, language background of students, ability level of students (including homogeneous or heterogenous classes), size of class, number of Latin sessions per week and length of session, length of the Latin program (one, two, or three years, or less), degree of integration with other second language programs, amount of homework, and grading required. Traditionally, foreign language programs at this level are put under the headings of FLES (Foreign Language in the Elementary Schools: introductory) or FLEX (Foreign Language Exploratory: with other languages introduced as well—see Strasheim 1984–85). These terms are subject to interpretation as to the degree of actual Latin language learning involved, ranging from very little to some degree of reading proficiency. The good news is that there are Latin programs available, both commercially and independently produced, that will satisfy the specific needs of most schools.

The following brief descriptions of available materials (in alphabetical order) are intended as a starting point. Care should be taken to explore the options thoroughly and thus assure a good fit. A packet entitled "Exemplary Latin Programs for Elementary Schools" has been compiled under the auspices of the National Committee for Latin and Greek and is available from the ACL's Teaching Materials and Resource Center (TMRC), catalog no. B911a. In addition to descriptions of materials that may be purchased from the TMRC and other sources, the packet contains publicity brochures, articles, background information, and a list of resource centers.

Discovering Languages: Latin (Ashworth and Robbins, AMSCO School Publications, 1995)

One of five books in a series of introductory language textbooks emphasizing limited language acquisition and extensive cultural awareness, the program, illustrated in full color, is organized by topic including names, numbers, days of the week, months of the year, parts of the body, the classroom, and so forth. There are Latin dialogues in a cartoon-strip format and Roman culture capsules written in English on areas of interest such as food, life and work, education, and fashion. Puzzles and games reinforce vocabulary and Latin-English cognates. The teacher's manual provides strategies for teaching all elements and supplementary activities, as well as a key to all exercises and puzzles.

First Latin: A Language Discovery Program (Polsky, Scott Foresman-Addison Wesley, 2nd ed., 1998)

A flexible and multi-faceted Latin program in which students practice all four communicative skills, *First Latin* helps students recognize word roots and learn a variety of language features and patterns in both Latin and English (see Polsky 1987 on the 1st ed.). Puzzles, games, reading stories, skits, and songs are integrated into a cultural context about a Roman family and a freedman.

Topics include Roman heroes, mythology, language families, and the variety of life in ancient Rome (the family, slavery, social class, dining, schools, clothing and grooming, neighborhoods, entertainment, and so forth). The teacher's books are self-instructing so that the teacher with little or no Latin background, as well as the Latinist who is unfamiliar with elementary-school instruction, can immediately begin teaching the course. There are two teacher's books (including test masters), two illustrated student activity books, a set of picture cue cards, and an audiocassette. *First Latin* can also be used at the middle-school level and serves as an introduction to the *Ecce Romani* Latin program (Lawall, et al.).

The Keepers of Alexandria (Montessori Teacher Partnerships)

This novel program, which started as a remedial program for inner-city school children in Beloit, Wisconsin, and spread to Montessori and other schools, is set at the time of the Roman Empire and centered in the multi-ethnic city of Alexandria, an important crossroads for trade betwen East and West. Students receive a "passport" to go back in time; they follow in Latin the adventures of an Ethiopian family of the second century, A.D. (Maiken). Latin is not the focal point of the curriculum but a vehicle to an inter-cultural journey in which literature, philosophy, arts and sciences, technology, and other human achievements are analyzed. Elements of the program include a timeline, language cards, slides, models, literary selections, Latin grammar material, and tapes. Contact person: David Kahn, Montessori Teacher Partnerships, 11424 Bellflower Rd., Cleveland, OH 44106.

Language Arts through Latin (Masciantonio, School District of Philadelphia and Los Angeles Unified School District)

This pioneering program developed in Philadelphia for inner-city students was adapted and expanded in Los Angeles through the Language Transfer Program to provide in-service material and a Spanish word-roots component (see the several articles by Baca and Masciantonio in the bibliography). The language teaching is primarily audio-lingual with a question/answer format, using picture cue cards and songs. The course emphasizes the Latin roots of English words and offers simple Latin stories about Roman daily life and mythology. There are two levels, for the fifth and sixth grades, respectively; these include teacher's manuals with the oral work and cultural material, student readers and workbooks on derivatives, visual cards, game kits, tapes, and filmstrips. Contact person: Prof. Frank Morris, Dept. of Classical and Modern Languages, Coll. of Charleston, 66 George St., Charleston, SC 29424.

Salvete! A First Course in Latin (Phinney, et al., Cambridge University Press, 1995)

This illustrated reading program in Latin contains stories about a Roman family in A.D. 9–10 that moves from Roman Italy to Roman Spain, to Roman

Gaul, and all the way to the German frontier. Students learn about the local customs and diverse viewpoints of people living in the provinces. They also study English derivatives from Latin and cognate words in Spanish, French, and German. There is extensive Latin vocabulary and grammar incorporated directly from Unit 1 of the *Cambridge Latin Course* (Phinney and Bell), to which *Salvete!* may also serve as an introduction. Points of grammar, with some formal Latin terminology, are presented and discussed in the students' books, along with exercises and activities on language and derivation and cultural discussions in English. There are two student books, a teacher's manual, and an audiocassette.

In addition to the several excellent programs described above, there is a considerable array of supplementary materials and teaching aids for use by teachers to enhance a child's experience with Latin and provide multimedia opportunities. Support of both the tangible and intangible varieties is offered, first and foremost, by the American Classical League (ACL) and its committee, the Elementary Teachers of Classics (ETC). Their publications, the *Classical Outlook* and *Prima*, respectively, provide many practical ideas for the classroom and keep the teacher up-to-date on new materials, and their annual National Mythology Exam (NME) helps to generate interest among youngsters in grades 3–9. The ACL's TMRC offers inexpensive materials by mail order (for information on ACL, ETC, NME, and the TMRC, write to the American Classical League, Miami Univ., Oxford, OH 45056). Teachers may also want to investigate local and state classical associations; their meetings and journals provide a forum for sharing ideas and promote collegiality in the field.

Another kind of resource that bears mention is assistance in preparing elementary and middle-school in-service teachers to present an introductory Latin program, since many districts are not able to hire a specialist teacher. Because a relatively limited knowledge of Latin is needed to teach most of the programs, a motivated teacher can acquire the necessary background in a short time. Some of the programs described above offer workshops and follow-up support.[2] A Latin teacher from a local secondary school or college might serve as a mentor. Once programs are in place, participating teachers might form a network in their city or state to bring in speakers in a conference format. The fact that Latin is easy to pronounce, I have found, makes the prospect of teaching it much less intimidating for the non-Latinist, especially in the lower and middle school, where the oral component receives special emphasis. Furthermore, many veteran teachers are eager to try something new that is time-tested and not just the latest "cure-all" for language deficiencies. The teaching population for elementary-school Latin is already out there; it is a matter of making the match and providing support from the resources that now abound.

IN THE CLASSROOM

It is probably no exaggeration that anyone who has had the opportunity to teach Latin to young children becomes reacquainted with the language in powerful ways. This is because children already know a great deal about language per se, their knowledge is largely intuitive, and they raise deep-level (read: "hard!") questions without being aware of it. They are also uninhibited and not afraid of being wrong. The Latin teacher must approach this population with open-mindedness and high expectations. Interest in an ancient people, with their funny clothing, their imposing architecture, their gods and goddesses, and their language that sounds sort of familiar, is easy to secure; it is apparent from the first day. Building upon that interest requires age-appropriate techniques and activities. The suggestions that follow derive from my experience in the elementary-school classroom, both as a supervisor of in-service teachers and as a teacher. Though I have focused mainly on grades 4–7 in my own work, I believe that most of the points made here can be applied to even younger students, with appropriate adjustments of curricular level. The methodology remains largely the same. It emerges directly from the children themselves.

Younger learners are open to learning and take intellectual risks. Imagine teaching students who have no pre-set categories or pigeonholes for language processes, no preconceptions. You show them a language process in Latin and compare it to English. For example, in English the adjective is not inflected; in Latin it is. You demonstrate this with familiar Latin vocabulary, family members, perhaps, or food names, any declension, and (to start) adjectives of the 1st–2nd declension. They accept it, matter-of-factly. No arm twisting, no "I know this is hard, but . . .." The truth is, you can do "hard" things linguistically; it's all a matter of presentation and expectation. One of my favorite examples happens very early on; students receive Latin names orally, then they go to the board, one at a time, to write their names. As each attempts to sound out the name, the teacher makes corrections orally and refers to the specific sound/spelling correspondences involved in that name. By the time student #17 or so comes up, the system is usually in place; other classmates start calling out the letters, even for diphthongs, *v*, and pre-vocalic initial *i*. Sometimes they get angry at English and comment on how much harder English spelling is (but they also pay more attention to English spelling).

Younger learners use different strategies for second language learning. For example, some have more of an aptitude for listening and others for the printed word. Children who already have a second language in the home, or for whom English is a second language, tend to have more highly developed listening skills then monolingual children. It is important to treat the same material with the four communicative skills—listening, speaking, reading, and writing—so that all students achieve some measure of success in their areas of strength and stretch their language skills in other areas. A popular audio-lingual device is showing picture cards and having students answer questions about them, such as *Quis est?* / *Lucius est*, and later: *Filius Claudi est, Frater Claudiae est; Qui sunt?* / *Lucius et Claudia sunt, Liberi sunt.* In my experience, those bilingual students who happen to be poor readers of English, when given a chance to shine audiolingually, develop enough confidence to test their language skills with the printed word; they want to read Latin stories. This transition is powerful and heartening for the teacher.

Younger learners see things in a literal way. You cannot be too concrete. These children are busy figuring out their place in the nature of things; they need to pin things down, constantly: "Well, did the Romans wear underwear? Did Roman girls choose their husbands?" These are the sort of questions a teacher needs to anticipate. A favorite example is in the area of word roots. It is very important to give the variant forms of a root; this uncomplicates matters, rather than the opposite. In fact, with little children, more information often helps, surprisingly. When I was new to this, and my students had learned *videt*, I elicited English derivatives: "video," "vision," "visible." Very nice. Then one little girl, waving her hand furiously, volunteered "vitamin." She explained, to my puzzled expression, that her mother had told her that vitamin A is good for your eyes. But of course the Latin root is not *vi-*, the commonality she had correctly seen between "video" and "vision," but *vid/s-*. Language processes are not scary when they are specific, especially when they yield the comfort of patterns: *vid-* and *vis-*, *sed-* and *sess-*, *lud-* and *lus-*.

Younger learners like repetition. You really cannot repeat things enough, regardless of ability level; how they love to respond, to chant. Also, the more varieties of media for reinforcement and repetition, the happier the class: e.g., picture cards, tapes, printed text, classroom games, puppets. The wonderful thing about oral repetition, particularly, is that you can introduce variants, and also have students create variants, following a particular structural pattern that they have practiced repeatedly. As their repertoire grows, they delight in giving alternative answers to the same question.

Younger learners are physical learners. Students want to act out stories and plays; this kind of activity is not a frill, but intrinsic to the learning process. In teaching a story I wrote about a fire in the *insula* of the freedman Quintus, children volunteered to be Quintus, members of the fire brigade, other tenants, passersby, and—the building itself, the flames coming out of it, and smoke. When we then looked at the story again in the book, the class was more than ready to explore the linguistic features and vocabulary. Also important are songs, both those relating to the cultural content and Latin versions of familiar favorites; students like standing up in different parts of the room for rounds. Many games and activities allow for movement; for example, *Simonus Dicit* (using classroom commands and/or vocabulary for parts of the body). Art projects to decorate the classroom can help; try a Latin graffiti wall, with Latin words and English derivatives in different lettering styles on rolled out brown paper, or let students make scenery for a skit or build models of important buildings in the city. Even having individual students come to the front of the room to lead a song or hold a picture card focuses physical energy.

Younger learners are emotionally involved. They come to the classroom with varied life experiences and with knowledge of life's harsher aspects. They react strongly to the cultural content of the modern Latin curriculum, which is no longer prettified. One student from the original Cornerstone Project (see Polsky 1986), responding to what she thought about the Latin program, wrote, "I didn't like that they have slaves"; another put forth, "I think they should let all the girls go to school." There was no separation of the learning process from the content itself. Students need the opportunity to express their feelings about the cultural phenomena. They might write stories and plays imagining themselves traveling through time to visit ancient Rome, or portray the reactions of ancient Roman characters coming to their town or city. To put themselves more tangibly into the earlier time frame, the class might produce a magazine or newspaper, put on a banquet with costumes, or create an ongoing Roman soap opera. I have not discovered a single thematic area in which students do not express interest and make their reactions known. Of course, even the topics that are common to most second language study—naming, dates, time, family, food, clothing, housing, professions, education, and so forth—will have a special twist in the ancient setting. Other topics, not generally encountered head-on by elementary school children in a modern foreign language program, are more provocative: violent heroes, slavery, class structure, the place of women, imperialism, ethnic diversity, urban problems. These aspects, interwoven as they are with the topics of daily life, require sensitivity on the part of the teacher regarding his/her particular student population. If they are treated from the historical perspective, they can yield benefits unique to the Latin experience: students not only witness and evaluate lifestyles different from or similar to their own, they develop an emotional bond with people from the past, they care about them, they may even want to change their circumstances. What if there were no slavery in ancient Rome? What if Romulus didn't kill his brother? How would the world be different? And then: How can I make it different today?

Younger learners thrive on spontaneity. As has already been shown, they readily get involved and immerse themselves in the material. The further along they are in their course of study, the more their natural responses reflect their learning. A productive area for spontaneity is allowing for substitutions in familiar songs and expressions. Students in this way engage in creative language play and can even be silly while learning. For example, in the song *Lucius edit,* to the tune of "London Bridge," students are called upon to provide a suitable food item in the accusative case, based upon pattern verses that have been oft-repeated (*panem, pullum,* etc.). Some of the playful answers I have heard are: *canem, stilum, flammam*! Spontaneity is also important from the teacher; in a FLES or FLEX curriculum, variety in presentation reinforces the material while keeping it fresh and exciting. Though each lesson might start with greetings and simple dialogue in Latin, to bring focus, what comes next should be unpredictable for the students, at least some of the time: songs, plays, puzzles, games, fill-in exercises, reading, art projects, discussion, story-writing, team activities, and the like are all part of the learning process. Shifting the content emphasis is also critical. In a program with a Latin language component, a good balance between linguistic practice (through oral dialogues, reading stories, plays, and written exercises), the study of derivatives and cognates, and cultural activities will keep students attentive and also meet the needs of different kinds of learners.

Younger learners are interdisciplinary by nature. They are intrinsically interested in how things fit together, and they are forever making connections between different areas of knowledge, both in and out of school. One of the strongest arguments for a Latin program at this level is that Latin study, too, is interdisciplinary by nature, and on two levels. Students are exposed to an ancient civilization in which the interrelationships among language, social structure, art, politics, literature, geography, values, and religion are clear to see, by contrast with their own era. At the same time, the interrelationship between this civilization and the students' own is also quite visible, through the influence of the Romans and Latin on the West. Therefore, curricular connections can be made both vertically and horizontally. Take *servus,* for example. Students learn the Latin vocabulary word and use it in sentences. They may also learn how to inflect it, in part. Perhaps, further, a *servus* is a character in the Latin family they are following. They imagine what it would feel like to be that character. They begin to explore the institution of slavery in Rome, its relationship to daily life and to political conquest. They compare slavery in other ancient civilizations and in the United States. They move from denotative to connotative meaning. Then they discover that "servant," "serve," "service," "servile," "servitude," "serf," and "subservient" derive from the Latin root *serv-*; they use some of these words in puzzles or sentences. Through this process, in which different areas of learning are related, students come to retain better each component, and they learn to make sophisticated connections themselves as they go forward.

Correlated to the interdisciplinary approach to Latin language learning is the extension of the curriculum outside the Latin classroom. The art teacher might be enlisted to develop a project based on a classical theme and display student work on bulletin boards and showcases in the halls throughout the school. A science class on volcanoes might include discussion of Pompeii. A school play might be based on stories from mythology or comic scenes from daily life written by students. An Olympics-style competition might be organized by the physical education teachers. Local museums and libraries often welcome the occasion to organize school programs around historical and literary themes. The more varied the settings in which Latin students are able to make connections to their course of study, the more vital the learning process becomes.

While certain factors—the teacher's individual style and the time constraints on the program, to name two—will determine the types of activities chosen and the particular emphases on different aspects of the curriculum, one outcome is virtually certain: the students will come away changed and empowered, and their parents will see it. In an era of dwindling monies for education, this is good news, for once a Latin program is started up, parental support (fund-raising, letter-writing, attendance at board of education meetings) may be needed to sustain it.[3] While tangible proof of the academic gains that derive from the study of Latin in the elementary school can be persuasive in building community support and commitment, the ultimate proponents are the younger learners themselves.

NOTES

[1]The articles by Mavrogenes contain summaries of the leading programs of the 1970s and 1980s and include useful bibliography. See also LeBovit, Baca, et al., Masciantonio 1972 and 1977a-b, and Polsky 1986 and 1987, for detailed accounts of the programs in Washington, Los Angeles, Philadelphia, and New York City.

[2]Teacher training and support are available: for *First Latin: A Language Discovery Program* through the teacher's books, which contain self-guiding instruction in Latin language and culture, and through workshops given by the author (Dr. Marion Polsky, 545 W. 111th St., Apt. 5C, New York, NY 10025); for *Language Arts through Latin* (in its Los Angeles version—the *Language Transfer* materials), through workshops given by Prof. Morris (address above) and by Albert Baca (4221 Agnes Ave., Studio City, CA 91604); and for *Salvete!*, through the annual Cambridge Latin Teachers' Workshop, which is regularly advertised in the ACL's journal, the *Classical Outlook*.

[3]Parents may be enlisted to make costumes and provide food for a Roman banquet, accompany class trips to museums, and the like, in addition to soliciting administrative and community support. Two examples of elementary-school Latin instruction that demonstrate strong parental involvement are: the "Latin and Classics for Children" program of West Caldwell, New Jersey, in which Latin and mythology are taught after school in a club format (contact person: Ron Ditmars, 29 Fairfield Ave., West Caldwell, NJ 07006) and the Thomas O'Brien Academy of Science and Technology in Albany, New York, which integrates a Latin curriculum in grades K–8 (contact person: Joanne B. Gascoyne, 289 Lark St., Albany, NY 12210).

7

Latin in the Middle Grades

LEAANN A. OSBURN
Barrington High School, Barrington, Illinois
Northern Illinois University

Students in the middle grades are unique learners. Neither the child-centered classroom of the elementary years nor the subject-centered approach of high school matches the learning characteristics of this age group, which begins before the onset of puberty and lasts through the early years of adolescence. This group of learners, sometimes called "pubescents" or "transescents," were once simply considered learners in transition from childhood to adolescence. The last decade, however, has witnessed an explosion of research into this neglected age group. While most of the research has focused on the general characteristics and needs of middle-grade learners, and a few articles have delved into foreign language education for this age group, little has been said about Latin and the middle-school student.

At the same time, however, Latin enrollments in the middle grades are on the rise. Increases were reported during the late 1980s (Gascoyne; and cf. Strasheim 1990; Osburn 1992), and recent data from the American Council on the Teaching of Foreign Languages document the growth of public-school Latin in grades 7–8 from 8,389 in 1982, to 12,179 in 1985, 18,897 in 1990, and 25,349 in 1994—a greater than 300% increase over 12 years (LaFleur 1997: 128 and Table 1). While complete national data are not available, evidence suggests that there has been comparable growth in private middle schools (LaFleur 1997; National Committee for Latin and Greek).

This increase in enrollments, combined with the paucity of information on Latin in the middle grades, makes it critical that Latin educators of all levels and pre-service teachers become well-informed about the characteristics of middle-grade learners, schools, Latin programs, instructional methods, extra-curricular activities, educational resources, and teacher preparation. As Sally Davis has remarked in *Latin in American Schools* (10–11), "Perhaps the most crucial age group of the student clientele for Latin is in the middle schools. . . . This is *the* currently critical area where classicists need to enlighten counselors, parents, and administrators better than previously, provide qualified teachers and establish attractive programs. "

MIDDLE-GRADE LEARNERS

Middle-level learners experience a host of developmental changes during transescence—physical, cognitive, social, and emotional. Unpredictable and variable physical growth occurs during transescence. At the same time, between ages 10 to 12, there is a period of expansive brain growth which is followed by a plateau from ages 12 to 14. This physical characteristic of transescence alters the cognitive abilities of the middle-level learner.

Socially, transescents feel a greater impact from peer persuasion than from parent, teacher, and adult persuasion. Emotionally, they feel the need to develop values and to accept and understand themselves. The progress through these changes is as variable as the changes themselves. While one student is learning to understand his physical development, another may be wrestling with forming values, and still another may be experiencing a leap in cognitive abilities. Some students in this age group will feel awkward about their appearance and thus be uncomfortable or exceedingly nervous about making a presentation to the class alone. Others will need to move freely around the classroom due to their physical growth. Some will need hands-on activities or manipulatives to help them learn, while others will want to help guide the decisions about what is being learned in class and how. Most middle-grade learners want to explore different aspects of themselves and the world but also want to make connections between what they see and learn in various subjects. The middle-grade teacher must be prepared to open the door to exploration to their students and to engage them in experiential learning opportunities. An entire classroom filled with these eager, enthusiastic learners all in different stages of growth is a challenge that must be met by the teacher while accommodating a variety of learning styles and responding to the students' development.

While transescents have their own developmental needs, middle-grade educators also know that it is at this age that the continued development of verbal and reading skills is most necessary to insure the students' foundation for secondary studies. Since the teaching of Latin can emphasize word and reading skills so easily, while at the same time providing for the transescent's needs for exploration, movement, hands-on activities, and a look at values, Latin is exceedingly well-suited to the middle grades.

MIDDLE-GRADE SCHOOLS

In elementary schools most students spend their day with one teacher. In the middle grades two to four teachers are with each student, while in the high school each day is spent with six to seven teachers. The exact configuration of the grades contained in each type of school varies from region to region and is affected by school size and enrollment.

Some middle-grade students are in K–12 schools, while others are in K–8 schools. K–12 schools in general de-emphasize advanced courses and foreign language courses such as Latin, while K–8 schools generally offer more reading, less physical education, and more exploratory courses. Especially in sparsely populated regions, some middle-grade students are in a 7–12 setting where the offerings mirror a high-school curriculum. Still other middle-grade students are in a 7–9 school, often called a "junior high." There are frequently more algebra, foreign language, industrial arts, and home economics courses and fewer reading courses in the junior high school. Other middle-grade students are in 6–8 schools and still others are in 7–8 schools, configurations usually termed "middle schools." In middle schools that contain grades 6–8, more reading, computer, and exploratory courses are offered, while in those that house grades 7–8 more computer and fewer science classes tend to be scheduled. While more advanced courses are typically offered in junior highs than in middle schools, a school in an upper-middle class area is more likely to incorporate advanced classes into the curriculum.

Junior highs are frequently modeled on traditional high-school patterns. Middle schools, however, are characterized in general by blocks of instructional time for interdisciplinary learning, a range of exploratory courses, a core of learning experiences focused on needed academic skills, a guidance system in which the student and counselor know each other well, and appropriate methodologies including cooperative learning and team teaching. Instruction in the typical middle school is innovative, active, and student-centered.

MIDDLE-GRADE LATIN PROGRAMS

Latin middle-grade programs, like other foreign language programs, vary according to the program mission, the teacher's goals, and the students' interests. The beginning Latin course in a given middle-grade school, whether in a FLES, FLEX, or sequential program, may begin anywhere in the middle grades from 6th through 9th. In addition, in some middle-grade schools Latin is designed for students with remedial English language needs.

FLES Latin Programs in the Middle Grades

A Latin FLES (Foreign Language in the Elementary Schools) program is more common in the elementary grades but also occurs in the middle grades. Such programs emphasize language and cultural awareness and are designed like elementary FLES Latin programs (cf. Chapter 6). In the middle grades a FLES Latin program typically exists in the 6th grade and may lead to a sequential Latin program in 7th, 8th, or 9th grade or, more rarely, to a FLEX (Foreign Language Exploratory) program.

FLEX Latin Programs in the Middle Grades

Latin FLEX programs are commonly offered in the middle grades, primarily because exploration is one of the key components of the middle-school concept. The goal of a Latin FLEX program is to introduce students to the language and culture of the ancient Romans. Latin FLEX programs typically contain several units of thematic study. For example, a unit on foods may introduce students to the Latin vocabulary that describes or names foods, while concurrently covering how, what, and where the Romans ate. The appearance of a Roman *triclinium* may be included as well, and students may sample a few Roman food items in the classroom or be encouraged to make a Latin recipe. The structure of the Latin language may be introduced, but grammar and syntax form a minimal portion of the usual Latin FLEX program. Many Latin FLEX programs stand alongside FLEX programs in other languages, and the students typically experience each language in a rotational schedule of varying lengths (six weeks, eight weeks, etc.). In this way the students are introduced to a variety of foreign languages and may use this experience to make an intelligent choice of which to study in later middle-grade sequential language programs or in high school.

Sequential Latin Programs in the Middle Grades

Sequential programs focus on the progressive development of Latin language skills and may begin anywhere in the middle grades. The sequential program may be the first course of Latin offered to students or may follow a FLES or FLEX program. Middle-grade programs commonly prepare students to enter a course higher than Latin I in high school, although some programs stand alone without further study of the language offered at the local high school.

Sequential programs may use proficiency-based instruction or content-based instruction. Proficiency-based instruction in the middle grades frequently has as its goal Latin reading proficiency. Oral/aural proficiency in Latin may also be a goal, but more commonly is an adjunct learning activity used to strengthen reading skills. Writing proficiency, that is student production of correct Latin sentences, is rarely a goal in proficiency-based instruction and is a concomitant exercise in fewer classrooms than previously. Instruction in a sequential program often relies upon the textbook to provide a Latin reading passage and the sequence of syntactical and grammatical items which lead toward Latin reading proficiency. The textbook exercises, however, are less commonly used in the middle grades than at the high-school level. Middle-level educators frequently design most of the learning activities and exercises themselves in order to meet the unique characteristics of transescents, a point to be discussed in more detail later in this chapter.

The other type of instruction in a foreign language sequential program is content-based rather than language-based. Proficiency is still the goal but is achieved by shifting the focus of the course from learning the language per se to learning other subject matter in the target language. For example, a 6th-grade science course may be taught in French, and the learner, while mastering the content of the science course, has heard, spoken, written, and read French throughout every class meeting and thus achieved a certain level of proficiency in French.

Other types of content-based instruction include the top-off module and the concurrent module, both taught in the foreign language. In a top-off module, using the previous example, the 6th-grade science class would be taught in English by the science teacher for most of the duration of the course. Meanwhile, the French teacher, who has the same students as the science teacher, would use proficiency-based instruction but tailor the vocabulary and syntax to fit what is being taught in the science class. Near the conclusion of the science course or a particular unit, the French teacher would teach the top-off unit by reviewing with the students the content of the science unit or course in French. By contrast, in a concurrent module, the French teacher would select from the science curriculum those content items which could also be taught in the French language and present them in French class at the same time that the science teacher is teaching them in science class.

Both the top-off and concurrent modules use the foreign language to reinforce the content matter of other subjects while advancing the language proficiency of the student. In this way content-based instruction is a logical extension of proficiency-based instruction. In some subject areas, such as social studies or literature, either the top-off or concurrent foreign language module may be designed to reinforce the foreign language cultural component, as well as to extend proficiency-based instruction and strengthen the content matter of the other subject. In fact, an enterprising teacher may select from the subjects taught in the middle grades a different subject for each season of the year, each quarter, or each six weeks and present a concurrent or top-off module for each subject. For example, a Latin teacher might select 7th-grade social studies for the first quarter school year, since it is during this time period that many 7th-grade social studies teachers present an ancient history unit, then schedule a science unit on planets for the second quarter, an appropriate English unit for the third quarter, and perhaps in the fourth quarter a physical education unit that corresponds to a Roman sport.

Latin is new to content-based instruction and appears to be rarely used in content-based instruction in its purest form. There is no reason to doubt, however, that a middle-grade Latin teacher with enough oral Latin training could teach such a course. On the other hand, Latin can be easily used in the top-off and concurrent modules. In a science unit on planets, the Latin teacher might teach the names of the planets in Latin, thus illustrating their connection to Latin. A classical myth which includes a deity whose name is a planet might also be taught and timed to coincide with a unit on mythology in an English classroom. The names of the planets might be presented orally, while a simplified version of a myth in Latin might be taught for reading comprehension. At the same time, the color adjectives (e.g., *ruber, albus*) might be taught in order to reinforce noun-adjective agreement while strengthening the scientific description of the planets. There are many, many ways to cross disciplinary lines in content-based instruction. The result is exciting for the students and allows the teacher to use creative approaches to curriculum.

MIDDLE-SCHOOL CONCERNS

Latin programs that are in grades 6–8 or 7–8 schools must respond to the special concerns of this type of school, including interdisciplinary instruction and teaming. Middle-level educators agree that the curriculum should not consist chiefly of separate subjects and skills taught in isolation. Thus interdisciplinary teaching is inherent in the middle-school concept. As Vars observes (3), "Efforts to interrelate and integrate the many strands of the school curricula have a long history and are supported by a sizable amount of research." A middle-school may use the thematic, fusion, or correlation approach in order to integrate the curricula and thus achieve interdisciplinary instruction. Each approach may be supported by various staff organizations.

The Thematic Approach

The most widely used method of integrating curricula is the thematic approach. In this method a theme is chosen based upon the needs and interests of the pupils and teachers. The theme should also support the goals of the school, as well as include organized knowledge, thinking skills, and personal development. A given theme may be used for the entire school year, but more frequently is used for a smaller block of time, such as a quarter or semester, and then another theme is chosen and addressed. An example of such a theme might be "conflict." Since middle-level learners are intensely interested in their changing selves and how they fit into the adult world, conflict addresses the needs and interests of these students perfectly. The transescent's need to understand the conflict that he feels between the influence of adults and the influence of his peers will be addressed by instruction on familial and global conflict. As this example shows, the transescents' quest to learn about themselves often mirrors versions of larger world questions. Each or certain curricular areas in the school will follow this theme for the given time period by presenting content matter that fits the theme.

A middle-school Latin teacher, for example, might do the following. The Latin stories in the *Ecce Romani* series (Lawall, et al.) focus on a Roman family, and different types of familial conflict are examined. In Chapter 16 the mother Aurelia responds to her daughter's complaints about the ward who is living in the house. In another chapter the children in the Cornelius family are upset by the move to Rome, occasioned by their father's job. Familial conflict is also present in the Oxford series (Balme and Morwood 1996–97). In Chapter 1, the mother Scintilla makes dinner and goes outside to call her daughter Horatia into the house. Meanwhile, her son Quintus grabs the food off the table. When Scintilla returns and sees that the food is missing, she calls for Quintus but he does not answer. Scintilla becomes angry and has to prepare more food. In other textbooks such as *Latin for Americans* (Ullman, et al.) or Jenney's *First Year Latin* (Jenney, et al.), for example, the Latin stories are not connected readings but deal with a variety of topics. Many of those stories represent various conflicts, such as in the readings about Spartacus, Quintus Fabius Maximus, or Aeneas. The job of the middle-school Latin teacher will be to connect the examples of conflict in whatever textbook is used to the interdisciplinary theme of conflict, make the connection evident, and encourage student thought and discussion.

Staff Organization

The staff organization of a particular school will affect how this theme is integrated into instruction. Three types of organization are commonly used in middle schools. In the total staff approach, all members will meet and decide upon the theme, its content, and the contributions of the various subject areas. This approach works well in a small school, but in a larger school the number of staff members will make it unlikely that all will agree on the theme and some may be reluctant to fit a theme with which they do not agree into an already overloaded curriculum.

In larger schools, interdisciplinary core teams function better. There may be one or more teams per grade level, and the members most frequently have a common planning period in which the design and goals of a theme are developed. Occasionally, for special purposes, a number of teams or even all the school teams may elect to follow the same theme. A core team frequently represents the four required subjects of English, mathematics, science, and social studies, but often teachers of elective or exploratory courses are also involved. Foreign language courses typically include, in addition to the language itself, the culture, geography, and history of the people who speak or once spoke the language. Thus by their own interdisciplinary nature, foreign languages, whether taught via sequential, FLES, or FLEX instruction, lend themselves well to the interdisciplinary team and the thematic approach. In fact, content-based instruction makes the foreign language teacher a natural member of a core team.

In other middle schools a third type of staff organization, called disciplinary teams, may be used. Disciplinary teams are essentially the same as the departmentalized organization of many high schools. A foreign language disciplinary team may design and implement a given theme alone or may choose to work cooperatively with another disciplinary group.

The Fusion Approach

Integrating the curricula of a middle school may also be accomplished by the fusion approach. In this way two or more subjects are fused into one subject that occupies a longer block of time. For example, American History and English might be fused into a new course entitled American Studies. Or Language Arts and Latin might be fused into Language Studies. There may be any number of fused courses in a given school. The teachers of the two fused courses design a new curriculum which emphasizes the interdisciplinary connections between the content of both subject matters. This approach is most common when the total staff organization is used in the school, but disciplinary teaming and core teams also work with the fusion approach.

The Correlation Approach

The correlation approach to integrating curricula involves any two or more teachers, whether on a team or not, in cooperative planning. One type of correlation approach is the curriculum connections method, which contains some of the same elements as the fusion approach. In this approach teachers make connections in the classroom when two or more subjects coincide. For example, when the world history teacher is presenting a unit on ancient Rome, the middle-school Latin teacher might reinforce the content of this course via special readings, assignments, or projects in the Latin classroom. The second type of correlation approach is the thinking skills development method, in which two or more teachers focus on developing a particular thinking skill within their respective content areas. A middle-school Latin teacher, along with a mathematics teacher, might focus on the skill of analysis. Both types of correlation are less structured than other approaches to curriculum integration and are feasible with any type of staff organization.

ARTICULATION WITH ELEMENTARY AND HIGH-SCHOOL PROGRAMS

Middle-grade Latin programs are the link between an elementary Latin program, if one exists in the area, and the local high-school Latin program. Elementary Latin programs most commonly are FLES programs with goals of language and culture awareness; high-school Latin programs are most frequently sequential, with a goal of progressive language acquisition. By contrast, middle-grade Latin programs may be FLES, FLEX, sequential, or a combination of these program types. Whichever type is used, articulation is the key to a successful overall K–12 Latin program. Each level must be aware of how and what the students learned previously and what will be taught afterwards. Whether the overall Latin program exists in a unit district, which may or may not foster articulation between teachers at different levels, or in a number of local districts, it is incumbent upon the teachers at all levels to work together to design the most effective Latin program possible in the given circumstances. The master plan which results from such articulation must be designed to reflect what is best for the learner at each level and must integrate the goals of each level of education. Cooperation and communication are the key elements. The educator must consider carefully how the middle-grade program can serve as an extension of elementary learning and likewise prepare the student for high-school Latin, while still meeting the social, emotional, and intellectual needs of the transescent learner.

The design of overall Latin programs varies from region to region and often even from city to city. The most commonly seen configurations follow. In any of these configurations at any level, a separate Latin course may exist to remediate students with identifiable problems in English language skills. Since this type of remedial course is not central to the purpose of a Latin FLES, FLEX, or sequential program, it should be scheduled and taught as a separate course with its own purpose.

Elementary School	The Middle Grades	High School
FLES programs in grades 4 and/or 5 or no FLES program (hereafter called optional FLES)	Latin I in grades 6, 7, 8 in a sequential program	Latin II and beyond in grades 9–12 (Latin I may also be taught for students entering from another system, hereafter called optional Latin I)
optional FLES	6th-grade Latin FLES Latin I in grades 7, 8 in a sequential program	Latin II and beyond in grades 9–12 (optional Latin I)
optional FLES	6th-grade Latin FLEX Latin I in grades 7, 8 in a sequential program	Latin II and beyond in grades 9–12 (optional Latin I)
optional FLES	6th-grade Latin FLES 7th-grade Latin FLEX 8th-grade Latin I in a sequential program	Latin II and beyond in grades 9–12 (optional Latin I)

optional FLES	9th-grade Latin I in a sequential program	Latin II and beyond in grades 10–12 (optional Latin I)
optional FLEX	8th-grade Latin I in a sequential program 9th-grade Latin II	Latin III and beyond in grades 10–12 (optional Latin I and/or II)
½ Latin I in grades 5, 6 in a sequential program	½ Latin I in 7, 8 in a sequential program	Latin II and beyond in grades 10–12 (optional Latin I)
optional FLES	8th-grade Latin FLEX	Latin I and beyond in grades 9–12

INSTRUCTION IN THE MIDDLE GRADES

Characteristics

Instruction used by middle-school teachers must meet the physical, social-emotional, and cognitive needs of the transescent learner. The physical growth of transescents necessitates hands-on, active instruction that allows for student movement in the classroom. Such instruction will capitalize upon the high activity level of middle-grade pupils. The social-emotional development of transescents indicates that activities which allow for peer interaction within the classroom are optimal. Cooperative learning, the use of oral Latin with student-to-student interaction, group task, and peer teaching are examples of such activities. In view of the cognitive growth that occurs during transescence, the teacher should clarify the purpose of each lesson and provide motivation, goal setting, and structure for students. Appropriate recall strategies should be used to help students connect the lesson to prior learning. Instruction should move from the concrete to the abstract in an inductive approach, in order to accommodate the differing cognitive levels of the learners, and enrichment activities should be provided for those students capable of a higher level of abstraction. Several activities in 10-minute segments will provide variety and be suitable for the short attention span of these pupils. Assessment of learning via questions or some similar activity should conclude the lesson.

The Council on Middle Level Education of the National Association of Secondary School Principals, in *An Agenda for Excellence at the Middle Level*, recommends that instruction at this level :

- include a variety of instructional approaches;
- be organized to match the attention span of the adolescent;
- accommodate individual student learning styles;

- maximize time on task with an emphasis on intellectually challenging activities, not trivial tasks;
- center on learning tasks and activities, not merely content coverage;
- provide feedback, both written and oral, that is specific and continual;
- stimulate creative problem solving and productive thinking through group interaction;
- emphasize cooperative learning activities rather than competitive tasks, thus enhancing time on task and improving the quality of the intellectual activity;
- use textbooks as organizers rather than as the sole core of instruction;
- utilize hands-on, involved, active learning as the preferred mode of instruction to capitalize on the students' natural activity levels.

Types of Instructional Methods

The various methods used by middle-school Latin teachers, whether in a grammar-translation or reading approach, should reflect one or more of the above general characteristics. The following methods are by no means a complete listing but instead represent those most commonly employed by middle-grade Latin teachers.

Drama and Role-Playing: Many types of stories, myths, and daily life activities can be converted into some kind of dramatic form. Students may convert a myth into a dramatic scene and then present it to the classroom, or the teacher may access myths and stories already in a dramatic form and have the students perform the mini-play. Drama and role-playing also allow for movement in the classroom, one of the characteristics of middle-level instruction. One year, when I was teaching 7th-grade Latin, a dramatized English version of Pyramus and Thisbe was in the *Pompeiiana* newsletter. I divided the classroom into several groups and each group performed this scene, using the exact dialogue given in the newsletter. Not surprisingly, each group gave quite a different presentation, due to the use of different props, gestures, and the like. The content of this myth, the love between two young people and their parents' role, prompted discussion about the emotional aspect of love and its effect on young individuals. In this way, the myth of Pyramus and Thisbe was directed toward the transescent's emotional development.

The increasing use of oral Latin in the classroom facilitates dramatizing a story in Latin. Even reading selections about a Roman family that are found in several Latin textbooks can be easily dramatized. Burnell's *Vesuvius and Other Latin Plays* was written for students learning Latin via the Cambridge series (Phinney and Bell) but may be used with any textbook. Or Latin phrases and sentences may be incorporated into a dramatic scene. When the Latin language is used, either for the whole presentation or peppered throughout the scene, students are given invaluable pronunciation and intonation practice and the repetitive nature of dramatization encourages student learning. Drama and role-playing may also be incorporated into learning Latin vocabulary. For example, the teacher lists, from previously learned vocabulary items, adjectives that express emotions or the verbs that express movement. The list may be put on the blackboard, overhead, or worksheet. A student or a pair of students then act out the word or phrase while the remainder of the class must guess the Latin adjective or verb. Playing charades is also a form of drama or role-playing. Roman historical, legendary, or mythological characters are a natural for playing charades in the middle-grade Latin classroom. Playing charades is also a good way for the students to learn the terms for professions (e.g., *pistor, raedarius, miles, agricola*). The student actor should conclude with *Quis sum?*

Total Physical Response (TPR): Children learn through their senses and through motion. Most TPR activities include an oral command, an oral response, and a movement. For example, a Latin teacher might review the first person singular of present tense verbs while introducing singular imperatives of the different conjugations through this TPR activity. More commands and responses, of course, would be included to facilitate practice.

Grammar	Teacher Command	Pupil Response	Pupil Movement
Conjugation 1	Ambula ad ianuam!	Ambulo ad ianuam.	The pupil walks toward the door.
Conjugation 2	Sede in sella hic!	Sedeo in sella hic.	The pupil sits in a designated chair.
Conjugation 3	Surge nunc!	Surgo nunc.	The pupil stands up.
Conjugation 3-*io*	Arripe librum!	Arripio librum.	The pupil picks up his book.
Conjugation 4	Veni huc!	Venio huc.	The pupil comes to the teacher.

Other TPR activities for the middle-grade classroom include commands and responses that illustrate accusative versus ablative prepositional phrases, as well as those that direct the student to place an object in certain locations in the classroom. Or various areas of the classroom can be given place names such as *Hispania, Gallia,* or *Italia*, and the pupils can be commanded to visit those countries. Thus TPR is an instructional method that allows for another learning style, as well as being another way to provide movement in the classroom for the active, transescent learner. TPR activities are also an excellent way to insert variety into the segments of a lesson; a good source for Latin TPR activities is Salerno's *Latin in Motion: A Handbook for Teachers* (and cf. Strasheim 1987).

Songs: Transescents also learn through singing. A Latin version sung in the classroom may exemplify a particular grammatical structure, illustrate a vocabulary item, or simply reinforce pronunciation patterns. *Adeste Fideles*, for example, exemplifies the use of present active plural imperatives, while the Latin version of "He's Got the Whole World in His Hands," in *Latine Cantemus* (Schlosser, 20–21), illustrates and repeats common Latin vocabulary items including *teneo, mundus, manus, frater, pater, filia, mater, sol,* and *luna.* "Today Is Monday," in its Latin version in *Learning Latin through Song* (Osburn 1995b: 36), not only reinforces pronunciation but also teaches the names of the months in Latin. There are also songs in English that teach language and cultural items in *Learning Latin through Song* and in the *Mythology Songbook* (Edwards, et al.). Hand movements or clapping can also be incorporated into these types of songs to meet the high activity level and natural enthusiasm of middle-school students. The song "Argus" (*Learning Latin through Song*, 42) is a Latin version of the childhood favorite, "*Bingo.*" This song contains clapping in the chorus and is a perfect activity when young students are restless.

Games: Middle-grade learners are enthusiastic about games, and there are many types suitable for Latin classes, including word games, bingo-type games, team games, guessing games, TPR games such as "Simon Says," number games such as "Buzz," prop games such as "Telephone," board games, card games, computer games, relay games, and charades. Many learning games feature a winner or a winning team, and middle-grade students love rewards or prizes. Many teachers routinely keep a bag of candy in their desks in order to have a prize ready for any occasion. Stickers and free homework passes also work very well. Examples of how to use some of these games in the middle-school classroom follow.

A favorite word game is scrambled words or sentences. A scrambled word or phrase from the previous day is an easy way to start or end a lesson. The pupil who correctly unscrambles it first wins. Bingo games do not have to teach only numbers. An easy way to play bingo is to make and photocopy a substantial quantity of blank worksheets. With any given topic, pass out the sheets and make a list of more than 30 Latin words on the blackboard or overhead. These words may all be part of one category, such as 30 different verbs, or may contain words from different categories, such as 15 Latin words from a unit on the Roman house and 15 from current vocabulary items. Instruct the students to choose 25 words and to write them in any square on the blank bingo sheet. The teacher or another student selects words from the list in a random order and says them aloud. The students draw an X over that word if it appears on their bingo sheet. The rest of the game proceeds as any normal bingo game. Some teachers prefer to have the students write the definition below the word on the bingo sheet instead of drawing an X over it.

Team games can include "Latin Wheel of Fortune" or "Latin Jeopardy," and team sports games such as "Latin Classroom Volleyball," which can be played inside any classroom with a nerf volleyball while a line of desks in the center of the room serves as the net. The server is the pupil who not only serves the ball physically but also announces a Latin word and a category. For example, the server might say "*puella*—person." The player who returns the ball from the opposing team must say another Latin word for a person. The first player who cannot say a Latin word which fits the category is considered to have dropped the ball and normal volleyball rules govern the game.

Relay games fit the inflectional nature of Latin very well. One common type can serve as a review for any or all of the Latin declensions. It may be played at student desks which are in rows or at the blackboard. The teacher or a selected student says a Latin noun in the nominative singular. The first person in each row writes that word down on a piece of paper along with the genitive singular of the noun. The first person then passes the paper to the second person in the row, who writes down the dative singular and passes the paper to the third person, and the game continues until a row has correctly completed the declension. In the blackboard version of the game, each player must run to the blackboard to write the form of the Latin word, and then run back and hand the chalk to the next student on the relay team.

Cooperative Learning: Much has been written on the theoretical framework of cooperative learning and its value in educating middle-level learners. It is sufficient to note here that cooperative learning serves the social development of transescents by allowing interaction with their peers and aids their cognitive development through the role that each learner has within the cooperative group. At Baker Demonstration School of National-Louis University in Evanston, Illinois, beginning in the late 1980s, cooperative learning groups were used to aid middle-school students in translating Latin selections from *Ecce Romani* (Lawall, et al.). Each group contained four learners: the vocabulary expert, the syntax expert, the translator, and the recorder. During the first class period, the students in each group read the Latin passage aloud to each other. Then on a copy of the text each group working cooperatively labeled in some instances the subject, verb, and direct object of the sentences and other times the prepositional phrases and modifiers. After the group completed both of these tasks, the translation began. The translator began translating, seeking vocabulary and syntax help as needed from group experts. The recorder wrote down the translation after all group members had agreed upon it. At the end of the first class period, the students in each group were responsible for completing, in written form at home, the portion of the translation which had not been finished in the classroom.

During the second class period, the same cooperative groups, using the written translations they had completed at home, agreed upon the correct translation of the remainder of the passage and the recorder produced the written version of it. The Latin teacher highlighted the incorrect parts of the group translation and the cooperative group then produced a revised and agreed-upon translation. The teacher continued to highlight the incorrect portions and the groups continued until a given group had a correct translation. Finally, copies of the correct version were made and given to each member of the group in anticipation of the unit examination. Initially, the students in each group divided up the homework portion of the translation among the members of the group. As a result, according to Baker Latin teachers Rebecca Crown and Elisa Denja, the students were not adequately prepared to do all sections of the translation on the unit test. In later uses of this instructional strategy, the teachers clarified that all members of each group were to translate all of the remaining section of the translation. Crown and Denja also reported that students were more willing to translate Latin as a result of the cooperative groups and that, as the school year progressed, these students began of their own accord to seek out other students with whom to work in small cooperative groups on other learning tasks.

EXTRA-CURRICULAR ACTIVITIES

Extra-curricular activities are an important part of the transescent's social-emotional development and allow for peer interaction. Many high-school enrichment activities are suitable to middle-level learners, and so readers should refer to Chapter 11 below for further details and recommended activities.

The National Latin Exam (NLE): The NLE offers an Introduction to Latin Exam that is suitable for those middle-level learners who have learned approximately half of a Latin I curriculum in a sequential program.

National Mythology Exam (NME): The NME is designed for students in grades 3–9. Learners in grades 6–9 take a basic exam of 40 items and then must choose to take at least one sub-test. Each sub-test on the *Iliad, Odyssey, Aeneid*, African or Native American myths contains 10 items.

The National Junior Classical League (NJCL): The NJCL sponsors a national convention every summer. The six-day event is held on a university campus in different regions of the United States. In addition to many types of activities which middle-level learners enjoy, academic tests on mythology, Latin derivatives, Latin reading comprehension, Latin grammar, mottoes, and other topics are administered during the convention. Middle-school students who have completed approximately half of a standard Latin I curriculum should register at the one-half level. Many states also hold a state JCL convention during the school year. Middle-level Latin teachers must find out from the state JCL chair whether any of the academic tests or other activities are suitable for transescents. There are numerous JCL chapters in high schools which host activities for their members and may include guests from local middle schools. Information on the NJCL, NLE, and NME is available from the American Classical League (ACL, Miami Univ., Oxford, OH 45056), whose Teaching Materials and Resource Center (TMRC) also distributes the very useful packet "Exemplary Latin Programs for Middle Schools," prepared by the National Committee for Latin and Greek (TMRC item B911b).

Certamen Meets: Certamen is an oral quiz-bowl type of academic game which focuses on various topics commonly taught in a Latin classroom, such as Roman history, mythology, mottoes and derivatives, Roman daily life, Latin vocabulary, etc. In a typical game, a team of four players from one school competes against two more teams of four from different schools. Correct answers gain points for the team. Certamen meets are rare in some areas of the United States and abound in others; many are sponsored by local JCL chapters, and Certamen is a major event at the annual NJCL convention. Middle-school Latin teachers will need to investigate whether or not meets are available in their area and whether middle-school students may play on a Latin I or novice team or whether that is against local rules. Middle-school students love games, and Certamen is a naturally attractive activity to them.

Trips Abroad: Like their high-school counterparts, middle-schoolers enjoy and benefit educationally from trips abroad. Many companies offer student tours to Italy or Greece, and these are often advertised in ACL's journal, the *Classical Outlook* (an excellent source of articles and reviews of interest to Latin teachers at all levels). The middle-level teacher must scrutinize the itinerary of such tours to insure that there are sufficient recreational and educational opportunities for the high activity level of transescents. In addition, some tour companies will combine a group from one school with a group from another. If both groups are not composed of middle-level students, it may be difficult to meet the needs of both groups on the tour.

EDUCATIONAL RESOURCES

Criteria for Evaluation of Instructional Materials: Whether considering a textbook for adoption or the use of supplementary materials such as books, videos, software, etc., the middle-level educator must insure that the social-emotional, physical, and cognitive characteristics of transescents are reflected in the materials. Thus, the materials should set goals that the middle-level learner can achieve and should contain closure. In addition, the materials need to be age-appropriate and flexible enough to accommodate the variety of learning styles, cognitive development, interests, abilities, attention span, and background of the students. Instructional materials should also show the multicultural aspects of Roman life. The ancient Romans themselves lived side-by-side with immigrants from many Mediterranean cultures and valued a global education through study of the language and culture of ancient Greece. Middle-level textbooks and materials should do no less.

Textbooks: The Latin textbook chosen for any middle-level Latin class must fit the goals of the course, which may be a FLES, FLEX, or sequential offering, as well as meet the criteria listed above and aid articulation among the elementary, middle-level, and high-school courses. There are many Latin textbooks suitable for the middle grades, and only those most commonly used will be mentioned here. The two most frequently adopted for FLES middle-level Latin classes are *Salvete*, Books 1–2 (Phinney, et al.) precursor of the Cambridge Latin series, and *First Latin*, Books 1–2 (Polsky 1998), part of the Scott Foresman-Addison Wesley Latin series (cf. Chapter 6 above). In sequential middle-level classes that follow a reading approach (cf. Chapters 9 and 14), the *Ecce Romani* (Lawall, et al.), Cambridge (Phinney and Bell), and Oxford (Balme and Morwood 1996–97) series are typically used, while middle-grade Latin teachers who follow the grammar-translation method (cf. Chapters 8 and 13) commonly adopt Jenney's *First Year Latin* or the *Latin for Americans* series (Ullman, et al.). The *Phenomenon of Language* (Florian) or Amsco's *Discovering Languages: Latin* (Ashworth and Robbins) are the usual textbooks in middle-level Latin FLEX courses. In fact, *Phenomenon of Language* was developed to provide materials for the Latin exploratory course at Harvard School in North Hollywood, California. Unlike most FLEX courses, the Harvard curriculum was designed as a 17-week introduction to Latin, after which the students rotated through four-week courses in French, Spanish, and Russian. In the majority of schools, however, each language FLEX course is of equal length. This concept is the basis of Amsco's Exploratory series in Latin, German, French, and Spanish. Also available from Amsco is *Latin Is Fun*, Books 1–2 (Traupman 1989, 1995). Although *Latin Is Fun* is in workbook format, a step-by-step progression toward reading Latin is used and, as a result, the book may be used as a basic text or as a supplement.

Supplementary Materials: In the middle grades it is especially important for the teacher not to rely solely on the textbook to provide instruction. Language and cultural topics, as well as hands-on and interdisciplinary instruction, are best served by a wide variety of supplementary materials in book, workbook, novel, video, computer software, board game, and card game formats. Only a few examples from the many that exist will be described here; addresses for many of the publishers and vendors mentioned here are listed in Chapter 24 below and others can be identified through your local bookstore.

Several supplemental Latin language books are suited to middle-level learners. *O Loca Tu Ibis* (Geisel) is based on a Dr. Seuss story, while *Tres Ursi* (Osburn 1995a) retells the fairytale of the three bears. Along with *Learning Latin through Mythology* from Cambridge University Press (Hanlin and Lichtenstein), these books are designed to meet the goals of reading proficiency. Traupman's

Conversational Latin for Oral Proficiency from Bolchazy-Carducci is useful for the oral component of language learning.

For hands-on activities, Lumina's overlay books are well suited to middle-grade Latin students, who love to look at the pictures of how Rome and Pompeii once appeared and then pick up the plastic overlay to see the state of the site today. Likewise transescents enjoy the Latin *Libelli* from L & L Enterprises (Osburn 1994a–b), which involve the origami project of folding paper, which is pre-printed with Latin on such topics as animals, numbers, mottoes, declensions, etc., into the shape of little books. A more involved hands-on activity, which is best managed through group work, is the construction of an Usborne cut-out model, such as *Make This Roman Amphitheater*. Other arts and crafts hands-on activities can be found in Alarion's "Look and Do Workbook" on the *Art and Architecture of Ancient Rome* (A. Campbell) and in Henrich's *Big Book of Roman Activities*.

Coloring books are also very useful in the Latin classroom. By removing the staples which hold most coloring books together, the pages may be cut and distributed to different members of the class. In one 6th-grade FLES class I taught, I took apart the *Coloring Book of Rome* (Bellerophon Press) and gave a page to each student. After coloring their pages with magic markers, the students constructed frames for their portraits with black construction paper. Using a computer program, they then generated a title and a description label for each portrait. The labels were affixed to the bottom of the construction-paper frames, and the framed portraits, hung in the hallway, formed a gallery through which the students took turns leading tours of other classes, as well as administrators, school support personnel, and parents. Other coloring books from Bellerophon, such as *A Coloring Book of the Trojan War* or *A Coloring Book of the Olympics*, may be used in a similar way to create attractive bulletin boards or classroom decorations as well as enhance and enrich student learning.

Another type of hands-on supplementary material is board and card games. *By Jove*, a mythology board game from Aristoplay, is a favorite with middle-schoolers, as is the *Greco* bingo-type game on mythology, which can be purchased from ACL's TMRC. *Greek Myths and Legends*, a card game from Aristoplay, fits the needs of the transescent learner very well. In this game, each player attempts to collect the four cards which together tell one myth. As in *Rummy*, the player lays down a completed set of cards on the table, and the first player to put down all the cards in his hand wins. Finally, classroom games such as Jeopardy and Certamen are also popular with this age group; a new teacher resource book, *Farrago Latina*, by Gaylan DuBose, contains many Jeopardy and Certamen questions ready for use in the classroom.

Many supplemental materials, including those already described, may contribute to interdisciplinary instruction. In addition, there are several colorful and eye-pleasing books available on the topic of Roman life which can form a link to a social studies class. Amery and Vanag's *Rome and Romans* and Wingate's *The Romans* are designed with the middle-level learner in mind, as is Garieri's *How Would You Survive as an Ancient Roman*. Other books may be useful to link Latin to a language arts class. Henrich's workbook *Story Starters on Ancient Rome* is designed to help middle-level learners write a culturally accurate story set in Roman times. Henry Winterfeld's two novels set in ancient Rome, *Detectives in Togas* and *Mystery of the Roman Ransom*, are written at the 5th/6th-grade reading level; teacher resource guides for these novels are available from L&L Enterprises. Other ways to link middle-level Latin classes to the language arts classroom is through the study of classical mythology or word elements. Ingri and Edgar Parin D'Aulaires' *Book of Greek Myths* is a standard, and can now be accompanied by *A Literature Unit for D'Aulaires' Book of Greek Myths* (Ross) from Teacher Created Materials Press and *D'Aulaires' Book of Greek Myths* audiobook from Airplay Audio. *Classic Myths to Read Aloud* (Russell), from Crown Publishing, indicates the number of minutes it takes to read a particular myth aloud (an excellent middle-level instructional activity). *Our Greek and Latin Roots* from Cambridge (Morwood and Warman) may be used by middle-level Latin or language arts teachers. Middle-school "foods" classes may be linked to Latin through any of these three books: *The Classical Cookbook* by Dalby and Grainger, John Edwards' *Roman Cookery*, and Giacosa's *Taste of Ancient Rome*.

The last two types of supplementary materials to be noted here are videos and computer software (but readers are referred also to Chapters 23 and 24 below for further details of classroom resources and addresses for many of the vendors and publishers mentioned in this chapter). There are many instructional videos on the culture and history of Rome. Of special interest to the middle-level Latin educator, however, is *Asterix vs. Caesar*, which is in animated format from Gaumont Dargaud/Rene Goscinny Productions, and *Wishbone: Homer Sweet Homer*, Polygram Video's retelling of the *Odyssey* in which the key role is played by a dog named Wishbone. For a complete discussion of computer software refer to Chapter 23, but the transescent's love of games is served well by these two computer games in particular: *Wrath of the Gods* (Luminaria), which allows the middle-level student to learn about the classical heroes and their quests, and *Escape from Pompeii* (Centaur Systems), both of which are simulation-type games.

CONCLUSION

With the accelerating growth of Latin in American middle schools experienced since the 1980s, more Latin middle-level educators will be needed in the upcoming years. About half of the 50 states require a special certificate to teach in the middle grades or require a middle-school endorsement on another type of certificate. Anecdotal evidence suggests that few trained Latin teachers in the U.S. hold this special certificate or endorsement, and very few schools, if any, have programs for training middle-level Latin teachers. Yet, middle-school principals, when interviewing candidates, look for teachers with a command of the subject area, the ability to increase student motivation, and an understanding of transescence, according to a national survey (Epstein and MacIver). Until teacher training programs begin to produce middle-level Latin teachers, it is most likely that high-school Latin teachers will fill middle-school positions. A high-school teacher in a middle-level Latin program must learn to understand and use the sorts of instructional methods that best meet the needs of the transescent. The various kinds of Latin programs that exist in many types of schools, along with the transescent's high-activity level and need for a variety of activities within one class period, make this a challenging task for a transplanted high-school teacher.

In the fall of 1980, after eight years of successful high-school teaching, I walked unsuspectingly into the first 7th-grade Latin class to be offered in my district. When the bell rang, I gazed at 17 faces, much younger looking than those of their high-school counterparts. Undaunted, I began class as I always had on the first day of school. What happened next is a scene indelibly printed in the pages of my mind. Suddenly, all 17 hands were in the air, all 17 students asking different questions. Some of them had remained in their seats, others were kneeling on their chairs, some were standing next to or near their chairs, and still others were clustered around me at the front of the classroom. And one young boy had positioned himself exceedingly close to my arm, totally violating the interpersonal space that is expected at the high-school level. When that student then tugged on the sleeve of my dress, I jumped with surprise. What I did not see that first day, but did consistently notice over my next 16 years in middle-level Latin classrooms, was the bubbling enthusiasm, the incredible curiosity and inquisitiveness, and the unceasing search for knowledge which transescents constantly exhibit. It is these characteristics that make middle-level Latin students a joy to teach.

8

Grammar-Translation And High-School Latin

KAREN LEE SINGH
Florida State University School, Tallahassee, Florida

Much has been written during the last 15 years or so comparing the traditional, so-called "grammar-translation approach" to teaching Latin with the "reading approach" (see Chapter 2 above for a discussion of the essential differences between the two methods). The object of this chapter is not to favor one system over the other but to survey the tools and strategies available for those teachers who feel most comfortable with, or who have experienced success with, the grammar-translation method at the secondary level (cf. Chapter 13 on using this approach in college).

Certainly the needs of students also play an important role in choosing a *modus operandi*. For instance, first-year students and their parents often see the Latin class as an opportunity to work on study skills, self-discipline, and logical thinking, in addition to increasing language skills and vocabulary for those all-important PSAT and SAT tests which lie a few years ahead (cf. Craib, 117–18). Therefore, the focus of my Latin I class, and most of my Latin II, is the study of *language* itself—how it developed, how it works, and how it can be made to serve the students best. Since this can be taught in a highly inflected language like Latin much more easily than in English, I emphasize thorough familiarization with the signposts such a language provides (cf. B. Campbell, 249). Obviously, at this stage, my object is not to read Latin but to give students the tools they need to become better speakers and better writers. Writing is surely a creative process, but only through a knowledge of the "nuts and bolts" of a language can a creative piece be fine-tuned.

The emphasis, then, should be on grammar and vocabulary acquisition in the early stages of Latin study (cf. Ball and Ellsworth 1989: 60–61) with a lot of comparisons to English usage and attention to word derivation. Students do learn lists of vocabulary words, but not *in vacuo*. They are used in sentence work needed to understand the grammar, and their derivatives are studied to increase the students' knowledge of English vocabulary. In order to ensure that these words become a *working* part of their everyday vocabulary, students use them in sentences on the vocabulary quizzes and, as an incentive, receive a bonus point every time these derivatives are naturally used in written work and casual conversation.

TEXTS

Once the "grammar-translation" approach is chosen, the next decision concerns the choice of a beginning text. The following are the most commonly used:

1) The third edition of *Our Latin Heritage* (Hines and Howard) is much more attractive than the earlier publications with the addition of colored pictures of ancient art and architecture. Its derivative study is built directly into the vocabulary lists, its reading passages consist of well-known stories from mythology or depict interesting events in Roman times, and a conversation piece begins each unit. However, the medieval "J" is employed, there is perhaps too much packed into each unit, and the text is rarely broken up by pictures, which makes it far less appealing to students. It remains, however, an excellent, if somewhat demanding, textbook.

2) The 1997 edition of *Latin for Americans* (Ullman, et al.) is pleasing to the eye and moves at a leisurely pace. The readings are rather pedestrian in the earlier part of the book, but the stories use the vocabulary and grammar already familiar to the students and stress the material introduced in the chapter. This eliminates much of the frustration which students encounter if they have to look up words continually and avoids extensive glossing, which is not conducive to mastering the vocabulary.

3) The revised "Jenney" (*First Year Latin*, by Jenney, et al.) is an attractive book with beautiful pictures, wonderful sections on culture, and excellent "relevance" pages at the end of every unit. Using it to teach the Latin language, however, is another story altogether. For example, in Lesson 1 it introduces the nominative case, the genitive of possession, and the ablative of place where, as well as all the first declension endings. I prefer to limit students' first exposure to nouns to the nominative case with a linking verb, adding the accusative case with action verbs in the following chapter. This allows students to concentrate on sentence structure and the basic building blocks of a sentence before encountering similar endings that signal different uses (cf. Stephens, 112). Many of the explanations are excessive; the vocabulary presented very soon gravitates towards the Vergilian, although most students in Latin I will not reach Latin IV; and at times confusing words are taught together (*vincio, vinco,* and *vivo* in Lesson 24). The readings rapidly become difficult for beginners because they have to look up so much unfamiliar vocabulary, and there are no superscripts in the text to refer a student to the footnotes. The manipulative exercises are

often quite good; however, the review sections do nothing but list the vocabulary covered in the unit. All of the grammar review exercises have been moved to the workbook or the teachers' manual which is *not* helpful (see further the reviews by Howard and Montross, cited in the bibliography under Jenney).

4) Manuals and Workbooks: Good manuals at the lower levels with extensive bibliographies and lists of audio-visual materials are available for these three text series. The manuals for Jenney in particular are very complete, although they contain numerous errors. However, those written in any series for upper level courses are largely devoted to mere translations, with no sections on background, interpretation, or relevance. New teachers and experienced ones alike often lack the knowledge necessary to lead fruitful discussions on the literature being studied, and the classroom often becomes a tedious hour of translation and grammar discussions. While college training is often at fault for this, publishers also are guilty for failing to provide teachers' manuals which address this problem.

Workbooks can be quite helpful (the new ones for *Latin for Americans* are excellent), although their usage will depend on the needs of teacher and student. I find them particularly indispensable when I have to be absent from the classroom, for they help the students review material and keep the class from being a wasted period or at best a study hall for other subjects.

THE LATIN I CLASS: TEACHING THE LANGUAGE

When a teacher has decided on the grammar-translation approach and has chosen a text, there are two things to keep in mind: 1) Grammar should *not* be the only thing taught, and 2) the textbook must not dictate *how* the material is to be taught.

A teacher does not have to use all the material in a chapter; he or she may perhaps decide to use none, group chapters together, or take them out of order. The caveat here is to be sure any exercises or readings assigned to the class do not include excessive amounts of untaught vocabulary or unfamiliar grammatical constructions.

In order to determine what material to teach, the instructor must first decide what are the *essentials* a student has to master before starting Latin II—in other words, the curriculum is outcome-based. The basic material usually covered in a grammar-based Latin I class includes the formation of nouns and adjectives of the first three declensions; adverbs; the first three conjugations active and passive, and *sum*, in all six tenses; and the present imperative. Syntax covers the basic uses of six cases (including the vocative and half a dozen ablatives). However, guides such as the *Standards for Classical Language Learning* and state curriculum frameworks (see Chapter 5 above), combined with district or departmental curriculum outlines, will help the teacher in deciding what to teach. The new standards allow for wide variations in methods, and benchmarks of accomplishment may now be reached at different times by different students. Other helpful sources are the syllabus for the National Latin Exam (NLE) and Junior Classical League (JCL) competition parameters.

Patterns of language and pyramidal instruction (reaching out to new material from what students already know) give a teacher ample opportunity to work on *logical thought*. For example, learning the future endings of the first conjugation has never been a problem for my students. The third conjugation present tense, however, seemed to engender an automatic mental shutdown, until one day I had them write down the future endings of the first conjugation, cross off the "B," and place the stem of a third conjugation verb in front of the remaining letters (*bit* to *it* to *ponit*). I knew it was successful when I heard comments like, "Oh, this is easy," or "What's so hard about that?" Of course, I had psychologically prepared them for the worst by telling them how difficult the third conjugation was to learn!

This is merely one example of using the structure of Latin to improve logical thought processes. Regardless of how early students begin reading Latin, there comes a time when they must recognize and differentiate between tense forms. Surely it is of some importance to the hero of a story whether *interficitur* or *interficietur*!

Memorizing forms and vocabulary is a comparatively low level skill which students can practice by themselves on the computer or at home. Understanding how these words and forms are put together in sentences to convey thoughts requires critical thinking skills, which I prefer to oversee in the classroom. Cooperative learning has made this possible. The methods I use to construct my system are given below (see "Setting Up Cooperative Learning"); a general overview of its use in my classroom is the focus here.

Reading and translations are now always done by groups in class instead of being assigned as homework. The "jigsaw" method seems to work best at this level, with students divided into "expert" groups to learn the material and then teaching it to their home-base "study" groups. It is during the "expert" phase that the teacher is very busy, moving from group to group assisting with the material, as well as monitoring group behavior. To preclude one student from doing all the work and to teach them to read Latin as we read English, students are instructed to take turns moving clockwise around the group, analyzing each word as it appears in the sentence and translating what becomes clear as they proceed (cf. Hamilton, 167–68). There is no "find the verb—now find the subject" (cf. Hoyos 1993: 127–28; Hoyos 1997). If a student does not see all the options or commits an error, other members may help, *not* by simply giving the answer but by using the Socratic method. This technique makes students think through the problem for themselves. They then must explain the point to the other members of the group. After completing the assignment using this process, the students may ask for clarification on any points the group could not resolve, and I in turn question the members about the work to make sure they all know the material equally well.

Students then move to their "study" groups. This is the most important part of the cooperative approach, for it is in the teaching that true learning takes place. It is also during this phase that even the weak and shy students can build self-confidence, for the knowledge they bring from their "expert" groups is needed by each one in their group. Although the teacher has some respite here, it is imperative that he or she move quietly around the classroom listening to each group and checking for correct group behavior. This is also a good opportunity for teachers to learn about their students by watching them present their material and observing their interactions with other group members.

The benefits of translating in this fashion become clear quite rapidly. The students do more work in less time and do it better than those students I previously taught in theater fashion and required to do translations as homework. For example, I used to assign 10 sentences on a particular day, and I was lucky if one or two students brought them all translated to the next class. The same pattern continued when I cut the assignment in half. With cooperative learning, each student now finishes a lesson having translated 12 sentences, four of which are English to Latin (cf. Saunders, 389–90). And they *all* understand everything about those sentences, for there is a final group check in which I can call on anyone to recite on behalf of the group, the entire group being awarded points based on that one student's performance. They are therefore all dependent on each other, and the motivation for joint success is strong.

This approach makes the Latin class a much more enjoyable place to be, and the teacher is available to help with any problems that arise. However, in Latin I the students must first be taught how to work in groups, and the process must be tightly controlled and closely watched at this level.

THE LATIN I CLASS: TEACHING THE CULTURE

A foreign language class involves not only learning vocabulary, grammar, and derivatives, but also studying the culture of the people. Culture can be taught in whole sessions devoted to it (e.g., every Friday), or it can be addressed whenever sentences, or readings, or even vocabulary signal an opportunity. A proper name can lead to a discussion of Roman nomenclature or result in a geography lesson; a common noun like *pecunia* gives insight into language development from early customs (*pecus*) and flows naturally into the invention of coined money in Lydia, with its concomitant influence on trade and exploration. At the Latin I level, this discussion may be rudimentary, but the mention of Lydia will, at the very least, lead to Croesus and the common use of his name today. The discussion might include the story about his visit to the

Delphic Oracle, which in turn brings up the role and practice of divination and Apollo's place in mythology. A study of the Delphic Oracle even allows an introduction to Hellenic history (Themistocles), which cycles the discussion back to Croesus. Connections like this are fun to make, and the culture is thus much more embedded in the study of the language—all this from one vocabulary word! The two strands should be inextricably woven together. National and state standards, including the NLE, will furnish some guidance on what to cover. However, the interests and knowledge of the teacher, coupled with those of the class, will determine how far and how deeply to go in any discussion, and the emphasis in any Latin class must always be on the language itself.

Studying culture is also a good way to acquaint students with the various areas of JCL competition. It can spark the students' interest in doing further work on their own, an essential for JCL involvement since there is not enough class time to bring their skills up to competition level. Regardless of a teacher's personal feelings about competition in general, there is no denying the holding power it can have on a student's commitment to the study of Latin. I therefore require all my Latin I students to participate in the Regional Forum held in early February. Their successes look good on a curriculum vitae, and they can then make an informed decision as to whether they wish to continue competing.

THE LATIN II CLASS

Where the Level II class begins its study of grammar depends on what was covered in Level I; where it ends depends on what the teacher deems essential to begin the reading of real Latin texts. Many teachers believe a full-scale review of Latin I is necessary *before* new material is presented; I used to be one of them. However, I found I had to rethink my approach completely when my school went to block scheduling. I now incorporate review into the daily class schedule of even my 50-minute year-long courses by giving the students assignment sheets which itemize the exercises to be used on computer programs like *Latin Flash Drill* (from Centaur Systems) and *Grammar Computerized* (from Lingo Fun) and include a due date on which a short quiz will be given; students are also encouraged for review purposes to use the computer games *Mare Nostrum* and *Cursus Honorum* (from the University of Delaware—see Chapter 23 below). This approach allows for individual pacing, and charts on the wall track a student's progress. Vocabulary reviews are held every Friday, followed by group work on easy passages of Latin from various Level I texts which illustrate and emphasize the review material assigned for that particular week.

The new grammar material to be covered in this class makes Level II by far the most difficult for both teacher and student, primarily because it focuses on grammatical concepts which are seldom covered in an English class but are absolutely essential for understanding Latin. It is the rare student who knows subjunctives or even participles at this level. The grammar covered in my Latin II class focuses on pronouns (with a lot of comparison and contrast to English) and the formation and use of comparatives and superlatives, infinitives (especially their role in indirect statement, an essential for reading Caesar), participles (including the ablative absolute), and subjunctives (cf. the guidelines in Chapter 5 above).

The other problem encountered in teaching this level lies in the plethora of relatively minor points to which the texts devote whole chapters—indefinite pronouns, special verb forms, impersonal passives of intransitive verbs, and the like. Although I dutifully used to teach all this material, I found that students could read a good deal of real Latin without encountering any of it. I therefore now delay teaching much of the usual Latin II grammar such as gerunds and gerundives until the students meet it in their reading.

Although I consolidate text chapters in teaching grammar and syntax, I do follow the vocabulary in each lesson quite faithfully with constant quizzes and considerable derivative work. Since this class is a termination point for many students, I really focus on vocabulary building and cull as many Latin-based words as possible from real SATs and JCL derivatives tests, organizing them on worksheets and quizzes to match the vocabulary in their textbooks. This reinforces the meaning of the words in both languages.

The study of grammar should continue to emphasize forms (e.g., the mood of the verb in a *qui* clause), for their identification is often necessary to understanding the fine points of a passage under discussion or the argument being presented. The focus, however, must always be on the use of grammar in understanding the language, not on grammar as an end in itself.

Cooperative learning is again the primary strategy in my Latin II classroom, and I find the jigsaw method is still the most effective. The teaching which occurs in the study groups forces the students to explain verb tense relationships and identify subordinate constructions, a technique which encourages the repetition necessary for mastery and requires each student to participate in the process.

Culture also continues to be a part of the Latin II class. If the teacher intends to read Caesar, the study of history and customs should focus on family life, the Roman method of calendar dating, and the politics of the late Republic. For instance, every Latin II student in my classes must memorize the calendar poem ("In March, July, October, May, / the Ides fall on the 15th day, / the Nones the seventh; and all besides / are two days less for Nones and Ides") and master the method of inclusive counting. The study of Roman family life in general gradually evolves into the study of Julius Caesar's life in particular so that, by the time I introduce students to the *Gallic War*, they have enough background to participate in discussions and appreciate the literature they are reading.

The last weeks of my Latin II curriculum are devoted to reading Caesar. Many teachers choose to introduce students to real Latin via other authors, often because they did not enjoy reading Caesar in their own high-school classes, because they find it boring, or because they believe its interest to teenagers is limited. However, thanks to a superb college professor, I learned to see Caesar as an exciting personality whose work is relevant to all times and all ages. His *Commentaries* have become a political pamphlet for me instead of a mere military manual, containing remarkable character delineations and loaded vocabulary, all presented in a beautifully precise style which students would do well to emulate in their own writing (cf. Buller 1994b).

The translation itself is done in groups, sometimes with jigsawing, sometimes with all groups translating the same passage. Students are monitored closely as they work; however, I have found it best to resist explaining each and every problem that arises. Instead, I encourage the groups to complete the assignment, leaving blanks where necessary, but coming to closure on the *substance* of the translation (cf. Hamilton, 170–72). We then reassemble and review the translation together. Very often a problem encountered by one group has been solved by another; I only assist, therefore, when everyone has the same problem. My biggest job at this juncture seems to be moving them from "classroomese" to equivalent, idiomatic English.

Once everyone is satisfied with the translation and understands the grammar, we approach the passage as a piece of literature, examining the use of vocabulary, sentence structure, nuances of meaning, political references, tone, and intent. For example, in Chapter 2 of Book 1, we examine the Roman attitude towards *regni*, the pejorative meaning of *cupiditate*, and the events of 63 B.C. which the words *coniurationem nobilitatis* call to mind. This leads to a discussion of Orgetorix—how Caesar depicts him and why.

As students gradually become more adept at such analysis, the focus turns to their own world, and they are encouraged to bring in examples of rhetorical devices, loaded vocabulary, or misleading information found in current newspapers and magazines. Advertisements, the editorial page, and political slogans are the best sources for this activity, and Caesar's art of pre-expletive narrative (explaining away possible failures before they occur) can be heard repeatedly every Friday in the fall during interviews with football coaches about the upcoming game.

This is, admittedly, a very sophisticated level of analysis for young students. Nonetheless, I believe an introduction to such analysis in Latin II lays the groundwork for the intensive exams that will occur in advanced Latin, and it benefits even those students who choose to leave Latin after two years.

A final exam on Caesar includes multiple-choice questions on his life and writings, several short "seen" passages to translate, followed by a brief discussion question on each of them, and a sight passage to be paraphrased. In addition, students are required to write an essay analyzing the Caesar they have read—a take-home assignment which they are given a week to complete. Since this is the first time most students have had to do such writing, I give some ideas on how to approach the task and share a couple of examples that demonstrate the type of information required. It is very important that the teacher give extensive feedback on everything from content organization and validity of the argument to proper sentence structure and pronoun agreement (cf. Harwood).

This, then, is the beginning of the process by which my Latin students are lifted above the nuts and bolts of the language to the sophisticated levels of learning and thinking I continue to develop and refine as they proceed through my advanced classes. Grammar ceases to be the main focus of my teaching, although reviewing of forms is constant, and unfamiliar grammatical constructions continue to be explained as they appear in the text. Vocabulary words for memorization and derivative study are now chosen from the passages being translated.

The techniques I use in teaching Caesar and the outcomes I expect are applicable to any good Latin author the teacher may select. My choice would be governed by a work's innate value as a piece of literature and as a model of good writing (cf. Dickison 1992: 394–95), the insight it furnishes about the Romans, and its relevance to our own time.

ADVANCED LATIN CLASSES

Many teachers who are fortunate enough to teach in schools with advanced Latin programs have to deal with the distinct problem of multiple-level classes. However, such a challenge can be met at this stage far more easily and with much greater success than at levels I and II where it can easily spell disaster.

There are several ways to handle this situation. Teachers may offer only Advanced Placement (AP—see Chapter 10 below) with all students studying for the same exam. Or they may decide to alternate the traditional Latin III–IV curriculum, with prose one year and poetry the next. A third solution keeps the levels separate in the same classroom, the teacher working alternately with the level III and level IV students. The main problem lies in the extra year of experience and knowledge the more advanced students possess over those who are just beginning Latin III. This difficulty is compounded by larger enrollments, which usually result in a greater disparity of talent among the students.

Cooperative learning is a real asset here. Although a great deal of time during the first year is spent on teaching group skills, since this is a new concept to them, the advanced class almost always becomes cohesive right from the beginning because I organize the students into groups which consist of an equal number of experienced and new students. Reviewing and drilling are relegated to computer assignments and homework. Students can be divided into expert and study groups, with a chapter in Cicero or a section of Vergil being divided among the groups. Or all groups can work on the same passage. Whichever method is chosen, each group breaks up its assignment into equal parts, with each member responsible for the vocabulary of his or her section. At first this exercise was done during class, but it quickly became a homework assignment at the instigation of the students, who then asked that penalty points be assessed against any group member who came unprepared. Students who are absent now often send in their lists through friends so their group will not fall behind! Group checks come in the form of short quizzes on translation, grammar, style, and content, instead of just class recitation. Whole class discussions are held upon the completion of each chapter or section, and a take-home essay, along with a final exam, concludes each speech or book.

As students who had been taught Latin through cooperative learning began to come up into the advanced levels, I found I had to do little or no monitoring, as by now they knew how to work together. Although I still hand-pick the groups, they now have more freedom to decide how to tackle an assignment. They have learned to give each other a share of the work and thus a share of the leadership; the more able students have learned patience when working with a slower student, and the teaching is almost always done by the Socratic method. Group testing and group grading are no longer necessary.

Block scheduling has been a real plus for these classes, for it allows the students more time to become involved in their work. Not only do they cover at least as much as in the year-long classes, but they learn it better and enjoy it more.

AUTHORS STUDIED IN ADVANCED CLASSES

Cicero is a delight to teach, especially during an election year, for students can read Cicero by day, go home and listen to our politicians at night, and return the next day with relevant comparisons and contrasts (cf. Lean). I have also had students analyze Jefferson's "Declaration of Independence," Martin Luther King's "I Have a Dream," and Mario Cuomo's nominating speech at the 1992 Democratic Convention. John F. Kennedy's inaugural speech is perfect for such an assignment and is even available in Latin (Hines and Howard, Book 3, 369–72). Nor is this an exhaustive list; teachers can use whatever applicable sources come their way. Since I believe we must help prepare students to be good citizens and therefore develop their interest in politics and government, I can think of no better way to accomplish this end than through a study of Cicero.

Vergil's elegant poetry, too, can be appreciated by students almost immediately. The relevance of his epic is both timely and timeless, and students do not always need a teacher to point it out to them. For instance, the success and psychology of the liar Sinon in Book 2 prompted my students to compare it to the motion picture *The Usual Suspects*, and a lengthy discussion ensued in which every trick of Sinon was examined and compared to those of the main character in the movie.

Students in my Latin V class set up their own curriculum with some guidance from me. One year I had a real Cicero afficionado, so we read large sections of the *De Imperio*; another student was an Empire expert in JCL competition, which led us to include the Third Satire of Juvenal and Seneca's *Apocolocyntosis of Claudius*, as well as *The Werewolf* and *The Widow of Ephesus* from Petronius. We ended the term with epigrams of Martial and selections from Ovid's *Ars Amatoria*.

Another class wanted to read selections from Sallust's *Bellum Catilinae* to get another perspective on the Catilinarian conspiracy. The essay question I set at the end of that study required them to assume the persona of a Roman senator who had to vote on the death penalty. The students had great fun creating their characters, including the influence of bonds engendered by *amicitia* and marriage. They had to draw upon a great deal of the material learned through several years of studying Roman history, reading Caesar and Cicero, and analyzing families and politics (cf. Hamilton, 173). Their final essays showed not only how well they had imbibed the spirit of the era but also how intellectually creative and clever teenagers can be. We then read several letters of Pliny, including the one to Tacitus on Vesuvius (which resulted in several days' study of Pompeii via filmstrips and recent videos, including the delightful production by *Forum Romanum*—see Chapter 11), and those between Pliny and Trajan about the treatment of the Christians. Students also spent some time on Catullus, read one play each in English by Plautus and Terence, and finished the term again with that perennial favorite, the *Ars Amatoria*. Such an exciting and challenging curriculum can easily be adopted as an alternative to the AP program. I prefer it because it introduces students to a wide variety of literature without sacrificing depth (cf. Davis, 17–18).

SETTING UP COOPERATIVE LEARNING

Cooperative learning requires an enormous amount of preparation by the teacher and a great deal of monitoring in the classroom during the initial phases. Once this plan is in effect, however, there is a marked improvement in student performance and more free time for the teacher to assist those in need.

There are many ways to set up such a system (cf. Williams 1991), but the groupings should not be made randomly or by the students. Three reasons for avoiding such procedures are obvious: 1) friends will want to work together and tend to socialize instead of working on the assignment; 2) people of similar ability will gravitate toward each other; and 3) the shy or unpopular student will be overlooked or intentionally excluded.

Cooperative learning works best if the groups number from three to five and are a cross-section of varying academic abilities, on-task and off-task students, extroverts and introverts. To accomplish this, teachers must learn about their students through a perusal of school records, discussions with other teachers, and close personal observation.

Teaching *how* to work in a group is at least as important as *what* is learned. This is why the teacher must organize carefully. It is essential that the group members realize they are jointly working toward a common goal. Certain ground-rules, such as staying on task and the prohibition of any negative comments, can be reinforced by a system of participation points which the teacher awards while monitoring the groups. Group grading is also a good incentive. For instance, group check results in a group grade even though the grade depends on the recitation of only one member. Since the object of group work is to have all members master the material, the brighter students will want to be more helpful to the less able in their group, and the latter will want to work harder so as not to let their group down. Tests on material covered in the groups can also be graded by averaging the individual scores of the members. Some teachers record both individual and group scores. I have found there are few problems with group grading if the students have input and are convinced they will be treated fairly.

Groups should be changed on a regular basis, e.g., after every unit test. In my experience, changing only one person at a time brings about the best results. The basic cohesiveness of the original group is not destroyed, and yet the new person makes the group different from what it was before. Group skills must be employed to make new members an integral part, and it is far easier for them to fit in when all the original members have a common purpose—to make the new person one of them as quickly as possible. By assigning letters, to indicate ability level, and numbers, to facilitate movement, I make a conscious effort to insure that the academic strength of each group remains about the same. This method also provides a means of keeping certain students from working together (I can provide charts outlining a variety of class configurations to interested teachers—please send a stamped, self-addressed envelope to Prof. Karen Singh, Florida State University School, Florida State Univ., Tallahassee, FL 32306-4420).

What does a teacher do with a member who consistently performs poorly despite the best efforts of the group? Such students can form a separate group with the teacher, who is freed up by cooperative learning for just such purposes. If and when these students begin to do better, they can be returned to the other groups.

What about the students who are capable but refuse to cooperate within the group? Those students should certainly be allowed to work alone; however, they must do *all* the work done by the groups, with no help from the other students. In my experience, the few Latin students who chose to work by themselves all decided to rejoin the others after only two or three days.

TECHNOLOGY IN THE LATIN CLASSROOM

Computer programs for Latin are easily available from the Teaching Materials and Resource Center (TMRC) of the American Classical League (ACL); several useful programs are also listed in the Applause catalogue (for addresses of most publishers and vendors mentioned here, see Chapter 24 below, and for details on these and other computer resources, see Chapter 23). Games such as *Cursus Honorum* and *Mare Nostrum* (see above) can be used during class and made available to students before and after school, as well as during lunch. Study and review materials from Quest on Caesar's Helvetian campaign, Cicero's First Catilinarian, and Vergil's *Aeneid* (Books 1, 2, 4, and 6) can also benefit the student. However, these programs not only contain some errors, but they frustrate students who are always obliged to start at the beginning of the program rather than at the point they stopped during a previous session. The *Tutrix* programs (from Centaur Systems) have an impressive format but at present are so limited in scope they are not worth the expense. Some of my students also like the *Lector* and *Translat* programs (University of Delaware) for working on sentence structure. The sets of Certamen questions available from the TMRC have vast amounts of information but are riddled with errors (including the spelling "Zues") and are available only in an Apple format of the antediluvian variety. A real advantage of most of these Latin programs, however, is the site license granted to the school when they are purchased. Finally, the development and upgrading of *Perseus* (see Chapter 23) has provided a most welcome classroom and library resource, and games such as *Caesar II* (Sierra-on-Line) and *SPQR* (GT Interactive Software) occupy many of my students during their lunch periods.

The Internet, of course, has opened the world to Latin students, and the ACL home page (www.umich.edu/ ~ acleague) provides several links to other useful sites. My students constantly bring in copies of relevant Latin materials they have found while browsing, and frequently make good use of pictures and maps which they download to illustrate their essays. This year they even designed their own Web page. Recently, a student and I were discussing an incident in late Republican history involving the man who had had molten gold poured down his throat and, much to my chagrin, I could not recall his name. My student went home, put out a call for help on the Internet, and returned the next day with the answer (Manius Aquillius) from a professor in Brazil. How did we manage before computers and the Internet!

BLOCK SCHEDULING

The trend toward block scheduling has been strong in the 1990s, and, if the amount of chatter about it on the Internet is any indication, it is affecting classrooms nationwide. Block scheduling can be managed in many ways, some more efficacious than others. Three plans keep the traditional year: 1) six periods can be split to cover two days and follow an alternate schedule, e.g., periods 1–3 on one day and 4–6 on the next, repeated throughout the year; 2) such an alternate schedule can be followed Monday through Thursday with all classes meeting for 50 minutes each on Friday; and 3) odd-numbered periods can meet on odd-numbered days and even-numbered periods on even-numbered days. The advantages of these three systems are obvious: they allow for longer periods of class time, yet have no adverse effect on foreign language competitions because the students remain in those classes throughout the academic year. The disadvantages are also clear: students and teachers alike become confused about the schedule, with younger students in particular having trouble with classes which meet only every other day; teachers, especially inexperienced ones, tend to double the homework load instead of using the extended class period more wisely; and, most importantly, students still earn only six credits a year.

Other forms of block scheduling alter the school year in some way. One popular system is the so-called "4 x 4" plan in which students attend four 90–minute classes a day and earn eight credits a year, thus having opportunities to take more electives or to re-take classes they have failed. Teachers have three classes each semester, thus producing six credits a year instead of the usual five, with a longer block for planning each semester. Since teachers teach more classes within the same time frame, classes can be smaller, which is indispensable for optimum results. If the plan results in teachers having more students rather than less because the system is used to save money, block scheduling is doomed to failure as soon as it begins.

The 4 x 4 plan is favored by administrators because it is the easiest to schedule. It has a debilitating effect on foreign language competitions, however, since regional and state fora are almost invariably held in the spring. Other systems of block scheduling attempt to solve such problems by including one or two 50–minute classes which last all year. This provides an opportunity to take additional electives, such as a foreign language class which focuses on humanities and social studies and can be taken by advanced students who want to participate in competition. One impediment to offering such a class is the temptation to use it solely to prepare students for regional and state fora. Competition study alone should not justify such a class, just as a study of Roman culture does not merit a language credit in Latin.

The key to successful block scheduling is the complete involvement of faculty, students, and parents. Plans should be introduced a year in advance, with small briefing sessions for parents, a feedback forum for students, and in-service programs for teachers. These should include not only workshops by experts from outside, but sessions in which teachers can exchange viewpoints, concerns, problems, and solutions. Only then will block scheduling result in effective and permanent change.

CONCLUSION

The 21st-century Latin class can be an exciting place to be, and instilling a love for the ancient world and a realization of its importance to modern life can be a thrilling experience. No two classes are exactly the same; consequently a technique or lesson plan that has worked with one may not necessarily be as successful with another. It is therefore imperative that even those teachers who continue to emphasize the traditional study of grammar in their classrooms remain flexible, creative, and, above all, enthusiastic.

9
Using the Reading Approach In Secondary Schools

DAVID J. PERRY
Rye High and Middle Schools, Rye, New York

INTRODUCTION

This chapter will examine in detail how secondary teachers may make the most effective use of the "reading approach" for teaching Latin. "Secondary" includes both middle and high schools, since the general principles of using the reading method apply to both levels (see also Chapters 7 and 14). Since a general description of this method and an account of its place in the development of Latin teaching have already been given in Chapter 2, I will turn directly to the question of how best to utilize the textbooks that are organized around this approach: the *Cambridge Latin Course* (Phinney and Bell), *Ecce Romani* (Books 1 and 2, Lawall 1994–95, and Book 3, Palma and Perry, reviewed by Polk and Staley, respectively), and the *Oxford Latin Course* (Balme and Morwood 1996–97). These three series, all well established and all recently revised and improved, are the most widely used reading-approach textbooks in American and Canadian schools (see review article by Gerda Seligson); details of workbooks and other ancillary materials for each series are included below in the bibliography. There are other reading method textbooks more intended for college use, such as *Reading Latin* (Jones and Sidwell) which might be used in high schools (particularly if students begin Latin in 10th or 11th grade). Most of the comments in this chapter would apply equally well to a teacher who is using one of these other reading-approach texts. Teachers should also be aware of two sources of support. For those who use *Cambridge*, there is the North American Cambridge Classics Project, which distributes a variety of materials developed by teachers and organizes workshops and trips for teachers (Resource Center, NACCP, P.O. Box 932, Amherst, MA 01004-0932; 800-250-6869; FAX to "Bill Gleason" 413-549-4418; E-mail wgleason@k12.oit.umass.edu; www.cambridgelatin.com); for those who use *Ecce*, there is the *Longman Latin Newsletter*, which appears twice a year and provides helpful articles and materials (subscriptions, at $5 per year, are available from Gilbert Lawall, 71 Sand Hill Rd., Amherst, MA 01002; E-mail glawall@classics.umass.edu).

THE CENTRAL ROLE OF READING

Given the fundamental tenet of the reading approach—that students learn best how to read an ancient language by doing extensive reading—it comes as no surprise that all three textbooks contain a great deal of reading, and that these readings form the central focus of each chapter. The readings are crucial, for not only do they provide practice in deciphering texts and introduce vocabulary, but they also serve as springboards for presentation of structure, culture, and all other aspects of the course. They also attempt to instill the attitude that reading a Latin text should, first and foremost, convey information about the events described and about Roman culture, instead of being a sort of abstract puzzle to be solved; that is, it is a communicative activity (see Hoyos 1993, 1997, for a good discussion of some issues regarding reading versus decoding Latin). The readings cannot be omitted or given only cursory attention as might be done—inadvisedly, in my opinion—when teaching from a grammar-translation textbook. The 1996–97 edition of the *Oxford Latin Course* has made a major break with tradition by putting the Latin readings, their accompanying vocabularies, and the cultural material in English in the first two-thirds of the book and placing the grammatical explanations and exercises at the back. The authors claim that "This has two advantages: first, the narratives present an uninterrupted story with social and historical comment in the essays; second, the presentation of the grammar is made clearer" (Balme and Morwood 1996–97, *Teacher's Book* 2: 5). Certainly such an arrangement makes it clear to students that reading Latin and learning about Roman culture are the primary aims of the course.

Teachers who come to a reading method from a more traditional approach often ask, "How can students do readings at the beginning of a chapter, when they have not yet learned the grammar and vocabulary in that chapter?" And indeed changing from a grammar-translation approach to a reading approach does require some modifications in a teacher's mindset. It should be clearly understood that the readings are *designed to be done first*, and so the authors provide the help that is necessary for students to deal with them successfully. Comprehension arises from a combination of carefully constructed aids, together with contextual clues and deductions that students can make based on their previous knowledge of Latin, obvious connections with English vocabulary, or their common sense. These points will be addressed further in the following paragraphs.

Since the readings are designed to introduce vocabulary, structure, and culture, the reading is normally the first activity that students undertake in a chapter. Very occasionally, one might present some other aspect of the chapter first, but this should be the rare exception rather than the rule. The practice of giving extensive reading before explanation is highly appropriate, since it emphasizes the communicative function, gives students more confidence in their ability to deal with a strange text, and provides more material to work with when the time comes to discuss structure.

Proponents of the reading approach regard reading as both the goal toward which we aim and the means of attaining that goal. The other linguistic skills—listening, speaking, and writing—are regarded as important to the extent that they support the development of reading skill. This does not mean that they should be ignored, however (see the New York State Education Department syllabus, *Latin for Communication*, for an excellent formulation of the relationship of reading and the other skills and of a communicative approach to Latin). The following discussion will provide some examples of how the other skills can be used to help students who are learning Latin through a reading approach.

INTRODUCING THE TEXT

How then does one present a chapter in a reading text? It is an excellent practice to begin with oral reading, since this provides a chance for students to look at the text prior to being asked to translate it. It also offers practice in pronunciation. At the very beginning of students' Latin experience, the teacher should read aloud and have students imitate, either chorally or individually. The teacher should model a clear, consistent pronunciation, including the distinction between long and short vowels, and should insist that students imitate accurately. Later on, students can read aloud on their own, although even during the second or third year the teacher's reading can provide a change of pace and can help students comprehend a difficult text if the teacher pays careful attention to phrasing. Barrett (1982) provides many excellent suggestions for teaching pronunciation and other oral activities. Another helpful technique is to use some of the pre-reading strategies that English and modern language teachers give their students: look at the accompanying picture and decide what may be happening in the story, look at the title, and so forth.

Sometimes it is helpful to have students look at a text as homework before translating it in class; the class activity is more meaningful and focused if it is not the first time they have seen the material. One can, of course, ask students to translate the text or a portion of it at home and then correct it in class. This may not be appropriate, however, either because of the difficulty of the text or the nature of the students. In such cases the teacher may ask students to read the text and look for certain information. For example, if adjective agreement was recently discussed, the homework could be to find all the adjectives in the story and tell what noun each modifies. This could also be related to the meaning: find all the adjectives that describe character A, and all the ones that describe character B. What does this suggest about the type of person each is, or the role each will play in the story? Here students must think about the meaning of the adjectives as well as about their endings. This type of activity forces students to look carefully at the reading, and they can do this even if their comprehension of the text as a whole is imperfect. This exercise can be varied in almost countless ways, depending on what vocabulary or structures the teacher wishes to stress, and on the content of the reading selection. One can make up *praelectio* ("pre-reading") sheets which contain a variety of questions designed to guide students into looking at certain aspects of the text that are important for comprehension or that the teacher will work with on the following day. *Responde Latine* questions and comprehension questions in English (about which more will be said below) can also be used as preparation for translation. These pre-reading activities can easily be individualized to accommodate students with a variety of ability levels. Another excellent activity is for the teacher to present a synopsis of the story orally in simple Latin, perhaps with the aid of pictures or props. This, along with oral reading, is particularly helpful for students who process information well through hearing but less well through reading off a page. A pre-reading activity may not be needed or desirable for every selection; the teacher must consider the difficulty of the reading, the nature of the students, the time available, the presence of certain structural features in the reading, and a variety of other factors.

THE MAIN EVENT

After completing whatever pre-reading activities are deemed to be appropriate, the teacher is ready to work with students to ensure that they comprehend the text at hand. What techniques are available? The old standby is translation into English. *Cambridge, Ecce,* and *Oxford* all seem to have been written on the assumption that most of the readings would be translated. The role of translation in the teaching of classical languages is a large issue which is best addressed elsewhere, so I will confine myself to a few comments relevant to using the reading method. First, I do not believe that one can use any of these books successfully without translating the majority of the readings. Those who want their students to learn by a direct method, without relying on translation, will probably be best served by a different book. The way the vocabulary and grammar are presented requires, in my opinion, a good amount of translation to ensure comprehension. (This is perhaps less true of *Cambridge* than of *Ecce* or *Oxford,* since *Cambridge* tends to repeat sentence structures in a more predictable way.)

Translation seems to be an efficient way of making sure that a student knows at least the surface meaning of a passage, which is its justification as a common pedagogical procedure in Latin classes. Note, however, that weak students may hear others translate a sentence and perhaps even memorize that translation without understanding what the words really mean. The major drawback is that students who are taught to translate everything may never learn to comprehend Latin without translating it.

What techniques beyond translation should the teacher employ? Probably the most widely used is comprehension questions in English; students show comprehension of many aspects of a reading by answering questions about it. This is a good alternative to translation, both for the sake of variety and to get away from the idea that every passage must be translated, although students accustomed to translation may well translate prior to answering the comprehension questions. *Ecce, Cambridge,* and *Oxford* all provide such comprehension questions. It is easy to vary the difficulty of such questions based on the needs of one's students. As mentioned above, one can also use English comprehension questions as an introductory activity. This is particularly helpful when dealing with unusually difficult passages. Students can comprehend the main points at home the night before by answering questions, and then acquire a more complete understanding by translating the next day in class with the help of the teacher.

Another technique employed in *Ecce* and *Oxford* is the use of questions in Latin, to be answered in Latin. Such questions have the advantage of letting students work in the language without recourse to English; its major drawback is that students may parrot answers from the text without understanding what they are saying. This can be overcome to some extent by careful construction of questions, but "parroting" remains a factor of which teachers should be aware. I find that such *Responde Latine* questions are most useful in two situations: as an introductory activity or as a review. As a preparatory activity, when one wants students to begin working with a passage, the fact that students may be answering without full comprehension is not a fatal problem, since the *Responde Latine* questions will be followed by other activities designed to ensure comprehension. This is likewise true of Latin questions used as a review activity, since students have already translated. Latin questions may be done either orally or in writing. When done orally as a review, an excellent alternative to having students look at their texts is to use visuals as the basis for the questions you ask. One can photocopy illustrations from the book and make them into overhead transparencies on a copier, or get students with an artistic bent to illustrate the stories. The publishers of *Ecce* produced a set of large visuals on cards, with the corresponding story text on the back for the teacher to refer to, to accompany the first revised edition; unfortunately, they have not produced these for the second edition, although the chapter illustrations can be made into overheads as mentioned above, especially if one has access to a color copier.

When students are reading, encourage them to attempt to figure out unfamiliar words through comparison with English derivatives, or with familiar

Latin words, or from context, instead of immediately turning to the back of the book. The authors intend that many such words be deduced, and some of these are listed in the teacher's guide. If a new form is being introduced, the first few occurrences will be glossed, but subsequent ones may not. For example, if the pluperfect tense is the new feature and the student translated *discesserat* as "left," point out one of the previously glossed examples of the pluperfect and help the student see the similarity and come up with the correct translation. But don't interrupt the flow of the story more than necessary; this sort of activity is preparation for the grammar lesson that will follow in a day or two, not the focus of the reading. Likewise, sometimes forms or structures that will not be formally taught until a later chapter are used. In such cases, give students what help they need and move on, but make a note for yourself that here is an example to use when the item is introduced officially. It is important for teachers to know which new items will be formally discussed in the current chapter, which are "seeds" for later chapters, and which will not be discussed formally. The teacher's guides clearly spell out this information. In fact, the guides for all three books provide many useful suggestions and should be consulted by every teacher new to one of the books.

FOLLOW-UP ACTIVITIES

After working through a story, the teacher may feel that some or all of the students need additional activities to make sure that they have internalized and will retain the material. This may be done immediately or later on, e.g., as part of a review for a test. In this section I will present some techniques that may be used for follow-up activities.

The use of *Responde Latine* questions as a means of review has already been discussed. Oral reading can also be used as a means of review; students must show their comprehension of the text by correct phrasing and appropriate expression, unlike oral reading done at the beginning of a lesson, which is mainly a means of introducing a text. The teacher will need to discuss where we pause in a sentence and why, since many students do not do this well in English. Expressive reading works best with passages that are in dialogue form, but may be applied to straight text as well. Dictation, when students write down the Latin as the teacher says it in short phrases, is another good review, since it forces students to look carefully at the Latin. For example, you can tell students to re-read the Latin passage while you walk around to check the homework, then give a short dictation.

The teacher may prepare a summary of the story in simple Latin and have students listen to it and answer questions in Latin about it. Students may also write their own summaries in Latin, or convert a narrative into a dialogue, or vice versa. They may illustrate stories—particularly good for stories that have lots of details. The teacher may tell a story in simple Latin, based on one students have just read, and have students draw a picture as they listen; then compare the various pictures. For some excellent suggestions about using visuals as the basis for oral skills in Latin, see Abernathy, et al. Finally, the use of TPR (Total Physical Response) activities, where students move around in response to commands in Latin, is excellent for practicing vocabulary and grammar (see Salerno, 85; Strasheim 1987; and Chapters 4 and 7 above).

The teacher may prepare a version of the story with certain words or endings replaced by blanks for students to fill in (known as the cloze procedure; see Thompson). When entire words are omitted, this focuses on vocabulary and the story line; when endings are omitted, it is more of a grammar activity. A word bank may be supplied, or not; one can make two versions, one with a word bank for weaker students and one without, for more capable ones.

Transparencies may be prepared for each story by photocopying the text from the book, enlarging it on a copier, and then making the transparency. These can be used to review specific vocabulary or to focus on grammatical items. An excellent review for a test on which students will be asked to translate a portion of a story is to have them close their books and translate from the overhead transparency. Water-soluble overhead pens can be used to mark up the transparencies; circle agreements, break up long sentences, and so forth, and then erase the markings and re-use the transparencies. Such transparencies can also be used when introducing a story.

THE QUESTION OF VOCABULARY

The reading approach, with its continuous storylines and readings organized around cultural topics, has an inherent advantage when it comes to teaching vocabulary, since students clearly learn vocabulary best when it is presented in a context of related words. With this advantage come some difficulties, however.

It is hard to tell an interesting story using a very limited vocabulary, so the number of words that students encounter in a reading text will be greater than in a grammar-translation text. Furthermore, some traditional textbooks were written specifically to prepare students to read Caesar and Cicero, and so the vocabulary in them emphasized military and historical/political topics. The reading method texts, however, focus on a variety of situations in everyday life, which means that a wider field of words will be needed. These two factors combined have led the authors of the various books to make use of a large variety of words, some of which may not be used much, if at all, in following chapters. For example, Chapter 33 of *Ecce* deals with a Roman dinner party and includes the word *boletus*, which does not appear in subsequent chapters.

In order to help students deal with this large vocabulary load, the authors of all three series present extensive running vocabularies in each story. These enable students to comprehend the story at hand, but the total number of words presented may be more than students could absorb and retain, and some of the words may not be needed for long-term retention. Both *Cambridge* and *Oxford* deal with this problem by selecting from the large number of words in the stories certain vocabulary for memorization. *Oxford* puts this vocabulary in shaded summary boxes, while *Cambridge* provides at the end of each Stage a checklist of words that students have encountered at least three times—an excellent approach, since students remember best words they have seen many times in the readings. *Ecce Romani* does not provide this kind of selection, leaving it up to the teacher to require certain words and skip others, based on experience with the book.

Regardless of the approach taken, it is the teacher's responsibility to focus on certain words and make sure that students know them by testing and by reusing the words as often as possible when constructing vocabulary worksheets and oral drills.

TEACHING STRUCTURE

All books that we describe as "reading-approach texts" have two essential tenets that affect the teaching of structure. The first is that *students should experience new structures in use, i.e., in the readings and perhaps through oral work, prior to analyzing and discussing them formally.* This is very different from the methodology of traditional grammar-translation texts, where one is expected to introduce a new structure formally, practice it in exercises, and finally encounter it in readings. When I switched to a reading approach several years ago, I found that this made a tremendous difference in how my students reacted to grammar presentations. The formal analysis of language is alien to many students, even in their native language (ask an English teacher!). I well remember that introducing new Latin structures out of the blue, devoid of context, was intimidating to my students and sometimes frustrating for me. In a reading method, when the time comes to discuss a structure formally, one can draw upon a wealth of examples with which students are already familiar. It is simply easier and less intimidating.

The best procedure is to put examples of the structure on the board or the overhead. These should normally come from the readings students have already encountered, so they will be able to understand them readily; if examples occurred in earlier chapters, bring them back and you will find that many students do remember them. It is usually preferable to elicit observations about the structure from students and guide them to formulate rules, although on occasion it may be simpler or more efficient for the teacher simply to provide the needed explanations. Discussion can then be followed by appropriate practice. One procedure that is frequently effective is to have students return to the readings they have done and find additional examples of the structure that is being taught.

The second tenet is that *grammar should be taught from the point of view of a reader, not a writer, of Latin.* The kinds of thinking that one needs to engage in when reading are in many cases different than when one is writing Latin. An excellent example of this occurs in Chapter 18 of the second edition of *Ecce*, which deals with adjective agreement. Students are shown how to use agreement clues to determine the meaning of a sentence which contains two nouns and one (or two) adjective(s). The question "How do you know which noun an adjective modifies?" is entirely relevant to a reader of Latin, and this is the type of teaching we should use as much as possible. There is certainly nothing wrong with exercises that ask students to put the correct ending on an adjective, or even with English-to-Latin sentences that contain adjectives; but the authors of the reading-approach textbooks help us by reminding us to keep the focus on what the reader needs to do in order to understand the text. Another excellent example of this reader-oriented thinking occurs in Chapter 54 of *Ecce*, where the various clues needed to correctly interpret the conjunction *ut* are brought together. We must keep in mind that learning the elements of a language (cases, tenses, types of clauses) is only part of our job; we must go beyond this and teach students how to read—what to do when they have a Latin sentence in front of them they don't understand.

Students clearly need to experience a certain amount of active, productive exercises in addition to the passive reading, if they are to have good control over the language. How much and what type this should be will vary with the age and ability of students and the time available. *Cambridge* provides relatively little in the way of practice exercises and many teachers find they need to provide additional activities. *Oxford* and *Ecce* provide more exercises, although even here the teacher may need to supplement. A wide variety of exercises, both written and oral, is recommended. The traditional English-to-Latin translation sentences are simply too difficult for some students; the use of guided composition, where students modify a model sentence, is a good alternative.

There are also differences over how much formal analysis and how much grammatical terminology should be used. Both *Cambridge* and *Oxford* tend toward the minimalist view and keep grammar discussion short and simple. This makes their presentations "student friendly," but many teachers feel the need to present more formal grammar. *Ecce*, on the other hand, offers very detailed grammar presentations, with full use of traditional terminology; some find this to be too much for students and soften the presentation a little. As always, the teacher's goals and knowledge of the students' needs and abilities will lead to the best teaching.

A final note about teaching structure: the reading method texts all provide a large amount of Latin for teachers and students to work with, undergirded by the two principles of extensive reading practice and seeing structures in use before formal discussion. As long as one adheres to these principles, one is not violating the essence of the method, and in fact is free to supplement with a wide variety of other techniques. Good teaching is eclectic, and teachers who use any of the reading method books should feel free to adopt the best techniques originally developed for other methods. The use of metaphrasing and various transformational activities from the linguistic school (see Chapter 3 above), a variety of oral activities from the direct method, the traditional analysis of grammar, all of these and more may have a place. In short, if it works, use it. The ease with which almost any activity can be incorporated into a course based on a reading method is an asset in this day and age, when teachers are often expected to accommodate students of all abilities and with different learning styles in one class.

CULTURE

One of the strengths of the reading method textbooks is the close link between readings and cultural topics. Culture is not an extraneous layer tacked on to fill up a Friday afternoon; it is part and parcel of the course. Students are fascinated by life in ancient Rome, and the teacher should help them come to see that the Latin readings, as well as cultural sections in English, are a source of information about Roman life. This reinforces the communicative aspect of learning Latin. Much worthwhile time can be spent on culture, and it should be taught through as many methods as possible: class discussion, reading, videos, models, projects, and others. The most recent editions of *Cambridge, Ecce,* and *Oxford* all provide greater amounts of cultural background and better photographs, in color, than earlier editions did. Teachers should, however, be careful not to let the Latin class become an ancient civilization class with a little Latin on the side; learning the language must always be the first priority.

TESTING

Testing in a reading-based class should reflect the teacher's goals and procedures. That is, if a great deal of time is spent with texts as the basis for vocabulary, grammar, and culture, then testing should be based on texts as well. It is convenient and simple to test vocabulary, grammar, and culture in isolation, but this does at some level violate the nature of what we want to achieve. If students never see a reading passage on a test, they will not consider learning to read Latin an important activity. How then can a teacher test in accordance with the reading method?

Many teachers ask students to translate on a test a portion of what they translated in class. This traditional procedure has the limitation that students may memorize the translation from their notebooks and not really understand the text. A better use of readings that students have seen in advance is as a basis for content, vocabulary, and grammar questions. Duplicate a passage and ask questions that require students to show comprehension of the Latin: "Cite two Latin words that show how character X reacted to seeing character Y, and give the English for each." For straight vocabulary, students may give the meaning of certain underlined words, and tell them it's okay to use the context of the story to help them. Or ask grammar questions: "Find four adjectives and tell what noun each one describes." "Circle three relative pronouns, underline the antecedent of each, and put brackets around the relative clause." Such activities should of course be practiced in class prior to the test; overhead transparencies as described above are excellent for this. Dictation from a familiar text is another good testing activity, especially in the early stages of Latin study.

One can also put reading passages that students have *not* seen before on tests. Such passages should be somewhat easier than those done in class with the teacher. They are time-consuming to compose but worthwhile, since they can be recycled in subsequent years. Again, vocabulary, grammar, reading comprehension, and culture can all be tested on the basis of such a passage. Reading comprehension, checked through questions in English or possibly in Latin, is particularly relevant as a test of whether students can truly understand the passage. The practice of using such unseen readings sends a strong message that learning to read a Latin text is the point of the course.

In my own testing, I tend to alternate the two. If the last test had a passage from the book, the next one will have a sight passage. On a long review test I might use both, together with other types of questions.

TIME FRAME AND TRANSITION TO AUTHENTIC LATIN

The preceding paragraphs have shown how the reading method offers many features that teachers can use to help their students become successful readers of Latin. There remains one important aspect to consider: the use of time. Teachers who have used other types of books, particularly the traditional grammar-translation methods, may find that they no longer "get through the material" as fast as they did. It is true that it takes time to do the extensive reading that is a feature of any reading approach; but this is time well spent, since students need to practice reading if they are to become proficient readers of Latin. The teacher should, however, be aware of time constraints and decide how to deal with them.

In high schools, many teachers find that Latin I and Latin II need to be devoted to the synthetic Latin found in the textbook, while Latin III is a transitional year in which students start to read short pieces of authentic Latin. *Oxford, Cambridge,* and *Ecce* all provide for this by including an anthology of short original Latin selections as the final book in the series. Latin IV (and V if available) is devoted to full-time reading of Roman authors, perhaps at the Advanced Placement level. In some schools, teachers find this program too ambitious and do not finish the synthetic Latin readings until well into the third year, while others dispense with the anthologies and move right into reading individual authors. The latter can be quite a jolt for students; some are successful with it, but this approach should be adopted only with caution. Most teachers find that there is a need for some kind of transition such as the anthologies provide. Teachers should do what works best with their students in a given situation, but should never expect to finish the teaching of basic grammar in less than two years.

All of the reading-approach books contain a great deal of material, and it may be necessary to omit certain items in order to finish the basic course in a reasonable time. The teacher must use experience and judgment in this area. Where more time is available (as when Level 1 is taught over a two-year period in grades 7 and 8), then the teacher can take full advantage of the materials provided in the books, with perhaps some supplements; in other situations some compression may be needed.

I will conclude with some discussion of the transition into authentic Latin. *Ecce, Cambridge*, and *Oxford* all provide some exposure to authentic Latin even during the first two years. If time permits, it is a good practice to provide additional examples of authentic Latin; short inscriptions and graffiti can be used (see Esler; McCarthy 1992), followed by short poems of Martial and Catullus, for example. This type of activity prepares students for reading beyond the carefully constructed synthetic Latin of the textbook stories. As mentioned above, the next step is usually a transitional anthology (Book 3 of *Ecce*, Unit 4 of *Cambridge*, or the *Oxford Latin Reader*). Another type of transitional book is a reader that contains adapted Latin which gradually becomes closer and closer to the original (see Balme 1973; Balme and Morwood 1976; and Perry and Lawall). A transitional reader can be followed by any of the good editions of standard authors now available (e.g., the Longman Latin Readers series), which provide enough help to enable students to cope with the text.

After I made the transition to using a reading method several years ago, I found that my students in Latin III had an easier time with Latin authors. They coped better with the readings, as might be expected given their extensive practice in reading Latin. For me, this was the validation of the method. This is not to say, of course, that none of my students struggle with Cicero or Vergil; but the focus on reading in the first two years does pay off in the upper levels. We are most fortunate to have for the 21st-century Latin classroom a rich array of textbooks that can provide our students an excellent start in reading the classic language.

10

Teaching AP Latin

MARGARET A. BRUCIA
Earl L. Vandermeulen High School
Port Jefferson, New York

The Advanced Placement (AP) Program is a cooperative, educational endeavor of secondary schools, colleges, and the College Board. Based on the premise that college-level material can be taught successfully to able and academically advanced secondary-school students, the AP Program provides an opportunity for such students to pursue and receive advanced placement and/or college credit for course work completed at the secondary-school level.

THE HISTORY OF THE AP EXAMINATIONS

The first AP Latin Examinations were administered in 1956. The two exams were called IV and V, with IV (fourth year) a Vergil exam and V (fifth year) an exam on prose, comedy, and lyric. There were no multiple-choice sections and no fixed syllabi. The make-up of the exam was varied and comparatively unpredictable to discourage "teaching to the exam." In 1969 the Latin IV and V exams were combined and the committee offered four discrete tests of one-and-a-half hours each (Vergil, lyric, prose, and comedy). Students were allowed to take one or two exams. Also in 1969, a syllabus-based multiple-choice section was introduced. The shorter passages used in the multiple-choice section allowed the Test Development Committee to obtain a wider sampling of students' knowledge. Using multiple-choice questions also made test equating (repeating some multiple-choice questions from one year to the next) possible, which facilitated the maintenance of consistent testing standards, an important concern as the volume of test-takers increased (for data on the number of participants each year since the 1960s, see LaFleur 1997).

Unfortunately, as Latin enrollments were then continuing to decline nationally (LaFleur 1997), the volume did not increase sufficiently and, consequently, the comedy option was dropped in 1972. The following year the Vergil, lyric, and prose exams lost some individual identity and were collectively renamed "Classics." The committee hoped to counter the threat of further declines in enrollment by appealing to the current trend towards "relevance" in education. Their concerns proved justified and low volume caused the discontinuation of the prose option in 1973. In 1978 the "Classics" title was changed to "Latin" (since this is what was tested) and "lyric" became "Catullus-Horace." In 1994, in response to a resurgence of interest in Ovid and a continued plea from secondary-school teachers for a reinstitution of prose, the Catullus-Horace Exam was renamed "Latin Literature" and expanded to include Catullus and a choice of second author—Cicero, Horace, or Ovid.

Today, AP Latin still comprises the same two courses, Vergil and Latin Literature (with some changes to the syllabi for the 1999 exams), the aims of which are, according to the most recent comparability study, in general conformity with college Latin studies at the intermediate to advanced level (fourth through sixth semesters). The Educational Testing Service and the College Board jointly oversee the work of the Test Development Committee, which includes publication of preparatory and informational material for teachers and students, setting the syllabus, and writing the exams. The committee consists of six members, three college professors and three secondary-school teachers, who meet twice each year (more often if needed) to make decisions regarding topics and assignments suggested by the Chair. A Chief Faculty Consultant, who has the responsibility of conducting the reading session and setting the standards for grading, also attends committee meetings.

The AP Latin syllabus is fluid; the committee may vary the course outlines and the material read as it sees fit. Each year the College Board publishes the *Advanced Placement Course Description: Latin* (often referred to as the "Acorn Book," due to the prominence of the College Board's logo on the cover). This booklet gives an overview of each course and offers sample exam questions; it also calls the teacher's attention to any changes in the syllabi or the structure of the examination. The Acorn Book and other College Board publications mentioned in this chapter are available from Advanced Placement Program, Educational Testing Service, Dept. E-22, P.O. Box 6670, Princeton NJ 08541-6670.

The designated lines or poems to be read in Latin on each syllabus as of the 1998-99 academic year are:

Vergil:

Aeneid 1.1-519; 2.1-56, 199-297, 469-566, 735-805; 4.1-448, 642-705; 6.1-211, 450-476, 847-901; 10.420-509; 12.791-842, 887-952.

Latin Literature:

Catullus (as numbered in Mynor's *Oxford Classical Text*) 1, 2, 2b, 3, 4, 5, 7, 8, 9, 10, 11, 12, 13, 22, 27, 31, 34, 35, 36, 43, 44, 46, 49, 50, 51, 53, 62, 70, 72, 73, 75, 76, 77, 83, 84, 85, 86, 87, 92, 95, 95b, 96, 101, 107, 109.

Cicero, *Pro Caelio* sections 1-9 (. . . *cum artibus honestissimis erudiretur.*), 21

(*Neque ego id dico . . .*)– 22 (*. . . ratio cum ratione pugnabit.*), 30 (*Sunt autem duo crimina . . .*)–43 (*. . . qui vellet excusatione defenderet.*), 47 (*Nihilne igitur illa vicinitas . . .*)–50 (*. . . ad se defendendum facultatem dabit.*), 72 (*M. vero Caelius . . .*)–77 (*. . . iam dies mitigarit.*).

Horace, *Odes* 1.1, 5, 9, 11, 13, 22, 23, 24, 25, 37, 38; 2.3, 7, 10, 14; 3.1, 9, 13, 30; 4.7. *Sermones* 1.9.

Ovid, *Metamorphoses* 1.452–567 (Daphne and Apollo); 4.55–166 (Pyramus and Thisbe); 8.183–235 (Daedalus and Icarus), 616–724 (Baucis and Philemon); 10.238–297 (Pygmalion). *Amores* 1.1, 3, 9, 11, 12; 3.15.

As of 1999 the AP Examinations in Vergil and Latin Literature will be three hours each. The format is as follows:

Multiple-choice Section:

50 questions in 60 minutes

Four passages: one syllabus-based (Vergil or Catullus); of the remaining three sight passages, at least one will be prose and at least one will be poetry.

Free-response Section:

VERGIL:

15-minute reading period; 1 hour and 45 minutes testing time

Question V1 (A and B): two translations (20 minutes)
Question V2: long essay (45 minutes)
Question V3: short essay (20 minutes)
Question V4: short essay on the parts of the *Aeneid* read in English and, where appropriate, on the selections read in Latin (20 minutes)

LATIN LITERATURE:

15-minute reading period; 1 hour and 45 minutes testing time

Catullus translation (10 minutes)
Catullus long essay (30 minutes)
Catullus short essay (20 minutes)

Cicero/ Horace/ Ovid spot question (10 minutes)
Cicero/ Horace/ Ovid translation (15 minutes)
Cicero/ Horace/ Ovid short essay (20 minutes)

For further details on format and discussion of actual test questions, teachers should see the annual reports of the Chief Faculty Consultant published in the *Classical Outlook* (*CO*—most recently Howard 1996, 1997).

SAT II AND AP

The SAT II Test in Latin (formerly known as the Achievement Test), graded on a scale of 200 to 800, evaluates a student's competency level in Latin (for further detail, see Crooker and Rabiteau, College Board 1997b). The test reflects general trends in high-school curricula and is independent of particular textbooks or methods of instruction. Most students taking the SAT II Test have studied two to four years of Latin in high school (the equivalent of two to four semesters in college). The best preparation for the test is the gradual development of competence in sight reading Latin over a period of years. Scores are not adjusted to reflect levels of study and colleges are advised to consider the amount of time a student has spent in the study of Latin when evaluating test scores. The Latin SAT II Test score is often used by colleges as an indicator for both course placement and credit.

The SAT II Test shares some noteworthy similarities with the AP Exam (cf. Crooker). Comprised exclusively of multiple-choice questions, the SAT II is designed to measure both the student's knowledge of Latin grammar and syntax and the student's ability to comprehend Latin prose (predominately) and poetry at sight. The AP Exam also measures, through multiple-choice questions, the student's general ability to comprehend Latin poetry (predominately) and prose at sight while, through free-response questions, it tests a student's ability to translate, interpret, and analyze syllabus-based passages written by specific, preselected authors.

A student who prepares for the SAT II Test can surely reap benefits from that preparation on the multiple-choice section of the AP Exam, and vice versa. Approximately half of the 70–75 multiple-choice questions on the SAT II Test are passage-based, compared to all 50 on the AP Exam. Here follows a comparison of sight passages and sight passage-based questions on each test.

On both tests, passages are introduced in English, on the SAT II with a brief title and on the AP with a short, explanatory "lead-in." The passages on the SAT II are shorter (about 8 lines, compared to 11–15 lines). Both tests use glosses. SAT II passages are adapted and employ macrons, whereas AP passages are taken unadapted from the Oxford Classical Texts or similarly authoritative texts. The poetry passages on the SAT II are limited to dactylic hexameter. Poetry passages on the AP Exam are either in dactylic hexameter or in elegiac couplets, but only the hexameter line is tested in metrics questions.

Passage-based questions on both tests are similar, except that the SAT II does not test figures of speech. In addition to the 30–37 passage-based questions, the SAT II contains 39 discrete items (8 morphological forms, 4 derivation, 14 sentence translation, 7 sentence completion, 5 syntax substitution). Common item types include: grammar, syntax, lexicography; translation, reading comprehension, interpretation; inference, reference; and metrics.

Because of its more general nature, some colleges prefer to use the results of the SAT II Test in awarding placement and/or credit to incoming students. Although both the SAT II Test and the AP Exam test the student's ability to read Latin, the AP also tests higher level skills of interpretation and analysis and assesses the student's familiarity with the style of a specific author or authors.

AP LATIN AS AN ADVANCED COURSE OPTION

The AP Program is nationally and internationally recognized for its high standards and accuracy in grade reporting. Successful participation in this rigorous program enhances the credentials of the student, the teacher, and the school. Although colleges and universities are free to draft their own policies regarding the acceptance of AP scores, most award placement and/or credit for scores above 3, and, in schools where there is a language requirement, a high AP score may exempt a student from further study of a foreign language. Since AP Latin courses are designed to mirror what is taught at the intermediate level in college, students gain a clearer idea of the amount and quality of work that will be expected of them. AP scores, ranging from a low of 1 to a high of 5, are a reliable indicator to both the student and the college of the student's ability to perform successfully at an intermediate or higher level of Latin in college.

The AP Latin Program, with its two courses, affords teachers and students the opportunity to select from a variety of authors: Vergil (AP Vergil), and Catullus combined with Horace, Ovid, or Cicero (AP Latin Literature). Once the course and the author(s) have been chosen, the syllabus is clearly delineated in the "Acorn Book." The reputation of the program, the variety of authors from which to choose, the clarity of the published syllabus and course outline, and the availability of resource materials for teachers make choosing to teach an AP Latin course an attractive option to many.

Drawbacks include the fact that the group of authors from which to choose consists (except for Cicero) exclusively of poets, that the amount of Latin to be read in any given syllabus may be daunting, and that, if AP Latin is the only course option for an advanced high-school Latin student, the struggling student may find the AP syllabus too demanding and choose instead to terminate his or her study of Latin. Sometimes the array of AP authors or the amount or selection of Latin to be read does not fit the particular style of a teacher or the needs of the students. Many secondary-school teachers, therefore, design entirely different, equally valid, and highly successful advanced level courses of their own. I would like, however, to address the case of the weaker Latin student in a school where AP Latin is the only option beyond the intermediate level of Latin instruction.

In my small, public high school, class size is crucial. Most of the students who pursue a sequence in Latin complete level three during their 10th-grade year. There is, of course, natural attrition at this point. In an effort to concentrate numbers and regroup, I combine all advanced students, 11th- and 12th-graders, into one class and alternate teaching the two AP syllabi. Some students read Vergil first, and then Latin Literature, and some the reverse. I have found that it makes no difference which comes first. There are always a few students who would like to continue with Latin but are leery about making the AP commitment. I encourage them to enroll in the class, but their transcript reads either Latin IV or Latin V, depending on their level, instead of AP. Although they will not take the AP Exam, they participate in all classroom discussions and complete all assignments. The only concession I make is that they may take exams with a dictionary and textbook notes and glosses. The system works and has allowed many students, who, under other circumstances, would have terminated their study of Latin, to continue to reap the benefits of advanced work.

TEACHING AP LATIN

Choosing a Course

After becoming familiar with each course outline in the Acorn Book, the prospective AP teacher must often choose between Vergil and Latin Literature. Each has features to recommend it. Most teachers, if they will teach only one course, choose Vergil. Reading a continuous narrative that is familiar, action-packed, and consistent in style and difficulty level is surely attractive. However, having students master 1,846 lines of Latin can create the feeling of a forced march through the *Aeneid*.

The Latin Literature syllabus, on the other hand, is somewhat shorter and easier to complete and is attracting growing numbers of participants (LaFleur 1997: Table 2). There are, however, more meters and different styles and difficulty levels with which to contend. Isolated poems are often harder to recall than lines in a larger context, and poems with similar themes are often easy to confuse. Catullus, the required author, is wonderfully appropriate for high-school students, who generally respond enthusiastically to his poetry. Similarly, the selections from Ovid's *Metamorphoses* are, for the most part, familiar, appealing, and easy to read (the *Amores* somewhat less so). Though I have always enjoyed teaching Horace, the difficulty of his style and the complexity of his imagery make translating his poetry somewhat challenging for high-school students (see Brucia 1995a). For teachers and students who are more comfortable with prose, there is, of course, the Cicero option (see Buller 1994a). Reading Catullus' poems as a backdrop to the *Pro Caelio* (or vice versa) provides a rich opportunity for students to view historical characters from different literary perspectives.

Resource Material

Once the choice of syllabus has been made, there are many resources to help the teacher. The College Board sponsors AP teacher workshops, ranging from one to several days, conducted at various locations throughout the country (College Board regional offices provide information and details), and AP sessions are regularly scheduled as part of the annual American Classical League (ACL) Institute each June.

In addition to the *Advanced Placement Course Description* booklet, there are several other useful College Board publications (available from the address given above). The *Teacher's Guide to Advanced Placement Courses in Latin* (Brucia 1995b) offers, among other things, "how to" information on teaching, sample syllabi from high-school and college courses, articles on topics of current interest on the teaching of Latin in general and AP Latin in particular, and annotated bibliographies for all AP authors that include textbooks, commentaries, translations, books and articles on literary criticism, and recordings.

A set of free-response questions used in recent years, in conjunction with the College Board publication *1994 AP Latin: Free-Response Scoring Guide with Multiple-Choice Section*, can help both teacher and students understand the nature of the free-response section of the test and the grading process. Since this guide includes the multiple-choice section, it is valuable as a tool to give students practice in answering questions of this nature as well.

As noted earlier, the *Classical Outlook*, ACL's quarterly journal, publishes many articles of specific interest to AP Latin teachers, most notably the yearly report of the Chief Faculty Consultant that assesses the performance of AP Latin students and explains the standards used to grade each question on the free-response section of a given exam. *CO* has also published "An Analysis of Candidate Performance on the Multiple-Choice Section of the Published 1987 AP Latin Examination" (Brucia and Rabiteau; cf. Crooker and Rabiteau), an article which offers hypotheses for why students chose incorrect options on certain questions and presents suggestions for teachers to improve their students' performance on this part of the exam.

The National Latin Exam (NLE), offered every year, is another useful tool for preparing students for the multiple-choice section of the AP Exam. The Level V Exam gives students the opportunity to practice answering sight passage-based questions. Like the passages on the AP Exam, those on the NLE are not adapted (for further details on the NLE, see Chapter 11 below).

Some Practical Suggestions for the Classroom

Because an AP Latin course is a literature course with incidental grammar instruction and review (rather than a grammar course with an incidental reading of literature), students need to adjust to new expectations. They must translate and analyze large amounts of Latin every day in order to complete the syllabus on time. I try to assign a manageable number of lines to prepare each day, with the intention of translating, analyzing, and discussing them in class, and then I attempt as much sight translation with students as the remaining class time permits. Perhaps the most difficult thing for me is to refrain from offering too many suggestions while students are translating aloud. Pulling translations out of students may help the class advance through the syllabus, but it does not train them to become better and more confident translators. I have found it best to help students in the beginning of the year, then gradually to step back and allow them to develop the ability to "unscramble" the words on their own.

Besides daily preparation, I also design long-range assignments for students. For example, I might select a passage or a poem of approximately 20 lines that the class will reach in a week or two and ask students to write both a literal and a literary translation, comment on unusual or noteworthy examples of grammar and syntax, point out significant figures of speech and stylistic devices and their effects, scan a few lines, and be prepared to read the passage aloud in Latin.

The question of translation deserves attention. In their written translations on the AP Latin Exam, students are expected to translate as literally as possible, thereby demonstrating that they have understood the Latin grammar. They are discouraged from writing "free" translations. For this reason, I often ask my students to translate twice. I grade their literal translation on closeness to Latin grammar and syntax; awkward English is acceptable if it can be justified by the Latin. I grade their "literary" translation primarily on its ability to convey the sense and spirit of the original.

Students keep a notebook, the form of which has evolved considerably with the passage of time. When I first taught AP Latin, I noticed that students slavishly copied down every translated word of the syllabus to have for study and review. This was a painfully time-consuming process, which allowed less time for classroom work and discussion. Try as I would, I could not convince them to rely on their ability to reread accurately the Latin they translated in class. Recently, students proposed a better method. We now have a different designated scribe for each class period. Only the scribe writes down the translation, after we have all agreed what it should be. Sometime during the school day a volunteer typist enters the translation into our Latin file on the computer in the foreign language office. As each page fills, I distribute photocopies to the class. This system allows students to spend more time looking at the Latin text in class. The depth and quality of classroom discussion has been greatly enhanced by freeing students from the drudgery of copy work.

Testing Ideas

Each AP Latin Exam free-response section follows a specific and predictable format. It is designed to measure the attainment of certain skills, among which are the abilities to translate literally, to put excerpted passages in their proper context, to interpret and analyze a passage's sense and meaning, to assess the characteristics of an author's style, to comment on the effects of stylistic devices and figures of speech, to scan and discuss meter, to recognize literary allusions, to place the literature at hand in its historical and literary setting, and to write both long and short essays in which observations based on a passage are made and appropriately supported.

These are all noble ends which are in harmony with my goals for my students. And so, I design my tests to mimic question types on the AP Exam, not to "teach to the test," but to train students to develop a facility with tasks that are appropriate for this and other college-level courses, and—most importantly—to sharpen my students' attention to, and appreciation of, every aspect of the Latin texts we are studying. A typical class-period test (47 minutes) will encompass approximately 100 lines and contain the following AP-type questions: both a long and a short passage-based essay which may include questions pertaining to context and literary analysis, a 6–10 line literal translation, and a few lines to scan. In addition, I may include brief identifications of proper names and a brief passage-based set of grammar questions. Tests are important and infrequent; I do not give quizzes. I average test scores and grades received on long-range assignments to determine quarterly grades.

A LOOK TO THE FUTURE

AP Latin is healthy. Enrollment continues to increase on a slow but steady basis. If this trend is to prevail, however, two areas are particularly worthy of attention: teacher training and cooperation between schools and colleges. Although secondary-school teachers have access to abundant workshops and printed material designed to train and inform them about the AP Latin Program, all too many college and university professors remain uninformed about the nature of an AP Latin course. New programs are needed that will encourage secondary and higher level instructors to forge partnerships that can be mutually beneficial (see Chapter 12 below on improving school-college articulation). I would like to see the creation of teams of high-school and college teachers who agree to teach the same syllabus. By designing a course outline together and visiting and teaching each other's classes, secondary-school teachers and college professors could help one another become better teachers and, at the same time, increase awareness of the AP Program at the college level. After all, the AP Program was created by the College Board to offer qualified secondary-school students the opportunity to complete college-level work in high school. An active and ongoing partnership between both educational institutions is essential in order to accomplish this goal.

11

Beyond the Text: Enrichment Activities for High-School Latin

JANE H. HALL
Chair, National Latin Exam

This chapter focuses on enrichment and extra-curricular activities for the high-school student, many of which are appropriate for middle-school students (see Chapter 7) and some for elementary-school and college students as well. These activities are in line with the *Standards for Classical Language Learning* (Chapter 5) and involve teachers and students in the national effort to establish broad goals and a framework for Classics programs. Included are specifics involving the National Junior Classical League (NJCL), the National Senior Classical League (NSCL), the National Latin Exam (NLE), the National Greek Exam (NGE), the National Mythology Exam (NME), the Bernice L. Fox Writing Contest, the Classical Association of New England (CANE) Writing Contest, the National Committee for Latin and Greek (NCLG), Advanced Placement (AP) Examinations, the SAT II Latin Test, scholarships, opportunities to travel abroad, summer academic programs, and other creative activities at the high-school level. Contact persons for these activities, many of which are sponsored by the American Classical League (ACL) are found at the end of the chapter.

THE NATIONAL JUNIOR CLASSICAL LEAGUE

The NJCL is an organization of junior and senior high-school students who are interested in the study of Latin and the Classics. Founded in 1936, and sponsored by ACL, it is the largest classical organization in the world. Its purpose is to encourage among young people an interest in and an appreciation of the civilization, language, literature, and art of ancient Greece and Rome, and to give them some understanding of the debt of our own culture to that of classical antiquity. The NJCL is composed of local and state chapters and has more than 55,000 members. Each chapter maintains its own program, participates in state and national conventions, and affords its members eligibility for NJCL scholarships. Seven student officers and the National Committee, composed of 12 adults, govern the national organization. Four annual issues of *Torch: U.S.* and five of *JCL Highlights* keep members apprised of individual and chapter news and activities across the nation.

A chapter may be formed by any local group of five or more students who are taking, or have taken, a course in Latin, Greek, or classical humanities. Each chapter receives a charter printed in purple and gold on parchment paper and a NJCL Chapter Handbook. In order for a chapter to be in good standing, it must affiliate each year with both the state/province and the NJCL. Properly qualified persons who wish to become members of the NJCL, but who have no local chapter, may join by affiliating with the state organization and applying to the NJCL at the ACL address; students who take Latin via distance education may also become members by applying to the NJCL.

Since 1941, when Texas held the first JCL state convention at the University of Texas, the NJCL has sponsored state conventions where students participate in a variety of academic and athletic contests, elect state officers following parliamentary procedure, and engage in many other stimulating activities. Attendance at these meetings, as the NJCL creed states, "fosters brotherhood, promotes enthusiasm, encourages competition, inspires dedication and enriches our total growth."

The NJCL also sponsors a five-day national convention, the first of which was held in 1954, in San Antonio, Texas. There has been a national convention every year since then, with attendance hovering around 1,300 for the last 20 years. College campuses are the sites for this culminating event, held each year in late July or early August; the use of college dormitories to house the delegates helps keep convention costs within a high-school student's budget.

The NJCL convention is one of the most important events for Latin students. They prepare all year to compete in a myriad of activities such as General Assembly, where delegations gather by state to engage in national, regional, and local chapter performances and presentations. They sing the NJCL song, recite the NJCL creed, listen to speakers, and receive awards. This is only one small part of the convention's activities, others of which include: seminars, academic and athletic contests, creative and graphic arts contests, oratory, costume contests, and publicity and publication contests. There is something for everyone at the national convention.

The projects displayed each year, from a model of a Roman bath or a musical instrument to intricate mosaics and jewelry copied from ancient artifacts, show evidence of painstaking research and careful workmanship. Each year, there are over 1,000 entries on exhibit. There are both individual and team awards. One of the most popular team competitions is Certamen, a rapid-fire question game much like "College Bowl" (see above, Chapter 7). A state may enter one novice, one lower-level, and one upper-level team, or a student may sign up for "Open Certamen" at the experienced or the inexperienced level. The benefits of being a part of this national convention are innumerable. Students return home with old friendships renewed and new relationships established. They exhibit an increased desire to learn, a new awareness of the civilization of Greece and Rome, and a desire to "hand on the torch of classical civilization in the modern world," a goal of the JCL Creed. A registration booklet, which includes all information on the upcoming national JCL Convention, is available from the ACL office in Oxford, Ohio.

The NJCL also sponsors the Latin Honor Society, which recognizes students who maintain a 90% or better average in any year of Latin, are members in good standing of the NJCL, and exemplify good citizenship. Parchment certificates with gold NJCL seals and membership cards are sent to the teacher registering these students to denote their success in the study of Latin.

Scholarships

Seven scholarships are awarded to members each year by the NJCL:

- The Belle Gould Scholarship, named in honor of Miss Belle Gould, the first editor of *TORCH: U.S.* and a Chair of the Committee on the NJCL; in the amount of $500.
- The Jesse Chambers Scholarship, named in honor of Miss Jesse Chambers, former Federations Chair, Committee on the NJCL; $500.
- The Rhea Miller Scholarship, named in honor of Mrs. Rhea Miller, the National Convention Coordinator for NJCL for many years; $500.
- The Red and Rhea Miller Scholarship, established in 1986 with a generous check from the Millers because of their devotion to NJCL; $500.
- The Margaret and Eugene Halligan Scholarship, funded by an endowment in memory of Mrs. Halligan's many years of service to the NJCL in Illinois; $1,000.
- The Maureen O'Donnell Scholarship, in memory of Mrs. Maureen O'Donnell, beloved Latin teacher and a Virginia JCL Co-Chair; $1,000.
- The NJCL Latin Honor Society Scholarship recognizes an outstanding member of the NJCL Latin Honor Society who has been a member of the JCL for three years, a member of the NJCL Latin Honor Society for at least two years, plans to be a Latin, Greek, or Classics major, and plans to teach Latin or Greek; $1,500.

All necessary forms for these scholarships are available from the ACL.

Over 2,000 high-school students participate in the "Pen Pal Program." Students feel that this is a great way to communicate with other JCL members across the nation. An application is available in *JCL Highlights* and an E-mail address is acceptable; the cost is $1, to be sent with the application.

College majors and future Latin and Greek teachers come primarily from high-school programs and so the NJCL has become an important part of a classical education. A local JCL chapter can make the difference between a student continuing the study of the Classics or dropping out of the program; as a national organization, the NJCL is a powerful force for the continuation and promotion of the Classics throughout the United States and Canada.

THE NATIONAL SENIOR CLASSICAL LEAGUE

The NSCL is an organization composed of high-school graduates and college students who wish to continue their affiliation with the Classics and the NJCL. High-school students need to be made aware that this organization exists and is active on many college and university campuses.

The purposes of the NSCL are to enhance and promote the appreciation of the Classics and classical scholarship in post-secondary education; to advise, encourage, and help the NJCL in its endeavors; and to provide its membership with a means of continuing and pursuing their interests in the overall purposes of the NJCL and the Classics.

The NSCL annual convention runs concurrently with the NJCL national convention, where the NSCL is responsible for publishing the *Convention Ear* (the daily newsletter), sponsoring informal athletic games, and running the "Olympika" under the direction of the National Committee Contest Chairs. NJCL delegates who join NSCL during their senior year or at the convention following their senior year are welcome at all SCL functions and are eligible to vote and hold office.

Scholarships

The NSCL awards two annual scholarships: the NSCL Scholarship, to be applied toward college tuition ($200 minimum—in 1997 $1,300 was awarded); and the Mark Shapler Book Award, to be used to purchase textbooks and supplies ($50 minimum—in 1997 $300 was awarded).

THE NATIONAL LATIN EXAM

The NLE, sponsored by a committee of the ACL, is open to all students enrolled in Latin. The philosophy behind the NLE is predicated on providing all Latin students the opportunity to experience a sense of personal accomplishment and success in their study of the Latin language and Roman culture. By taking the NLE, students are not competing with their fellow students on a comparative basis, but are evaluated solely on their own performance on the exam. The basic purposes of the NLE are to promote the study of Latin and to encourage the individual student.

Participation in the exam has increased each year since its inception in 1978, when approximately 6,000 students enrolled (see LaFleur 1997: Table 2). In 1997, more than 107,000 students from all 50 states and 11 foreign countries, including Australia, Belgium, Canada, the Czech Republic, England, Germany, Italy, Japan, the Netherlands, New Zealand, and Zimbabwe, applied to take the 20th NLE. The birth and growth of the NLE are all the results of a cooperative enterprise linking elementary, middle-school, high-school, and college teachers across the nation; the extraordinary success of the NLE has been both a cause and an effect of the resurgence of Latin over the past generation.

The exam is administered in individual schools the second week in March of each year. The majority of students who take the NLE are junior-high and high-school students, but elementary-school and college students also participate. Applications are available from ACL or from the NLE Committee; the deadline for submitting applications is 10 January each year.

There are six exams: Introduction to Latin, which is designed for Latin I students who cover approximately one-half the Latin I syllabus; Latin I; Latin II; Latin III–IV Prose; Latin III–IV Poetry; and Latin V. These exams are not based on any specific textbook. Exams Introduction–IV consist of 40 multiple-choice items on grammar, comprehension, mythology, life, history, and derivatives, as well as questions based on a short passage in Latin. The Latin V Exam consists of Latin passages with 40 multiple-choice questions on comprehension, grammar, historical background, classical literature, and literary devices. The syllabus and four previous exams are available for purchase from the ACL's Teaching Materials and Resource Center (TMRC).

Approximately 35–38% of the participating students win awards. A special hand-lettered certificate is sent to perfect paper winners. Gold medals and *summa cum laude* certificates are awarded to top scorers, silver medals and *maxima cum laude* certificates to second-place winners, *magna cum laude* certificates to third-place winners, and *cum laude* certificates to fourth-place winners. Ribbons and certificates of achievement are awarded to Introduction to Latin exam top scorers.

The Maureen O'Donnell Memorial Award, an *Oxford Classical Dictionary*, is awarded to students who win four gold medals. This award, named in honor of an outstanding high-school Latin teacher and founding member of the NLE, has been presented to over 500 students.

In 1984, the first four NLE $1,000 scholarship winners were announced at the ACL Institute. The NLE joined with the NGE in 1992 to offer a combined $2,000 Latin/Greek scholarship. In 1997, 16 students were awarded $1,000, and 33 students were eligible to renew their scholarships, for a total of $49,000 in scholarships. An anonymous donor has given $1,000 for an additional annual scholarship. Scholarship applications are sent by the NLE to gold medal winners in Latin III–IV Prose, III–IV Poetry, or Latin V, who are high-school seniors. Those who apply must agree to take one year of Latin or classical Greek in college. These scholarships are not based on financial need, but solely on the student's exam performance and completed application.

The NLE Committee offers several colloquia workshops each year. Under this program, committee members present a free workshop for a minimum of 20 participants. Possible topics range from the history of the exam and test-taking strategies to AP and oral Latin. The committee will design a half-day or day-long program tailored to the needs of the teachers involved. There is no charge—just provide lunch during the break! The committee has traveled from Florida to Alaska, from Maine to California, to discuss current trends in the teaching of Latin and classical studies, and has sponsored more than 30 workshops.

The NLE Committee also sponsors *Forum Romanum*, a series of 12 10-minute television programs conducted entirely in Latin, which present news from the ancient world "as it happens." Each show takes place on a particular date in Roman history. The purpose of *Forum Romanum* is to allow the audience to hear Latin spoken, within a realistic context. As an instructional tool, a suggested strategy is to 1) view the show for the first time straight through without preparation, 2) hand out copies of the scripts for study and review, 3) view the show again. VHS tapes and scripts of *Forum Romanum* are available from the ACL's TMRC.

The benefits of the NLE are realized in many quarters. Students who take the exam are encouraged both by their personal success and, perhaps as importantly, by the knowledge that they are participating in an enterprise that involves a large number of their peers. The NLE links Latin students across the continent and reaches out to an increasing number of them each year, making them aware that there are others who study Latin, and allowing them to compare their achievements on the exam to a national norm.

Another benefit of the exam is its effect on curriculum development. The NLE Committee makes its syllabus available in classical newsletters and journals, thus enabling both colleges and high schools to support current or proposed curricula by linking them with national goals and standards. The National Association of Secondary School Principals has placed the NLE on its Advisory List of National Contests and Activities each year since 1984.

THE NATIONAL GREEK EXAM

The NGE was initiated in 1978 by the late Ed Phinney, with 70 students taking six different exams. The following examinations are now offered yearly: Attic Greek, Levels I–III; *Iliad*, Level I; and *Odyssey*, Level I. Any student enrolled in classical Greek, from elementary school through college, is eligible to participate. Each test consists of 40 multiple-choice questions based on a passage in Greek; the questions cover content, comprehension, grammar, and sometimes metrics. Deadline for receipt of applications is the second Monday in January each year, and the exams are given in the individual participants' schools or colleges the second week in March. Ribbons and certificates are awarded to top winners; two $1,000 scholarships are offered each year, in addition to the combined NGE/NLE scholarship mentioned above.

The NGE is a valuable resource for all Greek students and teachers, and is a vital link in the preservation of the teaching of Greek in American schools. For almost 20 years, Ed Phinney responded to the needs of teachers and students and was personally involved in every step of the writing, editing, mailing, distribution of awards, and promotion of the exam. The National Association of Secondary School Principals has placed the NGE on the Advisory List of National Contests and Activities since 1988.

NATIONAL MYTHOLOGY EXAM

Sponsored by the Elementary Teachers of Classics (ETC), a committee of the ACL, the NME is available for grades 3–9 (see Chapters 6 and 7 above). The exam consists of 30 multiple-choice questions, with an additional 10 questions on a specific theme selected by the test committee each year, or a literary subtest on the *Iliad*, the *Odyssey*, the *Aeneid*, African Myths, or Native American Myths for grades 5–9. Every student receives a participation ribbon; the top 10% receive certificates, and the top 5% receive bronze medallions. Applications are available from the ACL.

BERNICE L. FOX CLASSICS WRITING CONTEST

Sponsored by Monmouth College, the Bernice L. Fox Classics Writing Contest is open to any student enrolled full-time in high school during the school year. An award of $150 will be given to the author of the best entry written in English on a specified theme. The entry may be an essay, a short story, a play, or a poem. Bernice L. Fox, in whose honor this contest is named, is the author of *Tela Charlottae*, the Latin translation of E.B. White's *Charlotte's Web*. Like the NLE and NGE, this competition is ordinarily announced each year in ACL's journal the *Classical Outlook*.

THE CANE WRITING CONTEST

The CANE Writing Contest is open to middle- or secondary-school students who are enrolled in Latin, Greek, or the Classics. The entry may be a poem, story, or essay of no more than 700 words, based on a specific topic. The winner receives a $200 savings bond and the winning entry is published in the *New England Classical Journal*.

NATIONAL COMMITTEE FOR LATIN AND GREEK

An excellent resource for support of Latin and Greek programs at any level, the NCLG was formed by ACL to act on behalf of its collective sponsoring state, regional, and national classical organizations for the promotion of Latin and Greek. Presently involved in the development of public policy on foreign languages at the national level through the Joint National Committee for Languages, the NCLG has available a number of promotional items, including posters, public relations materials, and information packets for exemplary Latin programs. These packets contain brief descriptions of lively and innovative Latin programs and may be obtained from the ACL's TMRC.

ADVANCED PLACEMENT EXAMINATION

The AP program, sponsored by the College Board, tests students on Latin material studied in an AP class, a college-level course available to students on the high-school level (see Chapter 10 above, and Howard 1996, 1997). Many colleges and universities grant credit, placement, or both to students who achieve a certain level on the AP examinations. Since credit and/or placement varies, students should contact the Classics department at the college/university in which they are interested to determine the credit and/or placement granted by that school. Materials such as the *1994 AP Latin: Free-Response Scoring Guide with Multiple-Choice Section* (College Board 1995) are available for study from the Educational Testing Service (ETS).

THE COLLEGE BOARD SAT II LATIN TEST

The College Board SAT II tests replace the College Board Achievement Tests (see Chapter 10 above, and Crooker and Rabiteau). For students who do not take AP exams, or in areas where AP courses are not available, this test gives students the opportunity to show how much they know. Some colleges require SAT II tests for admission. The current version of the one-hour SAT II Latin Test is geared toward students who have completed at least two years of Latin. There are 65–70 questions on the entire exam, 25–30 of which are based on three to five adapted Latin passages of about eight lines each. *The Official Guide to SAT II* (College Board 1997b) is available from ETS.

SCHOLARSHIPS

Many colleges, universities, and classical organizations offer scholarships to incoming freshmen in Classics, Latin, and Greek. A few sample programs, which present the diversity of scholarships available to high-school students, are mentioned below and contact persons are listed at the end of this chapter. Students should call or write the Classics department of the college in which they are interested and request current information about grants and scholarships.

The Classical Association of the Middle West and South (CAMWS): Offers book prizes and $500 scholarships to qualifying winners in its annual College Awards Translation Contest. The competition is open to advanced Latin students enrolled in high schools in the association's 31 states and 3 Canadian provinces. The teachers of the students must be members of CAMWS, or the school library must subscribe to the *Classical Journal*. In a two-hour time period, the contestants must translate at sight a passage of Latin prose and a passage of Latin poetry. The exam must be administered by a school official other than the Latin teacher.

The University of Arizona at Tucson: The Classics Department awards an annual prize of a Latin dictionary to an outstanding high-school Latin student in Arizona.

The University of California, Los Angeles: The Classics Department offers the Helen Caldwell Memorial Scholarship of $3,000 a year for four years to one freshman and one continuing student who have declared majors in Classics.

The Catholic University of America: Offers undergraduate tuition scholarships to incoming freshmen who are interested in pursuing Classics majors. The Martin Rawson Patrick McGuire Scholarships for Latin and Greek majors offer $6,000 each year for four years; the Shahan Scholarship awards $12,000 to Latin or Greek majors; and the Archdiocesan Scholarship offers full tuition for four years.

The University of Dallas: Offers merit scholarships in Classics and many other fields. These scholarships are open to incoming freshmen and are worth up to full tuition costs over a four-year period, renewable each year. About 20 are awarded annually.

The University of Georgia: The Department of Classics awards Warlick-Mannion Scholarships to five undergraduates, including incoming freshmen, who intend to enroll in either Latin or Greek courses at the University of Georgia. The scholarships carry a stipend of up to $1,000 for the first year, and may be renewed.

The College of the Holy Cross: The Department of Classics awards the Henry Bean Classics Scholarship, a four-year, full tuition scholarship, to two outstanding high-school seniors who will major in the Classics. The scholarship is renewable annually.

The University of Maryland: The Department of Classics offers the Steyer Scholarship in Classics for $1,000, renewable each year, to an incoming freshman.

The College of William and Mary: The Hogan Prize in Classical Studies is available to a student who has completed at least three years of Latin or Greek by high-school graduation. This award is for $1,000, renewable each year for four years.

TRAVEL ABROAD

Many college and high-school teachers sponsor trips abroad for high-school students (see Chapter 7 above). There are a number of travel companies that specialize in putting together trips abroad for teachers and high-school students.

The Vergilian Society, which offers three or four Classical Study programs each summer, will accommodate a group of high-school students, provided they are accompanied by a teacher or a parent. These programs are designed for persons with a serious interest in antiquity and include lectures, visits to museums, and on-site study of archaeological ruins.

The University of Dallas offers study programs abroad for high-school students. These three-credit courses are open to students who have studied at least two years of Latin in high school. Programs have included "Shakespeare in Italy" and "Latin in Rome."

SUMMER ACADEMIC PROGRAMS

The Governor's Honors Program in Georgia includes every academic area. Funded by the state legislature, it is a six-week academic program for high-school students which takes place at Valdosta State University. Every high school, both public and private, is eligible to submit nominations. A committee chosen by the State Department of Education selects the students, including 15 in Latin. The Latin program encompasses many activities not found in the usual curriculum, such as keeping a journal in Latin for the six-week period. There are cross-discipline projects and activities which enable students to see interrelationships among their subjects.

A similar program is offered in Virginia. The Virginia Governor's Latin Academy offers a three-week enriched Latin program at a Virginia college campus (Abbott 1992). This program is funded by the legislature and each Virginia high school has the opportunity to submit the name of a Latin student for consideration. A committee chosen by the legislature selects 45 students to participate in the program, which includes the study of Greek, oral Latin, presentation of a play in Latin, and many other multi-disciplinary activities.

OTHER CREATIVE ACTIVITIES

Archaeology is a subject that has great appeal for high-school students, who are fascinated by the mysteries of past cultures and how they relate to the present. The study of archaeology at the high-school level enhances critical-thinking skills, including the ability to evaluate, analyze, and synthesize. A visit to an archaeological site is an exciting experience, and many digs offer hands-on opportunities to scrape the trench wall with a trowel, screen artifacts, and learn to catalogue.

Students can be introduced to archaeological techniques in the classroom by "excavating buried artifacts" from a large dishpan or other container (see the material available from Elizabeth Fisher in the list of contacts below). A presentation by a local archaeologist, either in the classroom or on site, can make students more fully aware of methods and practices employed by the discipline.

The study of archaeology can be a year-long project or simply involve a one-day visit to an archaeological site. With the rise in the number and variety of sites open to the public, it is not difficult to find one that can be visited by students. The learning involved in a site visit will promote the comprehension of the importance of site preservation. The Smithsonian Institution offers a packet relating to many aspects of archaeology and anthropology, and the TMRC catalog lists a 48-page book containing many photos and diagrams of sites, excavations, and reconstructions in Britain. The reward of exposing young students to archaeology as a multi-disciplinary subject is an understanding of anthropology, culture, science, and history, and the relationship of these topics to one another.

Another creative enrichment activity is the study of architecture, one of the most visible indications of our classical heritage. Classical motifs are a part of public buildings, sports complexes, private homes, and modern buildings. Many museums prepare special talks and materials dealing with classical architecture, and basic information is readily available from the TMRC. One rewarding activity is a walking tour through a city, town, village, or neighborhood to discover the classical influences that can be found in and on many houses and buildings.

In Marietta, Georgia, when Prof. Bob Boughner and I were conducting a three-week Latin workshop, we devised a planned walk in the downtown district. We walked through an area of about six blocks to discover the houses and public buildings that would enrich our architectural "treasure hunt." We asked the workshop participants to identify the three basic styles of classical architecture—Doric, Ionic, and Corinthian—and various sculptural adornments such as griffins, pediments, and even Latin inscriptions. All were delighted to discover the classical heritage that existed in their own back yard.

Many students and teachers in the Washington area have benefitted from guided tours of classical Washington conducted by John Ziolkowski. Viewing the Capitol, the Supreme Court, the Post Office, and many other buildings and monuments, one realizes how many of these buildings reflect our cultural heritage from Greece and Rome. *Classical Washington: A Guided Tour* is available to teachers and students from Prof. Ziolkowski at the address provided below.

"Certamen/Latin Bowl" was begun in the 1960s by Sister Therese Marie Dougherty, at Notre Dame College in Baltimore. It quickly spread across the nation, becoming a major NJCL event (as discussed above), and today thousands of students spend countless hours studying questions and answers on every facet of Latin and Roman culture. Many schools host competitions after school, or on a Saturday, and award trophies and certificates to the winners. These contests bring together students from different schools who have common goals: participating in a competition and interest in and study of Latin. Any school can organize a Latin Bowl; it is an excellent project for the Latin club and the Latin honor society. Certamen practice is available on computer software from the TMRC, and a pamphlet on "How to Put on a Certamen" is also available from Susan Schearer (address below).

Enthusiastic high-school Classics students are a valuable asset to any Latin program. If they become involved in any of the aforementioned activities, the program will undoubtedly grow. The willingness of the teacher and the students to reach out and explore creative enrichment activities will further the cause of the Classics in our nation.

CONTACTS

Advanced Placement Program: Educational Testing Service, Dept. E 22, P.O. Box 6670, Princeton, NJ 08541

American Classical League: ACL, Miami Univ., Oxford, OH 45056; 513–529– 7741; E-mail AmericanClassicalLeague@muohio.edu

Archaeology:

Ann Kaup, Anthropology Out-Reach Office, NHBMRC 112, Smithsonian Institution, Washington, DC 20560; 202–357–1592

Roman Archaeology available from ACL TMRC, Miami Univ., Oxford, OH 45056

"Digging in a Dishpan," Elizabeth A. Fisher, Randolph Macon Coll., P.O. Box 5005, Ashland, VA 23005; 804–752–7249

Architecture: *Classical Washington: A Guided Tour,* John Ziolkowski, Classics Dept., George Washington Univ., Washington, DC 20052; 202–994–6127; E-mail ccojez @gwuvm.gwu.edu

Bernice L. Fox Classics Writing Contest: Thomas J. Sienkewicz, Capron Professor of Classics, Monmouth Coll., Monmouth, IL 61462; 309–457–2371; E-mail toms@ wpoff.monm.edu

Catholic University of America Scholarships: William Klingshirn, Dept. of Greek and Latin, Catholic Univ. of America, Washington, DC 20064; 800–673–2772; E-mail klingshirn@cua.edu

Certamen: "How to Put on a Certamen," Susan Schearer, 316 W. Whitlock Ave., Winchester, VA 22601; 540–667–2945

Classical Association of the Middle West and South Scholarships: Eddie Lowry, Jr., Classical Studies, Ripon Coll., P.O. Box 248, Ripon, WI 54971

Classical Association of New England Writing Contest: Bonnie Catto, Assumption Coll., 500 Salisbury St., Worcester, MA 01615

College of the Holy Cross Scholarships: Blaise Nagy, Coll.of the Holy Cross, Worcester, MA 01610; 508–793–2547; E-mail tmethe@holycross.edu

College of William and Mary Scholarship: James Baron, Dept. of Classical Studies, Coll. of William and Mary, Williamsburg, VA 23187; 804–221–2165; E-mail jrbaro@mail.wm.edu

National Greek Exam: Deb Davies, Chair, NGE, 1041 Arlington Blvd., Ann Arbor, MI 48104; 313–677–7045; E-mail drdavies@umich.edu

National Junior Classical League Convention: NJCL c/o ACL (see above)

National Junior Classical League Honor Society: NJCL c/o ACL

National Junior Classical League Pen Pal Program: Laura Giles, NJCL Scholastic Services, 6824 Rochelle Ln., Amarillo, TX 79101; 806–355–0122; E-mail lmgilrd@jenet.edu

National Junior Classical League Scholarships: NJCL c/o ACL

National Latin Exam Application and Information: National Latin Exam, P.O. Box 95, Mount Vernon, VA 22121; 800–459–9847

National Latin Exam *Forum Romanum*: TMRC c/o ACL

National Latin Exam Packet of Previous Exams: TMRC c/o ACL

National Senior Classical League Scholarships: NSCL c/o ACL

SAT II Latin Test: SAT Program, Educational Testing Service, 225 Phillips Blvd., Ewing, NJ 08628; 800–406–4775

Teaching Materials and Resource Center: TMRC c/o ACL

University of Dallas Merit Scholarships in Classics: Grace Starry West, Director, Classics Scholars Program, Univ. of Dallas, 1845 E. Northgate Dr., Irving, TX 75062; 214–721–5368

University of Dallas Study Programs Abroad: Community Education, Univ. of Dallas, 1845 E. Northgate Dr., Irving, TX 75062; 972–721–5225

University of Georgia Warlick-Mannion Scholarships: Dept. of Classics, Park Hall, Univ. of Georgia, Athens, GA 30602; 706–542–9264; E-mail crussell@parallel.park.uga.edu

University of Maryland Steyer Scholarship in Classics: Judith Hallett, Chair, Dept. of Classics, Univ. of Maryland, College Park, MD 20742; 301–405–2024; E-mail jh10@umail.und.edu

Vergilian Society Classical Study Programs: John Dutra, Exec. Sec., Vergilian Society, P.O. Box 817, Oxford, OH 45056; 513–529–1482; E-mail dutrajack@msmail.muohio.edu

12

School-College Articulation: Working Together For a Stronger Curriculum

SHEILA K. DICKISON
University of Florida

LATIN PROGRAMS IN ISOLATION

Although Latin currently thrives at all levels at which it is taught, elementary, secondary, and college programs often exist as isolated entities with interaction between the levels the exception rather than the rule. In this chapter I suggest some reasons for barriers between the different educational levels (as useful background to this discussion, see Davis, Chapters 4–5). The picture is not entirely bleak, because one can find some remarkable examples of school-college cooperation that deserve recognition, and some exciting developments, particularly in technology, promise to facilitate interaction in the future. In my conclusion, I list action items for faculty and teachers that have as their goal improving school-college articulation on both a personal and curricular level (and see Dickison, 1998, for some specific ways to improve the transition between high-school and college Latin courses).

A powerful indicator of the great divide between those teaching Latin at the college and other levels is the composition of the membership of the two national classical professional organizations. The American Philological Association (APA), "the principal learned society for classical studies in North America," counted barely more than 100 high-school teachers in its 1996–97 membership of nearly 3,200 (source: APA; and cf. LaFleur 1997: Table 2). Conversely, the American Classical League (ACL), with the "purpose of fostering the study of classical languages in the United States and Canada," had just over 200 college faculty among its nearly 4,200 members during this same period (source: ACL; LaFleur 1997: Table 2). On purely practical levels, these statistics suggest that at professional meetings, at least, there is little interaction between these two groups. Not surprisingly, the program of each organization's annual meeting directly reflects antithetical missions and membership.

The diametrically opposed missions of the two major professional organizations mirror very real differences in the goals of a Classics program at each level. Ph.D. programs are largely the responsibility of major research institutions, both public and private. Many more institutions, including small colleges, offer majors in the classical languages and classical civilization; some of these institutions also provide an M.A. Institutions with a Classics faculty but no major generally aspire to offering one. Most Classics departments and programs also teach a range of service courses to fulfill general education or distribution requirements, but this is often not recognized as central to the department's real mission of offering courses in the ancient languages. For faculty at almost every kind of higher educational institution, research has become a very important part of their job description.

In schools, on the other hand, Latin programs are generally considered an end in themselves: two or more years of a foreign language fulfill an exit requirement from high school or are part of an admission requirement to a college. A third or fourth year course might prepare students for the Advanced Placement (AP) examinations. Infrequently do teachers have the luxury to think in terms of preparing a student for a program in Latin that will continue through the undergraduate major. School programs are teaching programs and, except for AP or International Baccalaureate (IB) teachers, there is often little encouragement for professional development. While teachers in public schools are expected to upgrade credentials on a regular basis, state requirements do not always insist that this be done in the content area.

These fundamental differences in the goals of school and college programs are also reflected in curriculum and teaching approaches at the two levels. At the college level many institutions continue to use a very traditional approach to teaching Latin that emphasizes grammar first and reading only when grammar and syntax are completed (*Wheelock's Latin*, somewhat modernized in its revised 5th ed., is still highly traditional and remains the most widely used college text—cf. Chapter 13 below). A major reason for the persistence of this conservative approach is a practical one. As colleges have taught more and more beginning Latin to students who did not have the opportunity to take it in high school, expedience demanded that students be hurried through the fundamentals. A common perception is that reading programs require more time to accomplish the same goals (see Chapters 9 and 14). Some faculty also believe that reading-approach texts are less successful in teaching students to deal with real texts than the tried and true translation method. (I find no evidence that anyone has ever done a study to measure whether one method is superior to another.) Finally, many faculty, having been trained in the grammar-translation method themselves, seem to prefer it: "we teach as we were taught," the old adage goes.

Teachers, on the other hand, have been more receptive to reading texts such as the *Cambridge Latin* series, *Ecce Romani*, or the *Oxford Latin* course (see Chapter 9). The explanation for this may be as simple as the fact that the reading approach has a greater capacity to engage students in the learning process, and hence to hold the interest and attention of the younger learner. Teachers are also more likely to have encountered educational research pointing up the benefits of the active involvement of students in the learning process. Many recent educational innovations like collaborative learning had their origins in classrooms at the primary or secondary level. Higher education has been slow to adopt such advances.

There is also a college perception that school classes spend much more time on civilization and culture than on grammar, and that this is one of the reasons that students who have learned Latin in high school cannot translate Latin. It is true that secondary teachers have had to "enrich their classes by teaching more mythology, Roman culture and history, to say nothing of basic English sentence structure" (Davis, 14). Still, there are many indications that much high quality teaching goes on at the secondary level and that teachers have been very successful in working with motivated and unmotivated students alike.

SCHOOL-COLLEGE INTERACTION
AT THE PERSONAL LEVEL

Despite the somewhat gloomy assessment of the lack of articulation between school and college teachers and programs I have just painted, there can be found some impressive examples of successful and mutually beneficial cooperation between the two educational levels on an individual basis.

In its over 40 years of existence, the College Board's AP program has had an important impact on the secondary curriculum and has been responsible for bringing together faculty and teachers as no other program has (see Chapter 10 above). Development committees that oversee the curriculum for each discipline and write the exam are composed of teachers and faculty; the committee chair may be either a teacher or a faculty member. The annual exam reading itself provides an extended and remarkable opportunity for interaction between teachers and faculty. As a veteran of seven or eight readings, I can attest to the wonderful camaraderie and give and take that develop among fellow readers, as they carefully discuss question standards and then read their way through a seemingly endless pile of student test booklets. The shared experience, akin in some respects to a boot camp, creates friendships and memorable moments. (For a fun, yet realistic, re-creation of a reading see Margaret Logan's mystery, *C.A.T. Caper*.) Surely one of the most important by-products of this shared experience is the respect faculty gain for the expertise of teachers and the special insights they can bring to the reading of a Latin text.

The annual meeting of the ACL provides another example of productive collaboration between school and college teachers in an environment that promotes relaxed discussion and mutual discovery. The location of the meeting on a college campus allows for common meals and lodging, an important ingredient responsible for interaction of the kind that rarely occurs at other professional meetings. Additionally, the program itself is structured in such a way as to provide large blocks of time for workshops and interactive sessions. Glenn Knudsvig, President of ACL (1994–98), has encouraged the formation of task forces focusing on common concerns and issues such as learner and teaching portfolios, cooperative learning in the Latin classroom, oral Latin, distance learning, writing in and across the curriculum, and so on; these groups, composed of both teachers and professors, have provided a lively forum for discussion of common problems and approaches.

Regional meetings also provide occasions for interaction on all levels. Organizations such as the Classical Association of the Middle West and South (CAMWS) welcome teachers, specifically encouraging first-time attendees by providing a number of grants to do so. Small conferences, such as the biennial CAMWS Southern Section, have a well established reputation for being an enjoyable and relaxed occasion that emphasizes socializing and sightseeing, as well as the presentation of papers. There are any number of other regional, state, and local organizations with a reputation for encouraging interaction among teachers of Classics at all levels, but characteristically teachers tend to predominate in many of these groups.

Successful examples of interaction between faculty and teachers on a programmatic level may also be cited. The M.A.T. program at the University of Massachusetts at Amherst has worked very closely with the secondary-school system in the state in placing its student interns in classrooms as part of their curriculum (see Chapter 19 below). Some institutions, such as the Universities of Virginia, Florida, and Georgia, offer summer courses, specifically for teachers, on topics relating to the AP curriculum or other authors taught in schools. Others, the University of Maryland for example, reach a wide spectrum of students and teachers with Annual Latin Days (Hallett). Still others make an effort to provide appropriate courses at times when teachers can participate.

I would also like to mention a unique experience I had in Florida that involved extended and significant cooperation between school and college teachers. About 10 years ago, the Florida Department of Education decided to develop initial certification tests for K–12 teachers in-state, rather than contract with an external testing agency. Committees, composed of teachers and faculty, worked on all stages of test production from writing question specifications and developing a blueprint for the exam to validating questions. In all, the process involved over two years of meetings and work. Our final product, a test in multiple versions, has fortunately stood the test of time and is still in use. I am convinced that the test is as good as it is because of the intense and cooperative efforts of teachers and faculty.

NEW POSSIBILITIES FOR
SCHOOL-COLLEGE COLLABORATION

While articulation between college and university Latin programs may be characterized for the most part as hit or miss, on an individual level there are many examples of productive interaction. For the success of Latin in the 21st century, it is imperative that we continue these activities on a personal level and also work on a larger scale to increase cooperation between school and college programs. I will conclude with a look at recent developments that are likely to have a profound effect on articulation between the two levels of education.

In the last few years we have witnessed the birth of an electronic age that promises to have a major impact on all aspects of life, including education (see further Chapter 23 below). A particularly exciting and significant feature of the technological revolution is the means to bring teachers and faculty in contact with each other in ways that have not hitherto been possible. E-mail and computer discussion lists, for example, have already proven to be very useful in facilitating communication between individuals or members of a group. Both the CLASSICS-List and the LATIN-List have professors and teachers as active participants, although one group predominates in each (there are more teachers on LATIN-L than professors, and the reverse appears to be true for CLASSICS). Real-time conversation, enjoyed by the *Maius Reticulum* participants on America Online, is yet another example of the creative use of current technology to create community; subscribers gather at 8:00 p.m. on Tuesday evenings for an hour-long discussion on a variety of topics, and a weekly electronic newsletter announces the topic of the week. It is already clear that E-mail, discussion lists, and real-time chat provide teachers from different levels the means to share learning experiences, to problem-solve together, and to obtain a deeper understanding of the educational process at all levels.

Similarly, the World Wide Web will provide teachers access to the tools of our discipline that faculty have long been able to take for granted. *Diotima: Materials for the Study of Women and Gender in the Ancient World* (www.uky. edu/ArtsSciences/Classics/whither.html), for example, makes available college syllabi, bibliography, links to visual material from *Perseus* (see Chapter 23, and Chapman), and, in some cases, even the text of complete articles. The new "Roman *Perseus*," recently funded, proposes to provide Latin texts, translations, commentaries, Roman art (panoramas and rotations of objects in space), an atlas of the Roman world, the *Lewis and Short Latin Dictionary*, a 3-D walk-through of Roman space, and so on (www.perseus.tufts.edu/). We are really seeing just the beginning of the vast quantity and variety of information that the

Internet will make available to teachers, students, and the public. Other technological advances, such as video-conferencing from a desktop computer, will open up possibilities for distance learning and team- teaching with important ramifications for closing the gap between college and school programs.

A very imaginative project that takes advantage of capabilities of the Internet is the *VRoma* proposal with a goal of creating "an on-line community for the teaching and learning of Classics" (www.colleges.org/ ~ vroma). *VRoma* has two components that each emphasize collaboration and collaborative teaching projects between faculty from undergraduate programs and high-school teachers. A key component of the project is a virtual Forum, an electronic space where faculty and students meet and interact in a variety of ways: participants can talk to each other; hold class; access texts, images and teaching materials; do group projects; and so on. A second feature is two, intensive, two-week summer workshops in which participants design collaborative courses and course materials that take advantage of the tools provided by a MOO (Multi-user Object-Oriented) virtual environment/web server. The planners of this project anticipate that it will have a lasting and profound effect on the ways in which language is taught in schools and colleges (for a complete text of the NEH proposal for *VRoma* see the web site at hippocrene.colleges.org/ ~ vroma).

A different kind of development that may impact on articulation between the levels that teach Latin is the production of national standards for foreign language learning. The *Standards for Classical Language Learning*, produced as a collaborative project of the ACL, the APA, and regional classical associations, describe goals and content standards in an ideal K–12 program (see Chapter 5 above). How such descriptions of curriculum will influence the teaching of Latin in college remains to be seen, but, at the very least, they serve the purpose of providing a snapshot of what the profession believes important for the pre-college learning of Latin.

BRIDGING SCHOOL-COLLEGE CURRICULA

Although only about one out of 10 high-school Latin students choose to continue their study in college, it is important that the transition from high school to college be as smooth as possible. In this section I will look briefly at several programs that promote articulation between the two levels of education. Probably the most widely known is the AP program described above (and see Chapter 10), which has as its basic aim providing college credit and/or placement in the 16 academic disciplines that it offers. From its inception in 1956, the AP program has stressed the cooperative nature of the endeavor, involving teachers and faculty at every stage of the process from developing course descriptions through the scoring of the exams.

The College Board reports that AP courses are offered in more than 10,000 high schools in every state in the U.S., every province and territory in Canada, and 63 other foreign countries. Nearly 2,900 U.S. and foreign colleges and universities grant credit, placement, or both to students receiving a score of 3 or above on the examinations. Not surprisingly, there is a wide variation in college reaction to AP credit. Some colleges and universities automatically award credit for certain scores; other institutions or individual departments award credit under certain conditions (for example, with the proviso that a student take an additional course in Latin, or only after having reviewed the essay portion of the student's exam). Some give credit for scores of 4 and 5, but not for 3. Individual institutions vary widely also in their use of AP credit for placement purposes. A college's undergraduate catalogue often provides information on its practice; the registrar's office should also be able to clarify institutional policy. It is not unusual to discover that the Classics department is not familiar with its own institution's policy on AP, or that the current policy has been instituted with little or no departmental input.

When placement works as it should, students who have done well on the AP Vergil and/or Latin Literature exams should be able to continue Latin in the next appropriate college course at an intermediate or advanced level. At my own institution, the University of Florida, each AP score is given a UF course equivalent. Thus it is easy for students to see what credit they have earned for a particular score on a Latin exam, as well as what the next course in the sequence is. This policy also prevents students from earning credit for both an AP course and the equivalent university course. Students may also consult with a faculty member about the appropriate level course to take and even repeat the equivalent UF course (but without receiving credit for the AP score).

Students who have graduated from an International Baccalaureate (IB) program may also present credits in Latin literature, one of the electives in that curriculum. Many institutions now give college credit for IB courses, and, like AP, IB courses can easily be equated to equivalent college courses. As the popularity of the demanding IB curriculum increases, faculty can expect to see more students entering college with IB credit.

Another mechanism for placement into college Latin courses is student performance on the SAT II Latin subject test (Dickison 1998, and Chapters 10-11 above). Formerly known as Achievement Tests, SAT II tests measure student achievement in specific content areas; some colleges require a number of subject tests for admission and employ the scores for placement and advisement. The scores may also be used for exemption from college requirements, such as a language requirement. As with the AP examinations, a committee of professors and teachers writes the SAT II Latin test, which measures skills such as grammar and syntax, derivatives, translation, and comprehension. The Educational Testing Service then pre-tests new questions in college Latin classes from the second through the fourth semester. Participating in these pre-tests is an excellent way for college faculty to learn more about the test itself and to find out how their own students perform. An institution can also conduct norming studies on its own beginning Latin students. This involves matching student scores on the SAT II Latin test with course grades, in order to set appropriate institutional cut scores for exemption and placement.

Some colleges and universities prefer to rely on their own tests for placement. A frequent lament is that high-school students do not do well on these tests, which only confirms the belief that high schools are not doing a very good job of teaching Latin. For such placement tests to be reliable, they really need to be tested on native students at the different levels of beginning Latin and exemption scores related to scores and grades of those students. Testing experts on a college campus will be able to provide helpful information on how do the necessary statistical analysis of this data so that placement tests function properly.

One point about placement tests needs to be reiterated. Without a context, placement tests do not provide significant or reliable information. Such tests can really only do what they were designed to do if they reflect the achievement and expectations we have for the students we have taught in our own beginning Latin sequence. Articulating proficiencies we expect students to attain at the end of each semester of beginning Latin has a number of benefits. Such an exercise, while rarely done at the college level, is a very good way to determine whether we really accomplish what we intended to do in the beginning language classroom.

In the area of articulation there is much to be done at all levels. Here are my suggestions for ways in which each of us can begin to make a contribution to improving communication and cooperation. I challenge you to think of other activities that will serve the same end. College faculty are encouraged to:

- attend an ACL Institute or a regional meeting where teachers predominate;
- identify a local teacher to support and collaborate with;
- get involved with the AP Latin program as a reader;
- volunteer to pre-test SAT II Latin questions;
- provide opportunities for graduate students to become involved with Latin programs at all levels; and
- recognize teachers who have made an outstanding contribution to the teaching of Latin.

Latin teachers are encouraged to:

- join organizations such as the APA and attend annual meetings;
- participate in discussion lists that emphasize research topics;
- invite college faculty to participate in JCL events;

- seek help from college faculty in order to keep up with research trends in Classics;
- attend AP workshops and serve as a reader; and
- understand that they are making an important contribution to the vitality of Latin.

As educational institutions are increasingly faced with funding shortages and rising costs, it is crucial for teachers of the Classics at all levels to find arenas in which to cooperate. I am convinced that one of the keys to the survival of Latin in the curriculum of the 21st century is increased cooperation between school and college.

13

The Grammar-Translation Approach to College Latin

JAMES M. MAY
St. Olaf College

INTRODUCTION

Well, it happened to me again—this time at our commencement reception. A well-meaning relative of one of our graduates approached me with a broad smile on his face. "So you teach Latin?" "I sure do," I replied. "I took Latin when I was in school," he announced proudly. "*Amó, amás, amát . . . Portá, portaé, portaé, portám, portá,*" he chanted, stressing with gusto the inflectional endings in violation of the words' natural accent. "That's wonderful," I replied, smiling in return, while fighting against my impulse to wince and collapse on the floor.

People who have taught Latin for any considerable period of time—and I'm now approaching the quarter century mark—have heard that sort of comment literally hundreds, if not thousands of times, and for those of us who continue to use the grammar-translation approach in our teaching, it inflicts a certain amount of pain each time we hear it. Can we help but wonder whether this is the sole legacy that we Latin teachers have passed on to our students?

I must admit that, as a young teenager learning Latin, I too reveled in the ability to rattle off my Latin endings, duly emphasizing them in sing-song fashion. My confidence was somewhat shaken, however, after having at that time a conversation with my mother about languages. Although my mother was born in this country, her first language, spoken by her immigrant parents and family, was Slovak. Like so many of her generation, she grew up speaking the family's native tongue at home, and English at school and with friends. Shortly after I had begun learning Latin and had mastered many of my declensions and conjugations, I asked my mom about case endings in Slovak. Having not studied Latin, or Slovak, or any other highly inflected language formally in school, she had no notion of case. So, I took another tack and began constructing simple sentences in English, using the word "boy" in each sentence, but placing it in a different syntactical relationship on each occasion. To my amazement, my mother would instinctively change the case ending on the Slovak word; but when I asked her about changing that word, she would vehemently deny that she was doing so! After a brief mother-son altercation, mom finally did come to the realization that she was, in fact, altering the word's ending in each instance. I was flabbergasted that she could do this so readily, without even knowing or realizing what she was doing. On that day, this young junior-high schooler learned something that all serious students and teachers of Latin know: when the Romans learned Latin, they did so in the way that we all, for the most part, have learned our own native tongues—and not by memorizing inflectional endings! The image of a Roman matron quizzing her children on the endings of the first declension now seemed (rightly so) utterly absurd.

Since that time, in addition to ancient Greek and Latin, I have tried my hand at several modern foreign languages. Perhaps my most successful attempt has been at learning modern Greek. It took many years to gain the modicum of fluency I now possess in that language. I studied grammar, memorized forms, read Greek newspapers and magazines, and visited Greece on a regular basis. But the thing that really moved my abilities forward was the time I spent in an intensive advanced course in the language in Athens. Being in class for nearly six hours a day, doing several hours of written work every evening, and living with a Greek family for a month's time, allowed me to approximate learning a language through exposure and immersion, much as we do when we are growing up.

If, then, the grammar-translation approach (cf. Chapters 2 and 8) is not the most natural way of language acquisition, why, one may ask, do I and so many others in this country persist in using it to teach Latin to our students? The answer, of course, lies in the fact that teachers of foreign languages, particularly the classical languages, are faced with an almost impossible task. Here at St. Olaf College, a four-year traditional liberal arts college, every student is expected to learn a foreign language through the intermediate level. In Latin and Greek and the other less commonly taught languages, this generally means three semesters of language study; in French, German, and Spanish, four semesters. Our typical semester class meets three times a week, 55 minutes per class session, for approximately 13 weeks. Quick calculation will tell you that, in the course of three semesters, my direct, in-class contact with my students totals approximately 105 hours (not subtracting time taken for quizzes and tests). That amounts to roughly a score of hours less than my month-long intensive modern Greek class! In that span of time, we hope to expose students to the principles of language in general, to a different culture, and specifically to the details of Latin grammar and syntax to the extent that will enable them, by the third semester, to read real works of literature by real Roman writers.

This last point, I believe, is crucial. Holding out the reward of reading genuine Latin at some time in the future has been a tactic of Latin teachers probably since the beginning of formalized instruction in the language. A noble goal indeed! Few people who teach or learn a language are content with concentrating on the mere workings of grammar. We study languages in order to open new worlds; and these worlds open through communication, oral and/or written. Along the way, our colleagues in modern languages can offer their students newspaper and magazine articles in the foreign tongue, comic strips and cartoons, radio broadcasts, popular music, interactive computer activities with native speakers, piped-in television broadcasts on the satellite, and plentiful study opportunities in the target language and culture. Although we can simulate some of these situations (and there are, indeed, many good resources available), the real appeal of Latin is still its literature and its cultural legacy. Our students, even those who are with us only for the duration of their language requirement semesters, deserve at least a taste of the best that Latin and its writers have to offer. And after many years and much thinking and agonizing about it, I still contend that the grammar-translation approach (modified and expanded as much as possible), given the extraordinary constraints on time and contact-hours, can help us reach our goal in the most effective and expeditious manner.

THE TEXT

I was once told by a very wise professor of languages that a good teacher can be successful teaching Latin or Greek no matter what textbook is used for classroom instruction. I believe that statement, but I would add that a well-conceived, well-paced text that is (most importantly) compatible with the instructor's own philosophy, approach, and temperament will contribute much to the success of the course. The most commonly used college-level texts that employ the grammar-translation approach are the fifth edition of *Wheelock's Latin,* edited by R. A. LaFleur (Wheelock); *Latin via Ovid* (Goldman and Nyenhuis); *Latin: An Intensive Course* (Moreland and Fleischer); *Traditio: An Introduction to the Latin Language and Its Influence* (Johnston); *Latin for Reading: A Beginner's Textbook with Exercises* (Knudsvig, et al., 1986); and *Reading Classical Latin: A Reasonable Approach* (Ball). *Traditio,* one of the most recent of these texts, "is designed to give students at the college level a thorough introduction to Latin grammar and some experience translating Latin authors" (vii). Moreland and Fleischer's text, written specifically for the Intensive Latin Program at City University of New York, continues to be used in intensive courses, but also has a following among others who teach it over the course of several semesters. *Latin via Ovid,* as the name implies, teaches the grammar and syntax of the language by using illustrations and texts adapted, then later unadapted, from Ovid. *Latin for Reading* "attempts to combine the useful principles and descriptions found in textbooks representing the so-called traditional approach . . . with insights from linguistic research of the past several decades"(v). *Reading Classical Latin* eschews Latin composition and emphasizes reading Latin for comprehension. Wheelock is the oldest of these books, and over the years has certainly been the most popular text among college professors. Although its popularity has apparently waned a bit during this past decade, it continues to be used quite extensively, and it is the text that we have used at St. Olaf for more than a quarter century.

It is probably true that no teacher is ever entirely satisfied with any textbook. We all end up writing new exercises, borrowing from other sources, supplementing with other material, or perhaps ultimately writing our own text! Although I did not learn Latin from Wheelock's text, I came to know it already while in high school. I used it as a teaching assistant and teaching fellow at the University of North Carolina. When I came to St. Olaf in 1977, it was the text being used here, and I gladly took it up. Although generally very pleased with the text, my major criticism of Wheelock in those days (and I believe this was a criticism of most people who used the text) was its lack of continuous prose reading. The Practice and Review sentences, as well as the *Sententiae Antiquae*, provided plenty of practice on the grammar from that day's lesson, but each sentence was an entity unto itself, and there was seldom any opportunity for students to encounter connected thoughts in Latin. Even the *Sententiae Antiquae,* which were culled and adapted from Latin written by Roman authors, were presented entirely out of context and, as a result, often seemed to the students, who were largely unaware of the authors and their works, utterly senseless—or worse, even bizarre. These sentences did provide me with the opportunity to introduce Cicero or Catullus or Horace or Martial to my students, and to comment, as well, on specific works of literature or on cultural issues that a thought in any particular sentence might spark. Still, I found that, once my students had completed the 40 chapters of grammar and had begun reading Wheelock's selections in the back of the book (*Loci Antiqui* and *Loci Immutati*), they had great difficulty making the transition from one sentence to another in a paragraph, and from one paragraph to another in a story.

In an attempt to remedy this situation, my colleagues and I began developing over the years readings designed to supplement the sentences in Wheelock. After several years of teaching at St. Olaf, Anne Groton and I decided to organize these readings, write others, and adapt still more to correspond step-by-step with Wheelock's presentation of grammar and vocabulary. The results of this effort were published in 1986, *Thirty-Eight Latin Stories* (Groton and May). Now in its fifth revised edition, this reader provides a continuous prose passage for nearly every chapter of Wheelock's text (chapters 1–3 are covered in the first reading), with the vocabulary and grammar corresponding to Wheelock's presentation. The first 18 stories are composed Latin, each inspired by a generally well-known Greek or Roman myth. The final 20 stories are adaptations of passages from Roman authors (with poetic passages re-cast as prose), moving toward an increasingly unaltered (hence generally more difficult) state. I will mention in more detail below how I employ these readings, when I speak about using class time.

There were, of course, other complaints commonly lodged by critics (and even loyal proponents) of the Wheelock text. The grammatical explanations found in each chapter were minimal, sometimes barely existent, written at a time when students in college seemed to have a better grasp of the basic rules of English grammar and syntax. For some, the vocabulary selections were too limited and idiosyncratic. Excercises were considered too uniform in nature, incorporating no transformational or structural drills. Some of the sentences appeared blatantly sexist; others were rather strange, and seemed to make little sense to students. Many who used the book complained that the tone was too uniformly moralistic. These and other concerns were addressed effectively by Prof. Richard LaFleur in his comprehensive revision of the text, undertaken in 1995 (see the review by Wooten). Grammatical explanations were expanded, the vocabulary lists were enlarged, sentences were revised, and continuous reading passages were added to the end of every chapter. Ancillary aids to Wheelock have, for the most part, been revised accordingly. For example, a workbook by Paul T. Comeau and Richard A. LaFleur, *Workbook for Wheelock's Latin,* is available, and *Thirty-Eight Latin Stories* (see above) has appeared in its fifth edition, accommodating all the changes introduced in LaFleur's revision; computer software for drilling vocabulary and grammar introduced in the new Wheelock is available from Centaur Systems (see Chapter 23). Finally I should mention the *Comprehensive Study Guide for Wheelock's Latin* by Dale A. Grote. This work first appeared on the Internet, and has now been published (Grote). Teachers and students (especially those needing help with English grammar) searching for extensively detailed explanations of each chapter of Wheelock will find most of their questions answered here.

THE COURSE

As mentioned above, our ultimate goal in teaching Latin is the reward of reading original Latin prose and poetry, along with all of the other related benefits that are concomitant with such activity. On average, we enroll each year about 40–60 students in beginning Latin, divided into two sections. The great majority of that group are taking Latin in order to fulfill the language requirement. There are always a few who are studying Latin as a second (or third) language, and maybe only two or three who are planning to major in Latin or Classics. By the completion of the third semester, however, we generally add another three or four who have decided to pursue a major. Thus, our audience is varied, and we find ourselves faced with the challenge of presenting a course that will both equip those who want to continue beyond third semester with the necessary skills to do so, and at the same time appeal to those who will pursue no more than two or three semesters of the language. The course, then, must address both a general and a specific audience, so to speak, and do so without either "dumbing down" the subject matter to the lowest common denominator, or approaching it as if it were every student's major interest.

It is my hope that one of our graduates, 25 years after studying with us, might approach his or her child's Latin teacher, and rather than reciting the first declension, say something like this: "Yes, I took Latin in college, and it was one of the most worthwhile courses that I had. I not only learned the fundamentals of the language, which enabled me to read some original Latin prose and poetry, but I also learned how language works in general. I gained a great appreciation for the intricacies of grammar and syntax, and for expressing myself with precision and clarity. I learned to concentrate, to analyze, to think logically. I also learned a great deal about the culture and world of the ancient Romans, and came to appreciate how moving across time and culture can be a truly multicultural experience."

What, then, is the recipe for helping our students gain this kind of appreciation? First (and I believe this to be extremely important), we must proclaim these goals (and any others that we may have) to our students on the first day of class, and subsequently on as many occasions and in as many different ways as possible. It is important to remind our students, and ourselves, why we are doing this hard work. All of us who teach Latin have occasionally allowed ourselves to be consumed by detail. Those who teach the grammar-translation approach are particularly susceptible to the temptation of forgetting the forest for the individual trees: we sometimes lose sight of the real reason students are learning declensions and conjugations and the rules for indirect discourse. We need to remind them and ourselves continually of our ultimate goals. Every opportunity that we have to show our classes how some point of grammar, or some linguistic phenomenon, or some custom of the Romans relates in a larger way to their education and to their lives in general must be taken and capitalized upon.

I have a stock phrase that I use time and time again in class—"Latin (or Greek) is like life." The students guffaw at this, particularly the first time they hear it. But after I've illustrated to them, often very comically, but just as many times in a serious and meaningful manner, scores of ways in which Latin, and learning Latin, *are* like life, they begin to believe it themselves. I also firmly maintain that learning is a joy, and that learning even a difficult subject should be fun. There is seldom anything more enjoyable than exercising the intellect in rigorous activity through which we gain an understanding of a difficult or novel concept. Most of our students haven't thought much about this or experienced this kind of mental pleasure, and I do everything in my power to awaken their minds to it. The very last thing that I want to do in my daily life is to make students miserable while they learn the language that I love. Better to take up another profession than to have my pupils leave class hating Latin. All of us who teach do so, I assume, because we love our subject matter and we enjoy introducing it and sharing it with others. Our joy, enthusiasm, and love for the language, as well as our abiding appreciation for the richness of the Roman tradition, must imbue all of our lessons, whether we are talking about the Roman Senate, Roman roadbuilding, the love of Dido for Aeneas, or the endings of the first declension.

Equipped with such a philosophy of teaching, and determined to make it as apparent as possible to my students every day during class, I embark upon our beginning Latin sequence with enthusiasm and determination. As mentioned above, the task of learning basic Latin grammar will be completed in less than two college semesters, i.e., in about 75 to 78 class periods. We generally cover 23 to 25 chapters of the Wheelock text in the first semester, the remaining 15 to 17 chapters in the second. This enables us to end the two-semester sequence with a few weeks of readings, selected from Wheelock's *Loci Antiqui* or *Loci Immutati*. The pace is quick and steady. Normal written evaluation in the course of the semester consists of seven or eight quizzes, two hour-long exams, and one final exam, all (except the final) taken during regular class hours. This means that we average about two to three chapters in Wheelock per week. The quizzes are designed to cover two to three chapters each, and we devote approximately 30 to 40 minutes of a class period to them. The two exams cover approximately nine chapters each, and, although stressing the grammar and vocabulary of those particular chapters, they are, of course, comprehensive. The frequency of this written evaluation, while at first glance somewhat daunting, is, in the final analysis, greatly appreciated by the students. It forces them to keep pace with the material of the class, it allows them to keep an accurate accounting of their own progress, and it helps them to establish a routine for class preparation. Make-up exams and quizzes are not given, although students are permitted to drop their lowest quiz score. Finally, homework assignments are written and handed in to me every day. Although these are not corrected and graded, they are checked. If students turn in every assignment on time, they receive one quiz grade of 100%; delinquent and undone homework reduces the percentage of that quiz grade (which cannot be dropped) accordingly.

The concept of "routine" is, needless to say, not very popular in many educational circles today. I personally find this unfortunate. A routine need not be boring or monotonous. When constructed with care and administered with imagination, a routine, while offering a familiarity and security that most people enjoy, or even crave, can be exciting, fun, and educationally valu-able—especially in beginning language classes; and within any worthwhile routine, there should always be enough room for flexibility and originality. This is the kind of schedule that I try to establish in my Latin classes, and my students know the ground rules from day one. They have my pledge that I will operate in accordance with these rules, and they are expected to do likewise. As a result, I believe that they feel comfortable in class from the beginning, and this atmosphere contributes greatly to discussion and effective learning.

The normal rhythm of class proceeds something like this: After greetings are exchanged, I begin by putting what I call "Latin words for the day" on the blackboard. These are well-known Latin expressions, quotations, or mottoes, from *ab ovo* to *vox populi*. I make a big thing of these sayings, exaggerating their significance, and constantly insisting that, after a while, the class will become addicted to them. If the students have been particularly diligent, or have just taken a difficult quiz, I may give them three, rather than two. They get into the act, often begging for "just one more." This little gimmick actually serves many purposes. It's a bit of levity with which to start class; the aphorisms (many of which are or were commonly used in English, but today are generally not understood by students, e.g., *dum spiro, spero*, and *in vino veritas*) provide a stimulus for brief discussions about all kinds of topics, including the ways Latin has come down into and shaped our own tongue. I half-jokingly encourage the students to use some of the more esoteric phrases in their essays for other classes—to impress their professors. Surprisingly, these few minutes at the beginning of class make a tremendous impression on many. "Latin words for the day" have been mentioned many times on my teaching evaluations as one of the favorite parts of the class!

On most days, we then move to a review of the previous night's homework. Depending on the lesson, this might consist of the "Practice and Review," or *Sententiae Antiquae*, or portions of each, but always the selection from *Thirty-Eight Latin Stories*. From the start, I try to stress the importance of reading continuous passages. In the beginning, I generally read aloud a sentence or paragraph, and have the students repeat it together after me. I then call upon someone to translate. Later, students will read the Latin aloud without my prompting. It is very important for them to hear the language being recited—learning is easier when we involve as many senses as possible. It is also important for pupils to realize that Latin was primarily a *spoken* language. Unfortunately, I have not been able to introduce much oral Latin instruction into the classroom, mostly because of the crunch of time. But I do know of several professors who, while teaching the grammar-translation approach, have managed to do a great deal with oral Latin (e.g., Wooten, 188–89).

I realize that I have, over the years, changed my approach to teaching students how to translate/read Latin. As a young teacher, I was quick to point out to them that the Latin sentence is like a puzzle—figure out the verb and the endings on the nouns, and piece them together. As I grew in age, experience, and ability to read Latin, I came to understand that this was really the wrong technique. I now encourage students to approach a sentence in the way a Roman would have—starting at the beginning and proceeding to the end. The line that I used to hear from some teachers—that word order in Latin makes no difference whatsoever—only perpetuates bad habits and impedes students' ability to begin reading the language. The Romans composed their thoughts in a certain order for a certain reason, and the sooner students learn to approach a sentence in the way the Romans would have heard it, cultivating the ability to suspend their train of thought, the better readers of Latin they will become. With a little practice and discipline, it's amazing how well they adapt to this method, which, in the long run, will make them more capable readers. There are, of course, times when the Latin sentence is so long and/or complicated that we must resort to the "divide and conquer" method. At this point, a solid knowledge of grammar is indispensable for helping students out of trouble.

We almost always do the English-to-Latin sentences as well. Recently many objections have been lodged against doing Latin composition in elementary classes, and the debate has continued (see Ball and Ellsworth 1989, 1992; Newman; Gilleland). I will not rehearse the arguments pro and con here again, but simply say that I believe composition in Latin *does* serve an important pedagogical purpose. It exercises the students' minds in ways that reading Latin does not. I want my pupils to learn the subtleties of the language and its grammar, and I want them to know, rather than simply recognize, vocabulary and forms. In my classes, individual students place their composed Latin on the board, and we all critique it. From the beginning, I warn students that each and every one of us will make mistakes. This is nothing to be nervous or ashamed about; rather, it's the way we all learn. After a few trips to the board and a few critiques, we all find ourselves chuckling over silly errors and commending good performances.

Reading the story, which should be the most important activity of the day, gives us the opportunity to practice, in the context of a continuous passage, what we've learned. The natural impulse for students is to want to read the translations from their notebooks, paying no attention whatsoever to the Latin text as they do so. Again, this is counter-productive to the goal of reading comprehension. I encourage students to look only at their text while their classmate who is reading aloud tries to translate the sentence, also while looking only at the text. In this way, they have the opportunity to re-read what they had done at home, attempting to make sense of it again. Moreover, I encourage them, after class, to go back and re-read the story anew, looking only at the Latin. The more practice they have, even (or especially) on familiar passages, the better they will become. In addition to reviewing points of grammar and syntax, the continuous prose passages provide, of course, fruitful opportunities for discussion about topics of classical mythology, Roman life and manners,

Latin literature, and countless other things. Unfortunately, in a 55-minute period, ". . . I always hear / Time's winged chariot hurrying near." Still, these opportunities for discussion are often the most memorable moments of class for both pupil and teacher.

As a student of Ciceronian oratory, I have learned from the master that what he says in a "digression" is often more crucial to his winning his case than are the arguments strictly "relevant" to the point at hand. The same can be said for teaching. Often we do our most memorable teaching in our digressions. These are the vehicles through which we can offer our students glimpses into all aspects of the ancient world, as well as their connections to it. If I have to sacrifice a few choice grammar exercises to accommodate a good discussion about something that has sparked interest in my students, the trade-off is well worth it.

After having completed the previous day's assignment, I plan to have about 10 to 15 minutes of class time left for introducing the next grammatical concept. Obviously, the management of classroom time is crucial: poor time management often makes for poor teaching, and a class that is consistently behind in its syllabus, with both students and teacher juggling material and playing catch-up, can become frustrating and oppressive. Careful planning and experience will certainly help in this regard, but the wise teacher must know how to adjust the tempo of the class, when to add a digression (or resist adding one), when to encourage (or cut off) conversation, and when it's absolutely necessary to finish an assignment, or simply skip parts of it. I find this one of the major challenges in my daily teaching, for I have made it a principle not to send my students off to begin a lesson without first having introduced the new concepts in class.

During this portion of the class, which, for practical purposes, we might label "lecture," I forbid the class to open their books. I have found that, when books are open and I am speaking about some point of grammar, the students are often reading their texts rather than listening to what I have to say. So, in this section of the class, I have them open their notebooks for note-taking, and I attempt to hold their attention with what I say and write on the board. In my presentation of the lesson, I try to approach any given grammatical concept from an angle different from that taken in the text. I use different ways of explaining the point, and different examples in order to illustrate it. My goal here is to explain the essentials clearly enough to establish a rudimentary understanding. Then I instruct the students, before doing any written work at home, to read carefully the grammatical explanations in the text on these same points. In this way, what they have heard from me is reinforced and corroborated from a different perspective. They are then well-equipped to begin their written work.

Because most students today are not well-versed in English grammar, much of my lecture is spent discussing how any particular grammatical concept applies in English. I use many examples in English (some of them silly), then make the connection with Latin grammar. I point out parallels, and underscore emphatically the differences (helpful in this regard is Goldman and Szymanksi's *English Grammar for Students of Latin*). I promise my students on the first day that they will learn more in Latin class about their native tongue than they have learned in all their years of instruction about English. On the end-of-semester teaching evaluations, nearly all of them list this increased understanding of English as one of the real benefits of the class.

Although I opened this essay by poking fun at former Latin students who approach me reciting their paradigms, I am certainly a fan of paradigm-recitation. I tell students to invent songs, rhymes, and use mnemonic devices, in order to learn the forms more effectively. We recite endings aloud in class, chorally and individually. I encourage them to write out the forms in their notebooks, and to continue to recite them aloud at home. I use every gimmick in the book (short of doing acrobatics off my desk) to help them learn this material. I encourage them to study many times per day, in briefer sessions, rather than in long sittings, and I urge them to pair up with a friend or two in order to quiz and help each other in their study.

I have alluded several times already to the time constraints that we face in teaching college Latin. Learning a language is always a difficult enterprise, but when meeting only three hours per week, it becomes even more difficult and demanding. In order to give students more exposure to Latin, we offer supplementary sessions for practice and review on Tuesday and Thursday evenings. We call these "lab sessions," and draw the parallel with the language lab sessions required of students in the modern languages. Although attendance is not required, students are strongly encouraged to come at least once a week. Sometimes these labs are conducted by the instructors themselves; more often, however, our Latin tutor (usually one of our senior Latin majors), who is a paid work-study student, conducts the lab (in departments with graduate programs, teaching assistants can do the job). During this hour, the tutor reviews grammatical concepts, drills forms and vocabulary, answers questions, and assists with homework. In addition to these sessions, the tutor holds office hours two hours per week. Often students feel more comfortable asking questions of one of their peers than of their professors. Of course, I am always available for questions and consultation during my own formal office hours, which average about 5–8 hours per week, or during unscheduled hours by appointment. Thus, although our elementary Latin classes meet formally less than three hours per week and move at a rapid pace, students have ample opportunity for seeking help outside of regular class time.

Here I might add a few brief remarks about the format of my quizzes and tests. I have already spoken about their length and frequency. A typical quiz in elementary Latin is very traditional: it usually consists of a brief section with vocabulary words (both Latin-to-English and English-to-Latin—and yes, misspelled words are incorrect!), a section on forms (e.g., conjugate *habeo* in the imperfect, indicative, active), and a longer section on translation, mostly Latin-to-English, with some English-to-Latin also included. Although the translation section generally consists of individual sentences in the beginning part of the course, as soon as we've mastered enough vocabulary and syntax, the sentences give way to connected passages or stories. By the end of the elementary sequence, vocabulary and forms are stressed less on tests in favor of reading comprehension and sophisticated analysis of syntax. These reading passages are always unseen, sight-translations.

I have made it a personal goal over the years to grade and return papers in a timely fashion. This means getting quizzes and tests corrected and back to the student the following class period. If students can spend several hours studying and preparing diligently for their exams, I can spend several hours correcting them in order to insure a quick turn-around. Students appreciate this practice, and it is also pedagogically purposeful, since we can review the test during the very next class period, when the material is still fresh and familiar, and students can learn most effectively from their errors.

THE TRANSITION

It seems to be generally accepted by all who teach Latin and Greek that the most difficult learning period, for both students and teachers, is the intermediate level. It is usually at this juncture that students move from learning grammar and syntax to the higher level of synthesis that is necessary for dealing with substantial, uncut, and unaltered selections from classical authors. My friends who teach modern languages tell me that the intermediate level is also the most challenging for their students. This is not surprising, of course, especially in the case of Latin or Greek. Reading a passage of Nepos, Pliny, Cicero, or Catullus after only two semesters of learning the basic grammar is, of course, tantamount to reading any of the "classics" of British or American literature after having studied English only two semesters. Imagine reading *Hamlet* or *Great Expectations* or *Moby Dick* after six months of English instruction! The amazing thing is that most of our students do a respectable job of it.

As the second semester of our elementary sequence enters its last few weeks, we generally finish the 40th chapter of Wheelock and the final passage in *Thirty-Eight Latin Stories*. At that point, we take our second hour-long exam, concentrating on the last 9 or 10 chapters. We then turn to reading selections chosen from Wheelock's *Loci Antiqui* and *Loci Immutati*. The entire class period is spent reading aloud the Latin passage and translating it into English. Again, I try to stress reading each Latin sentence in its original order, as the Romans would have, rather than approaching it as a puzzle whose pieces need to be fitted together. We discuss sentence structure and syntax, and make certain that both the meaning and the structure of every sentence are comprehended. I often ask questions about constructions, e.g., why is this verb in this mood, or this noun in this case, or in what other way might this idea have been expressed? We also take time to discuss the passage in general, its context, its purpose, its author, and the circumstances of its composition. Here many opportunities present themselves to further students' interest in Latin and in the classical world in general, to draw meaningful comparisons and contrasts, and to give them a taste of the richness and depth of Latin literature.

When the students have read their first entirely unaltered piece of Latin prose, I make a point of emphasizing what an extraordinary accomplishment they have just managed. I take some time here to praise their hard work and diligence, and I try to instill in them a sense of pride for the task they have completed. I ask them to think back to the first day of class, when some of them barely knew the difference between nouns and verbs, adjectives and adverbs, and now to compare that day with this. In order to illustrate the point, I often tell them to turn back in their books to Chapter 5 or 6, and have them read off a few sentences or a short story. They are amazed at how things that seemed so difficult for them then, now seem almost ridiculously simple. Encouragement and positive reinforcement are essential at this point. Hard work deserves recognition. After so many hours and so much labor, we have finally realized a goal that we had set for ourselves at the beginning of the year.

Evaluation in this section of the course consists of a few pop-quizzes, always on the previous night's assignment before it has been covered in class. Students are asked to translate a short passage from the assignment and identify and answer a few questions about selected points of grammar and syntax. The final exam is almost entirely based on the reading that we have done at the end of the term. Passages are chosen from those readings, and students are asked to translate some, answer questions about others. Comprehension of passages is also tested. There is always at least one sight-translation passage included on the final, which is annotated according to the class' ability. There may also be some short answer questions about aspects of the passage which we have discussed in class.

During the last days of class, I always offer a few comments encouraging students not to abandon their Latin over the summer months. Of course, with an entire school year behind them, and finals just around the corner, this is the last piece of advice they want to hear at this point. On the other hand, knowledge of a language acquired over such a relatively short span of time will be lost quickly without any practice during the subsequent three months. Thus, I suggest some possibilities for reading over the summer, and beg them to open their books and read, if only for a few minutes, several times per week. I have discovered that those who do so, even only a few times during the entire summer, are at great advantage over those who allow their books to gather cobwebs in the corner.

When we return in the fall, the first few days of intensive review are painful, as students recall how much they have forgotten. Over the years, I have come to the conclusion that it benefits no one to linger very long over review. Some review, of course, is necessary and useful; but too much tends to be counterproductive and the students become bored with it. We move, then, fairly quickly to reading an entire speech by Cicero, several poems by Catullus, portions of another Ciceronian oration, as well as selections from his correspondence. In addition, six short Latin compositions are written by each student. The Catullus interlude is a welcome change of pace, and the class discussion, which emphasizes the interrelationships among the several protagonists involved—Cicero, Catiline, Clodius, Clodia, Catullus, Caelius, et al.—is lively and interesting (for a more detailed account of this course, see May).

The typical assignment, here and in our advanced reading courses, is calculated to take approximately two to three hours of preparation outside of class for every hour of seat time. As I tell my students, I want them to feel the hand of Prof. May on their backs, pushing ever so gently and steadily, not so hard as to make them stumble, but with just enough pressure to encourage them along to higher levels of reading. Our third-semester course is followed by a fourth-semester survey of medieval Latin (a schedule somewhat parallel to our Greek sequence, where we read Attic prose in the third semester, followed by New Testament Greek in the fourth).

Beyond the fourth semester, we offer six semester-long courses, based either in genre (e.g., Roman historians) or author (e.g., Vergil), offered on a rotating three-year cycle. Our purpose here, as in previous semesters, is for our students to read as much Latin as possible, while learning about the author(s) and their cultural milieu. Some reading is done in English, and some secondary literature is examined, but papers and exams still emphasize working with the primary texts in Latin. It is heartening to see that goal—established several semesters before—realized (albeit in lesser and greater degrees) in our students who continue on at this level. Like so many generations before them, they have learned Latin by the grammar-translation method, and are now reading the great Roman authors in their native tongue. Latin words for the day have taught them that *labor omnia vincit*. They have learned Latin *ab ovo* and have now reached *ad astra per aspera*. It is clear to them that *litterae scriptae manent*. The impressive thing is that, after only a few semesters of concentrated effort, they can read the "written word" with a modicum of fluency in the language in which it was composed. They have continued the tradition, and will help insure that the Latin classics remain vital for another generation. *Deo gratias!*

14

Toward Fluency and Accuracy: A Reading Approach To College Latin

JOHN GRUBER-MILLER
Cornell College

Okay, I admit it. I like grammar. I enjoy thinking of ways of explaining it, practicing it, and helping students learn to understand it, even if they are not willing to admit that they like it too. So why would someone like me, who learned Latin in high school with a traditional grammar-oriented approach and who taught college undergraduates from various traditional texts for 10 years, decide to change to a reading approach? Maybe it was frustration at my students' difficulty comprehending Latin passages except through a laborious, one-word-at-a-time, hunt-and-peck method. Maybe it was dissatisfaction that students could rarely read much more than 20–30 lines per night. Maybe it was unhappiness with trying to explain to my class yet another decontextualized sentence composed to practice some particular point of grammar. Or maybe it was disillusionment with the sporadic presentation of Roman culture presented in most traditional texts (for additional discussion of the reading and grammar-translation approaches, see above Chapters 2, 8, 9, and 13).

All these questions and more led me to the realization that I had been teaching students to focus primarily on grammar rather than communicating ideas. I was teaching vocabulary without providing the cultural context that gave those words different nuances than their English equivalents. I was instructing students to read by focusing on individual words instead of larger units of meaning: phrases, clauses, paragraphs. I was stressing grammatical accuracy to the exclusion of fluency. In short, I was presenting a limited view of what it means to know a language. Yet, as one influential definition formulates it (Canale and Swain; Canale), grammar is but one of four components needed for language competence:

Grammatical competence: mastery of a language's linguistic code, including pronunciation, vocabulary, word formation, morphology, and sentence-level syntax.

Sociolinguistic competence: the varieties of language appropriate for different social settings and different audiences, such as the range in tone, register, and dialect exhibited by Pompeian graffiti, Cicero's letters to Atticus, formal decrees of the Senate, Catullus' poetry, and Tacitus' *Annals*.

Discourse competence: the ability to understand and create a unified text through cohesion (e.g., pronouns, transition words, parallel structures) and coherence (e.g., repetition, progression, consistency, genre rules).

Strategic competence: strategies to compensate for a breakdown in communication, such as guessing in context, paying attention to discourse markers, using a dictionary, or making inferences from one's knowledge of the world.

Knowing a language, then, means more than grammatical knowledge. Now I understood why even my best students could usually explain the grammar, but could not always comprehend a text. Their knowledge of grammatical form alone was not enough. They needed experience linking it to function, meaning, and context. They needed to encounter extended discourse and to practice recognizing how a text progresses from one idea to another. They needed strategies for reading Latin fluently as well as accurately. In other words, they needed to treat Latin as a way to communicate and learn from others. I therefore switched to a reading approach and have successfully used it at the college level for several years. Such an approach comes closer to meeting Canale and Swain's criteria for meeting language competence than a traditional approach because "reading" texts emphasize meaning, use extended discourse as a means of comprehensible input, and integrate culture throughout the textbook.

In the rest of this chapter, I want to show some examples of teaching three standard components of a Latin curriculum—grammar, vocabulary, and reading—from a communicative perspective, a perspective that facilitates fluency and accuracy. The activities below have all been used successfully in a college classroom setting while covering most basic Latin grammar in the first two courses of a three-course language requirement.

Teaching Grammar as a Communicative Act

Students learn grammar best when they have the motivation to learn it. And the best motivation is the students' need to express ideas or to solve problems, especially ones that involve an information gap (see, e.g., Loschky and Bley-Vroman). Once they have been motivated to learn a new piece of grammar, students will succeed best if they can move through a series of stages from structured, form-focused, meaningful activities to more open-ended communication. Sequencing grammar exercises helps students make the shift from controlled to the more automatic processing needed for fluency (Higgs and Clifford; McLaughlin; Deagon). Littlewood sketches a continuum of classroom activities that move from a 1) primary focus on form, to 2) focus on form (plus meaning), to 3) focus on meaning (plus form), to 4) primary focus on meaning.

Using Littlewood's framework as a model, I present an example of what a typical grammar lesson would look like, followed by other activities that focus on form and meaning.

Sample Lesson Plan: Comparison of Adjectives

1. *Structured review: setting the context.* Copy the pictures without the captions from the *Oxford Latin Course* (*OLC*: Balme and Morwood 1996–97) 2: 53 onto an overhead transparency. For Picture 1, the instructor asks: *Quae navis est longa* (or *lata, alta, brevis*)? The class then responds, either chorally or individually, as the instructor points to the appropriate ship, *Haec navis est longa; illa navis est lata*, etc. For picture 2, the instructor may ask similar questions or may add, *Qui canis est saevus* (or *tacitus* or *territus*)? And the class responds, *Hic canis est saevus.* Then the teacher asks more open-ended questions about pictures 3–4, such as, *Quis est intellegens* (or *diligens, laetus, iratus, saevus, miser, territus?* etc.). As students respond, the instructor writes the adjectives on the board—providing visual as well as aural reinforcement. Students get involved by pointing from their seats, or coming to the screen, or adding second and third examples of each adjective (e.g., *Horatia et magister sunt intellegentes*). Of course, there might be some friendly argument for students familiar with the *OLC* whether the *magister* exemplifies *intellegentia*!

2. *Grammar presentation within a meaningful context (e.g. using pictures).* After students have reviewed adjectives, they are now ready to be introduced to the new structure, comparative forms. Begin by focusing on regular comparison first. Returning to the first two pictures, point to the appropriate ship, saying, *Haec navis est longa.* The class repeats in unison. Then ask, *Quae navis est longior?* After someone responds, the teacher sums up, *Haec navis est longior quam illa.* The class repeats the sentence. Then the teacher points to the other ship, following the same pattern, *Haec navis est lata. Quae navis est latior? Haec navis est latior quam illa.* The class repeats the answer. After similar statements about picture 2, substituting *saevus/territus* for *longa/brevis*, it is time to write the model sentences on the board.

3a. *Structured practice: focus on form (and meaning)—nominative singular.* Now the teacher invites students to come to the front and point to the appropriate people in pictures 3–4: Describe picturam. *Quis est intellegentior? diligentior?* etc. After each student describes the picture, the rest of the class repeats the sentence.

3b. *Pair work.* After at least one or two sentences for each picture have been formulated, then it is time for students to break up into pairs to describe the pictures. Using the adjectives written on the board as a prompt, the students alternate asking and answering questions. The sentence patterns on the blackboard help those students who might be unsure of the new structure while the instructor circulates from group to group to answer questions. If there seems to be general understanding, then it is time to move on to the next exercise. If not, it would be beneficial for the class to re-form as a group and to review the pictures again, this time by asking the less confident students to form comparisons after first hearing some examples from the more confident students. Pointing to the model sentences on the board or adding to them as students are speaking may help, too.

4. *Structured practice (sentence-builders).* On the overhead, place a new transparency that allows students to create sentences, using all three genders:

hic vir		altus		
		brevis		
haec femina		latus		
		laetus		ille
hic mons	est	felix	quam	illa
		tristis		illud
haec urbs		gravis		
		tacitus		
hoc flumen		saevus		
		audax		
hoc bellum		miser		

After showing the class how to create sentences—e.g., *Hic mons est altior quam ille; hoc flumen est altius quam illud*—group the students in pairs and ask them to take turns creating sentences.

5. *Grammar presentation: nominative plural.* To introduce the nominative plural, repeat steps 2–4, this time using new pictures which have pairs or groups of people, once again without captions. Picture 2 from *OLC* 2: 12 and pictures 2–3 from *OLC* 2: 25 would be suitable. Encourage the class to articulate which declension comparative adjectives take their endings from.

6. *Grammar presentation: irregular comparison (using classroom objects).* Employ the same statement-question-answer-write approach to introduce irregular comparison, only this time use classroom objects instead of pictures. Begin, for example, by comparing the size of two books: *Hic liber est magnus.* The class repeats in unison. Then picking up another, smaller book, say, *Hic liber est parvus.* Then ask, *Qui liber est maior?* After students have answered correctly, write the comparisons on the board. The same can be done to introduce *melior* and *peior*, this time comparing Vergil's *Aeneid* to a sleazy Gothic novel or an IRS tax booklet! Finally, to reinforce the new forms, ask students to compare other objects in the room, e.g., paper *(charta)*, notebooks *(tabula)*, bookbags *(capsula)*, pictures *(pictura)*, and so forth.

7. *Sentence builders: accusative case.* Sample sentence: *Numquam matrem fortiorem vidi quam hanc.*

	nautam	paratus			
		territus			
	militem	commotus			
		gravis			
	filiam	fortis	vidi		hunc
numquam		pulcher	cognovi	quam	hanc
	matrem	miser	audivi		hoc
		bonus			
	consilium	malus			
		parvus			
	onus	magnus			

8. *Focus on meaning (plus form).* Look out the classroom window or, better yet, take a brief walk across campus and ask students to write four to five comparisons. While the objects are still in view, students in small groups share their comparisons.

9. *Focus on meaning.* For homework, ask students to write a short paragraph describing their families (or roommates), asking them to make comparisons. The next day, in groups of two or three, students will share their paragraphs. After each member of the group has received feedback from the rest of the group, select students may share their descriptions orally with the entire class.

Certainly this is not the only way to introduce comparison of adjectives, but this sequence is one that I have used effectively in class. Since each activity above usually takes only a few minutes, the entire process can easily fit into one class period of 50–60 minutes. Yet in that time students have been introduced to a wide array of forms (regular and irregular adjectives, all three genders, singular and plural, different cases) in a step-by-step sequence that progresses from specific forms to more open-ended practice where the emphasis is on producing meaning, not simply on form. Since students have the opportunity to use and practice the new structures at each step, they begin the process of internalizing the new grammar immediately. As they continue to work with comparison over the coming days in other communicative settings, they can integrate it into their developing understanding of Latin grammar, and the new forms gradually become more automatic.

The superlative degree can be introduced in much the same way, with pictures or objects either inside or outside of the classroom. Once the superlative has been introduced, it is fun to ask groups of three good-natured students to stand in front of the class and ask the rest of the students to compare them. Another good review is to read a story such as *Tres Ursi* (Osburn 1995a), using comparatives wherever possible. Alternatively, after the students have heard the story, they could rewrite it with comparatives.

I now present a few more examples of other types of activities that focus on form and meaning. See Ur and Celce-Murcia and Hillis for more grammar activities, and Abernathy, et al., for more ways to use visuals in the classroom.

Other Exercises That Focus on Form (Plus Meaning)

1. *Acting out verbs.* Two students are asked to leave the room. While they are in the hallway, the rest of the students each choose a different verb to act out. For example, one student "stands up," another "sleeps," while a group of two "throw a ball." When the two students return, they must describe in Latin what each student or group is doing. The students who are acting confirm or deny the description. This activity is good for practicing most tenses of the indicative and participles (e.g., *Discipulum dormientem video*). Other activities based on TPR (Total Physical Response) can be found in Strasheim (1987) and Salerno.

2. *Role-playing.* To practice complementary infinitives, for example, one student takes the role of a young child who wants to do something and the other a parent or older sibling who says "no." *Materials needed*: multiple sets of cue cards with Latin verbs listed on them. *Instructions*: the student who has the cue cards takes the part of the young child while the other acts the part of the parent or older sibling. Using the card as a cue, the "child" will form sentences, based on the pattern *cupio* + infinitive phrase, e.g., *Cupio nunc cenare*. The "parent" responds, *Non debes nunc cenare*. As the students become more confident, they may expand the response, e.g., *Noli cenare: debes in agro laborare*. After students become acquainted with role-playing, they may write scripts and take the part of various mythological characters or historical figures. At this point, the role-playing becomes an activity focused more on meaning than on form.

3. *Sentence combining.* Give students pairs of sentences that repeat information or can easily be combined. This technique works best when all the sentences revolve around one particular cultural context. The sentences below focus on a Roman harbor. Students may solve these sentences in pairs or as a class. *Instructions*: combine the two sentences using the appropriate form of the relative pronoun.

Quintus Roma venit et naves spectavit. Illae portum intrabant.
Maximus erat portus. In eo plurimae naves stabant.
Ille nautas conspexit. Illi plurimas amphoras vini in navem ferebant.

This exercise not only focuses on the form of the relative pronoun, but also helps students understand word order and syntax as they learn where the relative clause may stand in a Latin sentence in relation to its antecedent.

4. *Understanding authorial choices: passive voice.* In a passage with several examples of the passive voice, ask students first to identify the passive

constructions, and then explain why the author chose the passive instead of the active voice. Reasons may include, for example, to emphasize the subject/topic, to emphasize the action, or to de-emphasize the agent. An exercise such as this will make it clear that the passive is not simply an inverted equivalent of the active voice, but is used in different contexts for different reasons.

Other Activities That Focus on Meaning (Plus Form)

1. *Interviewing members of the class: describing a typical day.* After students have learned expressions of time, they are asked to circulate throughout the room asking at least five people what they did, when they did it, and how long it took. Some questions that might be asked are:

Quid heri fecisti?
Quando surrexisti?
Quando cenavisti?
Tene exercuisti? Quando te exercebas? Quamdiu?
Musicamne audivisti? Quando audiebas? Quamdiu?
Quando studebas? Quid studebas? Quamdiu linguam Latinam studebas?
Quando cubitum iisti?

Students take notes and then report to the class or a group how a particular person spent the day. Alternatively, students could compare notes to discover similarities among students (e.g., Mike and Jen went to bed at the same time!). This activity is a good way for students to grasp Roman concepts of time. The interview can also be used to ask students about family, friends, likes and dislikes, dorm rooms, activities over the weekend, etc. When students first learn to interview, it is important to limit the number of questions asked. Once students feel more comfortable, the activity can become more open-ended.

2. *Problem solving: drawing a picture. Materials needed*: drawings of stick people (happy/sad, tall/short, big/small, intelligent, brave, etc.). *Instructions*: divide students into pairs. One student receives a picture card. Without showing the picture to the other student, she describes the person on her card (in Latin) while the other tries to draw a picture of what she hears described.

CONTEXTUALIZING VOCABULARY

Another traditional element of language teaching, vocabulary, can be enlivened and made more meaningful by highlighting connections between words. Research on reading stresses that vocabulary is one of the major stumbling blocks to fluency. Rote memorization of vocabulary lists, however, is one of the least effective ways for students to learn vocabulary. Vivian Cook summarizes research on learning and teaching vocabulary by offering several principles, paraphrased here with the addition of Latin examples:

1) Teach basic-level, picturable words first (e.g., *arbor*). Only after they have been mastered should the student try to learn more abstract, superordinate words (e.g., *planta*) or more concrete subordinate terms (e.g., *ilex*).

2) It is not so much how frequently words are encountered, but how deeply processed that matters most in remembering vocabulary. Processing the meanings of words within the whole meaning of the sentence is a deeper level than repeating words as strings of sounds.

3) Words need to be learned in relation to the entire cultural context. The word *vinum* in Latin has much different sense for Romans than "wine" does for Americans. Who drinks, on what occasions, and for what purposes each varies from culture to culture.

4) Knowing a word means not only how a word is defined but also how it functions in a sentence. For example, *omnes* may stand alone or may modify a noun. When it modifies a noun, it will usually precede it and the noun will agree with it in gender, number, and case—unlike English which may use a partitive construction with it (all of the people). A verb like *ambulo* requires a subject, but never an object—unlike English (walk the dog). And verbs like *audio* create multiple expectations: *audio* may have an object (*Canem audivit*), an indirect statement (*Audivit matrem ad casam advenisse*), or an indirect question (*Audivit cur mater ad casam rediiset*—see Lawall, et al., *Ecce Romani* 2: 240–41, for an exercise on creating syntactic expectations for verbs like *audio*.)

Activities for Contextualizing Vocabulary

1. *Visit Quintus' house: understanding words based on their component parts.* On the board or the overhead, draw two houses with arrows showing various stages of the journey. The trip could focus on compounds of *eo* or other compound verbs used to describe traveling. Compounds of *eo*: *exit, it, adit, init, ascendit, manet, descendit, exit, redit*. Verbs of motion: *discedit, procedit, advenit, intrat, ascendit, manet, descendit, exit, redit*. *Variations*: change who is going (person or number) or when they are going (tense).

2. *A visit to the baths: understanding words in their cultural context.* On the board or overhead, place a floor plan of a Roman or Pompeian bath complex. After the teacher describes the visit or students have read a passage about the baths from their text, divide students into pairs to describe what they would do (change clothes, swim, lie in the water, exercise, converse) and see (friends, vendors) and hear (shouts, arguments) at the baths. At the heart of their description, they would link different activities with different rooms of the baths, and understand the progression from warm to hot to cold rooms. This exercise can be adapted to the level of the students and their knowledge of vocabulary. It can be spoken in pairs (if relatively simple) or enacted in the classroom (by dividing the classroom up into different areas of a bath-complex).

3. *Odd one out: recognizing perfect stems.* Identify which word has a

perfect stem that does not belong to the group—*facio, fugio, venio, lego, dormio. Answer: dormio,* because it forms its perfect by adding a *-v-.*

4. *Semantic mapping: creating visual connections among words.* The teacher chooses a word or concept and asks students to brainstorm other words connected to it. The words are then arrranged visually on the board or on the overhead to show relationships. The semantic map below is designed to present graphically how Roman elections work by dividing the participants into recognizable groups and by displaying how supporters and opponents act and think about the candidates. For example, before the election the candidates have supporters and opponents, but at the election certain individuals take on the additional role of citizen. How they act (and feel) about the candidates depends on which role they play. Other semantic maps might be arranged by asking questions (who, what, where, when, how, why) or by representing different locations (spatial) or by emphasizing chronological stages (temporal).

This technique is most effective when it links new vocabulary with words and concepts already known. It is also more effective when it does not introduce too many new words or concepts. Besides being a good way to review old and introduce new vocabulary, it may be used to preview a reading passage or prepare for a writing assignment.

SEMANTIC MAPPING: *COMITIA* (based on *OLC,* Chapter 17)

Before the election
ubi in foro, in taberna, in triviis

	candidatus	
qualis	magistratum petere	**qualis**
bonus/optimus	orationes habere	malus/pessimus
gravis	omnia promittere	putidus
fautores		**adversarii**
orationem audire	**COMITIA**	candidato non credere
candidatum laudare		orationem (non) audire
candidatum comitare		candidatum vituperare

At the election
ubi in foro

cives
suffragium ferre
magistratus creare

5. *Facts in five: making personal connections* (Boyle). Five letters of the alphabet are chosen. Then three, four, or five categories are selected (e.g., school, family, baths, farming, love). Students are put in groups and given a strict time limit (five minutes) to come up with words of each category that begin with the letters chosen. The first team to complete all the categories (or have the most filled in when time is called) wins. Once students understand the game, students may choose the letters and the categories.

	ludus	familia	balnea	agricultura	amor
a					
c					
p					
s					
v					

See Gairns and Redman, Nation, and Boyle for further vocabulary activities.

READING FOR FLUENCY AND ACCURACY

The final area we need to rethink is reading. Traditionally, Latin teachers have focused on the text to the near exclusion of other factors. According to the way that many of us were trained, reading is a matter of recognizing words, endings, and sentence-level syntax so that we might decode the meaning of a text accurately. Such a text-driven model, known as bottom-up processing, assumes that a passage can be understood by building up the meaning from the simplest elements, by processing the letters into phonemes, phonemes into morphemes, morphemes into words, and words into sentences.

Such a model encourages word-for-word reading that emphasizes the smallest units of meaning within a text rather than the overall coherence of a text. It also leaves out the readers and their general knowledge about the world, about Roman culture, and about larger discourse patterns. Readers, in fact, bring to the text at least two types of background knowledge: content schemata and formal schemata. Content schemata refer to background knowledge acquired through life experiences, topic familiarity, and cultural knowledge. Formal schemata include such elements as the recognition of genres, rhetorical conventions, and patterns for structuring texts (Carrell and Eisterhold). Such a reader-driven model is known as a top-down processing model. Nowadays, most researchers describe reading as an interactive process in which readers depend upon their expectations and previous understanding of the topic to make guesses about the meaning of a text, and utilize their understanding of the words and morphemes on the page to verify their understanding. Top-down and bottom-up processes interact so that gaps in information at one level can be filled in by information from another level. Swaffar, et al., and Barnett review recent research on reading processes.

An analogy may help. Reading in a foreign language is like viewing developing film or reading a palimpsest. Only after successive viewings over a period of time does the picture or the text become clear. Only by a process of activating our prior knowledge, skimming the text for the gist, scanning it for specific information, and re-reading it for more detail do we fully understand what it is all about. In other words, to return to Canale and Swain's definition of communicative competence, efficient readers depend not only on their understanding of grammar and vocabulary (grammatical), but also on background knowledge of culture (sociolinguistic) and how a text is put together (discourse). Just as importantly, they need an array of strategies (strategic) to help them understand the text when the "palimpsest" is still not clear.

In what follows I would like to outline a process (based on Phillips and Rusciolelli) for teaching reading that encourages students not to rely on a word-for-word translation as their only reading strategy, but to become more flexible readers who use many strategies to read a text. The format for teaching a particular passage would typically contain pre-reading activities (activating prior knowledge), skimming and scanning practice, intensive reading (including guessing words in context), and post-reading activities (summarizing, transferring, integrating knowledge), so that students would gain practice not only in specific strategies, but also realize the importance of reading a text several times to come to a more complete understanding of it (for more reading activities, see Grellet, Phillips, and Barnett).

Pre-reading

In addition to the activities listed below, semantic mapping, as discussed earlier, is a good way to introduce the cultural context and vocabulary of a passage to help readers activate or create schemata with which to understand the text.

1. *Brainstorming: activating prior knowledge.* After introducing the topic of the text, ask students what they think might appear in the text or what they wanted to know about the topic. As the students respond (in Latin or English), the instructor lists the items on the board. The same can be done regarding text genre (e.g., a Pompeian election announcement, funerary epitaph, dedicatory inscription, battle scene, epigram of Catullus or Martial, *exordium* of an oration). Questions to be asked might focus on how the genre organizes information (what to expect at the beginning, middle, and end), what type of people inhabit this genre, or how close its events are tied to reality.

2. *Examining the title/pictures: inferring content.* Students read the title and look at the pictures (if some are presented with the text) to make predictions about the content or structure of the passage.

3. *Reading the first paragraph: making predictions.* After reading only the first paragraph, students, either as a class or in small groups, make predictions about the rest of the text. Predictions could focus on topic, characters, events, information, or genre.

Skimming

All the preceding activities lead directly into skimming for the gist of the passage. After students skim the text (a time limit may be needed), they verify their predictions, confirm the information on the board or in their notebooks, and add more ideas based on their initial reading. If the passage is quite long (several pages), students may try other skimming activities, which may include reading only the first sentence of every paragraph or selected paragraphs or only the first and last paragraphs.

Scanning

Scanning is a different skill from skimming. It is designed to look for specific information. It is therefore a good technique for a second reading of a passage. Here are some of the ways to scan a passage: 1) The instructor writes the main idea of each paragraph in mixed order and students read to put the ideas in sequence. 2) The class chooses the most interesting ideas and searches for details. 3) Individuals or pairs are assigned information to look for and to report to the rest of the class. 4) For a reading that recounts a journey, the class fills out an itinerary grid that lists basic information such as where, when, how long a stay. 5) Students may also look for words which signal overall text structure (e.g., chronological, comparison and contrast, description, argumentation—see Barnett, 202–03, for further suggestions on how to analyze text structure).

Intensive Reading

The third reading is slower because it is designed to understand the text in more detail, though not necessarily every detail. Two areas to work on during the intensive reading stage are for students to learn how to guess word meanings from context and to recognize cohesive devices and connecting words in order to predict meaning.

1. *Contextual guessing* (Rusciolelli). Begin by asking students to cover any marginal glosses. As students read at their own pace, they underline unknown words and then choose the ones that they think are the most fundamental for understanding the text. Because there is not enough time in class to discuss all unknown words and because efficient readers do not look up every word, students need to learn to make a conscious decision about which words are most important. The class may vote on which words are the most crucial for comprehension. Next, the class follows several steps to guess the meaning. First, identify the part of speech, divide the word into its component parts (prefix and base), and check to see if there is an English cognate. Next, examine the context of the passage, asking questions such as who, what, where, and when to help remind students of the context. Refer to the unknown vocabulary word with filler words like "someone," "something," or "someplace" in order to maintain the flow of thought. Elicit numerous guesses so that all students have a chance to learn the process. After several guesses, the teacher either confirms the correct meaning or directs the students to use a

dictionary. A variation on contextual guessing is to have pairs of students select three unknown words from the text. After they have gone through the steps in the guessing process, they report to the rest of the class their findings and explain how they reached their conclusions.

2. *Recognizing discourse markers.* The little words that organize a text (pronouns, demonstratives, adverbs, conjunctions) are crucial in helping readers construe the meaning of longer texts. There are a number of activities that would help students recognize these discourse markers. One activity is to ask students to read one to three paragraphs, note when there is a change in subject, and show what evidence they used to make their decision. Then they could classify the various possibilities (e.g., concrete noun, pronoun, person of the verb). Another is to have the pronouns and demonstratives already underlined in a section of a passage, and ask students to identify the words or ideas to which they refer. Students could then list the reasons for making the decision (proximity, gender, number, case, logic of the context). A third is to ask students, every time they come to a new connecting word, to pause and predict what they expect to read next. They might then list each connector according to its function (e.g., cause, consequence, sequence, concession, opposition).

Post-reading

There are many ways to check student comprehension of a text and to help make it more meaningful to them. To ascertain to what extent the students understand a text, the teacher could ask them to summarize it in Latin, draw a picture (or series of pictures) of the event(s) described, recall the text in English, or re-enact it through pantomime, drama, dialogue, or role-playing. Students can also go beyond the text by re-writing a scene, authoring a dialogue between characters, or writing a new beginning or ending for a text. Students may respond to the content of a text that focuses on a mythological character or historical figure by writing a character sketch of the person or by inventing an interview with the character (or his spouse or children). With texts that have many characters, groups of students may want to compose riddles ending with the phrase, *Quis sum?* to see if the rest of the class can identify the character. To return to Littlewood's list of types of activities, the primary focus in all these post-reading activities is on communicating meaning. Thus, they make an ideal way to end a chapter in a textbook, a unit of a course, or a section of a much longer text. Students are reminded that they are learning Latin to communicate ideas and feelings, and they can respond personally to the content of what they are reading.

In the preceding pages, I have tried to sketch out how to help college and university students read Latin fluently and accurately. I have found that by employing an incremental approach to grammar that moves from form-focused activities to more open-ended assignments that emphasize meaning, students begin to make grammar more automatic and understand it within larger patterns of discourse. By utilizing an approach to vocabulary that puts it in its semantic, cultural, and syntactic context, students better comprehend the meaning of a word within Latin discourse. By teaching reading within a sequence of pre-reading, skimming and scanning, intensive reading, and post-reading activities, students acquire the habit of reading a text more than once and also master an array of strategies for reading Latin. Yet fluency and accuracy are not the result of just a year or two of study. Choosing appropriate intermediate texts (including those in the Longman Latin Readers series, or narratives such as Hyginus' mythological tales, Eutropius' histories, stories from the Latin vulgate, and the romance *Apollonius, King of Tyre*) and continuing to work on grammar and vocabulary and reading at all levels of the undergraduate major are essential for Latin students to keep making progress in becoming the fluent, accurate readers we all hoped to become when we first began learning Latin.

15

Undergraduate Classics
At the University of Georgia

CHARLES PLATTER
University of Georgia

INTRODUCTION

My purpose here is to give a partial account of undergraduate Classics at
the University of Georgia (UGA), a program that has so far resisted some of the
trends that have weakened Classics departments across the nation. I will
concentrate on two basic aspects of our program: advising and mentoring, which
I have followed closely in my role as Undergraduate Coordinator (1990–97),
and curriculum development, a process to which the entire faculty has devoted
much energy (for an examination of other aspects of college-level Latin and
Classics, see LaFleur 1992).

The premise of this essay is that developing and promoting successful Latin
and Classics program remains a possibility in the last days of the 20th century.
This premise requires some justification. After all, one might have imagined
that such dinosaurs had already succumbed, either to the ahistorical "present-
ism" of our electronic media and computer cultures, or to one of the other
economic forces that threaten to undermine the tradition of critical thinking in
the humanities curriculum by replacing it with more "practical" courses
designed to transmit information but not to educate. Indeed, the imminent
demise of Classics as a course of study has long been feared by those within the
profession and all but assumed by those without. Recent articles in *Lingua
Franca* (Damrosch) and the *New York Times Magazine* (Wills) have registered
surprise that the discipline was still in one piece. Nor, despite some very
positive evidence to the contrary (see, e.g., LaFleur 1997), is the disappearance
of Classics simply a remote possibility. Classics suffered greatly in the 1960s
and 70s when enrollments sunk to all-time lows. Many programs were
eliminated or merged with other disciplines in departments of foreign languages
or literature. Even now it is rare that a year goes by when I do not hear of the
pending elimination of a Classics program.

It is in the face of such realities that I offer the following reflections, which, I should add, do not aspire to comprehensiveness in any form. Without a doubt many of the things that we have found successful at UGA would not be effective at institutions with different characteristics or educational missions. By the same token, much of what we do *is* transferable. I hope that one result of this essay will be a steady stream of advice, suggestions, and criticism that will allow us to improve our program at UGA. It is precisely this kind of ongoing group effort that has allowed our department to prosper as it has, and which will offer Classics the best chance to adapt itself to the demands of the new millennium.

UGA is a land and sea grant institution and the primary comprehensive research university for the University System of Georgia, a conglomerate of nearly 40 institutions and research centers governed by a Board of Regents in Atlanta. After several decades of growth, the enrollment stands at about 31,000 students with plans to increase that number to 35,000. This has come about partly as the result of a steadily rising population in Georgia, particularly in the Atlanta metropolitan area. Recent years, however, have seen the introduction and expansion of the extremely successful Hope Scholarship Program, funded by the Georgia State Lottery and providing four years of paid education to all Georgia high school graduates who have a B average in college-preparatory courses. In addition to increasing enrollment, the Hope Scholarship has led to a significant increase in admissions standards and a tendency for exceptional students, who previously migrated to elite universities in other states, to remain in Georgia. Thus the student population in general is quite strong, with a significant percentage of exceptional students.

The Department of Classics at UGA consists of 13 tenured and tenure-track faculty members (up three since the early 1980s) and two full-time instructors. The undergraduate curriculum includes three major areas: Latin, Greek, and Classical Culture (with no required language component), and a Classical Archaeology concentration (requiring a minimum of five courses in either Greek or Latin); minors are available in Greek, Latin, and Classical Culture. Latin and Greek majors must take an introductory course in either Greek or Roman civilization, depending on the major, as well as eight advanced courses, at least five of which are advanced author or genre courses. Up to three classes may be in related fields (ancient philosophy, ancient history and religion, art history, linguistics, etc.). The Classical Culture major requires introductory courses in both Greek and Roman civilization, as well as eight advanced classes, at least five of which must be advanced Classical Culture classes focusing on individual authors and genres in translation, archaeology, and various special topics. Up to three classes may be in related fields, just as in the Latin and Greek majors.

Double majors are encouraged by allowing students to complete the elementary civilization component and the five advanced courses required for each major, while requiring them to complete the three related courses only once. In effect, then, students completing double majors get a three course discount over students pursuing two unrelated majors (e.g., 13 advanced classes required for a Latin/Greek major versus 16 for Latin/Biology). This policy has been very effective in encouraging Greek enrollments, especially since students who enter UGA with strong Latin backgrounds can begin taking advanced Latin classes at an early point in their careers, and therefore can also complete a Greek major without special hardship.

In addition to the undergraduate curriculum, an M.A. is available in Latin, Greek, and Classics (both Latin and Greek required), as well as a B.S. Ed., M.Ed., Ed.S., and Ph.D. degrees in Latin Language Education, offered in collaboration with the UGA College of Education. The department sponsors a summer Studies Abroad Program in Rome, the UGA Excavations at Carthage, and a Classics Summer Institute designed especially for teachers pursuing certification or our "summers-only" M.A. degree, and also offering, in alternate summers, an intensive introduction to Attic Greek; all three of these programs are open to undergraduate majors and minors, as well as graduate students. The undergraduate Classics program has grown steadily, from a total of about 20 majors and minors in the mid-1980s to between 70 and 80 in recent years; typically, about half of these students are concentrating in Latin, 40% in Classical Culture, and 10% in Greek.

The success of Classics at UGA is attributable to a number of factors, but, most importantly, it is the cumulative result of consistent individual contributions made by faculty members, along with strong support from the college and university administration. Generally speaking, we aim to create on the departmental level the same kind of chemistry that exists in small private liberal arts colleges and probably does not conform to the stereotype of a large public university, where anonymity is the rule rather than the exception. The aspects of our program that have contributed to its strength in recent years, however, have been effective as much because of their consistent application as for their intrinsic importance. For example, all majors and minors have individual mailboxes in the department. This has the effect of not only establishing better publicity for departmental events but also of getting students into the habit of visiting the department regularly whether they are taking classes or not. We have a departmental library and reading room, to which majors and minors are provided keys and which serves as the meeting place for our very active chapter of Eta Sigma Phi, the national Classics honorary society. As a result, the Classics department becomes one of the relatively few domesticated spaces on a large campus where students feel comfortable just hanging out. In addition, the department, alone, and in cooperation with other UGA departments, the Archaeological Institute of America, and local colleges and universities, sponsors a wide range of conferences, lectures, and theatrical productions (20–30 yearly). The result is a particularly rich blend of offerings, which, in conjunction with our regular programs and facilities, make the Classics Department a very congenial place for students to be.

ADVISING AND MENTORING

It is difficult to overestimate the importance of advising for the health of our program. No one sees as many of the majors and minors (as well as prospective majors and minors) on a daily basis as the Undergraduate Coordinator. Consequently, he or she is in the position of speaking to students on behalf of the department on a wide variety of issues, both trivial and serious, professional and personal. Flexibility is a precious commodity here; certain issues, however, are very predictable. Despite the obvious sophistication of students in some areas, they generally have little idea of how to go about making a career choice, particularly if that choice involves Classics: How do I find out about high-school teaching? What can you do with a Classics major? How do I know if I want to go to graduate school? What are the best programs? When should I take the GRE? What should I do about that quarter I got two F's and a D? Is the job market really that bad? It is not necessary for the advisor to know the answers to all of these questions. Indeed, because of the subjective nature of some of them, and due to the limited experience of any advisor, students are counseled to seek out multiple opinions, a process that has the salutary effect of involving additional faculty members in the experience of every undergraduate. Moreover, if students believe that they can get reliable advice (or at least an attentive hearing) from the coordinator they will take advantage of the opportunity. This aspect of the position has its obvious drawbacks, especially when a knock on the office door represents one more obstacle to the grading of papers, or completion of that overdue chapter or book review. Nevertheless, despite the considerable time investment required, the kind of familiarity that we offer students is a clear advantage to the program, especially on a campus the size of UGA, where some departments have upwards of 900 majors and advisors cannot realistically deal with the students as individuals. Our assessment data (discussed below) strikingly confirm the point that this aspect of the department is viewed by students as a great advantage vis-à-vis other departments at UGA. Like everyone else, I too look forward to the day when we can teach Elementary Greek as a lecture class to a group of 300, but until that happens Classics departments should look to advising as a potential source of strength to the program, both as a vehicle for the recruitment of individual students, and as a means of retaining students who have sought us out on their own.

Assessment

The advising procedure has also been used to solicit student evaluation of the Classics program. Since 1992 we have conducted written "exit interviews" with graduating seniors as part of an ongoing self-assessment study. Students who are nearing graduation are required by the University to obtain from their major departments certification that they have completed all the requirements for the major. Each student in Classics is required to make an appointment with the Undergraduate Coordinator to check the certification letter for accuracy and to complete the department's assessment questionnaire. The usefulness of this method for data collection is obvious. Instead of being tempted to ignore a questionnaire found in the mailbox, students are asked to fill them out on the spot. Thus the amount of information collected is substantially larger than would otherwise be the case. At the time of this exit interview, students are also given a second form, identical to the first except that it is anonymous (the basic form has a place for the student's name and permanent address). The purpose of this second form is to allow students the opportunity to respond without having to divulge their identity. Students are asked to return the second form (it is of course optional) to the departmental secretary, who transcribes the information and eventually destroys the forms.

The data collected help us to plan for the future. We especially solicit information regarding shortcomings, information that we use, when appropriate, to improve our program. For example, a familiar theme in some of our early exit interviews was the relatively small number of courses offered during the regular academic year. In response to this criticism, and helped by rising enrollments, we have increased the number of advanced undergraduate classes offered over the past several years (as discussed below). Our assessment plans also call for students to be surveyed five years after their graduation and asked to comment in retrospect on their experience with the department; an alumni address list is maintained for this purpose, as well as for mailing our annual department newsletter, *Classics at Georgia* (which serves as a medium both for keeping alumni informed and for fundraising).

Faculty Mentoring

Traditionally, advising and mentoring in the Classics department at UGA have been the job of the Undergraduate Coordinator, with formal advising taking place during a two- to three-week period in the middle of every quarter, and mentoring all year round on a less formal basis. Recently, however, we have implemented a new system, involving all faculty in counseling majors while retaining most of the traditional structure of formal academic advising. Each of our 13 tenured and tenure-track faculty members have about six students to mentor each quarter. They meet with students individually, assess their interests, provide general academic information, and offer career advice. After these meetings the students sign up for an official advising appointment with the Undergraduate Coordinator, who then coordinates the mentor's advice with the various requirements at the department, college, and university levels.

This system has the salutary effect of increasing faculty involvement with our majors and reducing the Undergraduate Coordinator's heavy workload, without actually requiring the general faculty to be fluent with the minutiae of core requirements, graduation certification, and the like.

CURRICULUM DEVELOPMENT AND RECRUITMENT

Another important reason for the vitality of Classics at UGA is the ongoing interest and flexible attitude toward curriculum development exhibited by an active faculty. This attitude has allowed us to improve steadily the overall quality of the program, take advantage of opportunities for recruitment, and respond to student suggestions. Faculty have also taken the initiative by participating in special academic programs both inside and outside of the regular curriculum that promise to have a positive effect on the recruitment of majors and public perception of the department.

A substantial percentage of our majors and minors come from Atlanta area schools, many of which have excellent Latin programs and regularly produce students who arrive at UGA well prepared in Latin. A majority of our majors are nevertheless recruited from students already enrolled at UGA and come to the department with no particular training in the discipline. A major source of recruitment has been our series of lower-division (freshman-sophomore) Classics-in-translation courses which fulfill the literature requirement for the College of Arts and Sciences and some of the other colleges within the university: Greek Culture, Roman Culture, and Classical Mythology. These courses are limited to 36 students and require at least one significant writing assignment. The precise content of the classes is left to the discretion of the teacher, although Greek Culture typically has the *Iliad* on its reading list, Classical Mythology the *Odyssey*, and Roman culture the *Aeneid*. Honors versions of these classes are also regularly taught, with registration restricted to students enrolled in the Honors Program and class size limited to 15. These classes have been very popular over the years and have contributed greatly to our program.

Many majors and minors have also been recruited through the lower-division Latin program. The introductory component consists of four classes scheduled strategically to allow students as much flexibility as possible, with the succeeding course in the sequence always offered the following quarter. Thus, Latin 101 is taught fall and winter quarter (in a total of 9 or 10 sections), Latin 102 winter and spring, Latin 103 fall and spring, and Latin 204 winter and fall. In addition, the department has developed Latin 304: Vergil, which is open only to intermediate students and taught winter and spring quarters to accommodate those who have just completed Latin 204. This course seeks to help students bridge the always-difficult gap between elementary and advanced language courses, some of which are split-level classes taken by graduate students as well. Upper division Latin students choose from four classes yearly. Here, too, they are protected from registering for a class beyond their level of preparation by our requirement that graduate students who have passed the M.A. translation exam in Latin and who wish to enroll in a Latin class must sign up for the 800-level seminar offered each quarter rather than for one of the split-level courses reserved primarily for advanced undergraduates.

The elementary program has been an effective tool for recruiting majors for other reasons as well. Among them is the limited use made of graduate teaching assistants for elementary Latin instruction (just over 40% in recent years). Further, with only rare exceptions in the case of extremely experienced candidates, TAs are not allowed into the classroom before taking Latin 777: Latin Teaching Apprenticeship. This program covers all aspects of Latin instruction, from the dynamics of teaching and classroom management, to the construction of exams that are useful and fair. The apprenticeship program also gives prospective TAs an opportunity to teach several classes under the supervision of experienced faculty members and to benefit from both faculty and student feedback. By the time they are entrusted with their own classes, then, they are extremely well-prepared. Student evaluations are very high and Classics TAs are frequently honored by the University for their proficiency in the classroom.

Several aspects of this scenario are changing, with a potential long-range impact on recruitment. First, with our recent conversion to semesters, a new core curriculum has been instituted which has only a one-course literature requirement, vs. two in the past, and a slight reduction in the foreign language requirement as well. At the same time, however, the department has taken the opportunity offered by semester conversion to develop courses of interdisciplinary interest. For example, one aspect of our program that has been under-represented in our lower-division offerings is archaeology. In conjunction with the Department of Anthropology we have introduced Introduction to Classical Archaeology, a class which should appeal to majors and non-majors alike, and which we expect will eventually be accepted as satisfying part of the Social Science requirement under the new core curriculum. In addition, and again in conjunction with the Department of Anthropology, a new Program in Archaeological Studies has been proposed, which, if approved, will further increase the visibility of the archaeology program and stimulate interest in the Classics department as a whole. Thus while the cumulative effect of the semester conversion process is impossible to predict, the process has forced us to think about our introductory curriculum in an active way. As a result Classics at UGA may look quite different in 10 years than it does today, while remaining strong or stronger.

Other opportunities for recruitment have been explored by members of our faculty outside the standard curriculum. For example, the department has participated for decades in the Georgia Junior Classical League annual convention, contributing a wide range of tests as well as judging student projects. Faculty have also participated in an initiative developed by the College of Arts and Sciences called the Franklin College Outreach Program, which asks participants to offer one or more lecture topics suitable for general audiences, sending the list of proposed topics to schools and other organizations around the state. If a topic is requested, the speaker either travels to deliver the talk in person, or, on occasion, gives the presentation via a two-way television hook-up. The result is a greater awareness across the state that Classics at Georgia is active, not just in esoteric research, but in ways that the community can understand and value.

Recent curricular developments also are potential recruiting vehicles. An example is the requirement that incoming freshmen take a one-hour-per-week seminar on a topic of their choice. The seminar I have offered for the first year is called Mythology and Popular Culture. The seminar will attempt to show students a way of looking at the ancient world that is neither scornful nor adulatory, the premise being that mythology does not operate in a cultural vacuum and responds to the varying existential pressures and needs experienced by a given society at a particular time. Such a premise will allow us to look at various ancient and contemporary phenomena using the same template: for example, the increasing popularity of mystery cults in both the Greek and Roman worlds on the one hand, and the continued interest in millennial prophecy, UFO's, and urban legends on the other. My goals in designing this seminar in this way are twofold: to recruit majors to a department that will always be in need of them and to present Greek and Roman civilizations to an audience with little accurate knowledge of them in a way that does not romanticize but rather shows them confronting problems recognizably similar to those we face today. Both goals contribute to the goals of the department, for its immediate future in the recruitment of new majors and for its long-range well-being, by showing the continuing relevence of Greco-Roman antiquity in today's world.

Given the typical size of Classics programs, the number of available classes is likely to be a problem in most departments. Smaller Classics departments attempt to compensate for this situation by offering large numbers of guided reading classes. We have traditionally done a limited amount of this at UGA as well and will continue to do so; this sort of work amounts to extra uncompensated teaching for faculty members, to be sure, but this work is an unavoidable concomitant to strengthening or maintaining a strong undergraduate program. Nevertheless, we have succeeded in alleviating the problem of a relatively small annual course offering in a variety of other ways.

First, we have simply increased the number of classes taught at all levels: 25–30 sections of introductory-level Classical Culture courses are taught every year, as well as 8–10 sections of beginning Latin, multiple sections of the second-fourth courses, and two sections of Vergil's *Aeneid*, our intermediate/advanced bridge course. At the advanced level, courses have been added over the past decade in Greek, Latin, and Classical Culture. We now typically offer four split-level (advanced undergraduate/graduate) Classical Culture courses each year, two in archaeology, two on literary topics, and four advanced undergraduate Latin courses (in addition to three graduates-only seminars) focused on authors, genres, or thematic topics. The Greek program, though smaller than the Latin (a circumstance that parallels national patterns—see LaFleur 1997), has nonetheless been significantly expanded. Students can begin the elementary Greek sequence only in the fall, unless they have completed the summer Intensive Greek course, instituted in 1995 and taught in alternate years. In addition to the Intensive Greek, however, we have in recent years added a second section of the first elementary Greek course each fall, offering one in the morning and one in the early afternoon, so that students will not be prevented from enrolling because of a scheduling problem. We publicize these classes extensively in the spring of the preceding year, posting fliers and distributing announcements to our Latin and Classical Culture students, as well as to the Philosophy, Religion, and Art History departments, which have been very supportive of our program. We have also added an intermediate/advanced bridge course on Herodotus and Euripides, analogous to the Vergil course in the Latin program, to lessen the shock to students who had previously gone from our fourth-semester intermediate course directly into rigorous advanced courses with mixed undergraduate and graduate student enrollment.

A second step we have taken to provide our students a wide choice of courses has been to insure that these expanded offerings do not conflict with each other. All of our advanced courses are scheduled at different periods, in order to accommodate majors with upper-division standing who need to have the widest possible scheduling options in order to satisfy all their requirements. In addition, since a number of our students arrive at UGA with substantial Latin backgrounds but no Greek, it is of great importance that elementary Greek and advanced Latin, for example, do not conflict. The addition of the second section of elementary Greek in the fall, as well as the development of our summer Intensive Greek program, has made this problem much more tractable. Even so, other conflicts appear, and it is impossible to anticipate or remedy all of them. Nevertheless, by making the absence of course conflict a priority item, we have succeeded both in improving the quality of the offerings, and remaining attentive to the needs of undergraduate majors.

Third, operating through separate Latin, Greek, and Classical Culture committees (membership open to all interested faculty members), the department has instituted a series of rotating three-year curricula. The purpose of a rotation, of course, is to guarantee that a student who is taking advanced undergraduate classes for two or three years will be exposed to a wide range of authors and topics—that, for example, no Latin major should graduate with two classes in Horace or Pliny, and none in Cicero, Juvenal, or Livy. Thus we are attempting to reduce the difficulties students encounter in registering for the right number of classes by making certain that no student completing a degree within four years will encounter the same departmental offerings.

A fourth point where curriculum development represents an ongoing part of our activity is our close collaboration with other departments—Art History, Comparative Literature, History, Philosophy, Religion, Linguistics, Women's Studies, Language Education, etc., whose advanced courses we systematically advertise to our students when appropriate, and whose students regularly sign up for our classes. In addition, various team-teaching initiatives have been developed, both within Classics and in conjunction with faculty in other departments. The result has been extremely stimulating classes with students from diverse backgrounds, which have represented interdisciplinary learning at its best. Many of these initiatives have been made possible by the cooperation of the Classics Department and the University's Humanities Center, which coordinates a wide range of events. Such activities both enhance the offerings of the department and increase its visibility within the college and university communities, showing Classics to be intellectually active and commited to the goals of university education in the best sense.

CONCLUSION

In sum, the UGA Classics Department's success in recruiting new majors and developing its curriculum has not been an accident. Rather, by steadily promoting Classics, exploiting opportunities that arise, evaluating ourselves, and soliciting criticism from others, we have created a climate where change is viewed positively—one in which we will have a good chance of continuing to adapt both to the opportunities and the difficulties that the future will hold.

The Latin program has benefitted greatly as a result, with majors up significantly in the past decade and minors increasing at an even higher rate. Graduates of the program have had great success in their careers, both as teachers and in other professions such as law, medicine, business, and librarianship. Many have continued their training in graduate school, and have been accepted into excellent Ph.D. programs, both in the United States and abroad.

What we have done would not work everywhere, but the UGA program does show, I think, that Classics is not such a hard sell as it is sometimes portrayed, if it can be adapted both intellectually and logistically to the needs of our students. It should be particularly rewarding for those of us who care about Classics that it still has the capacity to attract some of the brightest students in our colleges and universities. These are not students who are nostalgically seeking us out to escape from contemporary society, or in a search for cultural purity in our fallen multi-cultural time. Instead, these are students who have the talent and dedication to keep Classics alive for another century, to approach the ancient world in ever new ways, and to show others why they should do so as well. In our respective colleges and universities, where we often feel under siege, where Classics frequently seems threatened by extinction, and where we are called upon to account for ourselves and our continued presence in the curriculum, we must set it as our goal to seek out those students, wherever they are, and to develop progressively new tactics for showing them what the Classics have to offer.

16

A Junior-Senior Seminar: Broadening the Latin Major's Experience of Classical Culture

PETER M. SMITH
The University of North Carolina at Chapel Hill

CHALLENGE AND RESPONSE

Like most college and university Classics departments, we offer several major programs—in our case Latin, Greek, Latin and Greek, Archaeology, and Classical Civilization—and these programs allow students to concentrate on that aspect of the ancient world they are most interested in. But specialization has a price, and we have become concerned that our undergraduate majors are studying *parts* of the classical world without being introduced to the range and variety of evidence which any serious student of the ancient world should know something about. Our response to this problem, and some of the unforeseen results it produced, may be of interest to those with similar concerns.

For example, a student majoring in Latin at Chapel Hill takes at least six semester-long courses beyond the second year of college Latin; minors take only four. Language majors, whether Latin or Greek, also take at least one course in Greek or Roman history. This leads a Latin major to read a respectable amount; but, as one might suspect, it allows that student to come away with an experience of the classical world largely limited to literature. The danger of narrowness is increased because, in view of distribution requirements and other electives, the student has to limit the number of non-literary courses about the ancient world he or she can take. It is even greater for those who add Latin as a second major. Similar specialization can threaten those who major in Archaeology or in Classical Civilization, and even those dedicated souls who undertake a combined Greek and Latin major.

Some time ago we decided that we needed to bring together our different undergraduate majors and ask them to share a course in which they might learn from one another more of the variety of approaches to the ancient world than they were getting by following our major requirements. We decided to offer a one-semester course and to ask all our majors to take it, if possible, in their junior year; we would let students share with each other their special knowledge, so that Latin majors, for example, would learn more of what archaeologists do—and how it can help them to understand the Roman world; Greek majors would learn what historians do—and how that can give literary texts the context they need; and archaeologists could see what it is that literature and history contribute to help them to a fuller understanding of Greek and Roman art and material culture.

This was already a tall order, but then we realized that our students are normally also restricted in the *periods* of ancient history they study. We decided they really should be exposed to the whole range of history studied by classicists, from the Neolithic to the Middle Ages. Three of us—Sara Mack, George Houston, and I—were set to figuring out how to do all this. We started with the idea of a survey-course in which everyone in our department could contribute her or his specialty. With a faculty of 17, including four archaeologists and two historians, it was tempting to think of drawing on each person's expertise to give students a more complete picture of our field. But of course our specialties are not chronologically arranged, so if the course were to be historically presented we feared it would become simply a historical skeleton with digressions on art, and literature, and philosophy—and with no more coherence than the Library of Congress cataloguing system. Some of us were also familiar with attempting an undergraduate course in which a major element was made up of "guest lectures" by multiple colleagues; the result had not been successful, because the contributors brought quite disparate interests to the classroom, and the students were given too centrifugal an exposure to the subject.

BUT HOW TO FIND A COMMON THREAD?

Then we turned to the possibility of finding a single area within the Mediterranean world, one which had periods of both Greek and Roman influence and which figured in the works of a significant number of Greek and Roman writers. But which area? One can make a case for Asia Minor, or the Bay of Naples, or the city of Athens. But it seemed to us that the most obvious answer was also the best one; and that was Sicily. After all, as soon as one begins to list the writers who can be included in a course on Sicily, one is surprised not by how many they are but by how few there are who can *not* be included. Among the Greek authors with a "Sicilian connection" are Homer, Stesichorus, Pindar, Aeschylus, Herodotus, Thucydides, Empedocles, Lysias,

Plato, Theocritus, Polybius, Strabo, Diodorus, and Plutarch. In Latin there are, to start with, Livy, Cicero, Vitruvius, Horace, and Vergil. And we have a large number of letters of Pope Gregory the Great dealing with the administration of church property in Sicily at the end of the sixth century. It is not just writers, of course: the historian's interest in colonization, in tyranny, in the growth and decline of the city-state, in the conflicts of Greece with Rome and of Rome with Carthage are only too well served by the violent history of Sicily. And the student of architecture, or of religion, has exceptionally rich materials to work with. In fact Sicily is so rich in things which should interest every classicist that, the more I came to work with them, the more I felt like the Athenians who, as Thucydides says, were at first unaware of the extent of the island and of the number of its inhabitants, both Greek and barbarian—and so did not realize they were undertaking a campaign not much smaller than the one they already had against the Peloponnesians. I should not have been surprised at the wealth of the material, or at the centrality of Sicily in the Mediterranean world; but, although I knew a little about the island in a scattered and fragmentary way, it had always lain for me, as it probably does for most of us, whether we are Hellenists or Latinists, on the periphery.

When I started to think in practical terms, I found that not only are our ancient sources rich, but the teacher is unusually blessed by modern scholarship as well. Among M.I. Finley's many contributions to our field is his *Ancient Sicily to the Arab Conquest*, which presents briefly, authoritatively, and of course highly readably, the whole history of the island in antiquity. It is an ideal book for a course such as the one I was planning, because Finley orients the student within each successive period and *makes clear the nature of the evidence we have and how our conclusions depend on it,* so that a teacher can then turn to larger or smaller examples of the primary evidence. On the archaeological side, I found Ross Holloway's recent *Archaeology of Ancient Sicily* invaluable: Holloway covers his subject from paleolithic cave-drawings to late Roman villas, presenting it with the knowledge and personal interest of a long-time participant. He also does it concisely, so that his survey can be used as an introduction to specialist publications on single topics, such as temple architecture, settlement patterns, sculpture, or coinage. There is also a quite detailed survey of material from the Empire by Roger Wilson, *Sicily Under the Roman Empire*, and I found my students not at all put off by Wilson's painstaking detail and encyclopedic coverage. Still, one can only sample Wilson's book, where Finley and Holloway can be used as constant guides. With so much ancient material at hand, and with excellent synoptic treatments by modern scholars, it was not hard to outline a set of readings for the course. (A sample of these readings, and of the topics for student reports which arose from them, is in the Appendix at the end of this chapter; E-mail the author at pmsmith@email.unc.edu for the full syllabus.)

WHAT WE LEARNED IN THE CLASSROOM

But all this is less interesting than what I learned from *teaching* the course, and it is that which I hope readers may find interesting about this project, and maybe even useful. We had expected that students would play to their strengths in volunteering for reports to their peers. But when I asked them to choose from my proposed topics-list, they did *not* want to stay within their "specialties" at all. Instead they seized the opportunity to learn about something new—not just new authors or new types of material, but topics entirely new to them: burial customs, the Presocratics, pastoral poetry, Carthaginian religion, Archimedes' engineering. We had been right in thinking that our students' picture of the ancient world needed broadening and complicating, but we were naive in not realizing that our students thought so, too, and would be eager to do the broadening themselves. I was also surprised by how undefensive our undergraduate majors are in admitting what they don't yet know, and how naturally they take responsibility for being learners rather than experts.

Another surprise, though, was not so much fun. That was to see how thoroughly these bright and interested young people have been trained to accept textbook presentations of material, especially on topics unfamiliar to them. I mean they have been ingrained through years of schooling, and not successfully un-trained by their college courses, to assume that authoritative knowledge in all fields is like that in the sciences, or in medicine: that is, that comprehensive knowledge of the subject is widely available, at least to the experts, and is relatively unquestioned in essentials; that available surveys incorporate in an objective way what can be known of a field; and that changes will come only from new evidence, or from new information extracted from old evidence by new technology. Most readers will surely know the sinking feeling a teacher has on realizing that his/her students look to him/her as the "expert" source of simple answers to their questions—authoritative, unambiguous answers that define and classify rather than analyze and explain.

I didn't know it, but help was already on the way, because what we were trying to do with Sicily forced on us just the right difficulties. We found ourselves at almost every step faced with ancient sources which were dependent on, or even largely drawn from, earlier writers whose work is known to us only indirectly. Thucydides used Antiochus of Syracuse for the dates of the earliest colonies; how good was Antiochus' information, and how did he calculate those dates? Plutarch used Plato's *Seventh Letter* for his life of Dion, but he also used other sources which we cannot know in detail. He used Timaeus of Tauromenium extensively and gratefully in his life of Timoleon; but Polybius disagreed with Timaeus and quarreled with him: what are we to make of the differences, and who was right? Then there is Diodorus; studying Diodorus is *largely* a matter of identifying and learning about his sources. In this and other such cases my students at first found themselves unsettled and frustrated: Does Cicero distort the record about Verres? How much can we know for sure from the design of a coin? What world is described in the pastoral poems of Theocritus? But they were becoming steadily more interested and challenged by seeing the problematic relations between evidence and conclusions. And this seemed to me wonderful. I hadn't planned it, but I was lucky: we were thinking and studying a great deal about the ways our knowledge of the past is constructed by other people like ourselves. As a result we found that ancient writers were no longer impersonal monuments to contemplate but became the first Users of Their Predecessors in a sequence of users and interpreters which extends from Thucydides to Sir Moses Finley and even to our poor selves.

This concern with sources and "source criticism" is something most classicists run into in graduate school, if they run into it at all. But in our case, I believe, it was wholly appropriate for a Junior Seminar, because we were simply doing something our students should have been doing for years: observing how interpretive conclusions are reached, looking behind the pronouncements of authority, and learning to live with the frustrating and seductive complexity of our evidence about the ancient world.

I have done my best to observe, and to ask for, students' responses to this Seminar. On the whole they like it: they *do* appreciate the chance to learn about parts of our field they did not know before. They *do* enjoy investigating new topics, especially when their doing so is part of a joint endeavor shared by their peers. They volunteer readily for reports, listen with interest and encouragement to their fellows, and even submit revised written versions more or less on schedule. Like most of us, they are specially turned on by any kind of direct contact with the ancients: by inscriptions,[1] coins, curse-tablets,[2] and graffiti. Students are intrigued, as Athenian audiences were, by overt rivalries and quarrels among the characters (when Polybius takes issue with Timaeus, or Strabo picks a fight with Posidonius).

One more surprise in teaching the course was a welcome one. I think the most exciting and intellectually engaged week of our semester has been the one spent closely with Finley's *Ancient Slavery and Modern Ideology*. If you know that book, you know what a marvel of scholarship, and of exposition, it is. All our students read it (it's not a long book), but individuals or pairs of students are responsible for each of its four chapters and lead our discussion of them. Each chapter makes a detailed, fascinating, and crucial argument, but that argument is not simply announced: with extraordinary mastery of the ancient evidence and of modern study of it, Finley shows us how to estimate the evidence and how to use it in controlling modern theories of the origin and nature of ancient slave economies—including his own theory. In studying this series of essays and in presenting their understanding of them to a supportive and knowledgeable audience of their fellows, my students have really stretched themselves, applying a lot of what they have learned about their major fields, and they have enjoyed it.

At least, I believe they have enjoyed it. Their evaluations, both written and informal, of the Seminar have been quite positive, which is interesting in view of the scattered and continuously changing nature of its subject-matter. I would, in fact, offer a caution in that regard: although it is all about Sicily, a course like this has really no unity of plot at all: as Aristotle says, don't write an epic about everything that happened to Heracles, because there is no necessary unity to be found in a set of events simply because they happened to the same person—or the same island. I think college courses ought when possible to have the kind of integrity of contents Aristotle goes on to recommend, and I think it is good to be sceptical about courses that are held together by some accidental device, such as being all about the island of Sicily. Such a course is only to be recommended if it is especially needed, as in our case I think it *is* needed in order to cross-fertilize and to broaden what our different undergraduate majors learn about Greece and Rome.[3] But if you do have a need at all like that, and if you want to organize a survey of the whole ancient world around a single place, then you might well find that Aeneas was on to something when he asked

> an sit mihi gratior ulla,
> quove magis fessas optem demittere navis,
> quam quae Dardanium tellus mihi servat Acesten,
> et patris Anchisae gremio complectitur ossa?
>
> (*Aeneid* 5.28–31)

NOTES

[1] My colleague George Houston made for us a selection of Latin inscriptions from Sicily and the neighboring mainland, and he added commentary and questions for discussion. Students were fascinated by the use of dedications, epitaphs, etc., as evidence for the work, and government, and beliefs of real Sicilians under both Republic and Empire. The need to *interpret* these documents they could see clearly and accepted eagerly.

[2] We are lucky to have in Chapel Hill a substantial lead curse-tablet from near Gela, written in the early fifth century; a student report on that tablet has been one high-point of the seminar.

[3] Just how broadened students' interest becomes is shown by the subjects those in our first offering of the Seminar chose for their final, entirely self-defined, reports: Maltese temples of the Bronze Age, the transition from temples to Christian churches, the location of the Cyclopes in Sicily, the pre-Christian religions of Sicily, Norman rule in the island, the temple of Apollo at Syracuse, Plutarch's *Marcellus*, and the Sicilian campaign in World War II.

APPENDIX: THE FIRST SIX WEEKS' READINGS AND REPORTS

	Secondary Reading	_Primary Reading_	_Student Reports_
29 Aug.	Finley 3–14	Strabo 6.2: the geography of Sicily	Strabo's accuracy? Strabo's sources? Strabo's interests?
31 Aug.	Holloway 1–42		Who _were_ the Elymoi? What _do_ we know of pre-Greek culture and society?
5 Sept.	Finley 15–42	Thucydides 6.1–5 Diodorus 5.1–10	Motives for colonization? Piracy and/or communism on Lipari?
7 Sept.	Holloway 43–96		Temple C at Selinous
12 Sept.	Finley 45–57	Herodotus 7.153–67 Pindar, _Olympians_ 1–3 Pindar, _Pythians_ 1–3	The Charioteer at Delphi Pindar's use of myth
14 Sept.	Holloway 97–120		The curse-tablet from Gela in UNC Rare Book Collection
19 Sept.	Finley 58–73	Pindar, _Olympians_ 4, 5, 12 Empedocles (in Kirk, Raven, and Schofield, _The Presocratic Philosophers_, 280–321)	Empedocles: philosopher? doctor? prophet? poet? shaman?
21 Sept.		Thucydides 6–7	The tragedy of Athenian imperialism
26 Sept.	Finley 74–87	Lysias 33 Diodorus 14.109	Who was Lysias, and how did he come to write speeches?
28 Sept.	_ad lib._ in D. Harden, S. Moscati, or S. Lancel on Carthage		Sicilian coins: art and history The temple at Segesta The temples at Acragas
3 Oct.	Finley 88–93	Plato, _Seventh Letter_ Plutarch, _Dion_	Is the _Letter_ genuine? What happened to the philosopher-king?
10 Oct.	Finley 94–106	Plutarch, _Timoleon_	Plutarch's use of Timaeus Plutarch as "biographer"

17

Graduate Education in Classics: From Quill Pens to Computers

MARK MORFORD
University of Virginia

Thirty years ago the late classicist William Arrowsmith published an article in *Harper's Magazine* with the provocative title, "The Shame of the Graduate Schools." His basic complaint was that graduate programs were deceptive, inhumane, and exploitative. While the article to-day seems rather querulous, Arrowsmith caught the attention of the public and irritated many academics sufficiently to bring into public discourse an area of university training that, until then, had been quietly assumed not to need reform. Many university faculty and administrators have, since then, moved in the directions advocated by Arrowsmith, and in this chapter I will attempt to survey the status of graduate education in the Classics three decades after the publication of his essay. Some of the old, intractable problems remain; some new ones (largely fiscal) have arisen; in general, however, there has been greater openness and flexibility, as Arrowsmith had recommended.

Difficulties there are. Here are a few:

- graduate education in the humanities is an easy target when budgets are being reduced;
- there is less clarity about the goals of graduate education in the Classics than at other levels of education;
- entering graduate students come with wide differences in previous training, experience, and achievement;
- after years of study the graduating student faces a job-market where the supply exceeds the demand and, in university teaching at least, where the barrier of tenure after another six years of effort may well disrupt the lives of even the most conscientious candidates.

Nevertheless, graduate education in Classics in this country has been largely a success story. I hope to show how this has come about and to suggest ways in which it can continue to be vital and flexible in a constantly changing educational climate that has become—and will continue to be—increasingly susceptible to budgetary and political constraints.

TENSIONS IN AMERICAN GRADUATE EDUCATION

Two characteristics of American graduate education in the humanities particularly distinguish it from European (especially British) graduate programs. First is the disjunction between the principles on which graduate programs have traditionally been founded and the actual level of pre-graduate preparation for most applicants. Second, is the conflict between the simultaneous goals of training research scholars, preparing future teachers, and staffing significant areas of undergraduate teaching in universities.

1) I will approach the first by recalling an episode in 1960 when I was a school teacher in Baltimore, having taught at the Oxbridge scholarship level for seven years before then and being about to publish my second book. I asked the chairman of the department at Johns Hopkins University—ironically, the cradle of American graduate education in the Classics—about entering the doctoral program. He was aggressive and inflexible, and he seemed to look upon graduate study as an initiation into mysteries that were best approached with a good dose of humiliation and inflexibility. Nearly four decades later this kind of arrogance is far less common in our profession, and good riddance to it. But we should ask why it was thought necessary in the first place and how it lasted so long.

In Europe, and in this country at the time when graduate programs were first introduced (in the third quarter of the 19th century), Latin and (less and less) Greek were typically studied at an early age, a pattern that continued well into the 20th century—for example, it was not at all unusual in the 1930s to begin Latin (as I did) at the age of 6 and Greek at 10. By the time one entered the university as an undergraduate, one had been writing compositions (in the plural)—Greek and Latin, prose and verse—every week for years, and translating Greek and Roman authors in secondary school at a level and in a quantity beyond the experience even of many graduate students today. Graduate programs were originally designed for scholars who could build on this impressive foundation in the languages and literatures, and many of the ambiguities in current graduate education have their origin in the huge difference between the limited experience of many beginning graduate students compared with the knowledge expected of an undergraduate as recently as 50 years ago. The reconciliation of the present reality and a past ideal is basic to the achievements and failures of American graduate education in the Classics.

The *heros ktistes* of graduate education in the Classics, Basil Gildersleeve, himself went to Germany for his doctoral degree and took German scholarship as his model (see Briggs; Briggs and Benario). In England and Scotland the focus was then, and until quite recently continued to be, on the gifted amateur, in this reflecting the basic goal of British higher education, which was to produce an administrative elite capable of undertaking varied and often huge responsibilities overseas. The focused professionalism of the German model has always been more attractive in the American system: it is appropriate to a more democratic system of education, and it fits in with the peculiarly American characteristic of seeing challenges as problems to be solved. If you want to put a man on the moon, you devote huge human and financial resources for a comparatively short period, and the problem is solved. If you want to become a scholar in Latin or Greek, but have not studied those languages until late in (or even after) your secondary education, you can complete a number of more or less intensive courses, earn high grades, and be admitted to graduate study. Unfortunately, the demands of graduate study do not admit of compromise: you cannot become a confident, or even adequate, teacher and scholar in Latin or Greek without having a firm foundation in the languages and literatures. Most American programs have been designed with this supposition as their basis, and the disjunction between the needs of graduate students and the principles on which their programs have been designed, continues to be the major challenge in maintaining academic integrity while allowing for flexibility in students' needs.

2) The second differentiating characteristic of American graduate study is inherent in the structure of the curriculum in research universities, many of them large, state-supported institutions and none of them free of government financial support. Even in some private universities (Johns Hopkins itself is an example), the teaching of undergraduate courses in the languages, at least at the first- and second-year levels, is wholly or largely assigned to graduate teaching assistants (on the subject of TA training, see the next chapter and cf. LaFleur 1992). The entire enterprise of elementary language teaching in universities would fall flat on its face if these indentured serfs were removed from the system. They provide a comparatively painless way for an institution to support graduate students financially, and to give them essential experience as future teachers. In many cases—especially where the graduate assistant is already an experienced teacher—the undergraduates benefit from excellent teaching by one who is often close to them in age. On the other hand, it is not uncommon for the pay for work performed by teaching assistants to be well below its value to the institution. This is an uncomfortable issue for deans and chairs to face, and it does not infrequently lead to the appointment of teaching assistants who are underqualified or incompetent. In large institutions with a foreign language requirement, the need for low-paid teaching staff sometimes outweighs the need

to maintain high professional standards, and the undergraduates, as well as the graduate assistants, are the losers.

PRINCIPLES FOR ADMISSION TO GRADUATE STUDY

These two characteristics of the American scene, then, require vigilance, flexibility, and time-consuming direction from graduate faculty. The foundation of graduate education in the Classics is a solid knowledge of the languages and literatures, which can only be gained by years of study of the texts and constant application. Because of the disjunctions noted above, it is essential that graduate faculty be flexible in assessing the qualifications of applicants. Yet they cannot afford to confer degrees on those who are not properly trained to become professional teachers and scholars. My impression is that graduate faculty in general are commendably concerned with academic standards and that few are prepared to allow deficient undergraduate preparation to be an excuse for inadequate work at the graduate level. For this reason I do not see an alternative to the traditional system of examinations as reality-checks along the road to the graduate degree, nor do I think that the thesis or dissertation is any less valuable now than it was decades ago. Despite the refreshing iconoclasm of William Calder's suggestions for "Fifty Monographs in Search of a Scholar," the traditional approach of studying major literary or historical texts still seems to be more effective in preparation for a professional career in teaching and research.

Graduate faculty, however, do find it hard to evaluate applicants for their programs. The typical applicant presents a transcript of previous work, an essay on his or her reasons for entering graduate study, Graduate Record Exam scores, and letters from two or three referees. The most consistent criterion in this medley is the GRE: although it may not always be the best predictor of success, I have found it to be more accurate than its critics would care to admit. Graduate faculty do not generally seem to take the selection of their future students as seriously as they do the planning and implementation of appropriate programs of study. Yet it is at this stage that the most difficult judgments often have to be made, for adequate study in one language only is now more likely to be expected of applicants, while standards vary as widely as ever between undergraduate programs, and the reliability of referees is uneven. There are no easy answers, and the temptation to admit more students than are properly qualified is strong, if there is a need for relatively cost-effective teaching staff and if a department needs to maintain its fiscal position through strong enrollments. In public universities there are the additional pressures of state supervision, which can take the form of demanding the ending of a degree program if the numbers of graduates drop below a certain level. Certainly some creative thought is needed in this unglamorous aspect of graduate study.

UNITY AND DIVERSITY IN PROFESSIONAL TRAINING

American graduate departments have customarily combined different professional goals. In Britain (more than in Germany) training for secondary teaching has traditionally been separated from training to be a teacher in a research institution, while in America the power of schools of education within universities and throughout the system of public pre-college education has been much greater than in Europe. This has led to the proliferation of professional education courses, theories, and faculty, and in all three of these categories the excellent has too often been suffocated by the mediocre. Further, the impatience of research scholars with the work of schools of education has generally had a negative effect, to the disadvantage of graduate students whose goal is to be good secondary-school teachers. To inflate technical and limited issues into university-level courses on a par with the potentially unlimited intellectual challenges of serious academic study is absurd, but it is all too common. On the other hand, it is equally common for graduate faculty in Classics to be contemptuous of professional courses that are truly valuable for future teachers at any level.

It seems that the M.A.T. degree has become an endangered species (for some notable exceptions, however, see Chapter 19 below), to be replaced by the M.Ed. (Master of Education) or the M.T. (Master of Teaching) degree, controlled by schools of education and available as a combined undergraduate and graduate five-year program, with graduate students from other undergraduate institutions admitted for the final two years. In these programs field experience and supervised classroom teaching practice is prominent, whereas it used to be possible for M.A.T. students to finesse the practice (and save a year's fees) by working in the schools as probationary teachers for a period (typically two years). Where the M.Ed. or M.T. program is administered cooperatively by the school of education it has proved to be very good. By "cooperatively," I mean that there is adequate consultation between the academic and professional departments in evaluating applicants for admission, and adequate space in the program's requirements for the proper training of future teachers in their academic fields, most typically by taking courses with other graduate students in the academic department, writing serious research papers, and being respected by the graduate faculty of the academic department as professionals whose work will be different from, but as valuable as, that of teachers and scholars in colleges and universities.

With few exceptions, I do not think that this ideal of cooperation is yet sufficiently accepted. For example, it is rare for an M.T. or M.A.T. graduate student to be offered financial aid, on the specious grounds that he or she is in a terminal two-year program, and I have known of cases (not in departments of Classics) where faculty have actually lowered the grades of M.A.T. students in

Ph.D. seminars. There is no excuse for snobbery of this sort. The would-be graduate student must be aware of the great differences between departments and institutions in their handling of a student whose goal is secondary teaching. They must ask: What is the structure of the program? Who controls it? What sort of relations does the department faculty have with secondary teachers? What is its record in placing its graduates, and what sort of careers have they had?

I do not think that the majority of graduate faculty in departments of Classics yet recognize how crucial to the profession—to their future colleagues and to themselves—is the proper integration of secondary and higher education. Very few research scholars have the right to inhabit the proverbial ivory tower (as an example of one who did have the right, I remember the powerful impression that Alexander Turyn made on me three deacdes ago in his sanctum in the library of the University of Illinois), and I would never suggest that those whose research defines what the rest of us will teach should give up significant time to pedagogical activities to the detriment of their research. Comparatively few great scholars also have the gift of making their time and intellectual energy freely available for those whose experience and goals are more humble: Robert Broughton was an inspiring example of such a caring scholar, and there are several distinguished scholars (for example, Gregory Nagy and Karl Galinsky) who have devoted significant time to National Endowment for the Humanities (NEH) summer seminars for school teachers. Most of us, however, in research institutions with graduate programs, need to be aware of the importance of giving time to professional activities shared with those in other constituencies, and, in the same spirit, respecting the work and the goals of those who will not become professional research scholars.

This principle of professional unity has been the policy of a succession of Presidents of the American Classical League (ACL), and it has become basic to the goals of the American Philological Association (APA). In 1986 the APA sponsored a conference in conjunction with the ACL with the title "Teaching the Ancient World." The methods and goals of the conference are relevant to the administration and development of graduate programs in changing times. The planning stage took nearly two years and was made possible in the first place by a grant from the then Chairman of the NEH, William Bennett, who has recently been energetically undercutting the principles that he then was championing. The planners came from different professional fields (ranging from research scholars in Classics through Modern Language Association administrators and a superintendent of a major urban educational system) and took a simple three-stage model for their plan: preparation, implementation (i.e., the conference), development. The conference itself was small and short: it was focused and hard-working. The development stage is still continuing and has already resulted in two major reports, the first written by Mary Ann Burns and Joseph O'Connor, and the second by Sally Davis. A group of university and school faculty met frequently with the authors in the preparation of these reports, which have been effective in focusing attention on the teaching of the ancient world and of Latin.

Some features of the planning and implementation of this conference are valuable for those who administer graduate programs. Amongst them are the following:

- Orderly stages of planning, with thorough preparation before putting the plan into action, and with time-consuming (but essential) attention to implementing and reviewing the results. Thus goals are defined, and changes in a program are evaluated.

- Consideration of the needs of both providers and consumers, that is, graduate faculty, on the one hand, and students, teachers, and taxpayers (and others who pay for the programs) on the other.

- Recognition of the value of the experience and wisdom of those outside the field to help in defining what classicists need and are expected to do. (This will upset many professional classicists, but *experto credite!*)

- Recognition that in the field of Classics there is no room for division between the different constituencies, different though their goals and methods may be. A distinguished philologist was a joint-president of the conference; a school teacher chaired the steering committee of university faculty and school teachers that assisted her in writing the report on the teaching of Latin.

While graduate faculty should not dilute their responsibilities for planning, developing, and evaluating their programs, the model suggested above would help in maintaining the discipline and vitality of graduate study. Like Janus it looks both ways—inward, at the scholarly enterprise of Classics; outward, at the diversity in the needs and goals of students and teachers. It is humbling to be reminded that what is being suggested here is essentially a return to the principles of Gildersleeve, enunciated in his Presidential Address to the APA in 1878, frequently reviewed by him, and triumphantly confirmed in his second Presidential Address in 1909.

WHAT SHOULD BE STUDIED?

There are 82 graduate programs listed in the APA's *Guide to Graduate Programs in the Classics in the United States and Canada* (1996 edition). Of these, 49 offer a Ph.D. degree, divided roughly equally between public and private institutions. It would be impossible and inappropriate to prescribe what curriculum these programs should include. Nevertheless, it is appropriate to address the basic contradiction in graduate study in the Classics between its philological goal and its wide range of subject-matter. Gildersleeve's closing words in 1878 (quoted from the version published in the *Princeton Review* for

1879 and reprinted in Briggs, 132) are still relevant:

> While it is very true that the transition from what may be called the formal side
> of philology to the study of history, antiquities, and art is much easier than the
> reverse, and should therefore form the staple of university instruction, no one,
> teacher or scholar, should so lose himself in grammatical and critical studies,
> as to become insensible of the deep truth which is embodied in the old term, the
> "humanities."

The "tendency . . . to over-specialization" (Gildersleeve's phrase) is inherent
in any program of graduate study, and the conflict between it and the broader
aspects of the humanities goes back at least to Seneca, whose 88th and 108th
Letters were widely read and admired in renaissance Europe. The disjunctions
noted in the first part of this essay make the old conflict especially pressing for
graduate study in this country, and it has been sharpened by the current
emphasis on accountability in higher education. We can mediate (to employ the
useful structuralist term) the tension by distinguishing between the different
functions of graduate study in the Classics.

First is training in the languages and literatures. The classical texts always
have been, and always should be, the foundation of graduate study. The student
who graduates without a firm grasp of the major texts (there seems to be little
disagreement as to which these are) is not properly prepared for teaching at any
level beyond elementary school. Nevertheless, some teachers find themselves
in this predicament, and many would-be graduate students find themselves ill-
prepared for graduate school. Sometimes local exigencies lead to the
appointment of such a person in order to save an endangered program, and
these teachers should justly be praised for their courage and devotion. While
some programs (including the University of Georgia's National Latin Institute
during the 1980s: see LaFleur and Anderson 1986–87, 1988) have attempted to
meet their needs, it is doubtful if graduate programs should regularly be adapted
to meet this sort of crisis. Instead we should look to an expansion of programs
such as the "Post-Bac" program at the University of Pennsylvania, which,
experience has shown, has been successful in preparing ambitious students
whose preparation for graduate school is in some way deficient. The financial
cost is high, however, and it may be that community and two-year college
programs could provide a practical and affordable way at least to provide a solid
grounding in Latin. Support for such efforts on the part of community college
faculty (for example, as in the program at Richland College in Texas: see
Pascal, and cf. Searles) has been sporadic and their success has depended almost
exclusively on the energy of individual faculty and their skill at lobbying for
scarce funds. Although the APA has given some attention to this important
segment of post-secondary education in the last few years, much more needs to
be done.

If we grant that the languages and the major texts are the foundation of graduate study, then how are we to apportion the limited time that remains in a degree program, two years in all for an M.A., M.A.T., M.Ed., or M.T., and at least three or four years more for a doctorate? Like the Professor in *The Yellow Submarine*, we have "so much to learn, so little time," and priorities have to be set—something that graduate faculties are not happy to do.

At any level ancient history should be high on the list, a field to which the structure of most American graduate programs has been inimical. Whether one is teaching in a secondary school, a college, or a university, it is virtually impossible to teach adequately without a secure knowledge of the historical and social background of the texts. Fifty years ago this was not necessarily so: in the rigorous training that I received at school, knowledge of the texts (including variants in manuscript readings) was the only requirement. Plautus was taught without reference to comedy or any aspect of drama or social circumstances, but we knew all about the *brevis brevians*; after studying Juvenal more intensively than many of today's graduate students, we knew the text and Housman's emendations, but there was no mention in class of the principles of satire or even of what life in early imperial Rome was like. This would be an unthinkable way of teaching today (except for a graduate seminar focusing on textual criticism), yet the structure of graduate programs (for the most part put in place 50 years or more ago) does not easily make room for present-day realities. The tension between the need to know the language and literature on the one hand, and to know about the historical context on the other, has been increased by the strange shibboleth, common in many graduate departments and vigorously defended by distinguished scholars, that ancient history belongs only in departments of history. In Europe (and especially in Britain) this rending of the body of Classics has traditionally been avoided, largely because of the structure of undergraduate degree programs in Classics, and the appearance of unity in the field has been easier to maintain because of the excellence of classical training in the secondary schools. This is changing: Classics no longer have their privileged position, and therefore no longer do university faculty have the luxury of teaching students who for the most part have had a proper grounding in the languages and literatures. In this country some departments have been more far-sighted in accepting the importance of ancient history in graduate programs in Classics. In some, ancient history has long been integrated; in some, the departments of History and Classics remain separate fiefdoms, to the detriment of their students; in very few (Princeton and Berkeley, for example) sophisticated programs in "Ancient Studies" have been devised, although how successful they have been in maintaining the essential basis of familarity with the texts remains yet to be seen. The ancient historian who cannot read Livy or Tacitus, or translate documents or epigraphic evidence, is no better off than the philologist who knows no history.

Literary texts and ancient history: the graduate student's time is already nearly full up, yet there is more! Firstly, no teacher should be unaware of the importance of social history in the Classics, especially in the light of the work of feminist scholars over the last 30 years. Yet I fear that even this mild formulation of the topic will displease traditionalists and feminists alike. I doubt if separate courses (with titles such as "Women in . . .") should be a necessary part of regular graduate programs, unless they are based on productive research and are offered by scholars deeply engaged with their issues. But equally, I do not see how a properly trained teacher of the Classics can study the ancient texts and ancient history without having at the very least to think maturely about the roles of women and the family—study of Homer, of Greek and Roman tragedy, Catullus and Vergil, to mention a very few texts, has been changed permanently by the work of feminist scholars.

Closely related to how we look at a text in relationship to all humanity—female and male—is the issue of critical approaches to texts. Here again, feminists and anthropologists have much to teach their colleagues in the Classics. I do not see the need for separate courses in critical theory, unless they are offered by a fully-engaged scholar, but it is essential that students be introduced to important schools of critical theory, for example, theories of the persona in satire or of narrative techniques in epic and historiography. My plea here is for a more broad-minded approach than has been traditional in many graduate departments, while I hope that classicists can continue to avoid the jargon that has threatened to suffocate much of modern critical writing.

So far I have left out art and archaeology, ancient civilizations, and mythology from the graduate student's training. The teacher at any level is going to be engaged with at least one of these areas, and at the university level probably with all of them. In universities, mythology is usually the most popular course offered by departments of Classics, yet the least attention is given to any systematic training in the area. In my experience, graduate faculties are quite resistant to any suggestion of offering a serious graduate-level course, based on the ancient texts, that would prepare future teachers to teach (or even to use) mythology in a systematic and disciplined way. More often, in the larger graduate institutions the graduate student assists (usually as a grader) in a course with a very high enrollment, which is fairly low in the academic priorities of the instructor. The instructor may be the only member of a department to teach the course, to the relief of his or her colleagues, who look upon it as a burden that they are glad to avoid. It would not be difficult to plan for a more systematic knowledge of the field through the texts that are being read regularly, and I doubt if some more attention to Ovid's *Metamorphoses* (to take but one example of such a text) would overload the graduate student's program.

With art and archaeology the issues are quite different, in part because the vast majority of faculty in departments of Classics are not experts in these fields, which are not (as ancient history is) based mainly on written evidence. Classical art and archaeology rightly are located in departments devoted to these subjects, although it should be noted that there are substantial differences in the methods of study of archaeology in departments of art and of anthropology. Where there are properly qualified faculty in these departments, students in Classics are being deprived of important experience if they are not encouraged to study with them. The availability of museum resources and the opportunities for travel to the Mediterranean world, of course, vary widely, but even here I suspect that more could be done to make it possible for students to enlarge their knowledge.

The teaching of Greek and Roman civilizations as a separate course (or pair of courses) calls for energy and skills that are quite different from those required for teaching most of the other topics that have been mentioned earlier. I doubt if time could be made for them in the regular graduate program, but experience as an assistant and responsibility for teaching a weekly session are invaluable, not least because they allow a graduate student to study a culture in its entirety.

MAKING A PINT POT HOLD A QUART: THE NECESSITY OF DATA-BASES

The previous pages have shown the need for establishing priorities in planning a course of graduate study. Taking the texts as the non-negotiable foundation, I have suggested that ancient history should be the first additional area to which substantial time should be devoted, and that social aspects of the field (particularly those involving race, gender, and family issues) and critical theory may best evolve from sensitive reading of the texts, unless qualified faculty are available to offer specific courses. Descending in order of priority, I have suggested that classical mythology be systematically studied, again in conjunction with reading of the texts, while the extent to which art and archaeology are studied will depend on the availability of faculty in other departments and of resources for visits to museum collections and overseas travel and study. Finally, I do not see time in a regular program for the separate study of "Ancient Civilization," except through the experience of assisting in courses with this broad rubric. To pack so much into the two years of a masters program (or even the five or six of a doctoral program) is impossible and undesirable, yet the judicious use of computer data-bases and other resources can make information available that until recently would have required more time, and probably more travel and expense, for access.

We should assume that any graduate program must be supported by an adequate library, and departments should be encouraged to make funds available for students to travel to other research libraries when their own is inadequate.

We should assume also that programs ought to be supported by adequate computer resources (see Chapter 23 for particulars on the programs mentioned here). At the very least, data-bases should include the Packard Humanities Institute and *Thesaurus Linguae Graecae* materials, the *Database of Classical Bibliography* (*L'Année Philologique*), and *Perseus*, and libraries (or instructional technology centers) should have the staff to train students in the use and development of computer materials. Students will thus be able to learn how to have access to other data-bases, for example in art and archaeology, and to create their own paths in specific areas of interest. Here at least is one way in which the gap between the time available and the amount of material to learn can be lessened. This aspect of graduate study varies a great deal from one program to another, and training in the use of computers and data-bases is fortuitous, often depending on the skills of particular graduate students. Students should also learn to use computers as a teaching resource, through the creation and presentation of interactive materials in classrooms. Classicists have been pioneers in a number of computer applications to scholarship (the data-bases named above are shining examples of such leadership), but there seems to be room in conventional graduate programs for ensuring that all graduate students are exposed to this essential area of scholarship and teaching.

CHOOSING A GRADUATE PROGRAM

I hesitate to offer generalities about the choice of a graduate program for study. Obviously the applicant must have some idea of his or her goal: secondary school teaching, research, teaching in a graduate or undergraduate institution, and so on. Some programs are focused more on one professional area than another. Applicants should write to a number of the departments in the APA *Guide to Graduate Programs in the Classics* and learn what they can about the faculty and their research; they should ask about the library and computer resources; and they should find out what the record of the department is in placing its graduates. Usually financial aid is a deciding factor, but even with that as a priority these other questions do not lose their importance. For those who have clear professional goals the choice is easier—not many departments, for example, have a really good program for the training and support of future secondary teachers, and fewer departments (than many would like to admit) have the faculty and ongoing research to inspire a future scholar for a career in which original scholarship is to be important. Having determined the programs best suited to their interests, applicants should apply to several of them—half a dozen at least—because opportunities for admission and especially for financial assistance fluctuate significantly from year to year.

An inescapable question is what happens after graduation. Many more graduate degrees are awarded than can possibly be absorbed into the profession (and this is especially so for careers in research institutions), and most graduates will be relieved to find a permanent job at all, let alone one in the kind of institution that they had aimed for. Those departments that do not value secondary teaching as a noble vocation are doing their students a disservice. For those who do enter a research institution, there loom the Scylla and Charybdis of tenure, for which publications are the *sine qua non*. Graduates therefore have to consider what sort of career they really wish to aim at: in all cases, however, the essential criterion in choosing a graduate program must be that it should allow the student to develop a level of knowledge and a capacity for further learning that will endure and grow far beyond whatever the immediate needs may be. This is a matter of fundamental integrity.

CONCLUSION: *IN FINE INITIUM*

This paper began with a list of difficulties. I conclude by returning to them and observing that the record of graduate programs in this country is remarkably good. To balance the competing, and often contradictory, pressures and demands from institutions (and, in public ones, from taxpayers) with the needs of students and faculty, is an impossible task—yet it is being done with extraordinary success, thanks to the vitality and skill of faculty in individual departments and the enthusiasm and courage of those who would join them in the profession. The suggestions offered in this essay have as their goal, for the most part, the orderly planning of programs, a realistic ordering of priorities and goals on the part of students, would-be students, and faculty, and a candid recognition by graduate students of the kinds of career in which they wish to spend their professional lives. And I would endorse Gildersleeve's plea, still a relevant one, for building on the languages and literatures as the foundation of study that will lead to the breadth and richness of all that an understanding of ancient Greece and Rome can be. Finally, the American word "commencement" is indeed significant: the good graduate program is one whose terminal degree is the key to the door of lifelong learning.

18

DOCERE DOCENTES:
A Methods Course for Latin TAs

CYNTHIA WHITE
University of Arizona, Tucson

Suetonius (*De Grammaticis* 2) tells us that in 169 B.C. Crates of Mallos first introduced the study of grammar and literature to Rome, when, as a legate to the Roman Senate, he broke his leg after falling into the opening of a sewer near the Palatine. While recuperating, he incidentally became a teacher of literature, a position known as the *grammaticus* when Roman education became formalized. Like many TA supervisors, I came to the development of a Latin methodology course almost as incidentally as formal instruction came to Crates, from my work supervising the Latin teaching assistants as Director of the Latin Program at the University of Arizona. Each fall we have five sections of Elementary Latin 101 and two sections of Elementary Latin 201, and in the spring, four sections of Elementary Latin 102 and two sections of Elementary Latin 202, all taught by TAs. Combined enrollments are about 220 in the fall and 160 in the spring. Latin TAs in the 101 classes often are first-semester graduate students in our M.A. Classical Philology program, with no prior teacher training.

As Director of the Latin Program, I initially developed (in 1992) a three-part sequence for TA training. This complements the University and Classics Department orientations, which cover general policies and procedures of the university and departmental employees, e.g., office hours, attendance, and academic honesty. The Latin Program training includes: 1) three days of pre-semester orientation meetings and the one-day Latin Workshop, 2) weekly coordination meetings throughout the semester, and 3) mid- and end-semester evaluations.

The regimen for the basic training program is short-term, reactive, and practical. To help TAs better contextualize this training, I subsequently developed a full-scale, discipline-based methods course, which was added to our curriculum in 1995. A survey of philosophic and theoretical readings on Latin pedagogy, the methods course both complements our practical training and fulfills College of Education requirements for TAs who are working towards teacher certification.

THE LATIN TA TRAINING PROGRAM

Pre-semester Orientation Meetings

At these initial meetings I first determine the levels of experience among the TAs (Nyquist and Wulff). This allows me effectively to manage novices, mentor the more experienced TAs, and encourage both levels to work collaboratively. We write a syllabus, talk in great detail about the first day of class, and begin to address interpersonal issues of, e.g., demeanor and confidence. At these meetings students prepare a mock presentation of some introductory grammar point from the first chapter of *Wheelock's Latin* (5th ed., Wheelock 1995). These presentations initiate the ongoing dialogue about the learner-centered classroom and effective teaching, both cooperative and collaborative.

Pre-semester Latin Workshop

In a morning and afternoon session Latin faculty review major grammatical points from Wheelock, chapters 1–22 in the fall semester and chapters 23–40 in the spring semester. Ample time is allotted for drills after each presentation and for TAs to ask questions. While there is some discussion of the *ars docendi*, this workshop is about Latin grammar. It attempts to anticipate difficulties that TAs may have in presenting new grammar, as well as the problems their students may encounter comprehending and applying it. TAs are asked to come prepared for an intensive review and are expected to recite forms, offer examples, and provide explanations.

Weekly Coordination Meetings

The core of the TA training program is the weekly coordination meetings during which we: discuss and demonstrate instructional methods that promote a learner-centered classroom; talk about, and test for, learning types; discuss a variety of testing methods; write tests; watch video playbacks of our teaching with a representative from the University Teaching Center (UTC) who critiques them; and, not least, study together the Latin grammar in each chapter of Wheelock. Once a month someone from outside the Classics faculty, e.g., from the University Composition Board or the UTC, conducts the meeting and addresses any of several vital issues. Among other things we spend full sessions on writing in the curriculum, classroom management, teaching styles and learning types, critical thinking in language training, diversity in the classroom, and cooperative/collaborative teaching (Walker).

TAs are asked to assemble a portfolio (Krause) as part of their training. This may include videotapes of their classes, materials they develop (e.g., syllabi, tests), as well as personal statements about their teaching goals. The portfolio should also include, however, materials from others, such as supervisors' critiques, teaching awards, student evaluations, papers presented on pedagogy, and collaborative and outreach efforts.

Evaluations

We have in place a whole battery of pre-observation conferences, classroom visits (by myself and by someone from the UTC), peer observations, and mid- and end-semester student evaluations. Novice TAs are expected to visit the classes of senior TAs, as well as the classes of the department faculty who are teaching in the basic Latin sequence. Senior TAs routinely visit and critique the classes of the novice TAs. They discuss their observations and recommendations both with the TAs and with me. I visit all the Latin classes several times throughout the semester and keep a detailed file of my own observations and recommendations.

While the end-semester student evaluations are essential, in that they provide a consistent instrument for collecting feedback, we have found mid-semester evaluations particularly useful for novice TAs. These reveal student reactions to instructional methods, learner-centered classroom activities, and the like. They also allow time for change of emphasis, or for redirection where necessary.

THE METHODS COURSE FOR LATIN TAS

The shortcoming of our Latin TA training program as originally designed, was that, much of the time, we were trouble-shooting. In our weekly meetings we were often reacting to some problem that had already occurred rather than anticipating problems and preparing for them. This led me to develop a course that would address the general issues of novice teaching as well as the unique requirements of teaching Latin. In this discipline-based methods course, Latin TAs read about Latin pedagogy in texts of ancient writers on education, especially Quintilian and Cicero. They then correlate ancient methodological issues, theories, and praxis with modern educational theories. Students who are working toward secondary teacher certification find that the readings complement those in their courses in the College of Education. But, whether or not the TA is working for certification, the premise is a useful one. Matching modern education/language theorists against ancient ones encourages TAs to compare methods and to compile comparative bibliographies. Such discipline-based readings allow them to confront the fundamentals of educational theory while continuing to improve their Latin reading skills and their research skills.

This kind of comparative reading is the result of a creative partnership we have established between the College of Education and the Classics Department, called an "association." Tracing these theories in the history of education through this interdisciplinary association encourages TAs to effectively combine research in Latin language with the practice of teaching. It requires them to have a command of a comprehensive bibliography of modern theories of education. It also requires them to research thematically a discrete body of ancient texts. That this interdisciplinary association between the Classics Department and the College of Education promotes excellence in both teacher preparation and in reading Latin hardly needs to be stated.

The first priority of the TA training program is to prepare them for the immediate tasks of teaching the basic Latin classes, but TAs must also engage in their own professional development, which is one of the goals of the methods course. In this course TAs learn ways to continue independently the process of reflective teaching, and they are encouraged to continue to experiment creatively with Latin texts, so that their teaching is fresh and effective. Ideally, the course should be completed before TAs begin instructing, but, because of limited resources for TA training, this has been impossible. Students at the University of Arizona take the course while concurrently teaching, as a complement to the ongoing pre- and in-service training.

At work in the methods course are three principles based on the successes and failures of our original training program. The first is that we are training TAs to teach and to think about teaching. For most of them, teaching is not an aside that will end when graduate school ends (Azevedo); rather, many will be teaching at the secondary or college level as careers. The second tenet of the methods course is that current theories of language acquisition may be anticipated in the teaching theories and techniques that we research in the works of Cicero, Quintilian, Suetonius, Tacitus, and Augustine. Finally, and perhaps most fundamental, is the principle that research and teaching ought not to be separated, either by the TAs or by those of us who train them (Barnett and Cook).

To state the obvious, learning Latin is not equivalent to learning how to teach it. Graduate programs in Classics ideally should require work in the principles of language teaching (as well as in the presentation of culture and literature), and not only in literary analysis, as was the Roman model. Indeed, in ancient Rome, education was largely the study of literature. Students learned reading, writing, and some rudiments of arithmetic in the school of the *litterator* or *magister ludi*. Then they progressed to the school of the *grammaticus*, from ages 12 to 16, where they learned *recte loquendi scientia* ("how to speak correctly") and were introduced to the *enarratio poetarum* ("exposition of the poets"). The *grammaticus*, as Juvenal tells us (7.234–36), was prepared to name the nurse of Anchises, or to quote the number of flasks of Sicilian wine Acestes presented to the Trojans, but having these arcane details at his fingertips by no means insured that he could teach effectively any more than having a mastery of literature today guarantees that one will be an effective instructor. In fact, there is much evidence to the contrary: Horace (*Epistulae* 2.1.70–71) calls his teacher Orbilius *plagosus*, "the flogger"; Ausonius (*Epistulae* 22.12) labels his "the frowner" (*tetrici praeceptoris*); and Petronius (*Satyricon* 2.3–4) goes so far as to accuse his teachers of "presiding over the ruin of eloquence" (*primi omnium eloquentiam perdidistis*). From Suetonius (*De Grammaticis* 9) we can even compile a rich vocabulary of tools of punishment for the classroom—rods, lashes, and whips—and their uses!

Ancient and Modern Theories and Praxis

Our Latin methodology course is designed to educate Latin teachers, not merely to instruct TAs for temporary assignments. It includes, even emphasizes, language proficiency, but it also stresses content, and, a novelty of the methods course, the readings in modern pedagogical theories and issues are compared, insofar as they can be, with similar theories and issues in Latin tracts on education. Students are asked to research modern theories in ancient texts. For instance, when we read about the place of Latin in the modern curriculum or about setting goals in the Latin classroom, we can compare what ancient writers on education may have said about the same or a similar topic. To Quintilian (*Institutio Oratoria* 1.4.5), for example, Latin literature was

> *necessaria pueris, iucunda senibus, dulcis secretorum comes et quae vel sola in omni studiorum genere plus habeat operis quam ostentationis.*

> a necessity for young people and a pleasure for old people, the sweet companion of our privacy and the only one of all branches of study which has more content than show.

Likewise, Cicero's views on the importance of literature are a *locus classicus* (*Pro Archia* 7):

> *Nam ceterae neque temporum sunt neque aetatum omnium neque locorum; at haec studia adulescentiam alunt, senectutem oblectant, secundas res ornant, adversis perfugium ac solacium praebent, delectant domi, non impediunt foris, pernoctant nobiscum, peregrinantur, rusticantur.*

> For other activities are restricted to time or age or place. But literature is a study that teaches young people, delights older people, allows us to have a deeper appreciation of fine things, and provides a solace in adversity. Moreover it is a welcome companion at home, at work, in evening leisure, while traveling, or while on vacation.

Or, to take another example, in one session we consider the profile of the Latin language student. How do we approach a Latin class with a student population of mixed preparations, abilities, learning styles, and any number of other variables? One way is to use instruments like the Myers-Briggs Type Indicator. These tests identify learning and teaching styles, and they give us strategies to assess our own style preferences. We can then develop teaching approaches that complement our style and respond to those appropriate to a wider range of students (Richards and Lockhart). Coupling these techniques with what we find in Latin texts about classroom psychology is doubly instructive. Quintilian (1.1.2), for example, speaks about the different abilities of students:

> *Hebetes vero et indociles non magis secundum naturam homines eduntur quam prodigiosa corpora et monstris insignia, sed hi pauci admodum fuerunt. . . . in pueris elucet spes plurimorum, quae cum emoritur aetate, manifestum est, non naturam defecisse sed curam.*

> Those who are dull and unteachable are as unusual as prodigious forms and monstrosities, but these are few in number. . . .Young people hold the promise of very many callings, and when that promise passes with age, it is clearly not due to a defect in their nature, but to lack of cultivation.

To the argument that there are degrees of talent, he replies that there are corresponding variations in actual accomplishments. But, he concludes (1.1.3), *nemo reperitur, qui sit studio nihil consecutus* ("everyone gains something from education"). Quintilian also writes about the need to meet students at their own level, presenting materials and activities that are accessible (2.3.7):

> *Oportebit summittentem se ad mensuram discentis; ut velocissimus quoque, si forte iter cum parvulo faciat, det manum et gradum suum minuat nec procedat ultra quam comes possit.*

> A good teacher will accommodate the student's level; just as a very fast walker, if he takes a walk with a small child, gives him his hand and slows his step so as not to go more quickly than his companion is able.

The benefits of positive feedback are well documented in modern educational theories, and we have all experimented with systems of reward to praise and encourage our students. Quintilian likewise understood this basic tenet of educational psychology, cautioning that without some levity and positive reinforcement, students might learn to hate their studies (1.1.20):

> *Nam id in primis cavere oportebit, ne studia, qui amare nondum potest, oderit. . . . Lusus hic sit; et rogetur et laudetur et numquam non fecisse se gaudeat.*

> Above all things we must take care that he does not hate the studies that he is not yet able to appreciate. . . . His studies should be a game: he should be questioned and praised and always take pleasure in what he has done well.

Another topic on the syllabus is the comparison of Latin textbooks and their methodologies. For this session students examine several language teaching methods, including the grammar-translation and audio-lingual approaches. They are then asked to review the presentation of some specific point of grammar in several corresponding texts and prepare a class presentation on that point using both these approaches. Closely related to this topic is the selection of Latin authors and readings appropriate to different levels of study. Quintilian's discussion (10.1.85–10.2) of the merits of several genres and authors provides an ancient *comparandum* (10.1.93):

> *Elegia quoque Graecos provocamus, cuius mihi tersus atque elegans maxime videtur auctor Tibullus. Sunt qui Propertium malint. Ovidius utroque lascivior, sicut durior Gallus. Satira quidem tota nostra est.*

> We challenge the Greeks in elegy. In this genre Tibullus seems especially on point and elegant. Yet, there are those who prefer Propertius. Ovid is more lascivious than either of them; Gallus more brusque. By contrast satire is a genre than belongs completely to us.

Augustine, on the other hand, in his well-known attack upon the necessity of learning Greek, condemns the canon of Latin authors as nothing more than a *dulcissimum spectaculum vanitatis* (*Confessiones* 1.13); he does tell us though, that he loved learning Latin, not the grammar but the literature (1.13: *Adamaveram enim Latinas, non quas primi magistri, sed quas docent qui grammatici vocantur*—cf. Imme). These are but a few of the many instances of a contemporary methodological debate anticipated in Latin pedagogical texts.

Teaching and Research

The approach used in our methods course has two important consequences. The first is that it invites TAs to participate in creative curriculum development through research. Secondly, it encourages TAs to reflect upon their own teaching methods. When they compare their own classroom strategies with both modern language teaching theories and ancient pedagogical *dicta,* they can make valid self-assessments. In reflecting upon experience, theory, and the wide range of readings required, they learn how to continue learning on their own, not only about the teaching of Latin, but also about the vast corpus of Latin texts they may use in their teaching. At their core, these scholarly and teaching activities are the same; that is, the research in ancient texts can be practically applied. A session on teaching prose composition may lead to a discussion about what ancient authors thought or taught about how to write well, noting, for example, Quintilian's remark at 12.10.50 (and cf. 1.9 and 2.4),

> *At quod libris dedicatum in exemplum edatur, id tersum ac limatum et ad legem ac regulam compositum esse oportere.*

> But what is written in books should be a model of a composition that is succinct and polished according to the accepted standard and rule.

This may lead in turn to a session about the presentation, in writing, of scholarly research, or how to critique the writing of one's students. In the methods course, teaching is research. We investigate the learning styles of our audience, we study techniques and methods of instruction, and we apply the pedagogical lessons from both modern and ancient texts. The TA in-service training, combined with the methods course, is an attempt to make our students conscious of the interdependence of applied techniques and pedagogical theory in teaching Latin. The course also aims at encouraging them to develop creative ways of integrating their teaching and research, just as they will have to do as scholars and teachers.

To help Latin TAs realize the importance of research in teaching, the course also involves a composition project, the production of a Latin reader for high-school students. The project is part of a coordinated effort among college and secondary-school Latin teachers in Arizona to set curriculum goals and develop classroom materials appropriate to those goals. Latin TAs produce, by the end of each semester, a lively Latin narrative aimed at high-school readers. The first, called "Happily Ever After," is the story of Demeter and Persephone, based upon Claudian's *De Raptu Proserpinae*. With the text is an addendum about Roman weddings, including related texts and suggestions for extra-curricular activies. Finally, the text has an accompanying commentary that reflects current scholarship and age-appropriate literary criticism. Such a compendium of texts, supplemented as they are by cultural material and literary criticism, aims at two important outcomes. The first is that appealing Latin texts and classroom materials will be accessible to younger students. These texts, combined with their interest in the cultural aspects of the narrative, will encourage them to continue to study Latin. Secondly, TAs learn to research and assimilate scholarship on a topic that will appeal to young students. In short, TAs learn to integrate their research and teaching in creative and practical ways.

The Latin methods course we have developed at the University of Arizona aims, as a complement to our TA training program: to educate Latin teachers, not merely to train teaching assistants; to examine and apply methodologies, strategies, and techniques culled from ancient texts as well as from modern pedagogical theory; and to insist upon the combination of sound teaching practices and careful scholarship in teacher preparation. For Quintilian the focus of education was spiritual at least as much as technical, and character development was a major goal; in the area of oratory, for example, he insisted that not only should an orator be a *vir bonus peritus dicendi* (12.1.1), but that "no one should be an orator who is not a good man" (12.1.3: *dico . . . ne futurum quidem oratorem nisi virum bonum*). A similar philosophy should motivate any Latin teacher training program: We should produce teachers who are at once skilled Latinists and skilled at teaching Latin. They should be committed professionals, reflective teachers, and effective researchers; they should be innovators, aware of the latest theories, methods, and resources available to the profession, but they should also have a sense of the history and classical origins of Latin pedagogy. While the training program and methods course briefly described here constitute simply one of many possible models (a detailed syllabus for our course is available from the author at the Dept. of Classics, P.O. Box 210067, Univ. of Arizona, Tucson, AZ 85721-0067—see Gibaldi and Mirollo for other examples), it has certainly been aimed at achieving these goals and at promoting the ideal that the *ars docendi* is indeed both an inspired and a practical art.

19

Graduate Latin Teacher Preparation Programs

GILBERT W. LAWALL
University of Massachusetts at Amherst

The demand for middle- and secondary-school Latin teachers is high. Positions are going unfilled, programs are being terminated when schools cannot find qualified replacements for Latin teachers when they retire, and desired expansion of programs into middle and elementary schools sometimes cannot be accomplished for lack of new teachers. Advisors of Latin and Classics majors in colleges and universities should urge their advisees to consider teaching careers in the schools. The opportunities are there, and an abundance of new teaching materials and new pedagogical approaches makes this a particularly exciting time for students to consider teaching Latin in the schools.

Interest in Latin and in the Classical Humanities, that is, the civilizations of the ancient Mediterranean world, classical society and culture, Greek and Roman art and archaeology, ancient history, classical mythology and folklore, ancient women's studies and ethnic studies, and the great works of Greek and Latin literature flourishes in our society, in the media, in the schools, and in institutions of higher learning. Classical studies are also expanding in the school curriculum, both laterally into history courses, social studies, English, and language arts, and vertically down into the junior high, the middle school, and the elementary grades. Latin is taught as part of exploratory language programs in the middle grades. Mythology and the epic poems of Homer, Vergil, and Ovid in translation have been introduced into the curriculum of the elementary schools. The American Classical League (ACL) now sponsors a group called Elementary Teachers of Classics, which in turn sponsors a National Mythology Exam for elementary-school students. The Classics profession, however, has not risen to the challenge of preparing teachers of Latin and Classical Humanities even to fill the need for secondary-school Latin teachers, much less for these other grade levels and in this broader context of language arts and classical studies (cf. LaFleur 1992: 178–79).

The following survey of graduate Latin teacher training programs will be followed by a description of the M.A.T. Program in Latin and Classical Humanities at the University of Massachusetts at Amherst (see Keitel), which may serve as a model for the development of new programs elsewhere.

SURVEY OF GRADUATE TEACHER TRAINING PROGRAMS

The 1996 American Philological Association *Guide to Graduate Programs in the Classics in the United States and Canada* lists 19 institutions offering an M.A.T. degree. While each of these programs involves teacher preparation in one way or another, the actual titles of the programs vary, e.g., M.A. in Latin, M.A.T. in Latin, M.Ed. in Latin, Master of Teaching, Master of Arts for Teaching, and Master's with Initial Certification. At the outset, however, it should be noted that some of these programs are inactive or marginal, producing few if any graduates per year. Often programs appear to be overshadowed by regular M.A. and Ph.D. tracks. The best programs are those in which there is a critical mass of M.A.T. students and those in which faculty members are heavily involved with secondary schools, secondary-school teachers, and professional associations that address the needs of secondary-school teachers.

Some programs are specially designed for those with a B.A. in Latin or Classics and no certification or courses in education. Other programs are for those who already have a teaching certificate. Some institutions offer a five-year program leading to a B.A. and a Master of Education degree. Some offer an M.A. in Latin and the possibility of spending an extra semester taking courses in education for certification. Some programs offer separate, carefully defined options for those who enter the program with and without certification. Hunter College will provisionally admit students with 18 instead of the normal 24 undergraduate Latin credits if they are already certified to teach a language other than Latin. This allows French or Spanish teachers, some of whom might actually be teaching Latin with the minimum of 18 credits, to develop their skills in the classical language and to become better teachers of Latin in their schools.

Some of the masters level programs in Latin teacher education require at least some acquaintance with ancient Greek. Some recommend completion of an undergraduate minor in English, a second foreign language, or some other subject commonly taught in the secondary schools prior to matriculation. Some programs require written and/or oral examinations, often the same as those for the regular masters degree. Some programs examine students on required reading lists. The program at the University of Michigan prides itself on its innovations in Latin teaching methodology, and the program at Texas Tech seeks to connect Latin with Spanish (see below, Chapter 20).

The length of programs varies from eight units without thesis or examinations to two and a half years. The programs at Hunter College in New York

City and at the University of North Carolina at Greensboro are primarily for part-time students who are already teaching, and completion of these programs can take up to four years. The University of Georgia's Classics Summer Institute is well attended by in-service Latin teachers from throughout the country needing to upgrade their certification or desiring to complete a Master's degree in the Classics Department's summers-only M.A. program. This institution, one of the most active in the nation in pre-service and in-service Latin teacher education, also offers a Ph.D. in Latin Language Education.

THE M.A.T. PROGRAM IN LATIN
AND CLASSICAL HUMANITIES AT THE
UNIVERSITY OF MASSACHUSETTS AT AMHERST

The program matriculated its first class in 1970 at a time when Latin enrollments in the schools were about to complete their catastrophic plunge to their lowest point in over 100 years. Some predicted that Latin would soon disappear from the schools; some college and university Classics professors even welcomed this trend, sure that *they* knew how to teach Latin better than high-school teachers, whom they criticized for spending too much time with Roman banquets and cultural trivia. The major Latin teacher training programs of the 1960s, such as those at Harvard and S.U.N.Y. at Albany, were closing up shop in response to declining Latin enrollments in the schools. Such were the bleak times in which, with the encouragement and blessing of the late John F. Latimer of George Washington University, we initiated a new Latin teacher training program at the University of Massachusetts at Amherst as the sole graduate program in the fledgling Classics wing of what was then a Department of French, Italian, and Classics.

In the early years we recommended that students complete courses in educational psychology and philosophy of education prior to entering the program, but the program is now designed for students with no previous preparation in professional education. The program grew from a one-year to a two-year program, and it has been responsive to changes in educational philosophy, state certification requirements, and changing expectations within our own Classics profession. The program began by offering an M.A.T. degree in Latin alone, with students receiving certification in Massachusetts for teaching Latin in grades 9–12. It now offers an M.A.T. in Latin *and* Classical Humanities, and state certification has now changed so that students receive provisional certification with advanced standing (a level of certification midway between the basic provisional certification and standard certification) for teaching Latin and Classical Humanities in grades 5–12. The program is approved by the Commonwealth of Massachusetts, the National Council for the

Accreditation of Teacher Education (NCATE), and the Interstate Certification Compact (ICC), which covers 31 states and the District of Columbia. Amid all of these changes over the years, three things have remained constant. First, although enjoying close and friendly ties with the School of Education on the campus and drawing on its clerical, instructional, and intellectual resources, the program has remained firmly based in what became an independent Department of Classics. Second, students in the program are fully supported with teaching assistantships. Third, faculty in the program and its graduates have worked hard over the years to reverse that catastrophic plunge of secondary-school Latin enrollments and to rebuild, reshape, and give a new lease on life to Latin and Classics instruction in American schools.

Eligibility requirements for admission to the program include a B.A. degree with a major in Latin or Classics or its equivalent with at least four upper-level Latin courses, 12 semester credits in ancient Greek, and 6 in Greek and Roman history. Applicants must submit a well-considered personal statement indicating a genuine commitment to a career as a teacher of Latin and Classical Humanities in grades 5–12. An undergraduate minor in a second teaching area such as English or a modern foreign language is highly recommended but not required and is, in fact, rarely found in applicants. We regard this as unfortunate, and we encourage undergraduate students at institutions throughout the country who are contemplating careers in middle- and secondary-school Latin teaching to complete a minor or a second major in some other widely taught subject, particularly Spanish, since the majority of schools now seeking Latin teachers want candidates who can teach Spanish as well. We are contemplating the addition of an optional third year for those wishing to earn certification in Spanish or French, as well as in Latin and Classical Humanities.

Efforts are made to locate and attract minority students, and during the 1995–96 academic year four of the 10 students in the program were from backgrounds underrepresented in the Latin teaching profession. Usually five or six new students are admitted each year, for a total of 10–12 students in the two-year program.

There are four strands in the program of studies: 1) academic courses in Latin and Classical Humanities, 2) methods courses in Latin and Classical Humanities, 3) field experiences, and 4) courses in educational theory and practice. Many practical and theoretical considerations have been weighed in the planning of the program over the years, not the least being the state requirement that those receiving certification must demonstrate not only competencies in the area of subject matter knowledge but also common teaching competencies in the areas of 1) communication skills; 2) instructional practice, including technology, addressing special needs, and making instruction relevant to students of diverse backgrounds; 3) evaluation; 4) problem solving; 5) equity, including consideration of special needs and diversity; and 6) professionalism.

ACADEMIC COURSES IN
LATIN AND CLASSICAL HUMANITIES

The required academic courses in Latin and Classical Humanities include two Latin literature courses, usually one prose and one poetry, chosen from courses in Vergil's *Aeneid*, Elegy and Lyric, History and Biography, and Cicero's Orations; a one-credit course titled Oral Interpretation of Latin Literature; Latin Prose Composition; Advanced Latin Grammar; and a Seminar in the History of the Roman Republic or the Roman Empire. To encourage an understanding of the relationship between study of Latin and other fields of knowledge, students must choose one course from a considerable list of offerings outside the department. If students have not studied Greek on the undergraduate level, they complete 12 credits of elementary and intermediate Classical Greek.

Many students take more than the required two courses in Latin literature, enrolling in a third and sometimes a fourth course for credit or audit in order to meet a programmatic expectation that students will have read extensively in Caesar, Cicero, Catullus, Horace, Vergil, and Ovid—the standard authors taught in secondary-school Latin classes—before completion of the program.

The course titled Oral Interpretation of Latin Literature is regarded as especially important, since most students come into the program with little or no experience with Latin as a living language, having learned Latin at a college or university in courses with a strictly grammar-translation approach. In teaching their Latin courses at the university, students in the program must become comfortable with reading passages of Latin and Latin dialogues aloud expressively, and they must teach their students to do the same. For most of the students in the program, this is a new experience that requires much practice and much attention to matters often neglected in undergraduate Latin courses—quantity and quality of vowels and accentuation of words.

The required course in Advanced Latin Grammar introduces students to linguistic analysis of language (phonology, morphology, and syntax) and shows them how to refine their own presentations of Latin grammar in their classrooms. An elective course in the History of the Latin Language teaches them how to present many aspects of Latin grammar (the formation of perfect stems, for example) as the result of easily traceable historical developments.

The graduate seminar in the Roman Republic or the Roman Empire is designed not only to emphasize the narrative history of Roman civilization but to reinforce knowledge of Mediterranean geography, ancient chronology, and the ancillary fields of classical study (epigraphy, numismatics, papyrology, etc.). Equally important, it emphasizes ancient and modern theories of historiography in an effort to give students an understanding of the methodology of the writing of history.

METHODS COURSES IN
LATIN AND CLASSICAL HUMANITIES

Effective and successful teaching has always been prized by the faculty in the department, and it is natural, then, that the department pays close attention to the teaching of its graduate students. In the first two semesters of the program, the graduate students teach Latin 110 and 120 at the university (the first two courses in the elementary/intermediate sequence); in either their third or fourth semester they teach Latin 230 or 240 (the courses in the intermediate part of the sequence). During two semesters the graduate students also serve as teaching assistants in Greek Civilization or Greek Mythology, where their role is to help the professor with audio-visual presentations, administering and grading of exams, and grading of students' essays.

Focus on teaching begins with the graduate students spending their first full day on campus in a university-wide orientation program for all new teaching assistants. This is followed by a day of workshops in the department, in which faculty and graduate students read and discuss the state competencies for educators and lay plans for teaching the first several Latin classes at the university.

Each course in the elementary/intermediate Latin sequence is accompanied by a one-credit, one-hour per week Seminar in Instructional Planning and Assessment, in which faculty members meet with the graduate students who are teaching each level of the sequence. In these weekly seminars, the professors and students study the chapters to be taught that week, plan classroom activities, generate handouts for supplementary grammatical material, exercises, and cultural background as needed, and discuss evaluation instruments such as quizzes and tests. As the semester progresses, there is opportunity to discuss problems that arise in the teaching of these courses and to plan strategies for coping with them. Selected pedagogical articles from journals and chapters of books on methodology are required reading, along with the teacher's handbook that accompanies the textbook series being used.

When graduate students serve as teaching assistants in the Greek Civilization and Greek Mythology courses, they enroll in one-credit seminars in Teaching Greek Civilization and Teaching Greek Mythology. Requirements for these seminars include attendance at all of the lectures in the Greek Civilization and Greek Mythology courses, reading of the textbooks assigned in these courses, and helping the professors who teach these courses in the ways described above.

In addition to these one-credit seminars in instructional planning and assessment and in teaching, all students are required to take three formal methods courses: Teaching the Latin Language, Teaching Latin Literature, and Teaching Classical Humanities.

Teaching the Latin Language, as taught by Visiting Instructor Richard Gascoyne in fall 1996, was correlated carefully with the state competencies for educators and covered the following topics: 1) overview of lesson planning and delivery; 2) resources, methodology, and textbooks; 3) learner strategies (including teaching the learning disabled); 4) classroom organization and management; 5) resources of technology; 6) standards and the proficiency movement; 7) teaching Latin in the elementary and middle school; 8) teaching and testing reading; 9) teaching and testing oral skills, listening, and writing; 10) teaching and testing culture; 11) teaching Classics in the elementary and middle school; 12) teaching and testing grammar and vocabulary; 13) testing: national, state, local, portfolio; 14) using authentic materials; and 15) professional resources and public relations. Each student was required to create and deliver two 10-minute mini-lessons, to study and review for the class a major textbook series, and to prepare six formal written assignments on the topics listed above.

Teaching Latin Literature will be redesigned when it is taught again and will begin with reading of the archaic epitaphs of the Scipios from an edition that instructs students at the secondary-school level in the conventions of Latin epigraphy and the skills needed to read and interpret Latin inscriptions. These early inscriptions presented in this way show how authentic material of this sort can be taught fairly early in the secondary-school Latin sequence to reinforce both the teaching of grammatical constructions and the teaching of Roman culture and values. In the next unit, students will read selections from Plautus' *Aulularia* and will explore various resources available for teaching this play and the cultural values that it embodies. This will be followed by selections from Cicero's *Somnium Scipionis* and Lucretius' *De rerum natura* and study of the diametrically opposed world views expressed by these contemporary authors. The course will conclude with the selections from Ovid's *Metamorphoses* and *Amores* that have been chosen for the Advanced Placement (AP) Examination (above, Chapter 10). Each student will observe a master secondary-school instructor teaching Latin literature, and as a final project teams of two students each will teach episodes from Ovid's *Metamorphoses* in schools.

The last methodology course, Teaching Classical Humanities, typically includes presentations by more than a dozen middle-school, junior-high, and high-school teachers from western Massachusetts and professors from the university and focuses on five areas of instruction in Classical Humanities in the schools: 1) general Classics courses, 2) mythology, 3) history, 4) classical literature in translation, and 5) social studies (in particular the influence of ancient political thought on the American founding fathers). The 10–12 students in the M.A.T. program divide into five teams, and each team chooses one of the five topics listed above and is assigned to work with one of the school teachers. During two weeks in the middle of the semester, the teams observe classes in the schools. Each team prepares a week-long unit of material of its own, which it teaches at the school of the teacher to whom the team has been assigned.

FIELD EXPERIENCES

For many of the students in the M.A.T. program, the field experiences are its most important component. These begin with the graduate students teaching in the elementary Latin classes at the university, using the newest textbooks and methods—an experience that most of the graduate students find very different from the way they learned Latin in high school or in their undergraduate years. A four-skills approach is used that privileges development of skill in reading, with this skill reinforced by the development of skills in listening, speaking, and writing. Much Latin is read aloud by teachers and students in these classes, an activity that develops reading, speaking, and listening skills simultaneously. Comprehension questions and translation from Latin into English are also used, and sentences of connected narrative are translated from English into Latin to develop writing skills as a check on knowledge of morphology and syntax and ultimately as a means of strengthening reading skills. Much vocabulary and grammar is learned in the process of reading, and it is then rigorously reinforced through memorization of vocabulary lists and paradigms of grammatical forms and study of syntactical patterns. Culture is carefully integrated into the Latin readings and developed further through essays in English, so that the Latin language is set in an authentic cultural context. The graduate students' teaching of these classes is guided and supported by the accompanying seminars in instructional planning and assessment discussed above, and faculty members observe each graduate student three times per semester, with each observation followed by discussion of the graduate student's progress and by completion of a standardized form that addresses the common teaching competencies expected of certified teachers.

The next field experience takes the graduate students outside the university during January intersession. This is the pre-practicum, which consists of 75 hours of observation and other experiences, which may include teaching, in at least three schools of different types and grade levels ranging from 5 to 12, and including observation of classes in Classical Humanities, as well as in Latin. The graduate students keep daily logs, build a portfolio of reflective essays on how they see the common teaching competencies described by the state evidenced in the teaching they are observing, and write brief critical essays on six short booklets that discuss current pedagogical topics.

After one or two more semesters of teaching at the university, students undertake their practice teaching or practicum, consisting of at least 200 hours of experience in schools, with at least 150 hours at one school (usually a high school), of which at least 135 hours must involve taking full responsibility, and with at least 50 hours in one or more of grades 5 to 8. This usually results in experiences at two different schools, a high school and a middle school or junior high, and prepares the graduate students for their certification that now includes grades 5 through 12. Some observation and some teaching are done outside of Latin classes in social studies (ancient history), English (mythology and Greek and Roman literature in translation), or other departments where classical materials are taught. The graduate students again keep a log and a portfolio, and their teaching is again observed and critiqued by a supervisor from the university, as well as by the cooperating teacher at the school.

After completion of all of the requirements for the M.A.T. degree, students receive their diploma and provisional certification with advanced standing in Massachusetts with the NCATE and ICC stamp of approval. Those who obtain teaching positions in Massachusetts may then pass through the final hurdle and obtain standard certification by completion of a clinical experience. This consists of one semester of full-time teaching, with the teaching again being supervised by a faculty member from the university and by a cooperating teacher at the school. One of the criteria for a successful clinical experience in Latin and Classical Humanities is evidence of mastery of the material being taught on the part of the students receiving instruction, with each student's progress being tracked throughout the semester.

COURSES IN EDUCATIONAL THEORY AND PRACTICE

The fourth strand of the M.A.T. program consists of courses directly related to the common teaching competencies. Four courses are required: 1) Educational Psychology or Psychology in the Schools, 2) Issues in Instructional Methods in Special Education or Historical Perspectives in Special Education, 3) Introduction to Multicultural Education or Curriculum Development for Heterogeneous Classes, and 4) Principles of School Law or Seminar on Law and Educational Policy. These courses are taught in the School of Education and the Department of Psychology.

EXAMINATIONS

As of January 1, 1998, all candidates for teacher certification in Massachusetts are required to pass a two-part state examination testing communication and literacy skills and subject matter knowledge.

ET CETERA

Students are required to assemble an on-going portfolio containing material such as syllabi for courses they teach, lesson plans for all classes they teach, handouts used in classes, quizzes and exams, evaluation forms, significant sets of materials prepared for courses they are taking, reflective essays on special events they attend, and reflective essays on their progress at the middle and the end of each semester. There is a recommended reading list containing standard selections from Cicero and Caesar and the selections on the AP syllabi for Catullus/Horace, Vergil, and Ovid. Each student must complete a research project, which often involves preparing a week-long unit of lessons on some readings from Latin literature. At the beginning of each year there are three two-hour sessions introducing new students to the computer resources in the department, conducted by an experienced second-year student; students also take advantage of workshops given by the university's Office of Instructional Technology and of the materials and equipment available in the university's Foreign Language Resource Center. For students wishing to continue their study of Greek, seminars meeting every other Sunday afternoon are available, which are attended also by school teachers from the area. The topics covered are relevant to the teaching of Latin literature, including, for example, Greek lyric poetry as background for the Catullus/Horace AP syllabus, Apollonius of Rhodes as background for the Vergil AP syllabus, and Theocritus as background for Vergil's *Eclogues*.

Three M.A.T. seminars in Latin and Classical Humanities are offered each semester, meeting from 3:30 to 6:00 in the afternoon and bringing together the graduate students in the program, faculty from the department and from the School of Education, and teachers from schools in the area. The topics covered in the seminars in 1996–97 were: "Constructive Discipline and Developing a Caring Classroom Community"; "The Keepers of Alexandria: An Innovative Multicultural and Interdisciplinary Curriculum for Upper Elementary Grades"; "An Elementary *Odyssey*: Children and the Classics"; "The Articulation and Achievement Project: Connecting Standards, Performance, and Assessment"; "The Roman Gladiator in the Latin Classroom"; and "Antigone: Tragedy and Ethico-Political Consciousness." Students may also attend a variety of public lectures sponsored by the Classics Departments of Amherst, Mount Holyoke, and Smith Colleges and the Western Massachusetts Chapter of the Archaeological Institute of America. The program underwrites memberships in and attendance at meetings of the local Pioneer Valley Classical Association, the Massachusetts Foreign Language Association, the Classical Association of Massachusetts, and the Classical Association of New England, and membership in the American Classical League. Two scholarships are available each summer for study abroad in Italy or Greece. The New England Latin Placement Service, co-directed by a member of the faculty, in cooperation with other regional and national placement services, locates abundant opportunities for employment.

The faculty in the program have been highly active in outreach and networking. They have offered courses, workshops, conferences, and study tours for teachers—at local, state, regional, national, and international levels. They have held positions of leadership in classical associations at all levels. They have revised and updated sets of teaching materials that are now among the most widely used in the schools, and they have created or sponsored the creation of numerous other textbooks and instructional materials, often in collaboration with students in the program. They have edited and distributed numerous newsletters for professional associations and publishing houses, and they have built and maintained a resource center in the department that is utilized by teachers throughout New England. Last but not least, they maintain contact with the graduates of the program and support their professional development as educators.

Anyone wishing further information on the M.A.T. Program in Latin and Classical Humanities at the University of Massachusetts at Amherst or wishing help in developing similar programs elsewhere may contact the Director of Graduate Studies, Dept. of Classics, Univ. of Massachusetts, Box 33905, Amherst, MA 01003–3905.

20

Latin and Spanish: Roman Culture and Hispanic America

EDWARD V. GEORGE
Texas Tech University

Latin and Spanish? *Together* in the classroom? How? When? Why? How much? Many Latin teachers have made brief excursions into the Latin-Spanish link, if only through occasionally pointing out, for instance, the relationship among *amicus*, *amigo*, *amico*, and *ami*. Much more is both possible and inviting. I offer four reasons why systematic attention to Spanish in the Latin class, enhanced by cooperation with Spanish-teaching colleagues, promises to provide rewards for students and benefits for the Latin program.

The Hispanic, and hence Spanish-speaking, portion of the U.S. population is expanding rapidly.

In 1995 persons of Hispanic origin in the United States totaled an estimated 26,936,000, or 10.2% of the total population. A recent U.S. Census Bureau report projects that by the year 2020 these figures will rise to over 52 million and 16.3%. A continuation of this trend is anticipated until 2050, when over 96 million Hispanic origin persons will constitute 24.5% of the population. Further, the expected proportionate rise among the young will be sharper than for the general population; for instance, the number of non-Hispanic whites age 5-13, projected at 23,125,000 in 2000 will drop to 21,186,000 by 2030. In the same time period Hispanic origin persons in this age bracket will rise from 5,651,000 to 10,362,000 (U.S. Dept. of Commerce, 12, 14, 17).

For the future this means a rise in the percentage of students with Spanish in their background—a reality which, with preparation, Latin teachers can use to the advantage of all students. The growing importance of Spanish in American society will put students in more and more situations, whether in business, public service, or private life, where Spanish will be useful; and Latin teachers have a wealth of ways to show their students that Latin training, among other advantages, brings people measurably closer to a command of Spanish.

Students with a year or two of Latin have acquired important tools for the study of Spanish.

Study of a compact set of sound and spelling changes is an easy first step to a systematic grasp of the evolution of Latin into Spanish. Some common, though not universal, changes are illustrated below:

	LATIN	SPANISH	EXAMPLES
Word beginnings:	sc-	esc-	scribere > escribir (to write)
	sp-	esp-	sperare > esperar (to hope)
Word endings:	-us	-o	amicus > amigo (friend)
	-ire	-ir	aperire > abrir (to open)
Vowels:	e	ie	herba > hierba (grass)
	o	ue	porta > puerta (door)
			fortis > fuerte (strong)
Consonants:	c	g	lacrima > lagrima (tear)
	p	b	lupus > lobo (wolf)
	t	d	sitis > sed (thirst)

Another example of easy movement from Latin to Spanish occurs in the descent of Spanish verb forms, extractable from the books *201 Latin Verbs* and *301 Spanish Verbs* (Wohlberg, Kendris), especially in *a*-stem verbs; compare, e.g., Spanish *canto, cantas, canta, cantamos, cantáis, cantan* with Latin *canto, cantas, cantat, cantamus, cantatis, cantant*. A few comments on what some teachers have done with this Latin-Spanish connection will suggest possibilities.

Donalee Harris (Spanish) and Susan Robertson (Latin), of Frenship High School in Wolfforth, Texas, have formulated a multi-session series of 60- to 90-minute joint meetings, spread out over the year, in their first-year, 9th-grade Latin and Spanish classes. Often students work in small mixed groups. For instance, on one day the focus is a theme-clustered exercise in animal vocabulary. Each student receives some two dozen cards picturing various animals, with captions in Latin or Spanish. Students play a number of games (e.g., "Concentration") with the cards, associating the Spanish and Latin names and observing recurring sound and spelling changes. Another lesson focuses on a short, original melodrama involving villain, heroine, and handsome rescuer; the playlet is acted out in Latin, Spanish, and English, again allowing chances to observe similarities and letting Latin students experience *lingua Latina* as a spoken language. In general, although these SPLAT lessons (as they are called: acronym for "Spanish-Latin") are presented only a few times a year, they provide experiences which may be referred to at other times, while generating widespread interest and even envy in those students whose Latin and Spanish classes are not selected for the SPLAT experiment. These sessions are frequent enough to provide substance and continuity, yet rare enough to avoid encroaching unduly on the remainder of the year's pre-set curriculum.

Harris and Robertson (1997b) report a high level of retention of specific material covered. They attend to other objectives as well. Among the aims of the program is "to break down cultural barriers and promote unity of participants and teachers within the foreign language department." Robertson observes:

> In one Latin class, only two students were willing to admit a knowledge of Spanish in September. Now a majority would like to learn more about Spanish. The general attitude that Spanish is an inferior language spoken by non-college-bound students has begun to soften. SPLAT has given students permission to to respect Spanish as a language which offers valuable advantages to its speakers.

Harris and Robertson also perceive a growing closeness between the Spanish and Latin programs among the teachers in the school.

Harris' comments should be equally encouraging to Latin teachers: "The addition of Latin to the Spanish curriculum has eased the acceptance of Spanish grammar. I was delightfully surprised to see how students transferred SPLAT knowledge to Spanish by remembering the spelling/sound change lessons." Spanish "stem-changing" verbs, which exhibit stem vowel changes (e.g., inf. *volar* [= "to fly"], present indic. *vuelo;* inf. *perder* [= "to lose"], pres. indic. *pierdo*), become much easier to teach to students who have studied a core list of regular Latin-Spanish transformations—in this case, $o > ue$ and $e > ie$. "Because of SPLAT lessons," Harris says, "a one to two week unit was shortened to a two day unit. After testing, I found that students [with exposure to SPLAT] had retained the concept of stem-changing verbs with greater acuity than did those students who had not experienced SPLAT lessons." Other Latin-Spanish teacher teams in Texas have had similarly successful cooperative experiences. In support of such efforts I have devised for teachers a graduate course at Texas Tech University, "Roman Culture and Hispanic America," which Harris and Robertson used as a resource in developing their program.

Many tools for Latin-Spanish instruction, either by the Latin teacher alone or, preferably, in cooperation with the Spanish teacher, are easily accessible. Lathrop, a readable survey of the Latin > Spanish linguistic evolution, stands out. Wilkes' *Latin for Beginners* (1985) and *Spanish for Beginners* (1987) provide a matched pair ripe for use together. For example, the page on family terminology is virtually the same in the two books, down to the illustrations, except for the language of the captions. Harris and Robertson (1997a) have assembled a packet of lesson plans based on their experiences described above. Traupman (1997) is a storehouse of conversational expressions in Latin for which the Spanish teacher may easily supply equivalents. Williams (1995) provides a short list of linguistic change rules and two simple Spanish paragraphs with keys to recognizable antecedent Latin vocabulary. Chapter 11 of *Salvete*, Book 2 (Phinney, et al.), "In Colonia Emerita Augusta," takes the reader to Roman Iberia and introduces valuable background material. Dee provides a listing in five columns of Latin words alongside selected English, Italian, French, and Spanish derivatives.

Other material, though valuable, is either out of print, expensive, or produced overseas. Patterson contains lists of frequently used Spanish words, including concentrations of inheritances as well as borrowings from Latin. Segura Munguia is more than just a Latin-Spanish dictionary: it tracks derivatives of each Latin word through Spanish and the other Romance languages. Mateos Muñoz is a vocabulary development text, based on Greek and Latin stems and affixes, for Spanish speakers. Royo, a Latin grammar for Spanish speakers, includes simple Latin paragraphs on topics like Roman myth or history, conveniently accompanied by Spanish translations in the teacher's manual. Corominas is a Spanish etymological dictionary, entirely in Spanish.

Latin is employable as a bridge between Spanish and English, and hence as a medium for improving English language skills.

One longstanding exploitation of the Latin-Spanish-English triangular connection is the Los Angeles Unified School District's (LAUSD) widely-used Language Transfer Project, begun by Albert Baca and others in 1972 (see Chapter 6 above). LAUSD data showed that blacks and Hispanics tended to score lowest on standardized tests of English language skills. The District implemented a project aimed at 5th- and 6th-graders. Latin roots and affixes were taught as a means of extending English vocabulary. For speakers of Spanish, a study of the Latin-Spanish relationship was included to form a bridge from Spanish to English. Baca (1991: 404) notes:

> Implicit in these goals is the understanding that English skills can be significantly improved through pupil participation in a specially designed course in Latin and Roman culture employing the principle of transfer and the results of contrastive analysis between Latin and English and between Latin and Spanish.

The first-level book, *Marcus et Julia* (LAUSD), contains a series of dialogues involving a fictitious Roman family. Each of the nine units provides the teacher with trilingual lists of vocabulary occurring in the dialogues, with entries such as *flamma - flame - llama*; *caballus - cavalcade - caballus*; *unus - unit - uno/único*; *piscis - Pisces - piscina/pescado*; etc. In each *lectio* (*lesson - lección*), the teacher can resort to the word list as appropriate for expanding students' vocabulary in all three languages.

Versions of the LAUSD project have spread to other sites in and beyond California. Frank Morris of the College of Charleston (South Carolina) has instituted intensive two-day Latin workshops, for school teachers who need not have Latin background, based on a revision of the LAUSD material. Upon completion of a workshop, teachers can conduct simple dialogues in Latin with students, and direct activities which extend their English or Spanish vocabulary.

Robin Polasek, a Spanish teacher and one of Morris' students, exemplifies the program's value as a stimulant to original variations. Polasek, of Buist Academy, a Charleston public middle school, conducts her Spanish class in Spanish and Latin, just as an elementary Latin teacher would work in English and Latin. After the Latin dialogues, songs, mottoes, etc., she adds activities which explicate the common ground between Spanish and English as discovered through Latin roots and affixes, with the ultimate aim of boosting students' PSAT and SAT scores. Informal observation indicates that the strategy has worked. Buist teachers in sciences, social studies, and other areas note improved technical vocabulary among Ms. Polasek's students who are taking courses in those other fields. Continuing administrative support also suggests success.

Eilene Marston of the Burbank (California) Unified School District uses Latin to build skills in both Spanish and English for elementary-level children, most of whom have English as their second language after Spanish. Marston uses picture cards illustrating Roman family activities, which she describes verbally (e.g., *Marcus sedet, Marcus edit*):

> After students have demonstrated their understanding of the action verbs, they see an overhead transparency with three headings written across the top: Latin, Spanish, and English. They see the connections that join their native language, their second language, and Latin (American Classical League, 30).

Turning to collegiate instruction, Baca has also implemented, at California State University, Northridge, "Classics 115," a variation on the ordinary vocabulary development course; as Baca has remarked:

> CSUN must deal with the problem of [students'] deficient language skills. [Further,] since a significant number of our students are speakers of Spanish whose language skills in both English and Spanish may be deficient, there is clear need for a course that can address the special needs of this segment of our student population. The basic justification for offering this course, then, is the need for a course that will train students in the techniques for acquiring a larger, more effective vocabulary through word analysis and through an introduction to English-Spanish comparative linguistics.

Thus, among the course's objectives is "To explore the relationship between Spanish and English through a comparison of words in both languages stemming from Latin and Greek roots."

A study of the culture of Hispanic America discloses roots that reach back to the Greco-Roman world.

Teachers have learned much about the influence of the classical tradition in North America. Similarly, the Roman impact on Iberia is an obvious focus of study (Astin, et al., 118–42; Curchin; Phinney, et al., Book 2, Chapter 11; Keay; MacKendrick). Less common is an awareness of the stream of cultural continuity between ancient Greece and Rome and Hispanic America, including affected regions of the United States (Grafton). *The Classical Tradition in the Americas* (Haase and Reinhold) includes a series of recent essays. Kubler (1948, 1959) opens the door to the classical inheritance of Spanish colonial architecture, while Foster (21–49) and Stanislawski touch on the Greco-Roman backgrounds to New World colonial town planning. MacCormack, Moffitt and Sebastián (173–247), and Todorov are examples of literature which examine Spanish preconceptions of indigenous New World cultures, as affected by the Greco-Roman inheritance. Sources illustrating this range of topics are scattered, and mostly await adaptation for use in Latin teaching, but following are a few examples of material that could be used to make the Roman-Hispanic cultural connection.

Notions of Empire

In creating their New World empire, the Spanish did not so much depend on the Romans for ideas of how to exploit conquered territory as they did employ Roman imperial imagery as a means of justifying or authenticating their conquests (Pagden 1990, 1995; Palencia-Roth; Seed, 181–84; Yates; see Gibson 1966, 1968, and Bethell for a general introduction to Latin America, and Gonzalbo on colonial education). A prime example is the aura surrounding the Spanish monarch ruling at the time of Cortez, Charles V, who was simultaneously the Holy Roman Emperor, a title which put him (however spuriously) in the line of the Roman emperors of antiquity. To Charles were attached two myths that might strike us now as bizarre, but which in their day carried weight in the public sphere: the myth of the Holy Roman Emperor as the "last descendant of Aeneas," and the myth of the "last world emperor," who will subdue the world and then lay his crown at the feet of Jesus in Jerusalem (Tanner, 113–17, 120–27). Both of these ideas spring from the example of the Roman Empire, especially as transformed by the Christian church and invigorating a Christian-sponsored world power. The Spanish came to the New World for wealth and souls; the myths behind the monarchy—and even the tradition of the papacy as heir to the Roman Empire (Volz, 76)—promoted the Roman-rooted Spanish belief in the rightness of their dominating presence in these boundless, unheard of dominions. Teachers who touch upon either mythology or the afterlife of Roman culture will find in this pair of myths an avenue for understanding something of the mentality with which the Spanish approached the New World.

The Colegio de Santa Cruz:
A Classical Education in Early Colonial Mexico City

The Spanish had not been in Mexico long when, in 1536, the Franciscans opened an extraordinary school, the Colegio de Santa Cruz de Tlatelolco (Mathes, 13-21; Heath, 28-31; Steck). Its original purpose was to train the young sons of indigenous chiefs in a completely European format, including the traditional liberal arts curriculum and instruction in Latin. Reports describe remarkable Latin proficiency among some students. Scholarship such as the celebrated cultural studies of Bernardino de Sahagún survives, along with other achievements. Emmart and Cruz are two editions of a fascinating manuscript from Santa Cruz: an herbal, with accomplished illustrations of medically beneficial plants, and a text in clear, simple Latin providing directions for use. Emmart, harder to find, includes the English translation; Cruz, in paperback but expensive, provides a splendid facsimile of the manuscript. Meanwhile, Fernandez-Armesto suggests a striking example from Santa Cruz of Greco-Roman influence on our conventional picture of the conquest of Mexico, in which the Aztecs are said to have been immobilized by superstition, thus enabling the tiny Spanish invading force to prevail. Fernandez-Armesto argues that the ancient lore of omens, as found in Lucan, Plutarch, and other classical sources, acquired by indigenous scholars through the Colegio, provided many of the crucial details of this conventional picture, which he believes is mistaken. In any event, the Colegio de Santa Cruz was influential in transmitting the Greco-Roman cultural tradition to earliest colonial Mexico.

Aristotle and the Struggle over How to Treat the Indians

The Spanish, having determined that the inhabitants of the newfound lands indeed possessed souls needing salvation, raised the question: how was conversion to be effected? Should the gospel be preached without coercion, and the indigenous peoples allowed to consider the message of the gospel and freely accept or reject it? Or was it legitimate to exert force, subdue the prospective Christians, and communicate the gospel and the sacraments in a compulsory manner? The Spanish crown actually declared a moratorium on colonizing activities for a period in the early 1550s, while a disputation on this matter took place at Valladolid in Spain (Hanke 1949, 1959, 1974). The protagonists were Bartolomé de las Casas, a Dominican priest and defender of Indian rights, and Juan Ginés de Sepúlveda, likewise a cleric and a famed Aristotle scholar. The argument was conducted with the documents in Latin, and centered on Aristotle's notion that some people are born naturally free and others (in this case, of course, the Indians) naturally slaves. In other words, at the time of the creation of the culture of New Spain, the world view and ideas of classical antiquity were still regarded as authoritative sources for considering the most pressing political questions of the time, and for deciding how the Europeans were to conceptualize the peoples they met.

Colonial Period Latin Literature from and about the New World

Latin, associated in most people's minds with the two centuries before and after Christ, continued to serve as a medium of communication in many parts of the world through the Middle Ages, the Renaissance, and beyond. Among the less widely known works of these later eras is a body of writings from or about the Hispanic New World (Osorio; IJsewijn, 296–307). Latin works in scholastic philosophy, theology, law, popularizing chronicles, religious and secular poetry, and other fields form a considerable corpus. The edition of a Latin epistle of Columbus (Marx) is a small and rare exception to the absence of annotated texts of these works suitable for school use. Many sources of potential interest could be profitably edited for intermediate or advanced courses in upper high school or college. Peter Martyr of Angleria's multivolume *De orbe novo* of the early 16th century (1892, 1912), narrating the Spanish voyages of discovery, was an important work through which Europe at large heard of the exploits. Other examples are the Jesuit missionary José de Acosta's *De natura novi orbis* (Acosta 1596), the Latin version of part of his longer work on the natural and moral history of the Indies; Acosta's and Las Casas' revealing books on how best to convert the Indians (Acosta 1984; Casas); Francisco Cervantes Salazar's unique Latin dialogue detailing a stroll through early colonial Mexico City; and Rafael Landívar's *Rusticatio Mexicana* (1948, 1965), the highly regarded long hexameter poem of scenes from life in Mexico.

A passage in Landívar's account of the 1759 eruptive birth of the Mexican volcano Jorullo provides an example of vivid and usable source material. Preliminary earthquakes have died down, and the inhabitants of Jorullo think the worst is over, but they are deceived (*Rusticatio Mexicana* 2.170–79):

> Tempus erat, quo clara suos Latonia currus
> aethereas emensa plagas declivis agebat;
> quin tamen interea roseos Aurora iugales
> annueret rapido segnis submittere plaustro,
> cum subito tellus horrendo rupta fragore
> evomit Aetneas furibunda ad sidera flammas,
> ingentesque globos cinerum, piceasque favillas,
> obscura densans totum caligine caelum.
> Flammea saxa volant rutilis decocta caminis
> et crebro tellus casu tremefacta dehiscit.

It was the hour when bright Latonia [the moon] had traversed the ethereal regions and was driving her chariot horizonward. Meanwhile Aurora was just giving the orders to hitch up her lethargic yoke-animals to the wagon. All of a sudden, the earth rips open with a horrible roar, furiously belches Etnean fires to the stars along with huge balls of ash and pitch-black firebrands, and thickens the air with a dark gloom. Flaming rocks fly, heated in the ruddy furnaces, and the trembling ground gapes in collapse after collapse.

Landívar combines an eye for physical detail with humanistic embellishment, and adds a New World twist. Figures from classical mythology are evoked, although Aurora's vehicle is not a chariot but a wagon, not drawn by more conventional horses but "by lethargic yoke-animals"; thus Dawn is drawn into the sky on a lumbering Spanish colonial oxcart! Besides illustrating a moment in the afterlife of classical hexameter poetry, the piece introduces the reader to aspects of geology, and (since the volcano appeared on a hacienda) of colonial Mexican socio-economic life, which itself has roots in attitudes that reach back to ancient Rome. I have taught successfully the 355-line Jorullo narrative in a text annotated by myself and Deborah Moczygemba for use with a second-year college Latin class; I have done the same with brief excerpts from Peter Martyr and José de Acosta.

In sum, while the value of Latin as a gateway to Spanish and the other Romance languages is readily acknowledged, the Latin curriculum's traditional focus on Latin literature from 200 B.C–A.D. 200 needs reassessment. Familiarizing teachers with potentially useful and appealing later texts is an important unfinished task.

Classical Echoes in Hispanic Life of the American Southwest: The *History of New Mexico*

A final example of the classical tradition in the New World is a work not in Latin but Spanish, which touches the southwestern U.S. directly: *Historia de la Nueva México* of 1610, a largely mediocre poetic narrative by Gaspar Pérez de Villagrá, a member of Don Juan de Oñate's colonizing mission to New Mexico in the late 1590s. "Reflecting, as do all *Siglo de Oro* epics, the overwhelming presence of Virgil and, to some lesser degree, of Lucan" (Villagrá, xxi), the work takes the relatively minor capture of the Indian village of Acoma Pueblo and elevates it to an epic campaign. It is an example of how the colonial Spanish could use a literary form from Greco-Roman antiquity to embody their perception of the New World natives, and to exhibit some of the attitudes they adopted in pursuing the conquest.

Allusions to classical history, mythology, and literature dot the epic, not always felicitously, but there are passages worth noting. Villagrá fuses three Vergilian descriptions of night-time (*Aeneid* 3.147, 5.721, 8.27–28) to describe the moment of the escape of a captured Indian:

Y luego que en mitad del alto Polo,
Según aquel varón heroico canta,
Los Astros lebantados demediaron
El poderoso curso bien tendido,
En el mayor silencio de la noche,
Quando las bravas bestias en el campo
Y los más razionales en sus lechos
Y los pezes en su alto mar profundo
Y las parleras aves en sus breñas
En agradable sueño amodorrido
Reposan con descuido sus cuidados ...

And when in the midst of the lofty Pole, / as that heroic man [i.e., Vergil] doth sing, / the lofty stars were 'minishing / their mighty, wide-extended course, / in the most silence of the night, / when the brute beasts throughout the fields / and those more rational in their beds, / the fish in their great, profound deep, / the chattering birds upon their boughs, / all sunk in agreeable sleep / repose in freedom from their cares . . . [at that moment the watchmen cried out that the captive was gone]. (Villagrá, Canto 13.19–29—orthography of translation adapted)

The Spanish text, besides being richly embroidered with Vergilian motifs, is alive with words that recall their Latin originals (*altus, cantare, maior, silentium, bestia, lectus, piscis, mare, profundus, somnium, avis,* etc.)—all of this providing ample grist for the clever Latin teacher's mill.

CONCLUSION

This chapter only scratches the surface. The time for more ample exploration of connections is ripe. Linguistic study of the Latin-Spanish link finds a place in the new *Standards for Classical Language Learning*, where Marston's elementary-school Latin-Spanish program touches on no fewer than six of the standards (American Classical League, 30). The situation is similar for the Roman-Hispanic cultural continuum. For example, when standard 4.2 advocates that "Students compare and contrast their own culture with that of the Greco-Roman world" (6), the unique place of Hispanic culture in our own society is part of the picture. Spanish programs are found in most of the schools that teach Latin, and census projections tell us that the number and proportion of students with Spanish in their personal background will rise sharply. Latin teachers who poise themselves to explore the connections in their discipline to Spanish and Hispanic culture will find close at hand a wealth of opportunities for cultivating contact with the growing minority audience, while enriching the experience of all students in the Latin program.

21

Latin for Special Needs Students: Meeting the Challenge of Students With Learning Disabilities

ALTHEA C. ASHE
Louisiana State University

One of my favorite cartoons depicts a man standing in front of a duck. The man is addressing the duck with, "Sprechen sie Deutsch?" The duck makes no reply. The man tries again with, "¿Habla Español?" Again, no response from the duck. The man tries yet another time to ask the same question but in a different way, "Parlez vous Français?" Only silence from the duck. In one last desperate attempt to speak in a language which the duck understands, the man says, "Quack?" The duck responds excitedly, "Quack!" Since the man has found a language which the duck understands, communication finally begins.

Latin teachers must often exhibit this type of persistence in dealing with students with learning disabilities, as well as with students who, although not identified as having a learning disability, are "at risk" because of previous difficulties in learning a foreign language. A learning disability (LD) is a disorder which adversely affects the manner in which individuals with normal or above-average intelligence take in, retain, and express information (National Joint Committee on Learning Disabilities). Students with a diagnosed LD (such as dyslexia) or attention deficit disorder exhibit a discrepancy between potential to perform and actual performance. At Louisiana State University (LSU) a student can be classified as learning disabled when a 15-point discrepancy is found between a student's IQ and performance score, indicating that a student's capacity to perform exists but that skills are weak in one or more areas, such as written language, oral expression, or mathematics.

WHY ACCOMMODATE?

Federal law (Section 504 of the Rehabilitation Act of 1973)[1] prohibits discrimination against those with handicapping conditions, including learning disabilities, and guarantees the right of every child to receive benefits from public education programs. The Americans with Disabilities Act of 1990[2] expands the scope of the Rehabilitation Act of 1973 and prohibits discrimination against people with disabling conditions even by institutions receiving no federal financial assistance.

Academic institutions, in complying with this legislation, are not required to make fundamental changes in essential elements of their programs in order to accommodate the student with LD. Academic adjustments which do not pose an "undue hardship" on the institution and are considered "reasonable accommodations" range from granting extended time for taking tests to modification of the tests themselves. The purpose of such accommodations is to assure that achievement, and not the student's disability, is being measured (Brinckerhoff, et al.).

The question that presents itself is whether students with LD, given appropriate accommodations and assistance, are able to benefit from foreign language study. Vygotsky, in a book considered seminal on the topic of the interrelation of thought and speech, claims that understanding of one's native language is enhanced by learning a foreign one. A more recent study has shown that the native language and foreign language aptitude skills of students with LD can improve with foreign language study (Sparks, et al., 1995).

WHY LATIN?

For LD students faced with the necessity of fulfilling a language requirement, Latin may be the best choice. Because many students with LD have difficultly breaking down and putting together the sounds of a language (Sparks, et al., 1992), Latin may be preferred to a modern language since the primary emphasis in the Latin classroom is upon reading and translating rather than oral communication. This emphasis provides ample opportunity for students to see a printed text at the same time the language is spoken and heard (Ancona).

The fact that Latin is an inflected language in which verbs and nouns can be broken down into smaller units (base plus ending) makes the task of deciphering words easier for the dyslexic student who transposes letters. This is particularly beneficial in dealing with verbs, since the endings themselves can be further analyzed according to tense indicator and personal ending (e.g., *lauda-ba-mus*).

Because Latin is a phonetic language in which there is simple co-relation of sight and sound, the student's ability to associate the written and spoken word is greatly facilitated (Ashmore and Madden). This phonetic nature of the language also facilitates correct spelling (Ancona), an area in which students who are at risk for foreign language learning generally have difficulty (Sparks and Ganschow). The consistency of pronunciation for specific letters (e.g., one sound only for *c* or *t*) makes Latin a language accessible for students with hearing impairments.[3]

Latin vocabulary is manageable for students with LD because Latin has a relatively small lexicon and few idioms (Hill, et al., 49), and more than half of English vocabulary is derived from Latin (Ashmore and Madden, 64).

ACCOMMODATIONS, ATTEMPTS, AND ALTERNATIVES

Eileen was a puzzle to me. A sophomore in my beginning Latin class at LSU, she was obviously intelligent, she expressed herself well in conversation, and she had a B average on the first half-semester's work. But now, two days before the mid-term exam, she was sitting in my office almost in tears because, in her words, she was no longer "getting it." She couldn't "put it all together." She was also holding in her hand an Accommodations Letter from the on-campus Office of Services for Students with Disabilities which stated that she had a learning disability entitling her to time and a half on examinations.

I had noticed that in Eileen's written work she frequently reversed letters. For example, she could recognize the tense of *laudabamus*, but when asked what the tense indicator was, instead of answering "b-a," she would reverse the letters and respond with "a-b." She also had difficulty connecting the written word with the way it sounded. Even though she would recognize the tense of *laudabamus*, she would often omit a syllable in pronouncing it, saying it as *laudamus* or *laubamus*. In reading aloud, she often substituted a familiar word with unrelated meaning but with similar form, e.g., *multitudines* for *militibus*. Connecting the written word with the spoken word was for her at best disagreeable and at worst agonizing.

In questioning Eileen about her past experience with foreign language study, I learned that she had made poor grades in French in high school. When she entered college, she decided to enroll in Spanish to fulfill her foreign language requirement; she dropped out just before mid-term. Armed with the documentation of her learning disability, she petitioned the College of Arts and Sciences to waive the foreign language requirement for her degree. The associate dean told her that a substitution of a culture course for the language course would be considered only after she made a "good faith effort" in attempting to pass the language course. This "good faith effort" was defined as consistent class attendance and completing or attempting to complete all class assignments and tests. If she was not earning a passing grade by the date for dropping courses, she would be allowed to withdraw without penalty to her grade point average and to take a culture course in place of the foreign language requirement. We still had four weeks in which to work together before the drop date.

We began meeting outside of class for 20 minutes per day. I quickly discovered that Eileen knew more Latin than she thought she did. When she could not answer a question on a practice test, she could frequently produce the information if I read the question aloud or asked it in a different format (using fill in the blank instead of true/false). We progressed mostly by trial and error, trying different techniques and discarding what did not work.

I suspected that there were other students in my classes who could benefit from using the same methods that Eileen and I were using. I contacted the Office of Services for Students with Disabilities and learned that there were 123 students registered with that office who had entered the university with documentation of a learning disability. The majority of these students needed to fulfill a language requirement for their degrees.

Because it would be impossible to incorporate an extra 20 minutes per day into the 50-minute class period, and because the majority of non-LD students do not need the extra reinforcement, I proposed to the Dean of Arts and Sciences that we institute a three-semester sequence of Latin courses designed primarily for students with learning disabilities. The class was not to be remedial, which would imply a substandard level of preparedness; the students with LD, in order to earn credit for the course, would have to pass the same departmental final exam administered to non-LD students. The class was to be modified, in that accommodations of time and alternate test-taking formats were automatically incorporated into the class structure, and different teaching methodology was to be employed. "Modified" meant a change of approach rather than diminished quality or expectation.[4]

During the year in which the proposal for the modified section of Latin was making its way through the proper channels, I attended workshops and conferences, took classes, and interviewed teachers who taught a foreign language to students with LD. Continuing to work individually with LD students throughout the year, I noted which techniques proved helpful and led to grade improvement. What follows is an account of the way in which I incorporated these techniques into the modified Latin class of 15 students with LD.

Response Journals

In the first semester of Latin study, these LD students became my co-researchers from the first day of class. Since the disabilities represented were wide-ranging (including dyslexia, attention deficit disorder, hearing impairment, and neurological impairment as a result of an accident), I asked the students to write, in their own words, a description of their disability as well as the effect it had had upon their attempts at prior language study. Thus began a written dialogue in the form of a response journal which continued throughout the three-semester course sequence. Topics were assigned on a weekly basis for which a one-page response was required. I responded in writing to their comments, questions, criticisms, suggestions, and ideas. In this way we learned from each other. As soon as a student began having trouble in a particular area (e.g., grades dropping on vocabulary quizzes), we addressed the problem through the dialogue of the response journal; I discarded techniques proving ineffective and tried different techniques until there was improvement in the problem area. What was found to be helpful to one student invariably proved beneficial to others as well.

In the journal entry describing their disability, each student expressed some degree of anxiety about learning a foreign language. Since anxiety appears to affect one's perceived difficulty with foreign language study (Ganschow, et al.), I considered it important to acknowledge and attempt to allay their fears. The main concerns expressed were having a "mental block" against learning a foreign language, fear of being called on in class, fear of appearing incompetent in front of classmates, fear of not being able to keep up with the assignments, and fear of test-taking. One student had so dreaded the idea of enrolling in a foreign language that it was her only remaining requirement for graduation.

For those who were anxious about foreign language study in general, we spent some class time examining the layout of the textbook so the students could see that the study of Latin progresses in small building-block steps in the areas of vocabulary, grammar, and translation. I discussed with the students the reasons why Latin is suited for students with LD, and we spent some time placing Latin in its social and historical context. I asked questions designed to help students draw parallels between ancient and modern culture, and the initial interest sparked by these early discussions of the Latin language and Roman culture remained throughout the course.

To address the fear of appearing incompetent in front of classmates, I used the reasoning that no one in the class had studied Latin, so no student was starting at a more advanced level in the learning curve (cf. Block, et al.). The fact that they would not be required to "speak" Latin in the way that a modern foreign language is spoken was reassuring to those visual learners who preferred to work from prepared texts.

Daily Road Map

Structure, organization, and predictability were essential for keeping the students on task yet flexible enough to move efficiently from one task to another. Every two weeks I gave the students a syllabus with homework assignments as well as an outline of the main daily class activities.

One day we had a particularly large and varied agenda. In an effort to let the students see exactly where we were going, I listed in detail the activities on the board:

- return and review Quiz 6;
- translate story assigned for homework, p. 92;
- sightread worksheet sentences on imperfect tense;
- recite vocabulary words, p. 98;
- preview outline for unit test 3.

Placing a check beside each task as it was finished, we completed the planned work in the allotted time. The students let me know in their response journals that seeing a visual "road map" of where they were going was helpful for three reasons: they were reminded to stay "on task" until the checkmark indicated completion, the list helped prepare them for the upcoming task, and having a record of "where they had been" contributed to their sense of accomplishment. They began using the daily "road map" as a checklist when reviewing for unit tests as well.

Accountability Log

What began as a way of keeping track of whether a student was making a "good faith effort" by means of an attendance log turned into a more detailed record of a student's efforts. At the beginning of the semester, I took attendance during the first few minutes of class and glanced over the students' written work to check for preparedness. This proved to be too time-consuming. Also realizing that disorganization often contributed to an LD student's tardiness as well as not having the materials needed for class, I included those aspects in the daily Accountability Log. At the beginning of each class I passed around the Log, which consisted of a rollbook (with personally assigned numbers instead of names) and three labeled columns in which each student placed a check to indicate preparedness or an "x" to indicate lack of preparedness in three areas: On Time, Homework Assignment, and Materials (text, notebook, auxiliary aids such as noun and verb charts). This method proved efficient for several reasons: the late arrival of students, which distracted the attention of those with attention deficit disorder, decreased; homework preparation became more regular and thorough because "preparation" was defined as having attempted every sentence of an assignment; and valuable time was saved and confusion avoided when students came into class and automatically took out the materials necessary for the day. Throughout the semester, if a student's average began to slip, I could tell at a glance if a lack of homework preparation was contributing to the problem. When calculating a student's accountability grade, I simply added up the checks, giving one point per check.

Multisensory Approach

Whether presenting new grammar, introducing vocabulary, giving instructions, discussing culture, or reviewing for a test, a multisensory approach was necessary in teaching the class of students with various learning disabilities. I presented all information in at least two ways: orally for those who learned best by listening, and in writing for those who were more visually oriented. The overhead projector proved to be a more efficient method of visual presentation than the chalkboard when I had to face the class while speaking because of the presence of students with hearing impairments. This also afforded other students the simultaneous opportunity of hearing me speak and write the words as they copied the information into their own notebooks.

Prepared handouts of grammar explanations with space allotted for personal notetaking proved to be a timesaver for students with handwriting difficulties. Included on these handouts were simple patterned-drill sentences with blanks which were filled in orally by students as I wrote their responses on the board or overhead projector. For instance, in introducing the accusative case, the sentence "_____ *video*" might be completed with the accusative form of all vocabulary words (with the nominative case of each word on the handout or written on the board) for that chapter.

Body movements which students could watch while Latin was spoken helped indicate meaning of speech as well as giving an additional associated memory aid. For example, in practicing the first and second person endings of verbs as in *Ego cenam coquo* and *Tu cenam coquis*, each time *ego* was spoken, I pointed to the written word on the transparency, and to myself as well, before making a stirring motion to indicate cooking. In speaking the word *tu*, I would walk toward a student to indicate the subject *tu*.

Including body movement in teaching direct objects stressed the concept that the direct object is acted upon. In illustrating the sentence *Magistra librum portat*, pointing to the accusative ending while saying the word and holding the text emphasized the meaning as well as the sight and sound of the accusative singular masculine ending. Picking up an additional book and changing *librum* to *libros* emphasized the change in form from singular to plural.

The concept of inflection was difficult for one student to grasp until he understood the importance of word order in English. This was accomplished with a visual component of colored index cards on which had been written single words in English, e.g., the/dog/bit/the/boy. As the student physically changed the position of subject and direct object, the different colors emphasized the change of word order with the attendant change in meaning.

Even though students had a typed syllabus of homework assignments, previewing the following day's assignment orally helped bring closure to class as well as introducing the next day's class structure.

Vocabulary

Students often addressed in their response journals the difficulties they were experiencing with vocabulary study and retention; this led me to experiment with more effective methods of integrating reading, writing, speaking, and listening into the study of vocabulary. After students prepared for a vocabulary quiz, I gave a practice quiz which served two purposes: it familiarized students with the form that the first graded vocabulary quiz would take, and the score indicated the effectiveness of the student's method of studying vocabulary. At the bottom of the practice quiz I asked that students describe the manner and amount of time spent in preparation for the quiz. The following procedure for introducing new vocabulary to the class, as well as suggestions for further individual study, evolved from the discussion, analysis, experimentation, and integration of students' learning styles and preferences.

- I pronounced the vocabulary words while students listened, followed along with the vocabulary list, and then pronounced the words.
- Using an overhead transparency, I placed a mark over the accented syllable for students who wished to pronounce words while studying outside of class.
- Students suggested and wrote one English derivative per word. They enjoyed this exercise and often vied to see who could come up with the most unusual derivative. When no derivative could be found, I drew a simple illustration of the word.
- Using the vocabulary list and definitions given in the text, I read each Latin word aloud, this time including the English definition in the oral practice. Students repeated both the Latin word and English definition.
- The students identified words according to part of speech as I wrote the correct response beside each word. Conjugations of verbs as well as declensions of nouns and adjectives were noted.
- For homework students wrote vocabulary words either on color-coded index cards according to part of speech or in a divided notebook with sections for each part of speech. All parts of words to be memorized (i.e., principal parts of verbs) were included on the cards or in the notebook.
- On subsequent days, I pronounced the words with students repeating while looking at their text or an overhead transparency.

Individual study strategies suggested and used by students in the class included: studying from shuffled index cards with the Latin written on one side and the English on the other, clapping out the rhythm of words while pronouncing orally, tape recording the vocabulary practice in class and replaying the tape, and writing out a practice quiz on the blank form provided.

Verb and Noun Paradigm Charts

Verb and noun paradigm charts were used throughout the course to indicate the place in "the big picture" where tense endings or case endings belonged. In the *Cambridge Latin Course* (Phinney and Bell—the textbook used for the class), the nominative and accusative cases are the first noun cases formally introduced, but the paradigm chart in the Review Grammar lists the cases in more traditional order: nominative, genitive, dative, accusative, ablative. I therefore provided a noun chart with all the cases listed in the same order as in the Reference Section of the text, but with blanks for each ending to be filled in as it was introduced in the readings. Visual learners appreciated having the entire paradigm picture with all case names listed but blanks left for endings not yet encountered; this avoided the confusion of changing the arrangement of the "mental picture" of a noun paradigm chart when subsequent case endings were introduced.

The same concept facilitated the integration of verb endings in the full conjugation chart. Even though the first verb ending encountered in the text and the first filled in on the student's blank verb paradigm chart was the third person singular, the subsequent introduction of first and second persons necessitated no rearrangement of the original visual image of the paradigm outline.

Students referred to the paradigm charts during class, and they requested blank paradigm charts for use during tests. In testing situations, some students filled in the charts immediately with the required endings, and some simply kept the blank chart before them while working. When a student began having difficulty with written translation passages, it took only a moment to check whether an inability to recall endings contributed to the problem.

Students who learned best by listening and speaking were helped by the oral repetition of paradigm endings. In keeping with the multisensory approach, endings were displayed either on the chalkboard or an overhead transparency when repetitive practice took place. The "chunking" of material (*bam-bas-bat* or *a-ae-ae-am-a*), both audially and visually, helped students memorize endings in proper sequence. One student made up hand motions to accompany the repetition of personal verb endings and mentally rehearsed these when attempting recall.

Testing Accommodations

Test anxiety was greatly reduced and performance improved when students with LD were given a practice test using the same format as the actual test. Not only did this require a review of the material prior to the night before the test, it also gave students a preview of the way material would be tested so that there was opportunity for clarification of instructions before encountering them in the testing situation.

Frequently I asked students, as part of the assigned practice test, to construct questions in the practice test form for their classmates to answer. This exercise proved to be an effective form of review, as it helped students focus on and become clear about main points of the material. Response journals indicated that students continued to utilize this question-construction form of review even when not specifically assigned for class use.

Students' recall of information improved when tested in the same format as the original presentation of the material. For instance, when teaching the steps for declining a noun, part of the practice was to separate the genitive ending from the base and to identify the declension before declining began; providing space on the test for these steps served as a reminder of the steps involved.

Visual cues associated with the original presentation of the information were helpful when provided on tests. Each time I introduced a new verb tense, I drew a time line on the board so that the students could "see" where the new tense belonged in relation to the other tenses (i.e., the future perfect between the present and the future). Along with the name of the tense, I wrote the translation. Reproducing this time line on a test with only the tense names served as a memory aid to "getting the tense translations straight," as one student put it. On tests containing prepared translation passages, it was necessary for me to retype the Latin in very large print for students with visual impairments; however, providing a photocopy of the entire page from which the passage was taken stimulated the recall of students who were visual learners.

Since institutions must provide methods of testing that do not magnify a student's disability (Moore, 60), and since spelling is often a problem for students with LD, I provided an alternate form of vocabulary quiz which did not require the active reproduction of Latin forms. This alternate form consisted of sentences containing underlined vocabulary words. The student had to translate verbs in the correct tense (to test recognition of infinitive form, perfect stem, and participial stem) and nouns in the correct case. Seven of the 15 students consistently chose this alternate form of vocabulary testing.

Tests became a learning tool when students made corrections on the test in a different color ink and analyzed their errors. Students became adept at analyzing whether a mistranslation resulted from a lack of knowledge of vocabulary, an incomplete understanding of a grammatical concept, or inattention to word endings. These analyses provided clues to how best strengthen a student's weaker areas. For example, on a multiple-choice test one student with a neurological impairment was convinced that he knew and recognized the correct answer but wrote the incorrect letter in the blank. Since he did not want to be tested in a different format, he thereafter circled his choice instead of writing the corresponding letter. Circling his answers eliminated the step which he perceived as causing the problem, and his grades on multiple-choice grammar items showed immediate improvement.

The most common legally-mandated accommodation requested by students with LD is extended time (generally time and a half) for test taking. This proves to be a problem when students have other classes to attend immediately after Latin or the room is unavailable for extended test taking. The most satisfactory solution lay in dividing the longer unit tests into two portions and administering the portions on separate days (since our class met five days a week for 50-minute periods, there was generally sufficient time to allow two periods per test). An alternate solution was to assign an out-of-class translation as part of the unit test and have students bring the prepared translation on the test day.

Quizzes were alternated between the first 15 minutes of class and the last 15 minutes. Some students preferred taking the quiz at the beginning of class after a few quiet minutes of review; they felt that they could not concentrate on new material presented during class if they were anxious about the quiz. Other students preferred being quizzed at the end of class because they felt less rushed and less as though they were holding up the students who worked at a faster pace. Whether the quiz was given at the beginning or end of class, a few minutes were given for individual review before the quiz, and students who worked more quickly were allowed to begin working on homework assignments after finishing their quiz.

Translation Enhancements

Students in the class were able to work through a translation (both in class and as homework assignments) more quickly when the print was larger, there was lots of "white space" with less crowding than normal textbook material, and there was room to work between lines. The pace of in-class translating of passages assigned for homework picked up noticeably when I began typing the homework passages from the book using a larger size print and leaving space between lines for translation. This served two purposes: when a student could not make sense of a sentence, there was room above the words to analyze each word according to case of nouns or tense and personal endings of verbs. This information was then readily available to the student as translation guidance was provided in class. Secondly, there was no time lost "looking for the place" when students were asked to re-examine the Latin form of a word used improperly in translation. In an effort to avoid having to type the Latin text, I asked students to number each line in their textbook and use the corresponding number in the margin of their written translation. This proved unsatisfactory and confusing for them. Asking students to copy the Latin before translating proved equally unsatisfactory because frequent errors were made in transcription, and it was not unusual for a student to skip a whole line of Latin text. The two students who chose to write out their translations on lined paper still preferred working from the larger reproduction of the material rather than the textbook itself.

As sentences for translation became more complex with multiple subordinate clauses, visual dissection of the sentence proved helpful. We isolated the main clause from subordinate clauses and identified subject, verb, and object or complement for each clause. Relationship between main clause and subordinate clauses was indicated visually, e.g., a relative clause connected by an arrow to its antecedent.

Translation of a passage was facilitated when previewed in terms of subject matter, vocabulary, and relevant grammatical structures. Students were often eager to explore the contents of a passage where there was a physical representation of an object used in previewing, i.e., a reproduction of an ancient coin in connection with a passage dealing with soldiers' pay.

Students with LD who are rule-bound learners had difficulty rendering literal translations into more natural English. To overcome the fear of making mistakes when practicing this step, students were allowed to offer the literal translation but encouraged to attempt a more "polished" translation; if they were unsure whether the more natural English represented what the Latin indicated, they were allowed to offer that translation in parentheses without penalty. I would validate or correct the translations so offered, and gradually students became more confident in their interpretation of meaning. One student was so fearful of making an error that she would not use articles (a, an, the) or possessive adjectives (his, her) without a specific corresponding word in Latin. For this student, an added written step in translating was necessary. After attempting an initial translation with virtually a one-to-one word correspondence, she was required to write the translation in paragraph form on a separate piece of paper while referring to her initial attempt.

When there was a need, due to time constraints, to omit a reading whose storyline was necessary for following the plot of the chapter, the class worked with the passage using what I call "guided translation." As students looked at the Latin, I asked questions about the content to guide understanding of the grammar. For the sentence *Amico dixi* I would ask, "Who did the speaking?" After eliciting the correct response, the answer to "To whom did I speak?" was quickly forthcoming. The class enjoyed working together and felt a sense of accomplishment in covering a large amount of information in a short period.

AIMS, ACHIEVEMENTS, AND ASPIRATIONS

One of the goals of our course was to prepare the students with LD to take the departmental final examination, which covered Units 1 and 2 of the *Cambridge Latin Course*. In an attempt to provide additional instruction time outside the daily 50-minute class period, a Latin tutor was hired by the Office of Services for Students with Disabilities. It quickly became clear that scheduling a time when all students could take advantage of the out-of-class instruction was impossible. The tutor remained available for individual and small-group instruction, but this did not solve the problem of needing more in-class time for translation.

When the class lagged behind the departmental syllabus, we continued to cover all grammar, vocabulary, and practice drills but began omitting some translation passages. Response journals indicated that students retained more when concentrating on a smaller number of translation passages, taking the time for in-depth analysis, discussion, and translation rather than covering a greater number of reading passages in less detail. This approach allowed time during each class period for review of endings, vocabulary, and grammar, as the need arose. The two students who felt the need for more translation practice simply wrote or typed translations for the passages we did not translate in class, and

I provided written feedback. Proceeding in this way, we were able to complete Unit 2 by the end of the semester.

Thirteen of the 15 students in the beginning class of Latin for students with LD successfully completed the course; 12 of those 13 continued in the second-semester course for students with LD in which Unit 3 of the *Cambridge Latin Course* was completed. Eight of those 13 continued with the third-semester course, even though it was not a requirement in every case. Since funding was available for only the first three levels, the one student whose curriculum required a fourth-level language course enrolled in, and passed, a non-LD section of Latin.

The success of these students in completing their language requirements in lieu of a course waiver or substitution has been a significant factor in continued funding by the College of Arts and Sciences for the three-semester sequence. The beginning course is offered in alternate years, and there is a waiting list for students wanting to enroll.

As the number of students with identified LD increases, it becomes more important to concentrate on what these students are able to accomplish and to structure accommodations and teaching strategies accordingly. Student feedback via response journals, individual consultation, and class discussions proved invaluable in matching teaching strategies to learning styles. Given the appropriate accommodations and teaching strategies, perhaps more students with LD will be able to say, as Eileen did upon completing her third semester of Latin and fulfilling her requirements for graduation:

> I was afraid to attempt a foreign language because I never believed I could pass, but Latin class has been a real learning experience. It enabled me to fulfill my foreign language requirement and to really understand the way another language works.

I began this journey with the question of whether students with LD, given appropriate accommodations and assistance, are able to benefit from foreign language study. If the purpose of the foreign language requirement is to familiarize students with the mechanics of language as well as to expose students to another culture from the intimate perspective of that language, then students with learning disabilities can, and do, benefit from the study of Latin. Just ask Eileen.

NOTES

[1] Public Law 93–112: The Rehabilitation Act of 1973. 29 United States Code (USC) 701-794, 29 USC 706(8); Code of Federal Regulations CFR 102.61.

[2] Public Law 101–336: The Americans with Disabilities Act of 1990. 42 USC 12101.

[3] Latin is taught to the deaf at Gallaudet University, and it is the language of choice

at the Rhode Island School for the Deaf in Providence, RI. Students with varying degrees of hearing impairment have successfully completed their three-semester language requirement at LSU by taking advantage of the accommodations and methodology used in teaching Latin to students with LD.

[4] Other universities, e.g., the University of Colorado and Georgia Southern University, share this philosophy and offer similar classes. The University of Colorado's successful Foreign Language Modification Program (Hill, et al.) served as a model for the modified classes taught at both LSU and Georgia Southern University (Seaman), which are in turn models for a course recently funded by the Franklin College of Arts and Sciences at the University of Georgia.

22

Latin Distance Learning And the Electronic Classroom

CATHY PHILLIPS DAUGHERTY
Hanover County Public Schools, Virginia

Since the 19th century, and indeed from antiquity onward (Sherron and Boettcher, 1), some form of distance learning (DL) has been used to instruct students who are physically removed from their teacher. In its earliest manifestation, DL took the form of correspondence courses, relying on the nation's postal system for delivery of lessons to the student and the return of completed work to the instructor. Intermittent phone calls between the student and teacher supplemented comments made on graded work. In many locations, such correspondence courses are still used to instruct people unable to meet classes on a university or college campus.

In the field of Classics, numerous correspondence courses based on this model have been taught at such leading institutions as the University of North Carolina and the University of Georgia (which has enrolled nearly 300 students in Latin correspondence courses over the past five years, 25% of them current or prospective Latin teachers). *Correspondence Courses in the Classics,* compiled by Prof. Kenneth F. Kitchell, Jr., offers the most complete listing of such programs and information on their make-up; his web site lists addresses for both the more traditional correspondence courses, as well as those now available through electronic means. *The Independent Study Catalog* (published by Peterson's) is another valuable resource.

Technological advances over recent decades have greatly altered the traditional correspondence course. Now, they use computer software, E-mail, and CD-ROMs both for instruction and for delivery of materials to the parties involved. The resulting availability and the number of resources and delivery systems from which to draw have broadened the appeal of Classics taught via this route. No longer are correspondence courses primarily filled with adults pursuing a college degree or advanced certification. Of increasing significance is the enrollment of the ever-growing population of home-schoolers in pre-college level courses. Such series as Waldo Sweet's *Artes Latinae* (1966, CD-ROM edition 1996–97) are experiencing a new-found popularity through a programmed-learning approach coupled with workbooks and visually and audibly-enhanced CD-ROMs.

DL, however, is not limited to correspondence courses or instruction via programs designed for the home computer. During the last half of the 20th century, technological advances in television, satellite, and cable transmissions have created an entire industry devoted to educational programming. From a privately owned facility in Texas, to a university-supported site in Kentucky, to numerous local broadcasts within individual school systems throughout the nation, DL is providing students with courses in Latin. Although originally there were few teachers and students engaged in such DL instruction, the numbers of both grow steadily each year. The lack of certified and qualified personnel for Latin instruction coupled with administrators' desires to offer a wider range of courses has threatened Latin programs nationwide in recent years. DL, whether via the Internet, satellite up-link, closed-circuit system, or other electronic method, not only provides courses for training Latin teachers (like those at the University of Georgia), but also saves programs.

THE ELECTRONIC CLASSROOM

One such DL program which meets the needs of students who otherwise would not have a Latin course in their school is the "Electronic Classroom," produced by the Virginia Satellite Education Network (VSEN). In Virginia, Latin is among the most popular of the DL offerings, consistently topping the enrollments in AP Calculus and AP English. For over a decade, these Latin courses offered via satellite have allowed students throughout Virginia (and a few in other states) to study the language of the Romans, their culture, and their history at levels I–III. My Latin III class is described in detail below (and see Allen); two sections of Latin I are also regularly offered by VSEN (each with 200–250 students) and one of Latin II (with 150–175 enrolled).

The challenges of teaching a DL class are many and varied. First and foremost is the teacher's experience. A DL classroom is not the ideal place for a neophyte but is best suited to a seasoned teacher who has a thorough knowledge of the content, has past teaching experiences from which to draw, and knows the behavior patterns of the age level being taught. To understand one needs only to "walk a mile" in the shoes of a DL teacher.

The Morning Rounds

I usually arrive at school about an hour before my three colleagues and the office assistant. Being the early bird enables me to organize the day's program for my Electronic Classroom Latin III, which typically goes out to 75–85 students in 30–35 schools around the state. It also allows me to monopolize the two office Fax machines, insuring that my students receive yesterday's graded work before class today. For a DL class to work, students must receive graded work in as timely a fashion as possible. My policy is to return materials within 24 hours, a standard I have rarely broken. Getting work back to my Latin students spread out over 30 schools in Virginia and other states makes Fax time precious. This is especially true when you realize that there are almost always at least five people using the machines constantly from 8 a.m. until 4 p.m.

While those last pages from yesterday's grammar quiz slide through the machine and out to cyberspace, I read the daily E-mail and ready any work for the office assistant. Having an assistant to photocopy materials, stuff envelopes, post the mail, and run any number of errands is a godsend! As I draw in macrons on a future quiz and print out the calendar for next month's work, I think about life before this support existed. How did I do it all? Easy! I stayed at school until well after 6 p.m. each night. The great myth among regular classroom teachers is that DL teachers spend their days styling hair and manicuring nails. Even with a course load of one 50-minute class per day, there is little downtime. Without help with the basic chores associated with teaching, DL instructors find their time devoted to the mundane, rather than to their students and the content of the course.

As my photocopy requests hit my assistant's folder, I receive a call from the technicians letting me know that the studio is ready for another session. This is my cue to test out the *PowerPoint* file I will use in class later that day. Some days the file may not be ready to test in the morning. Some days I simply have had to leave school before the next day's class has been prepared. Whenever that occurs, I must wait to test the file during the 10 minutes between the AP Calculus class and mine—chancy, but necessary. Our studio broadcasts Latin I, AP Statistics, and the calculus course with only a minimum of downtime between each. Before we had *PowerPoint* (one of a variety of computer presentation software programs on the market), all of my teaching samples were laminated pages prepared on a computer and projected though an overhead camera high above the teacher's console. For teachers in smaller DL programs and closed-circuit school systemwide set-ups, the Elmo projector serves the same function. Regardless of the apparatus used, you want to test out your final product as far from air time as possible. Typos, color clashes, and the dreaded wrong-sized font can spell doom in your class later in the day. No DL teacher should have to worry about unreadable print when trying to introduce the indirect statement. The students' response to the lesson itself is enough of a worry!

Since my Latin III class airs fourth in the day's line-up, I have the morning to revise my script, look over my overheads, and re-work or complete the presentation software. If my class were earlier, all of the day's work and revisions would have to be done the day before. After checking the day's lesson plan for any problems, I put it aside and begin to think about tomorrow. But, just as my thoughts are turning to Friday's class, I realize that I have forgotten to have copies of today's activity worksheet photocopied for my studio class. The off-site students' materials were Faxed out yesterday or mailed out earlier, but the on-site students must get theirs separately. A quick revision of the day's orders to the office assistant with an "Urgent" note attached remedies the situation.

Most DL courses via satellite do not have a live audience. Since my program is supported by both the state and a local school district and since it is housed at a high school, the classes double as part of the school's regular offerings. This presents an added wrinkle in DL: not only must you attend to the students viewing you through the camera, but you can never ignore the ones who are seated in front of you. The same dilemma must be addressed by teachers who have two-way video hook-up with students offsite. The result is that your attention is divided several ways during a broadcast class.

With the clock showing 8:35 a.m., the phones begin to ring and the Fax machine begins to churn out more papers to grade. By now colleagues have arrived, and concentration in an office bursting with five to six people all attending to their various tasks is an effort. It is between now and class time at 11:20 a.m., and in this environment, that I juggle several tasks at once. For someone who lives to address one item at a time on her "Things To Do" list, this is a Herculean task.

Of prime importance during the morning hours is the personal contact with students, parents, and the facilitator, an adult who monitors your students at the various sites while they are viewing the class. Most DL teachers, even those on closed circuit hook-up, will be required to keep office hours so that their students can reach them via phone or E-mail outside of the class time itself. If the telephone is the mode of communication, those calls will be taken as they come in throughout the day of the hours set aside for them. With E-mail or voice-mail on your phone, time devoted to reading and answering requests must be part of the daily schedule. Facilitators and students alike will contact the DL teacher with a wide range of requests which may or may not need to be addressed immediately. Keeping requests straight, knowing which students are at which sites, accommodating facilitators' requests, and being pleasant through it all can boggle the mind. Again, being organized is of paramount importance. While I address each item as it comes up, several of my colleagues find it more effective to keep a list of these phone/E-mail requests to answer after their class for the day has aired. If the request has to do with a worksheet or other item needed for the day, they alter their plans and Fax it at once. Establishing a system that works for you and sticking to it is essential.

Back to Grading Papers

While the regular classroom teacher may feel comfortable letting papers pile up on the desk, the DL teacher discovers quickly that such practices prove catastrophic. I grade throughout the day between phone calls, during lunch, and after working hours. Even during those years when class enrollment warrants hiring a grader to assist with the sheer volume of papers, I wield my red pen at every opportunity.

The DL teacher does not have the luxury of seeing the questions on her pupils' faces. She sees the correct and missed items on their papers. To address their needs and to maintain the needed comfort level in their learning through this medium, it is imperative to grade daily, to return work immediately, and to personalize and individualize instruction. Alterations to your lesson plans and your instructional methods need to be put into action immediately, if students have not grasped the concepts of the previous day's or week's work. Plowing ahead with content and then re-teaching it later may work in a regular classroom, but it will not in a DL environment. The loss in time spells more than a loss to your students. It also translates into a monetary loss in a delivery system where operational fees are high.

Along with immediate grading, the issue of the delivery of papers is crucial. Early in my DL teaching, the only route of receiving/returning student work was through the United States Postal Service. The time involved made this method most unsatisfactory. As much as two weeks lapse was normal in the receiving, grading, returning of work to students. With the advent and widespread use of the Fax machine, the situation vastly improved. Each school subscribing to my class has a Fax machine, dedicated for the most part to sending/receiving materials from my office. In Virginia the General Assembly has funded a Fax, a dedicated phone line, a VCR/monitor, and a satellite dish for each high school and middle school in the state to use for DL classes produced through VSEN. Now, as soon as a set of papers has been graded it is Faxed back to the school. A 24-hour turnaround in work is optimal. With this technology it is realized. An additional plus in using this method is that both teacher and students have a hard copy of the work. This is especially useful for parent conferences via phone or student calls requesting help on specific problems.

The use of electronic delivery via E-mail is also a route becoming available to DL courses of all types and at all levels of instruction. With a light pencil, student work E-mailed to the instructor can be graded while projected on the teacher's computer screen. The graded work then is returned electronically to the school. This method eliminates the use of reams of paper, but requires advanced technology, additional training, and more financial support from administrators. Without a hard copy, teachers must choose to save to a student file on their computers or delete the work and run the risk of needing it later when students/parents request information. The pros and cons make this an item to consider carefully when determining how best to serve your Latin students.

Planning the Class

When the grading bin is empty and while the Fax machine is broadcasting work to students in your class, planning the next day's class begins. Even after a decade of DL teaching, I have found that a good class incorporating a variety of instructional methods requires one hour of planning per 10–15 minutes of air-time. For a 50-minute class, that involves anywhere from four to five hours. While I base this on my experience of a class produced in a television studio with producer/director technicians, the rule holds true with classes taught via closed circuit and other electronic routes. This is why teachers who are asked to teach regular classes, in addition to a DL class, need at the very least a reduction in their courseloads. Sufficient planning time, at the school where all the equipment is located, is mandatory. Teaching the same course over a period of time will cut this somewhat, but not much. As with any teaching, lessons must be varied from one year to the next to accommodate the abilities and interests of students. The DL teacher has the added responsibility of annually upgrading the appeal of the class through new technology and activities such as games and projects designed to personalize the DL experience.

The content of a DL Latin class is the same as that of a regular Latin class. It is the course syllabus and textual considerations that may vary from previous teaching experiences, and time may be lost both through the nature of the medium and the changes in the daily schedule unique to the school. "Wait time," dictated by the phone system your off-site students will be using to contact you during class, and the use of more visuals in teaching may cause the DL teacher to cover less material than in a regular classroom situation. Added to this may be the usual school schedule alterations, i.e., assemblies, fire drills. While my class must air 50 minutes a day, five days a week, DL classes aired through a closed circuit within a school system or via computers may not be so rigid in their programming.

Beyond changes in the syllabus due to time constraints, the DL teacher may need to change texts to accommodate the more visual approach to teaching. The reading-approach texts (see Chapters 9 and 14) lend themselves to DL instruction more than traditional grammar-translation texts. The continued story line generates an added appeal, which grabs and maintains the interest of the audience. However, good planning on the part of the instructor using a traditional text can do the same. Just be aware that additional resources and, therefore, more time allotted to lesson planning may be required. Whatever text is used, the DL teacher must obtain permission to employ the visuals within that text and any other materials for broadcast use before a class airs. Copyright laws are clear about this (see Crews, and other articles cited online by the

Regional Center of the DL Multimedia Development). Your text selection may, thus, be dictated by the willingness of the publisher to accommodate your needs. The publishers of the *Ecce Romani* series (Lawall, et al.), which I employ in my course, are generous in their copyright provisions for DL classes, allowing the use of all pictures within their texts gratis. Others may require a fee; some refuse to grant broadcast rights for any situation. Investigate this issue thoroughly before committing to a text.

Consideration of how and by whom your lesson plan will be used must be made before you put pen to paper or cursor to screen. Initially, my lesson plans were for my own use and the perusal of my supervisor alone. Through the years use of the materials by others has necessitated a change in format. Now, each day I write a detailed script. It is as close to a word-for-word account as I can make it. Cues in the left-hand margin indicate where a change in a visual or an effect will occur, as well as when I want the camera on me or the studio class. My opening, *Salvete, discipuli et discipulae* and *Hodie est . . .*, lead into a regular format of daily announcements to students/facilitators, objectives for the day, the lesson itself, and homework due next class, ending with a *Valete, omnes!* I have found that the regularity of this format is comforting to the students, the producer/director, and to myself. It feels like home to all involved. Spontaneity is not sacrificed, but the basic structure within the class as it appears on that piece of paper puts me at ease in front of the camera. I know what comes next and which visual to show for maximum impact at each point in the lesson. I even type in the word "Questions" to cue myself to pause and give students time to reflect on what has just been covered. The on-air confidence of the instructor in turn projects confidence to the students, both on-site and off-site.

The daily script also serves as an instructional tool for those students who may miss class or who have special learning problems. Varying schedules at off-site schools, technical glitches, and human error may all conspire to create problems in the delivery of your class to a site on any given day. If a detailed script is at hand, you may elect to Fax it rather than to send a tape of the lesson to the student (students in my class are allowed to opt for both). In this way the student will not fall behind waiting for the mail service to deliver tapes of the missed class(es). My hearing-impaired students have found the script particularly beneficial when closed-captioning has not been available. Having a script ready to send can help all parties involved—the student, the facilitator, the technicians, and the teacher.

How much can I cover in a class period? There is no way that anyone can answer that question for any DL or regular classroom teacher. Your teaching style and the emphasis you place on components of your lesson dictate the amount you cover. As with any teaching situation, you must overplan. Eventually, you develop a feel for what is "enough" for you and the students in your class. Even when you reach this point, I again urge you to overplan. Unlike a regular classroom, there is no room for downtime in a broadcast situation, unless it is a part of your lesson plan and a visual has been scheduled to display during the time set aside for seatwork. Ad-libs are expected on late-night television; they will undermine your credibility on daytime educational programming. I can think of no worse crisis than running out of material with 5–10 minutes left in class. A DL teacher cannot run to the closet and pull out another worksheet nor can she say *Valete!* Time must be stretched out until the technicians indicate "Cut." Without visuals to show or content planned, those last minutes are excruciatingly painful for all involved. Be safe. Overplan!

Technicalities and Techniques

Planning a DL lesson involves using equipment and strategies different than those used in planning for a regular classroom. In place of an overhead projector or chalkboard, the DL teacher has an overhead camera or an Elmo and may have computer on-screen capabilities using such software as Microsoft *PowerPoint* or Aldus *Persuasion*. Using these items involves careful attention to the size of the projected area and the use of text, color, pictures, and/or clip-art to fill that space. Great care must be taken to keep your text and artwork within the confines of the space being projected. The same is true for any writing done on that overhead or computer slide. What you see on your monitor may not be true to what your students see. Television and computer monitors vary in what is being viewed from one model to another. As a rule, it is wise to leave space all the way around the image you are projecting.

The fonts, point sizes and colors of text, and background of visuals must be carefully thought out by the instructor. A white background, like wearing white clothing, creates a serious glare problem and must be avoided. Colors for backgrounds and fonts must be checked to see if they project true or in an altered shade. Practice and feedback from students and technicians train the eye as to what works and what does not. Instructors often develop a preference for particular colors and fonts; type style, however, is dictated in part by the legibility of the text for the students who are viewing. Fonts with serifs are more easily read. Also, you cannot put many lines on one computer screen slide or on one paper overhead. Break up the content into small segments easy for students to see. Consider what size television or computer screen they will be viewing and how far away from that screen each student will be seated. More overheads and/or computer screen slides that are easy to view are better than fewer that cannot be viewed easily.

Lessons and visuals can be made more appealing with the addition of pictures, clip-art, and music. The first consideration when adding any of these elements will be copyright (see above and Crews). Permission can easily be obtained by writing the copyright holder of the picture/musical score or the publisher of the material. Most computer clip-art can be purchased with a license to use in broadcasting. Some items may be in the public domain and will not require written permission. Presentation software is designed specifically to be used this way and requires no written approval for broadcast use. Music licenses cover many different tunes for one fee. Pictures used to create a *Chromakey* effect (color separation effect using a blue or green screen behind the teacher), where you appear to stand at the base of an arch, for example, or in the Roman Forum, generate the most impact in your class. Unless the pictures to be used were taken by you, they, too, must meet copyright requirements. Here is where your supervisor and/or media specialist can help. Promising a simple acknowledgment of your sources at the end of the lesson being broadcast is usually sufficient to gain permission for most items.

With your script complete and your visuals prepared, only organizing them for the broadcast remains. Cues added to the left-hand margin of your script will indicate where you will go to a particular picture, overhead, or computer screen to enhance the elements of your lesson content. If you are going over an exercise from the text, a cue will indicate which overhead to place on the overhead camera platform. I always laminate my paper overheads and write on them with water soluble colored pens so that they can easily be used year after year. The answers to the questions on a given overhead are typed to the side, away from the camera's view, as a back-up. Next to running out of plans before class goes off the air, my greatest fear is giving the wrong answer. It could easily happen. Distractions do occur which may cause your mind to wander even for a split second—time enough to lose your train of thought. All paper visuals are put in order and kept in a folder along with the day's script and any other materials needed for the class, including a computer disk with my presentation software files for the class. In addition to this disk which travels with me to the studio, I keep an extra folder for my *PowerPoint* files on the studio computer itself. Power glitches do occur. Files can be lost: expect the unexpected, and be prepared!

Lights, Camera, Action!

It has been a full morning of grading, phone calls, and planning. With 20 minutes left before the day's broadcast begins, I have all calls held so that I can rehearse one last time with my script, overheads, and *PowerPoint*. Quite often this is when I discover a typo or two to correct, or when I may pencil in the names of students who want to call in with news about their winning football team or an award recently given to their school. I may even add a last-minute thought on how best to emphasize a grammatical element or to remember a new vocabulary word. With my focus set on the lesson at hand, I grab my studio bag filled with pens, lesson folder, travel disk, kleenex, and a water jug and head to the studio.

Load the computer disk. Get slide one on the *PowerPoint* file ready to project. Arrange script and overhead visuals on the console. Test the focus and zoom on the overhead camera, mike up, and stand tall. *Quinque, quattuor, tres, duo, unus*, opening theme, and credits lead to my saying, *Salvete!* Class begins by my looking straight into the camera and "breaking the lens." Simply put, this means that you must visualize your students, not the camera lens, when looking into the camera. If you are not "seeing" a warm body out there, your students will know it. For everyone there is a moment when you first "break the lens"—once done, you can always do it. For me, it was hearing that first student's question. I knew from then on that there were live people out there who were listening and eager to know about the Latin language and the Romans who spoke it.

Careful planning produces a well-run class, with perhaps a missed cue here and there. This is a live broadcast. Perfection is not possible nor expected. Also, this is a classroom where flexibility is the norm and "rolling with the punches" is as certain as sun-spot interference with your satellite reception. Some days the phone rings constantly with all three lines lit up at once. On other days when the phones are deadly quiet, the studio class earns its keep by answering most of the day's questions. It is on these quiet days that I most appreciate having students in front of me. Many DL situations do not have a studio class. The instructor must rely solely on the calls from off-site students to keep the class flowing with interaction. While this may be problematic on occasion, the plus side to that set-up is that the instructor's attention is not divided between a studio class and the off-site students. Students on-site may be entering and leaving the studio or, as can happen from time to time, the instructor may even have to deal with a discipline problem.

Class Dismissed

Following class and a lunch break away from my desk, I note on the day's script what worked well and what did not. I mark "save" if it is a script I want to archive for use next year. Over the years I have saved many classes and segments of classes to use in preparing for the next year or to use as roll-ins. The Roman history lessons I teach as part of my syllabus are 30–45 minute tapes of classes prepared several years ago. By using them as pre-taped segments, I free up valuable planning time for other needs. Spending a moment or two now making these notes while the class is fresh in my memory saves time and energy later.

During my break the Fax machine spits out papers to grade, homework/ attendance reports, requests for notes where classes were not taped for a variety of reasons, etc. The afternoon is filled with answering each item, grading each paper, and continuing the planning for tomorrow's class begun earlier in the day. This is also the time when most phone calls from students are received.

Weekly participation in the form of at least one personal contact is required in my class. Experience has shown me that it is far too easy to have a student slip through the cracks of a DL situation if contact is not mandated. For my students who watch live, this means a call during class time while we are on the air. They volunteer to answer questions, read from the Latin passage, correct an exercise item, select and answer an item when we play "Latin Bowl" or "*Periculum.*" Students who watch delayed, that is, at a time other than the original air time, use another route to satisfy their participation requirement. Their contact is either by a call to my desk phone during office hours or by Faxing the answer to a weekly question, the *Mihi da*, posed to them on the air on Mondays and Tuesdays. The correct answer is due in the office by Friday noon. Completion of the weekly participation, in whatever form is most convenient to the student, results in a grade of 100 or 0 each week of the grading period.

At 3 p.m. my phone usually ceases to ring and my lesson for the next day is complete or far enough along that I can put it aside. For the next 45 minutes more "behind the scenes" chores begin. Some days I am typing up tests and quizzes, or putting together the monthly calendar I send to each student/facilitator. Other days I am filing papers or re-filing used visuals and lesson materials. On Fridays, however, without fail, I update student grades. First, I record scores as papers are graded in a regular grade book according to the marking period set-up of my several schools. Some use six-week periods, others, nine-weeks. When these grades are typed into the computer, the spreadsheet formula clicks in and gives me a reading of individual progress for each pupil as of that date. At a glance I see who is up-to-date, who is behind, who is working, who needs a gentle prod. Missing work is noted and messages asking for its prompt return or an explanation are Faxed out that afternoon. This process helps at the end of the marking periods, when grades for at least half my students must go out within a 24-hour period.

GOING THE DISTANCE

The working days and weeks of a teacher offering a traditional correspondence course, maintaining an Internet course, or broadcasting via satellite or cable are both similar and different from those of a regular classroom teacher. How each is organized, the medium used in imparting information, and the proximity of the students to the instructor are the biggest differences. DL teachers must be flexible and deal with change in ways that regular classroom teachers do not, but the content and the importance of meeting the needs of all students as dictated by their situations are similar for both types of teachers. The Latin instructor in a DL class and a regular classroom both strive to convey their love of Latin to their students. Using the medium of technology just requires re-thinking strategy without sacrificing content.

Latin instruction delivered via DL will become increasingly common during the 21st century. Easy access to computers will encourage more "mixed-media" Latin correspondence courses such as those now in place at the University of Georgia. Fiber optics and other delivery systems yet to be invented will facilitate development of more electronic classrooms such as those currently in operation in Virginia (VSEN), Texas (STARNet, formerly TI-IN), Georgia (GSAMS—see "Distance Learning: A Latin Language Collaborative"), Kentucky (KET/SERC), and the University of Minnesota (see Sonkowsky). Becoming aware of what DL instruction involves and the challenges facing the DL teacher (see especially Lorraine Sherry's "Issues in Distance Learning") is rapidly becoming essential, as more and more classicists teach their ancient languages to a modern-day audience via technology-based delivery systems.

For additional information readers may contact: Cathy P. Daugherty, 11174 Elmost Rd., Ashland, VA 23005, E-mail cdaugher@pen.k12.va.us; Cindy Pope, STARNet, Region 20 ESC, 1314 Hines Ave., San Antonio, TX 78208, 800-234-1245, E-mail cindyp@tenet.edu; Jane Smith, KET–The Kentucky Network, 600 Cooper Dr., Lexington, KY 40502, 800-333-9764; Robert Sonkowsky, Univ. of Minnesota, E-mail sonko001@maroon.tc.umn.edu.

23

COMPUTAMUS: *We Compute!*

ROB LATOUSEK
Centaur Systems Ltd.

INTRODUCTION

Classics and computers may well sound like the most unlikely of partners. Most people I talk to outside of our field find it both amusing and fascinating that such a combination actually has been tried. The two topics seem at opposite ends of more than one spectrum—from the ancient to the ultra-modern, from the deeply literary to the superficially technical.

Ironically, Classics has been proudly in the vanguard of research and development in educational computing almost since its origin. We may not have the same abundance of materials available to other fields, due to our relative size, but we do have some of the most distinguished examples of software available to any discipline, and we have a fairly good sampling of materials in all the typical subject areas. The aim of this chapter is to acquaint the reader with those categories, some of the strongest examples in each, and other sources of information to keep in touch with as the field of "classical computing" continues to evolve.

THE BIG PICTURE

I would like to begin with one strong cautionary note. There is no absolute guarantee that using computer applications in teaching the Classics will become an automatic advantage for either you or your students. I do know several teachers who have attracted immediate attention and increased enrollments because they were the first in the foreign language department to incorporate computers into their curriculum; but this is not the norm, and the initial excitement can quickly turn into a nightmare if you don't plan carefully. Computers are powerful tools; and, like any good tool, they can be used well or abused. The old "double-edged sword" metaphor applies well here. For a more detailed discussion of potential negative effects of computer use in education, see Bowers and Muffaletto and Knupfer.

There is as yet no conclusive research indicating that any particular types of educational computer applications are any more effective than a good teacher. In general, the literature suggests that tutorial software can be as effective as one-on-one tutoring and drill-and-practice software can be as effective as group instruction, but the most productive results have been achieved through a well-coordinated combination of teacher-directed and computer-assisted instruction (Crown; Kulik, et al.). This is probably due to the fact that computer applications can provide opportunities outside of the scheduled class time for students to apply themselves to the curriculum in a structured environment.

Some computer programs can appeal to learning styles and sensory modes different from those targeted by a teacher in the classroom. Some students respond well to working independently on a computer, as opposed to the performance pressures of the classroom environment. Others prefer the social interaction of the classroom over the mechanical limitations of the computer (Sloan; Taylor 1980). There are countless variables involved in successfully integrating computer applications into any curriculum, so don't expect miracles overnight!

EDUCATIONAL VS. INSTRUCTIONAL

As we begin a review of the development of "classical computing," let us start by defining some terms. The first delineation that I have found useful is that between educational and instructional software. Educational software can be any software with educational applications, which would include wordprocessors, spreadsheets, and databases. Instructional software is a sub-set of educational software, made up of those programs which are specifically designed for interactive support and guidance within an instructional curriculum.

Educational software which is not considered instructional can be divided into two categories: 1) reference materials and 2) productivity tools. Productivity tools for education are much the same as those for business and other fields: wordprocessors, spreadsheets, desktop publishing software, and database-handling programs. This is often the first type of program that anyone is exposed to on a computer. Most often it is a wordprocessor, the software which turns a computer into a glorified, correcting typewriter for many, a typesetter for some. In this area, you should be aware that there are several wordprocessing programs which have been specially adapted for foreign language work, such as *Nota Bene* and *Gamma Universe* (for more information on software programs mentioned in this discussion, see the postscript on "Keeping Current" at the end of this chapter). These programs can facilitate the creation of anything from macron-marked worksheets to fully annotated book manuscripts with Greek passage excerpts.

For those who are already committed to a particular wordprocessor, it is usually possible to install separate font software which most standard wordprocessors can utilize for the desired effect. Font software can be very specific to a computer's operating system and printer type, so be careful in making a selection. Examples include: *GreekKeys*, *TransRoman*, *LaserGreek,* and *WinGreek*.

TEXTUAL AND VISUAL DATABASES

Reference materials include a number of various types and formats: 1) electronic texts; 2) text-search utilities; 3) image collections (usually on videodisc or CD-ROM); 4) electronic dictionaries; and 5) cultural, historical, or literary references in electronic form.

Some of the largest and earliest software development projects in Classics have been devoted to the conversion of texts into electronic form. The *Thesaurus Linguae Graecae* Project began in 1972 and spent close to 20 years organizing, manually inputting, and proofing nearly all of extant Greek literature up to 600 C.E. for publication as the TLG CD-ROM (Brunner). Concurrently, the Packard Humanities Institute was building up a substantial database of Latin texts, ending up as the PHI CD-ROM #5. These disks are constantly being updated; they can be licensed by either institutions or individuals.

Several more specialized databases have also been created by long-term, grant-supported development projects. The Duke DataBank of Documentary Papyri (DDBDP), the Lexicon Iconographicum Mythologiae Classicae, AMPHORAS, and the Database of Classical Bibliography (DCB) are all well enough named to give a sense of what they are attempting to catalog (for a detailed examination of any of these, see Solomon).

Some of the best image collections (or visual databases) available in the humanities are videodiscs done by art museums and cultural foundations. Two of these which have generous applications to Classics are the ones from the Louvre in Paris and the National Gallery in Washington, D.C. Another excellent source for maps and slide-quality photos of Italian sites and artworks is the *De Italia* videodisc, developed in Italy and imported by the University of Wisconsin Department of Classics. These videodiscs can be accessed through their own software indexes or by using a simple bar-code reading tool to call up images from the printed index.

THE PERSEUS PROJECT

Saving the most impressive, multi-media database project for last, we come to the *Perseus* Project, a well-organized collection of text, art photos, site maps, historical mini-encyclopedia, lexicon, and parser—all devoted to classical Greek civilization. *Perseus* is the culmination of an intensive development process begun at Harvard in the early 1980s by Gregory Crane and a number of others, who eventually gained major funding from the Annenberg/CPB Project to complete the task they had set out for themselves (Crane and Mylonas). The goal of *Perseus* was "to put the information traditionally used in the study of Classics and archaeology into electronic form and to disseminate it in a system that not only facilitates familiar ways of using these materials but also makes possible new types of research that may not have been feasible previously" (Mylonas). Most who have seen the outcome of this endeavor seem to agree that the goal has been largely achieved, though it may have taken a bit longer to execute than they originally projected. The work continues, as of this writing, and will expand into the area of Roman civilization (the so-called "Roman *Perseus*") under a new National Endowment for the Humanities (NEH) grant.

The concrete form of *Perseus* is contained on CD-ROM disks. The first version fit on one disk, the second now takes up four. There was a supplementary videodisc for the first version, but all of those images have been transferred to CD-ROM. *Perseus 2.0* contains 3.4 million words of Greek literature, 24,000 images, and 179 archaeological sites. The CD-ROM interface was created in HyperCard, making it Macintosh-based up until recently. An IBM-compatible, Windows-based interface is still under development, but many of *Perseus'* resources can now be accessed via the Internet, which is "platform-independent" (www.perseus.tufts.edu).

One thing that makes *Perseus* unique among all of the reference materials discussed so far is its capacity to straddle the dividing line between instructional and non-instructional software. Besides putting all of the aforementioned databases and tools at the disposal of a student/user, *Perseus* has a handy utility for creating "paths," which allows a teacher to set up a specific sequence for students to follow, customized to a particular issue or theme and including original notes or directions which can be "tagged" to pictures and text along the way (Chapman). This facility has indeed proved so useful and popular that Mark Morford and Robert Lenardon have published a *Companion to Classical Mythology* (1997) to help users of their well-known mythology text (Morford and Lenardon 1995) create correlated *Perseus* paths; and Wendy Owens has established a business, Classical Technology Systems, to provide support tools and services for *Perseus* (home.earthlink.net/~clastechsym).

FROM PLATO TO PERSEUS

The *Perseus* Project and its resulting materials have set some new standards for the potential of software development in our field. There is, however, a big difference between software that puts an abundance of reference materials and tools at your disposal for research or self-instruction and the purely instructional software which tries to interactively guide you through a set curriculum, coaching and assessing your progress along the way. The standards for instructional software have actually changed very little in the last 25 years, while development has moved from one "platform" to another and user interfaces have improved somewhat. This fact should serve to reassure those teachers in fear of being replaced by a computer. Indeed, most of the promises made by artificial intelligence researchers 20 years ago have proved relatively fruitless. Natural human language has shown itself to be a terribly tough nut to crack.

At the same time, just as science and math have been the most obvious places for computer-assisted instruction (CAI) to apply itself, Latin appeared early on to be one of the easiest languages with which to attempt CAI, because of its inherently logical structure and "crystallized" grammar (at least, in its classical, literary form, as opposed to the colloquial, conversational form evidenced by Plautus). In fact, some of the earliest applications of CAI to Classics teaching occurred in the late 1960s and early 1970s. This was the time when access to the old, bulky mainframe computers was beginning to be extended beyond their original computer science domain.

Some of the earliest attempts at CAI for Latin were those made by Stephen Waite at Dartmouth College (Waite), Richard Scanlan at the University of Illinois (Scanlan), and Gerald Culley at the University of Delaware (Culley 1978). While Waite was working with the BASIC computer language, since Dartmouth was its birthplace, Scanlan and Culley were working on the PLATO system, with its own TUTOR language and "touch" screens. PLATO (Programmed Logic for Automatic Teaching Operations) had been specifically developed for instructional applications, mainly on large university campuses; and the software developed for it was very sophisticated and effective.

Microcomputers started to appear on the scene in the late 1970s and immediately became popular with primary and secondary schools, which had never been able to afford the large mainframes, like PLATO. The Apple II set the first powerful standard for microcomputers in 1980, soon to be followed by the IBM-PC in 1981. One of the first pieces of software to appear in Latin for the microcomputer was *Latin Skills*, a successful conversion and expansion by Gerald Culley of programs he had earlier developed for PLATO (Culley 1984–85).

Drill and Practice vs. Tutorial Software

The very earliest programs developed for Latin—and for almost every other field actually—came to be referred to as drill-and-practice, and the majority of instructional software still falls into this category. Drill-and-practice software is characterized by the following qualities: 1) a simple "question-and-answer" format, 2) immediate "right-or-wrong" feedback, 3) a pre-set or randomized sequence. Current examples of drill-and-practice software include: *Latin Grammar Computerized*, *Latin Vocab Drill*, and *MasterLatin*.

When a drill-and-practice format is adapted to provide more sophisticated feedback than just right-or-wrong, and the sequence is customized or directions are given based on user performance, we cross the line into tutorial software. These programs depend on careful recordkeeping by the program, which can then be compared against a computer model of expected performance. In this way the program can recommend (or require) that a student either proceed to the next level of instruction or return to a lower level for remedial work. Current examples of tutorial software include: *Latin Skills: Verb Factory*, *Tutrix*, and *World History Illustrated: Rome*.

SIMULATIONS AND NATURAL LANGUAGE DIALOGS

While drill-and-practice and tutorial software programs are generally designed with a tightly controlled structure, simulations and natural language dialogs try to provide a little more freedom within the broader limitations of computer technology. Simulations attempt to create an artificial environment or context in which a student will attempt to solve a problem or attain a goal, with many possible paths to that end. The program will define parameters and provide tools with which to work. This category of software includes several sub-categories, two of which are important for our purposes: 1) interactive fiction and 2) community management.

Interactive fiction programs try to maintain a narrative sequence by putting the user into a role-playing situation within a simulated environment, which may change in both predictable and unpredictable ways, based on the level of the user's acquired knowledge. The goal may be to simply "stay alive," find a specific object, or get to a certain location. Current examples of such a program include: *Wrath of the Gods*, *Denarius Avaricius Sextus*, and *Rome*.

Community management programs put the user in charge of creating a new, artificial community from scratch by allocating resources and planning out changes to the environment. As time passes, various challenges will arise which affect the community and require a response from the user, using the tools available. The goal may be to see how long the community can survive or how prosperously it can grow. Current examples of such software include: *Caesar*, *Populous*, and *SPQR*.

As I have discussed earlier, the promises of the artificial intelligence researchers have not panned out very well over the last 25 years. The programs that such research is aimed toward are often referred to as natural language dialogs. Basically, such software is expected to converse with a user in a natural, human language. The complexity and flexibility of human language has proved incredibly difficult to convert into the rule-based structure of computer languages. So far, every attempt to create a prototype of such a program has been heavily restrained in the range of vocabulary and grammar that can be used. There are no commercial programs of this type currently available for Classics; however, a valiant attempt to create such a program in Latin was made by Gerald Culley at the University of Delaware in the mid-1980s. His program, called *Saltus Teutoburgiensis*, came close to handling a vocabulary of 75 verbs and a few hundred nouns within the confines of elementary grammar, but it was so large that it could not be transferred from a minicomputer to the most powerful microcomputer of its time (Braidi; Culley, et al., 1986).

EVALUATING EDUCATIONAL SOFTWARE

Once you have a grasp of all the types of educational software delineated above, it should be easier to approach the evaluation process. The first question that needs to be answered in selecting software for a given class (or individual) is one of hardware compatibility: will it run on the computer(s) available to use?

Everyone understands that it would be much simpler and more convenient if there were one standard, so that all new software could run on any new computer, just like the standards for VHS videotapes and audio CDs. Ever since microcomputers appeared, there has been talk of such a standard, but reality keeps getting in the way. The IBM vs. Apple division has been the most consistent over the years. First, it was IBM-DOS vs. Apple II; now it's IBM-Windows vs. Apple Macintosh. Even though IBM and Apple tried to team up together to create a new, single standard for the new PowerPC computers, it has not yet come to fruition.

Therefore, it is still important to determine the type of hardware with which you will be using the software. Besides the big question of "IBM or Mac," it will often help to know the amount of RAM (Random Access Memory), the operating system version, and the space available on the hard drive. If you are dealing with both Mac and IBM-compatible computers, it may be reassuring to know that some programs are available in both formats, but they usually need to be purchased separately. Some of the newer "hybrid" CD-ROM programs even provide both versions on one disk.

Besides the technical hardware requirements, you may be limited by certain administrative criteria. If your school's computer lab is controlled by a network system, you will want to know if a program can be installed on a network and if a special license is required to do so. Some programs are available with a network or site license, which allows for installation on a network or multiple computers at a single site. Another common option is a software lab pack, which provides multiple copies (5–10) at a discounted rate. An individual or single-user package is the most typical option, but there may also be different prices for consumer and academic purchases. To provide an opportunity to "test drive" software, many publishers will offer either a free 30-day preview period or a demo version at a nominal charge.

SETTING UP SCENARIOS FOR COMPUTER USE

While we are covering administrative criteria, it would be appropriate to discuss the variables in computer use which are determined by the school, the teacher, and sometimes the family or student. The various environments mentioned above—school lab, classroom, or home—are one important factor in the creation of any specific scenario for computer use, besides the software resources themselves. Another important factor is the social atmosphere. In a school lab, students may be using a program in concert with an entire class during a regular class period, or on their own during a study hall or after school.

Similarly, in a classroom students might be working alone or on a group project. In either situation, students might also be working with a partner, depending on the student-computer ratio. Many teachers have found that working in pairs on a computer can, in fact, be very productive in the area of collaboration and peer tutoring. Certain types of software, such as simulations or game-style drill-and-practice programs, can be very effective in a paired or "work group" arrangement. Some teachers also use a computer in front of a classroom with a projection device to conduct software-based demonstrations or conduct group drills.

I have tried to list all of the potential combinations of location and grouping, so that teachers can determine which ones are available and then, through experimentation, determine which work best for their situation. The curricular structure of a school will often eliminate some of these options, and student personalities and learning styles can also make a big difference. Don't be afraid to let students with strong computer experience help out. They will be proud to demonstrate their skills in an area outside of Classics, and you might learn a good bit from them. Some teachers are afraid of "turning the tables," when the students become teachers and vice versa, but it can be a valuable and empowering experience for both sides.

BACK TO THE EVALUATION PROCESS

The next question to ask relates to curriculum compatibility. Will this program correlate with the textbook used, or does it cover a suitable area for enrichment? Some programs may offer textbook-specific versions, and others may offer editing modules which allow users to customize a program to their needs. Still others may include material that is common to many textbooks, and it will be up to the users to decide how well it ties in with their plans. There are a number of programs that cover the most popular areas of classical studies, such as mythology, archaeology, and architecture. Many of these could serve the purposes of enrichment in a Latin or Greek class.

Once the issue of curriculum compatibility is resolved, you can move on to the broad topic of user-friendliness. Some may feel that this term has become overused or outdated, but I think it is still a helpful umbrella term for a host of issues related to the program's practical design and "personality." One software characteristic that can create a strong first impression and encourage continued use is attractive presentation. Standards for graphic design are constantly being raised by improvements in technology and increased public exposure to state-of-the-art software.

Another factor which should be evident in any piece of good software is consistently clear instructions. There should be "help" options available on screen at all times, and the user manual should support the program by providing clear installation instructions and other helpful material that is not provided within the program. This might include suggestions on how to use the program or a teacher's guide on incorporating it into a curriculum.

A very practical issue is the ease of movement into, out of, and throughout a program. There should not be too much introductory material before a menu or list of options is presented to help you get to the specific part of the program you need. A "quit" option should be available on screen at all times. There should always be obvious methods to obtain access to central menus and quick ways to return to screens or areas that have recently been used.

Finally, the most important characteristic for instructional software is useful feedback. This refers to the responses the program gives when answering questions (drill-and-practice, tutorial, dialog) or making decisions (simulations). The complexity and intelligence of the feedback is probably the most difficult aspect of software to program.

A drill-and-practice program may only tell you whether the user is right or wrong, perhaps giving a hint or providing the correct answer when the user is wrong and offering some encouragement (or "positive reinforcement") when the answer is correct. More refined feedback for a drill might point out a specific part of the answer which needs correction or make a point of redrilling items until the user gets them right. A tutorial should incorporate most of these types of feedback, offer context-sensitive feedback for expectable errors, and provide a more detailed evaluation upon completion, with specific directions for subsequent work.

A simulation might offer context-sensitive feedback whenever crucial decisions are made (or actions taken). This feedback is often optional and may be given in cryptic form, or "hints," that must be deciphered. In simpler and less educational simulations, the only feedback may be the consequences that result from the user's decisions; only through repeated attempts and learning from mistakes can the user acquire enough experience to reach an intended goal.

In a natural language dialog, feedback must be judged on how close it approximates what would be expected from a human tutor. All feedback must be context-sensitive, useful, and appropriately phrased. When all four of the major qualities of user-friendliness are executed successfully, you will understand how a good program can work.

THE EXPANDING WORLD OF THE INTERNET

The most important and influential trend to affect computer use in education currently is the phenomenal growth of the Internet and its applications. Begun by the U.S. Department of Defense in the 1970s as a handy and efficient method of communication among researchers, contractors, and government officials, the Internet went public and commercial in the 1980s. Originally supported (physically) by universities and other research institutions, the Internet now also includes a large private, commercial infrastructure, which is paid for by service fees, much like the telephone and cable systems. Indeed, telephone and cable companies are already trying to offer themselves as an alternative to the now specialized "Internet Service Providers."

The Internet has been touted by some as the "Great Equalizer." It provides unprecedented access to many kinds of information, and it has been called instrumental in the crumbling of the Berlin Wall and the protests of Tiananmen Square. Unfortunately, it has also become famous for extended "outages" and a terribly confusing initiation process. Many businesses who thought they were going to get rich quick are now struggling to find users to pay fees for information services that have usually been free on the Internet. For the most part, though, the general impression has been positive enough that the Internet will surely be around for a long time in one form or another, and its applications will expand.

The most common use of the Internet still seems to be electronic mail, or "E-mail." It can be very convenient for sending short notes or entire articles to colleagues anywhere in the world in the blink of an eye, with no paper involved, and for much less than the cost of a stamp. Discussion groups (or lists) can be set up for any specialized topic and messages posted (much like the earlier "bulletin board" systems) for all to read and respond to as desired. This utility allows teachers to send out unique requests for information or direction with a much broader base of sources to hear from within their own subject area. Many college teachers are already using E-mail to keep in better (and more frequent) touch with their students and are even conducting correspondence classes online (see Chapter 22).

There are a few common methods of "subscribing" to a list, but the simplest way to be certain is to send a brief inquiry to the "moderator" of the specific list for instructions. Be sure to hold onto those instructions; they will be useful when you need to "unsubscribe" or put your mail on hold while on vacation. Lists especially useful for Latin teachers include CLASSICS and

LATIN-L, both moderated by Linda Wright (weber.u.washington.edu/ ~lwright: see the catalog of related lists on this home page, and cf. Chapter 12 above).

Another new type of discussion group—this one in "real time"—is the Latin Chat Night on America Online (AOL), which has been running for a few years now. To subscribe to their newsletter and/or join the "conversation," contact the moderators (msmagistra@aol.com).

THE WIDE, WIDE WORLD OF THE WEB

Methods of interacting with the Internet have evolved over the years in much the same way that operating systems have, moving from the "command-line" interface of DOS to the "graphical user interface" of the Macintosh and, later, Windows. Accessing information on-screen and downloading files on the Internet used to be done by the former method via Gopher and FTP (File Transfer Protocol). These operations have now been made simpler and more convenient by the graphical interface of the World Wide Web (WWW), or just "the Web," for short.

The standard upon which the Web is based is HyperText Markup Language (HTML) and its correlative, HyperText Transfer Protocol (HTTP). Most Web addresses (or URLs, "Universal Resource Locators") used to begin with "http://," but you may still find a few using "ftp://" or "gopher://." Most Web "sites" are accessed through an introductory "Home Page," which acts as a graphical table of contents for a site; and many will contain additional "links" of their own, which can be used, as desired, to jump to other sites, without needing to know the exact address.

There is a substantial list of Web sites in the *Software Directory for Classics*, cited at the end of this chapter. Among them can be found sources for electronic texts and collections of material on special topics, like Vergil or ancient theater, as well as useful E-mail directories and other references; many sites will be cross-linked. A good place to start any information search is usually one of the general Index-Search sites, like Yahoo (www.yahoo.com) or WebCrawler (www.webcrawler.com). For a Classics-oriented search, try Maria Pantelia's "Electronic Resources for Classicists" (www.tlg.uci.edu/ ~tlg/index/ resources.html), Jim Ruebel's "Repository of Classical Texts and Publications" (www.public.iastate.edu/ ~flng_info/classics/resources.html) or the "Library of Congress Classics Links" (lcweb.loc.gov/global/classics/claslink.html).

One of the current favorites for classicists is the *Perseus* site (www. perseus.tufts.edu), which provides online versions of much of the *Perseus* literature database, its lexicon and parser, and a significant collection of maps and images. The Roman version of *Perseus* now underway will also be online. Another new NEH-supported Classics project, called *VRoma*, is attempting to create an online, simulated city of Rome, in which students can meet with teachers or conduct their own research within the cultural context of the civilization they are studying (www.colleges.org/~vroma: see Chapter 12 above). Other Web sites that offer instructional support specifically for Latin teachers include Mark Keith's "Forum for Latin Teachers" (www.pen.k12.va. us/Anthology/Pav/Classics/Forum.shtml), Ross Scaife's "Internet Resources for Latin Teachers" aka "Lupa" (www.uky.edu/ArtsSciences/Classics/schools. html), and Jim O'Donnell's "Tools for Teaching" (ccat.sas.upenn.edu/teach demo).

The next area of expansion for the Internet will undoubtedly be the realm of online interactive applications. At this point, the Java language has become fairly well accepted as a new standard for Web-based applications. Just like the Web itself, Java is "platform-independent," meaning that it can be accessed from any hardware platform (such as Macintosh, Windows, Unix), as long as your computer has accessing software (such as Netscape's *Navigator* or Microsoft's *Internet Explorer*) for a platform. The development of this opportunity may indeed be the long-lost answer to the compatibility conflicts of the past.

The actual logistics of how this sort of online access might work are still a bit sketchy, but it will most likely involve a "pay-as-you-go" methodology, similar to phone calls or videotape rentals (the latter may be replaced by an online access method in the not-too-distant future). If Internet access does not achieve the convenience of making a telephone call or flipping on the VCR, this trend may be thwarted or postponed; but the flexibility of being able to use a wider variety of software for short periods of time, paying only for what is used, could prove to be a very attractive option in the long run.

CONCLUSION

As I expect you will have easily gathered from reading this chapter, if you are not already aware of it experientially, the face of computer applications in the Classics—and in general—is constantly changing. However, most of the basic criteria that teachers can employ to assess the usefulness of computer-based tools for their own classroom should remain fairly constant. When the opportunity to try a new tool or program arises, ask yourself a few simple questions: 1) Does it appeal to the learning style of one or more students in the class? 2) Does it provide more convenient access to information previously unavailable or less accessible? 3) Does it assist students in learning how to structure and analyze their own work? 4) Does it facilitate and expedite the learning process?

Answering these questions is no simple task. It may depend on a certain amount of experimenting with different scenarios in the context of your own school's curriculum and structure. Like any other curricular adjustments, it will help to compare notes with other teachers who have already tried a few experiments of their own. Be sure to ask the students directly about their own critical impressions. And don't get carried away by all the hype and the hoopla. Computers are, by no means, a panacea for school productivity issues. They are merely one more tool in a teacher's workshop.

Postscript: Keeping Current

Software, URLs, and other electronic resources seem to be constantly changing in one way or another, and interested teachers need to know how to keep current. The *Software Directory for the Classics* (Latousek 1997) is a listing and description of available software programs and Web sites, including those cited in this chapter, updated biannually and available from the American Classical League (ACL) Teaching Materials and Resource Center (Miami Univ., Oxford, OH 45056; 513–529–7741; E-mail: AmericanClassicalLeague@ muohio.edu); a concise listing which is updated more frequently can be found on the Web at www.centaursystems.com/soft_dir.html. Updates on computer resources for Classics are surveyed twice yearly in the "Random Access" column of ACL's journal, the *Classical Outlook* (*CO*), and readers may wish to consult the entire series of columns beginning with the 1989–90 volume of *CO* (Latousek 1989–98, also archived at www.centaursystems.com/archives. html). You can also get a free subscription to the *Computing and the Classics* newsletter in either its online or print form by E-mailing the editor, Joseph Tebben (tebben.1@osu.edu). Finally, the ACL Committee on Educational Computer Applications coordinates both a program of hands-on computer workshops and an ongoing software display at the ACL Institute held in late June each year, and the American Philological Association also sponsors a substantial "Technology Showcase" exhibit and program at their annual conference at the end of December.

24

Teaching Resources
For the Latin Classroom

KENNETH F. KITCHELL, JR.
Louisiana State University

"Teachers of Latin have not generally urged upon the school authorities their need of classroom equipment and consequently this has received little attention. It is quite as important for the Latin teacher to have modern equipment for his work as it is for the teacher of any subject in the course of study." So, over 80 years ago, wrote Josiah Bethea Game (108), professor of Classics at Florida State College for Women. His words are even more true in this day than they were in his. A look at his list of equipment confirms the vast difference that exists between the classrooms of 1916 and those of today. In order, Prof. Game treats charts, books for the class and books for the teacher's use, wall pictures, sculptures, lantern slides, photographs, coins, and homemade illustrative materials. In many respects today's needs are similar to those of Dr. Game's students, yet in this world, when our students are besieged on all sides and at all times by multi-media stimuli, teachers are in even greater need of assistance to make the "mere" written word come alive—the more so if that word happens to be in Latin.

Before going on, it would be wise to stress what this chapter is not. First, it is in no way all-inclusive. Considerations of space and the limitations of personal experience demand that there be selection and omission. Secondly, computer resources are excluded, since they are thoroughly surveyed in the previous chapter and the *Software Directory for the Classics* (Latousek 1997) cited there. Finally, any list of materials must assuredly go out of date in its specifics, for companies come and go, addresses change, and products are removed from catalogs. This piece should serve only as an introduction to the many and varied types of resources that are available to the Latin teacher today and to provide the conscientious teacher with the means by which to stay current; teachers in the elementary and middle grades will want to review the additional materials referenced in Chapters 6 and 7.

THE CLASSROOM ENVIRONMENT

Bulletin Boards

Dr. Game knew the importance of having Rome and its greatest achievements always before our students. To this end he suggested posting photographic enlargements of Rome and its monuments and adorning the room with plaster copies of classic sculpture, especially busts of authors. I could not agree more that such things enliven a classroom; in addition, they also give a sense of reality to those voices from the past which otherwise can remain "dead."

It is important to realize that bulletin boards must be changed frequently to be effective. In order to do this you need a large number of pictures, prints, maps, and the like. If you need a cheap source that will enable you to post numerous pictures throughout the year, try University Prints, a company that Dr. Game undoubtedly knew (addresses for University Prints and other resources mentioned here are provided in the list at the end of this chapter). The prints come in thematic sets such as "Etruscan-Roman Art and Architecture" or "Greek Art and Architecture." The prices are so reasonable that you can change your bulletin board frequently or can give the plates to students to study. It is most useful if you select the pictures to match other classroom decorations thematically. One month could be "myth month" and the next could feature Aeneas or Athens. Some bulletin boards will be teacher-generated, featuring material you have gathered together. You may want to consider having a small section of one board devoted entirely to "Classics in the News." I have such a board outside my office on my college campus. To keep it stocked, I have a clutch of dear friends who act as a clipping service, dutifully cutting out and forwarding items they find in such places as the *New York Times, Newsweek, Time,* and the like. Archaeological finds, book reviews, new translations, earthquakes, and similar articles come to me in a steady flow. You can also help yourself out with a few careful subscriptions to well-illustrated magazines. The best for this purpose is surely *Archaeology* (discussed below); you may also want to include *National Geographic* and *Smithsonian.* If you cannot afford all the subscriptions, rely on the good will of relatives and friends. Once the word gets out, you will be inundated with materials. Do not omit *Aramco World,* a magazine published by the oil company Saudi Aramco, "to increase cross-cultural understanding." I have been a subscriber for almost 20 years now and have observed that it always seems to have an article about antiquity in it. Incredibly, it is free for your request. To obtain a subscription, merely write. Your students and your bulletin boards will thank you.

Before leaving this subject, remember that it is the clever teacher who enlists the aid of the student in decorating the classroom and the bulletin board. Small bits of extra credit will inspire your students to augment the efforts of friends and relatives at finding items for display. Likewise, when creating and assigning projects for students to do, be sure to factor in the eventual display of the projects in and around the room. To give a few brief examples, you could assign students to produce photographs of classically influenced buildings in town, to copy down the names of car brands which are really Latin words (e.g., *Lumina, Taurus*), or to bring in examples of Latin found on product labels. Posted, these make excellent bulletin boards.

Walls

Every classroom has at least four of them, and if they are lively and hung with appropriate materials they can do a great deal for the learning environment. The need for maps in the classroom is fairly self evident. How can we appreciate Catullus' voyage to his brother's grave unless we have some firm idea of just how arduous it was? And how far from home was Pliny the Younger when he went to his post in Pontus, or just how far from civilization was Ovid in exile? Nothing shows this as clearly as a map. What is less obvious is where teachers can obtain maps geared just for their purposes. Moreover, once you begin to investigate a bit, you find that maps are more than just large things to hang on the wall. For example, Hammond offers a series of world history transparencies for grades 6–12. One set is entitled the *Growth of Civilization to 1500 AD*, and three titles in the set sound very intriguing: the *Beginnings of Civilization, 3500 BC-AD 1500*; *Classical Greece, 600-400 BC*; and *Trade Routes and Great Empires of the First Century AD*. Rand McNally offers a series of 8½ " x 11 " outline maps which are printed on both sides of the page. One side is a relief map in two colors, while the reverse is a one-color outline map. The *Ancient World, Alexander's Empire*, and *Roman Empire* come in packs of 50 and are moderately priced, enabling each student to work with an individual map. Another title, *Mediterranean Lands*, comes in this size, but is also available in the "Project Size" of 11 " x 15 ". Still, there are times when only a wall map will do, and their Breasted-Huth-Harding Series features 44 " x 32 " full-color maps, some in a folded format and others spring-roller mounted. There are many titles for Greece and Rome, so contact Rand McNally for a catalog. Most recently Routledge has produced two new maps sponsored by the Classical Association of Great Britain. Each is 35 " x 55 ", is laminated, and comes rolled in a tube. One is entitled *Greece and the Aegean*, the other *Roman Italy*.

National Geographic is known to most of us, and I own many of their maps myself. I continue to be amazed by their reasonable prices. Titles of interest: *Early Civilizations of the Middle East, Classical Lands of the Mediterranean, Greece and the Aegean*, the *Mediterranean Seafloor* (a favorite of mine), and the *Historic Mediterranean Sea—800 B.C. to A.D. 1500*. By the way, if there is a used book shop around, it is generally easy to find these maps on old issues that tend to sell for a quarter or so a piece.

Be sure to look beyond the language arts catalog of a given company. For example, the social studies and geography catalog of Opportunities for Learning offers *World History Map Activities*, consisting of 70 photocopy masters and a teacher's guide. The sheets can be used for in-class work, review, testing, or homework. The chronological range is wide, covering the period from Ancient Egypt to just after World War II. It might be the sort of thing you and the history teacher could split with minimal pain. Likewise, Facts on File's *Historical Maps on File* (selected by *Library Journal* as one of the best reference books of 1985) has over 300 maps ranging from the Ice Age to 1980, and photocopying is encouraged. Pomegranate Artbooks might not be the first place one would look for classroom materials, but they have a wide variety of postcards, books, and calendars featuring old maps. One series stresses maps of antiquity.

A word of advice: do not post a map on day one only to have it hang there for the entire semester. Change them often, moving their position in the classroom. With materials from the sources listed above, you can easily bring out just the right map for a given lesson, making it an integral and useful part of the learning process.

Nor are maps all we can hang. Posters are generally available cheaply enough to enable you to change them every quarter. Try companies like L&L Enterprises, Lumina, Perfection Form Co., and museum catalogs such as those from the British Museum or the Metropolitan. Gessler Publishing Co. and Éditions SOLEIL have carried vocabulary posters as well, and, of course, the American Classical League's (ACL) Teaching Materials and Resource Center (TMRC) is a treasure house of inexpensive and widely varied posters and charts. Finally, do not be afraid of asking tourism agencies such as the Italian Government Travel Office, the Cyprus Tourism Organization, or the Greek National Tourist Organization for posters, pamphlets, and brochures. Results vary depending upon who fields your request but you often are well rewarded for the effort, especially if you identify yourself as a teacher of Latin or Greek. Closer to home, you may wish to cultivate the good wishes of a local travel agency for posters.

BOOKS AND PERIODICALS

What books should a good classroom have in it? The list could be endless, of course, for Latin teachers are among the world's greatest bibliophiles. Let us instead discuss four main topics: reference texts, both for the students' classroom use and the teacher's preparation work; textbooks; a collection of books to have on hand for your students' pleasure reading; and journals and other periodicals.

Reference

Every class should have a collection of books which students can use to help with their oral reports, projects, and Junior Classical League (JCL) or Latin Club activities. Remember that, while I may list some titles by name, there are many more out there for you to find by writing to the publishers listed below in the resource list. You will want an atlas to accompany the maps we just discussed. Some treat antiquity in a general context (*Past Worlds*; Palmer; Manley; Talbert 1985), while others focus on Greece and Rome, either together (Grant 1995a–b) or separately (Scarre). Some, like Grant, are notable for their many, clear maps, while others include different sorts of cultural and historical data (Levi; Cornell). No one atlas fills all needs, so you should have several on hand. When choosing, you will want to weigh factors such as age-suitability, layout, and durability. There is a nice juvenile market, for example, for this sort of book (*Atlas of Ancient Worlds*). Atlases seem always to be in demand and most have short publication lives. In an interesting article, Richard Talbert (1992) outlines the history of our attempts to map the classical world.

You will find it useful to have several basic reference works in the classroom as well. These need not be as elaborate as the *Oxford Classical Dictionary* (Hornblower and Spawforth), which is now in its third (expensive) edition, although that is a work you will want for yourself. Your students might profit more from the new version of the *Concise Oxford Companion to Classical Literature* (Howatson and Chilvers), which sports more information, a larger format, and an expressed desire to appeal to the general reader and not just the specialist. Originally published in 1937 and unchanged until recently, it now has many articles which have been updated.

Other useful titles might include the older though still useful *Lemprière's Classical Dictionary*, but more modern books are available (Radice; Bowder; Sacks 1995, 1997; Bunson). Mythology books are important, of course, and these too come and go rather quickly. Of special note is an excellent small reference work which each student could own (Zimmerman), or your classroom may prefer *NTC's Classical Dictionary* (Room), which has more than 1,200 entries on the names in the legends and literatures of Greece and Rome, or a book such as those by Grant and Hazel, Morford and Lenardon (1995), Pinsent, and Stapleton. Here too pay very careful attention to the age level of your students.

Before moving on, let me suggest that you may wish to have several inexpensive Latin dictionaries around. *The New College Latin & English Dictionary* (Traupman 1994) is an excellent choice, as are the larger Cassell's dictionaries (Simpson 1977, 1987). Each of these is clear, inexpensive, fairly sturdy, and each has an English-to-Latin section. For your own use you should probably have a Lewis and Short's *Latin Dictionary*, the *Oxford Latin Dictionary* (Glare), or *Chambers Murray Latin-English Dictionary* (Smith).

Textbooks

The vast majority of school systems require that classroom texts be taken from a state-approved list if they are to be provided free of charge to the school. Such lists traditionally are narrow in scope, and many teachers complain that they are woefully out of date. Yet there is still room for maneuvering, for teachers can assign supplementary texts to accompany the main texts or, at some schools, can assign what they wish, since the students buy the textbooks. It is crucial, then, that the Latin teacher be familiar with the major sources for textbooks and the places they are reviewed.

I strongly recommend that you subscribe to *Classical World* (*CW*), which publishes annotated surveys of textbooks arranged in such categories as dictionaries and word lists, grammars and grammatical aids, readers, beginners' books, and individual authors. Currently *CW* offers a full survey in even-numbered years and supplementary surveys in odd-numbered years. The full 1996 survey was over 50 pages long (Sebesta). In recent years, as a response to the increased visibility of Latin in our secondary and elementary schools, several publishers have increased their offerings. Bolchazy-Carducci Publishers is among the most devoted to our field, with a complete and innovative line of books for use at all levels. Focus Press not only has its own selection of fine books, but is also the American distributor for Bristol Classical Press and Duckworth. The Focus catalog features translations, editions, commentaries, textbooks, vocabulary lists, scansion exercises, composition exercises, and grammars. An innovative approach has been taken by Gilbert Lawall as editor of a series of small, inexpensive books which can be combined to produce, in essence, your own reader; they are published, along with other useful texts, by CANE Instructional Materials. Of the larger commercial publishers, Scott Foresman-Addison Wesley has one of the most extensive listings of Latin textbooks in the country (including all the former Longman publications) and the company regularly adds new titles.

Several university presses also carry sizable collections of classical offerings. Some of the best include Cambridge, Chicago, Cornell, Harvard, Johns Hopkins, Oklahoma, and Oxford. A postcard will bring you their catalogs. Further, many publishers have smaller, but still quite excellent, offerings. I list a few names here (Ares, Aris and Phillips, Bryn Mawr Commentaries, Francis Cairns, Caratzas, Coronado, National Textbook Co., Prentice-Hall), but there are others listed at the end of this chapter as well.

Pleasure Reading

The warmest memories I have of classrooms involve those that had book collections. When our work was done, or simply as a treat, we were allowed to wander among the teacher's books and read whatever we wished. I have believed ever since that this is an invaluable adjunct to a true learning environment and one that encourages students to learn ever more about antiquity. Rather than list a great number of titles here, let me encourage you to purchase certain types of books. You will be the best judge of which particular ones suit the age and ability of your students. By all means, have many books on mythology and art. Since students will often be looking at them during off moments, choose titles with excellent pictures. The J. Paul Getty Museum produces several splendid books in these areas. I suggest a book or two each on ancient coins, ancient armies, and daily life (be sure to have some on the lives of children and women). Add a few archaeology books which show students how we dig up the past, and have some "then and now" titles showing the ruins as they appear now as well as how they looked when intact. Let your imagination be your guide. Depending on the reading level of your students, do not forget the historical novels by such authors as Steven Saylor, John Maddox Roberts, Lindsey Davis, and Colleen McCullough. If you are unfamiliar with these authors, you may want to check Jeffrey Buller's article on the subject (1989—available from the TMRC, item B806). Add a few of the excellent comic books (e.g., *Asterix*) and activity books that are now available, and your book corner will be complete.

With the increase in enrollments in elementary- and middle-school Latin classes, many companies offer books for a wide range of age levels. For younger readers, consider companies such as Cobblestone, Peter Bedrick, Wayside, Opportunities for Learning (see their *Expanding Horizons* catalog), National Textbook Company, HarperCollins *Children's Books*, and Puffin Books (division of Penguin). You should also investigate other catalogs from the same publishers, since much material for younger students is to be found in sections aimed at teachers of social studies, geography, and literature. Put yourself on the appropriate mailing lists, and offerings for these titles will soon be flooding your mailbox.

With careful buying you will have a fine collection in two to three years. When parents wish to "do something for the Latin program," suggest that they add some books to the collection—it will be ever so much easier if you have a list ready—or use proceeds from JCL or Latin Club activities to add volumes.

Periodicals

Naturally, I would suggest that you put out copies of the magazines your friends and relatives have collected for you, so that your students can read them. But you should also consider subscribing to a magazine or two for your students to peruse. The *Pompeiiana Newsletter* is a must. Its newspaper format and quick articles (some in Latin) are definite hits with students, and the puzzles and games are equally popular; there are even bulk discounts that allow you to use this as a supplementary text if you choose. *Aramco World*, a free magazine mentioned earlier, is published bimonthly and aimed at a general audience. It features excellent photographs and reconstructions, and nearly every issue has something concerning antiquity. *Calliope* is a magazine on history published by Cobblestone Publishing and aimed at high-school and younger students. While not all articles are about Greece and Rome, it is still worth investigating. Another fine journal is *Archaeology*. You can buy it on the newsstands, but it is better to join the Archaeological Institute of America (AIA) and choose it as your membership option. Remember that you can also display a three-ring binder filled with articles your colleagues, friends, and students bring you. This is a space saver, enabling you to keep just what you need from various journals and magazines for your students.

Finally, any teacher can profit from keeping up with the field through judicious personal subscriptions to journals. There are several journals one could mention specifically, but *Classical Outlook* is among the best, with a wide variety of features to help the teacher. You receive a subscription when you become a member of the ACL, as you surely must (more on this below). Note also that membership in ACL brings you *Prima*, a newsletter devoted to those who teach Classics in the elementary schools. I recommended above that you subscribe to *Classical World*, and here I will add *Classical Journal*, which you will receive when you join the Classical Association of the Middle West and South (CAMWS). *CJ* offers excellent scholarly articles, but also has a section called the "Forum" which regularly offers articles on pedagogical matters. Moreover, the *CAMWS Newsletter* is specifically designed to publicize information about resources, meetings, and funding sources for teachers. Likewise, if you join the Classical Association of New England (CANE), you receive the *New England Classical Journal*, which regularly has articles that are very useful to teachers.

REALIA

This rather broad term refers to replicas or reproductions of objects, or the actual objects themselves, which are representative of the lives and culture of a civilization. Latin teachers suffer, after all, from a distinct disadvantage in this regard. The German teacher can readily bring in a menu from a fast food outlet in Frankfurt. Spanish teachers need not even leave the country to find Spanish food labels. A clever French teacher can devise an entire lesson, both linguistic and cultural, around a handful of francs left over from a trip to Paris.

How can the Latin teacher compete? A single silver coin from antiquity can cost hundreds of dollars. A simple, unadorned lamp can cost over $50. But all is not lost, for there are several outlets where Latin teachers may find exactly what they need. Small items such as coins are frequently copied and sold. Several sets are offered by the TMRC, and L&L Enterprises is another excellent source. Moreover, if you subscribe to *Archaeology*, as recommended above, you will find several advertisements for independent companies that offer a wide range of archaeological replicas. Museum Replicas Limited specializes in full-sized reproductions of ancient weapons—you'll want to use these with care!

What of actual art? In the 19th century, full plaster copies of ancient sculpture were quite the rage. The museums at the University of Texas and the University of Missouri, in fact, still exhibit theirs. Today we can do the same thing, if only in miniature. The first and best option is to visit museums which have ancient art. A trip to Greece or Rome will bring you many such items, but local museums can also make excellent field trips, and invariably their museum shops will have replicas for sale. Since few of us have the luxury of the museums of Greece or Rome at our disposal, and since most of us do not have a local museum with any ancient art to speak of, it is often a good idea to have replicas on hand to show our students. One excellent source for such *realia* is catalogs of larger museums. I have already mentioned the British Museum, but you should also be aware of the Boston Museum of Fine Arts, the University Museum of the University of Pennsylvania, and the Metropolitan Museum of Art. Be sure also to contact the Smithsonian Institution and Museum Publications of America, the latter being an independent company with an excellent and broad collection.

The Biblical Archaeology Society often has items from antiquity, and remember that membership in AIA will also bring you the *EUREKA!* catalog, containing all sorts of items you will be able to use in the classroom (AIA members receive a 10% discount). Eleganza Ltd., Star River Productions, and World Treasures are some of the many private companies that often have fine replicas, and many others are regularly advertised in *Archaeology*.

I offer some final tips. When you see such materials, buy them immediately as they are often only available for a short time. If it is a piece of art you know about, do not be shy about bringing in a picture of the original to compare for accuracy. Finally, archive your material carefully—do not merely toss it in a box. Whether you use a computer data base or index cards, you should create a filing system. Number each item you buy and then, on separate cards, create headings under which you might bring out the item for classroom use. For example, you may purchase a replica of a Roman coin of Nero. It should be noted on cards marked "Coins," "Emperors," "Nero," "Roman Persecution of Christians," and abbreviations like "Pontifex Maximus." The small set of Roman soldiers sold by the British Museum would serve equally "Army," "Caesar," or "Tacitus." Noting these things down helps me use my replicas more often.

MOTIVATORS, PRIZES, ASSISTANCE

It is surprising how important instantaneous gratification is to learners of all ages. A story exists that two prominent classicists once attended a teaching demonstration by the late Maureen O'Donnell. Maureen routinely awarded prizes for right answers and one of these was a "magic pencil," guaranteed not to write wrong answers in Latin. After the session, one of the classicists was overheard complaining that, although his hand had been up, he had not been called on and he never got a pencil. I once taught a class in intensive Latin attended by four fellow professors. If I forgot to put stickers on good papers, they were the first and loudest to complain.

In short, such devices make learning fun and they are to be encouraged. Our field is fortunate to have many outlets where we can obtain a wide variety of reasonably priced items to make the classroom a more lively place. There are stickers and stamps to put on good papers, buttons that proclaim the value of Latin, Latin rulers, calendars, games, crossword puzzles, note cards, note pads, napkins, pencils (presumably the magic variety), comic books, workbooks, bookmarks, and page clips. Many of these are adorned with appropriate quotes in Latin. Numerous model assembly kits are available too, ranging from the Parthenon to an entire Roman military camp. There are excellent sources that offer a wide variety of all these sorts of adjunct materials—Lumina, L&L Enterprises, ACL's TMRC, CANE's *Emporium Romanum*, and Small Potatoes Press. Note also that Bolchazy-Carducci offers a large set of buttons with quotations in Latin or Greek. These work very well when worn, and explained, by the teacher. Good Impressions specializes in rubber stamps and inkpads, many of which can readily be used by a Latin teacher.

Students are not, however, the only people with whom we deal who need encouragement. The Latin teacher is frequently found convincing administrators of the need to retain a program or telling parents why their child needs to take Latin. The same holds true when teachers try to recruit students at their own school. Fortunately, help is available here as well. Each of the companies just listed carries materials with which to advertise during your school's registration period or which will serve to make your Foreign Language Week all the better. The National Committee for Latin and Greek (NCLG) also can help with its informational packet, "Latin in the 90's." It consists of a sturdy folder of over 70 pages of camera-ready, copyright-free, promotional materials to help Latin teachers start, build, or maintain programs, and it is available from the ACL's TMRC (item B908); materials in the packet are regularly updated. Note too that NCLG has recently produced "Beyond Greece and Rome: Teaching Cultural Diversity in the Roman Empire." Designed to help teachers integrate a multicultural approach into their classrooms, it can be ordered through the CANE Instructional Materials service.

If your program needs specific help, whether with getting started, expanding, or avoiding cutbacks, there are various places to which you may turn. The CAMWS Committee for the Promotion of Latin has long been a supporter of programs in its geographical area, and the ACL's Classics Action

Network works to protect programs on a national basis. Likewise, the American Philological Association (APA) has become increasingly concerned with Latin at the pre-college level; its Education Committee has been especially active in this regard. Contact the parent organizations for information about the current heads of each committee.

AUDIOVISUALS

It is fair to say that a classroom that does not include audiovisuals is sadly misjudging the learning styles of contemporary students. Gray's 1929 book on teaching Latin contained only three pages on such aids (175–77). Today's Latin teacher must be conversant with a vast array of media and the companies that distribute them. Be sure to request their foreign language catalogs, of course, but you will also find much of use in catalogs directed toward teachers of social studies, geography, and literature. I will list in some detail several companies with large holdings to give a sense of what is available, and then I will mention other sources more quickly. Once more, I encourage you to subscribe to *Classical World*, which, in addition to its textbook reviews, also features periodic surveys of audiovisual materials. The 1996 survey (Bender) featured almost 50 pages of information, and Buller's work (1991) is another rich source (TMRC item B303).

Many films and tapes come in complete packages. For example, Alarion Press offers programs (for grades K–4, 5–12, or for grades 9 to adult) on Greek or Roman architecture and civilization that contain a teaching manual, poster, and a video. CLEARVUE/eav touts itself as "the most complete source for curriculum-oriented A-V materials" and its holdings are indeed vast, including videos, enhanced videos, and filmstrips (although most of these have now been transferred to videotape). I cannot begin to list all the relevant titles, but look at the sections in the catalog that we could use: History through Art, Ancient Civilizations, World History, World Literature, Mythology, Drama. A comparable selection is offered by Insight Media.

Visual Education specializes in slides and videos of all cultures and its catalog has a section on "Classical Greece and Rome." There are five titles for the series *Greek Art and Architecture*, and 11 titles comprise *Roman Art and Architecture*. Most contain about 40 slides. Visual Education also provides Latin flashcards, a staple from my college days. Bolchazy-Carducci has produced the excellent "Monumenta Romana Nostra," a collection of slide lectures fully supported with commentary, ground plans, and bibliography designed for high-school or college-aged students. See also the offerings of the American Library Color Slide Co.

Audio-Forum specializes in oral tapes and carries many of the tapes which Stephen Daitz and Robert Sonkowsky have produced illustrating the pronunciation of ancient Latin and Greek. Vocabulary cards are available for both Latin and Greek, and there are films such as the *Iphigeneia*. Opportunities for Learning, mentioned above for their maps, also offers many videos; ask for the social studies and geography catalog. Another useful but often overlooked company is Time-Life Video, but the single most fertile source of audio-visual materials for the Latin teacher must be Films for the Humanities. Their collection is huge and deals with history, literature, archaeology, and virtually any aspect of antiquity that may interest you, and the quality is consistently first class.

If you are trying to work in an archaeological unit, the AIA has two excellent resource books. The first is *Archaeology in the Classroom: A Resource Guide for Teachers and Parents* (O'Brien and Cullen), which contains information about all sorts of educational materials available in North America, including books, magazines, curriculum and resource packets, films, videos, kits, computer programs, and games; it also includes resources and sites listed by subject area, and ends with an excellent bibliography. The second book, *Archaeology on Film* (Downs), catalogs over 700 films on archaeology, and each listing includes synopsis, distributors, and purchase and rental prices.

Finally, be aware that many of the companies listed as sources at the end of this chapter may have only one or two items of interest to Latin teachers, but these items can be of great use. Be sure, then, to write for brochures. Several universities, such as Indiana and Kent State, have excellent collections of audiovisuals.

STAYING CURRENT

"The rapidity with which new Latin texts and new books and articles on various phases of the teaching of Latin are appearing makes any bibliography incomplete within a short time after its appearance." So wrote Mason Gray in 1929 (173). It is as true today as then. The above survey represents a sampling of what is available today, but the resources available are constantly changing, and how does one stay current while teaching five or six classes with nearly as many preparations? The trick is twofold—first, get the information to come to you rather than vice-versa; second, keep involved with organizations that help you find this information.

First and foremost, as I have stressed repeatedly above, you should join several organizations for the quality of assistance they offer. All secondary, middle, and elementary Latin teachers should belong to the ACL. Its journal, *Classical Outlook*, is indispensable for its regular columns designed to help keep you up to date. Among the more useful are the "Clearing House," which appears in every issue and serves to pass along information on the latest classroom materials and teaching tips, "Random Access" (on computer resources—see Chapter 23), "*Quid Novi?*" (with news of meetings, special events, and resources of interest to teachers), and especially the "Reviews" and

"Audio-Video Audit" departments, which offer extensive reviews of new books and audiovisuals. Next, you should join your regional Classics organization. Some, such as CAMWS, CANE, and CAAS (the Classical Association of the Atlantic States), publish journals, and most have newsletters especially aimed at teaching issues. Further, the annual meetings of these groups are replete with pedagogical panels, talks, and displays of current books and materials. The time it takes to go to a meeting is more than amply repaid. Perhaps most importantly, you should try to attend an ACL Annual Institute at least every two or three years. Here you will find more useful information in just a few days than you thought imaginable. And, by all means, join your state Classics organization. Most have newsletters and many have their own meetings with appropriate displays; moreover, membership and attendance in such organizations will insure that you are informed when new and relevant items appear of which you might not normally be informed.

Do not forget the power of the World Wide Web. There are numerous home pages devoted to resources for Classics teachers and discussion groups that will enable you to "throw open a window and yell for help," as it were (see Chapter 23). I can not overestimate the assistance that can be found this way in the electronic age. Be sure also to be on the mailing lists of major publishing houses and suppliers of materials; the cost of postcards will put you in touch with them all (if you miss one or two, or if new ones emerge, fear not, for your name will be passed on as companies buy and swap mailing label lists). An occasional purchase now and then will keep you on these lists—but when you see what a rich array of materials is available, the only burden will lie in not being able to afford everything that you know can enrich your teaching!

SOURCES OF MATERIALS

Alarion Press, P.O. Box 1882, Boulder, CO 80306-1882; 800-523-9177; FAX 303-443-9098.

American Classical League/*Classical Outlook*, Miami Univ., Oxford, OH 45056; 513-529-7741; FAX 513-529-7742; E-mail AmericanClassicalLeague@muohio. edu.

American Council on the Teaching of Foreign Languages, 6 Executive Plaza, Yonkers, NY 10701-6801.

American Library Color Slide Co., Inc., P.O. Box 5810 Grand Central Station, New York, NY 10017; 800-633-3307; FAX 212-691-8592.

American Philological Association, Executive Director, Scholars Press, P.O. Box 15339, Atlanta, GA 30333-0399; 404-727-2345; FAX 404-727-2348; E-mail scholars@emory.edu.

Amsco School Publications, Inc., 315 Hudson St., New York, NY 10013-1085; 800-969-8398 or 212-886-6565.

Applause Learning Resources, 85 Fernwood La., Roslyn, NY 11576-1431; 516-365-1259 or 800-253-5351; FAX 516-365-7484.

Aramco World, Box 469008, Escondido, CA 92046-9008.

Archaeological Institute of America/*Archaeology*, Boston Univ., 656 Beacon St., Boston, MA 02215-2010; 617-353-9361; FAX 617-353-6550; E-mail aia@bu.edu; www.csaws.brynmawr.edu:443/aia.html.

Ares Publishers, 7406 N. Sheridan Rd., Chicago, IL 60626; FAX 312-743-0657.

Aris and Phillips Ltd., c/o The David Brown Book Co., P.O. Box 511, Oakville, CT 06779; 800-791-9354 or 860-945-9329; FAX 860-945-9468.

Audio-Forum, 96 Broad St., Guilford, CT 06437; 800-243-1234; FAX 203-453-9774.

Peter Bedrick Books, 2112 Broadway, New York, NY 10023; 212-496-0751; FAX 212-496-1158; E-mail bedrick@panix.com.

Biblical Archaeology Society, 3000 Connecticut Ave., NW, Ste. 300, Washington, DC 20008; 202-387-8888 or 800-221-4644.

Basil Blackwell, 238 Main St., Cambridge, MA 02142.

Bolchazy-Carducci Publishers, Inc., 1000 Brown St., Wauconda, IL 60084; 847-526-4344; FAX 847-526-2867; E-mail latin@bolchazy.com.; www.bolchazy.com.

Boston Museum of Fine Arts, 465 Huntington Ave., Boston, MA 02115.

British Museum Connection, c/o Unit A, Chettisham Business Park, Ely, Cambridgeshire CB6 1RY, ENG.

Bryn Mawr Commentaries, Bryn Mawr Coll., Thomas Library, Bryn Mawr, PA 19010-2899.

Francis Cairns Publishers Ltd., c/o Univ. of Leeds, Leeds LS2 9JT, ENG.

Cambridge Univ. Press, 40 W. 20th St., New York, NY 10011-4211; 800-872-7423.

CANE Instructional Materials, Prof. Gilbert Lawall, Ed., 71 Sand Hill Rd., Amherst, MA 01002.

Aristide D. Caratzas Publisher, P.O. Box 210, 30 Church St., New Rochelle, NY 10802; FAX 914-632-3650.

Univ. of Chicago Press, 5801 South Ellis Ave., Chicago, IL 60637-1496; order dept.: 800-621-2736, FAX 800-621-8476; E-mail rdo@press.uchicago.edu.

Classical Association of the Atlantic States/*Classical World*, L.E. Gaichas, Dept. of Classics, Duquesne Univ., Pittsburgh, PA 16282-1704; E-mail gaichas@duq2.duq. edu.

Classical Association of the Middle West and South/*Classical Journal*, Gregory Daugherty, Dept. of Classics, Randolph-Macon Coll., P.O. Box 5005, Ashland, VA 23005-5505; E-mail gdaugher@rmc.edu.

Classical Association of New England/*New England Classical Journal*, Ruth Breindel, Treas., CANE, Moses Brown School, 250 Lloyd Ave., Providence, RI 02906; E-mail grmbt017@llwsbe.wsbe.org; www.hnet.uci.edu/classics/cane.html.

CLEARVUE/eav, 6465 North Avondale Ave., Chicago, IL 60631-1909; 800-253-2788; FAX 800-444-9855; www.CLEARVUE.com.

Cobblestone Publishing, Inc., 7 School St., Peterborough, NH 03458; 800-821-0115.

Cornell Univ. Press, 124 Roberts Pl., P.O. Box 250, Ithaca, NY 14851-0250; 800-666-2211.

Coronado Press, Box 3232, Lawrence, KS 66044.

Cyprus Tourism Org., 13 E. 40th St., New York, NY 10016; 212-683-5282.

Dorling Kindersley Publishing, 95 Madison Ave., New York, NY 10016.

Éditions SOLEIL, P.O. Box 890, Lewiston, NY 14092-0890; 905-788-2674.

Educational Video Network, 1467 19th St., Huntsville, TX 77340; 409–295–5767; FAX 409–294–0233.

Eleganza Ltd., Magnolia Village, 3217 W. Smith St. #1205, Seattle, WA 98199.

Emporium Romanum, Donna Lyons, 11 Carver Cir., Simsbury, CT 06070; FAX 860–253–5555 (Enfield H.S.); E-mail DonnaLyons@AOL.com.

Facts on File, 460 Park Ave. South, New York, NY 10016.

Films for the Humanities and Sciences, P.O. Box 2053, Princeton, NJ 08543–2053; 800–257–5126 or 609–275–1400; FAX 609–275–3767.

Focus, P.O. Box 369, Newburyport, MA 01950; 508–462–4856; FAX 508–462–9035; E-mail pullins@pullins.com; www.pullins.com.

Gessler Publishing Co., Inc., 10 E. Church Ave., Roanoke, VA 24011; 703–345–1429 or 800–456–5825; FAX 540–342–7172.

J. Paul Getty Museum, P.O. Box 2112, Santa Monica, CA 90407–2112; 800–223–3431.

Good Impressions, P.O. Box 33, Shirley, WV 26434–0033; 800–846–6606.

Greek National Tourist Org., 645 Fifth Ave., 5th Floor, New York, NY 10022; 212–421–5777; E-mail gnto@eexi.gr; www.1travel.com/greece.

Hammond Inc., 515 Valley St., Maplewood, NJ 07040; 800–526–4953.

Harcourt Brace Jovanovich, Dowden Rd., Orlando, FL 32887; 800–225–5425.

Harper and Row and HarperCollins Children's Books, 10 E. 53d St., New York, NY 10022–5299; 800–242–7737; FAX 800–822–4090.

Harvard Univ. Press, 79 Garden St., Cambridge, MA 02138–9983; customer service dept.: 800–448–2242; FAX 800–962–4983 or 617–495–5898.

Johns Hopkins Univ. Press, 2715 N. Charles St., Baltimore, MD 21218–4319; 800–537–5487.

Indiana Univ. Audio Visual Center, Indiana Univ., Bloomington, IN 47405–5901; 800–552–8620 (in IN 800–942–0481).

Insight Media, 2162 Broadway, New York, NY 10024-6620; 800–233–9910 or 212–721–6316; FAX 212–799–5309.

Italian Govt. Travel Office, 630 Fifth Ave., New York, NY 10111; 212–245–4822.

Kendall/Hunt Publishing Co., Order Dept., 4050 Westmark Dr., Dubuque, IA 52002; 800–228–0810 or 319–589–1000.

Kent State Univ., Audio-Visual Services, P.O. Box 5190, Kent, OH 44242–0001; 216–672–FILM or 800–338–5718; FAX 216–672–3463.

L&L Enterprises, 401 Towne St., Gilberts, IL 60136; 708–426–5311 or 800–426–5357; www.home.aol.com/LandL800.

Lumina, 520½ S. Pitt St., Alexandria, VA 22314; 800–358–9015.

Macmillan/McGraw-Hill Coll. Div., 445 Hutchinson Ave., Columbus, OH 43235; 800–228–7854.

McGraw-Hill School Div., Corporate Headquarters, 1221 Ave. of the Americas, New York, NY 10020; 212–512–2000; www.mmhschool.com.

Metropolitan Museum of Art, 255 Gracie Sta., New York, NY 10028; 800–468–7368.

Museum Publications of America, 306 Dartmouth St., Boston, MA 02116; 800–442–2460.

Museum Replicas Ltd., 2143 Gees Mill Rd., Box 840, Conyers, GA 30207.

National Committee for Latin and Greek, Virginia Barrett, 11371 Matinicus, Cypress, CA 90630-5458; 714-373-0588; FAX 714-890-0862.

National Geographic Society, Educational Services, P.O. Box 98019, Washington, DC 20090; 800-368-2728; FAX 301-921-1575. Membership, 1145 17th St., NW, Washington, DC 20036-4688; 800-NGS-LINE; www.national geographic.com.

National Textbook Co., 4255 West Touhy Ave., Lincolnwood, IL 60646-1975; 800-323-4900; FAX 708-679-2494.

Univ. of Oklahoma Press, 1005 Asp Ave., Norman, OK 73069-0445; 800-627-7377; FAX 405-325-4000.

Opportunities for Learning, 941 Hickory La., P.O. Box 8103, Mansfield, OH 44901-8103; 800-243-7116.

Oxford Univ. Press, 200 Madison Ave., New York, NY 10016; order dept.: 2001 Evans Rd., Cary, NC 27513; 800-451-7556.

Penguin USA, Academic Marketing Dept., 375 Hudson St., New York, NY 10014-3657; Consumer Sales, P.O. Box 999, Dept. 17109, Bergenfield, NJ 07621; 800-253-6476.

Perfection Form Co., 1000 N. Second Ave., Logan, IA 51546; 800-831-4190.

Pomegranate Artbooks, Box 6099, Rohnert Park, CA 94927; 800-227-1428.

Pompeiiana, Inc., 6026 Indianola Ave., Indianapolis, IN 46220-2014; 317-255-0589; FAX 317-254-1380; E-mail Pompeiiana@aol.com.

Prentice-Hall, School Div. of Simon and Schuster, Englewood Cliffs, NJ 07632; 800-848-9500.

Questar Video, Inc., P.O. Box 11345, Chicago, IL 60611-0345.

Rand McNally, Educational Publishing Div., P.O. Box 1906, Skokie, IL 60076-8906; 708-673-9100.

Routledge, 29 W. 35th St., New York, NY 10001-2291.

Scott Foresman-Addison Wesley, 1900 E. Lake Ave., Glenview, IL 60025; order processing: 800-552-2259; Cathy Wilson, Product Manager, Modern and Classical Languages, 847-486-2213; E-mail cathy.wilson@aw.com.

Small Potatoes Press, P.O. Box 274, Hales Corners, WI 53130.

Smithsonian Institution, Dept. 0006, Washington, DC 20073-0006.

Star River Productions, P.O. Box 6254, North Brunswick, NJ 08902; 800-232-1733.

Teaching Materials and Resource Center: see American Classical League.

Time-Life Video, 1450 E. Parham Rd., Richmond, VA 23286-4257.

Univ. Museum, Univ. of Pennsylvania, 33rd and Spruce Sts., Philadelphia, PA 19104-6324.

Univ. Prints, 21 East St., P.O. Box 485, Winchester, MA 01890; 617-729-8006.

Visual Education, 133 Smart Ct., Encinitas, CA 92024; 619-942-8405.

Visual Education Association, 581 West Leffel La., P.O. Box 1666, Springfield, OH 45501; 800-243-7070.

Waveland Press Inc., P.O. Box 400, Prospect Heights, IL 60070.

Wayne State Univ. Press, 4809 Woodward Ave., Detroit, MI 48201-1309.

Wayside Publishing, 129 Commonwealth Ave, Concord, MA 01742; 508-369-2519.

John Wiley and Sons, 605 Third Ave., New York, NY 10158-0012; FAX 212-850-6088.

World Treasures, 23016-A Del Lago Dr., Laguna Hills, CA 92653; 800-262-4382.

Author Biographies

MARTHA G. ABBOTT is the Foreign Language Coordinator in Fairfax County Public Schools, Virginia, and has taught Latin at the elementary and secondary-school levels for 14 years. She has served on the National Latin Exam Committee, as well as the Task Force that developed the *Standards for Foreign Language Learning* and subsequently the committee that developed the *Standards for Classical Language Learning*, and is Vice-Chair of the Northeast Conference on the Teaching of Foreign Languages. *mabbott@walnuthill. fcps.k12.va.us*

ALTHEA C. ASHE is an Instructor of Latin at Louisiana State University. While teaching at the high-school level, she became involved in working with students with learning disabilities; interested in the practical application of teaching Latin at the post-secondary level to students with LD, she designed and teaches the three-semester sequence of Latin courses for at-risk students at Louisiana State. Her doctoral work at the University of Georgia focuses on theory and research in second-language teaching and learning. A recipient of the American Classical League's Arthur Patch McKinley Scholarship, she is a past President of the Louisiana Classical Association and served for five years as managing editor of the *Louisiana Classicist*. *ashe@homer.forlang.lsu.edu*

MARGARET A. BRUCIA received her Ph.D. in Classics from Fordham University and teaches Latin at the Earl L. Vandermeulen High School in Port Jefferson, New York. A consultant for the Educational Testing Service and the College Board, she served as Chair of the AP Latin Test Development Committee for five years. She is a member of the New York State Latin Regents Examination Committee and the Education Committee of the American Philological Association. Her publications include *Teacher's Guide to Advanced Placement Courses in Latin*, "An Analysis of Candidate Performance on the Multiple-Choice Section of the Published 1987 AP Latin Examination" (with Kathleen A. Rabiteau), and "Horace and the High-School Latin Student." *mabrucia@aol.com*

CATHY PHILLIPS DAUGHERTY is the Lead Teacher/Specialist in Foreign Language for Hanover County Public Schools and Adjunct Instructor in Classics at Randolph-Macon College in Ashland, Virginia. For 10 years she taught Latin for the Virginia Satellite Education Network (VSEN). A former director of the

Virginia Governor's Latin Academy and past Chairman of the CAMWS Committee for the Promotion of Latin, she has attended programs at the American School in Athens, at Cambridge University, and as a Fulbright Scholar at the American Academy in Rome. Most recently she served on the committee writing the *Standards for Classical Language Learning. cdaugher@ pen.k12.va.us*

SALLY DAVIS teaches Latin at the H.B. Woodlawn Program and Yorktown High School in Arlington, Virginia, and pedagogy courses at the University of Virginia. She has worked on the National Latin Exam Committee from its inception and been a writer and reader of the AP Latin Exam. Her publications include *Latin in American Schools, Cicero's Somnium Scipionis* (with Gil Lawall) and *Review and Test Preparation Guide for the Intermediate Latin Student*, and she is editor of Paratext's *Vergil Reference* CD ROM, from the Romanitas Reference Series on Latin authors. *saldavis@erols.com*

SHEILA K. DICKISON is Associate Professor of Classics and Director of the Honors Program at the University of Florida. A past Vice-President of the American Classical League, President of the Classical Association of the Middle West and South (Southern Section), and a recipient of the Florida Latin Teacher of the Year award, her publications include an edition of Cicero's *In Verrem* 2.4 and articles on Tacitus, women in antiquity, and Latin pedagogy. She has served as a member and Chair of the AP Latin Exam Development Committee and was AP Latin Chief Reader from 1987–91. *s125@nervm.nerdc.ufl.edu*

RICHARD C. GASCOYNE chaired the national Task Force on Standards for Classical Language Learning. He is retired from the New York State Education Department after a full career of teaching in secondary schools and at the State University of New York at Albany. In retirement he has taught Latin in grades 5–8 at a private boys' school, Latin Methods to graduate students at the University of Massachusetts, and is currently teaching Latin at SUNY, Albany. *rgascoyne@aol.com*

EDWARD V. GEORGE (Ph.D., Wisconsin) is Professor of Classics at Texas Tech University, where he served (1974–97) as Graduate Advisor in the M.A. program in Classical Humanities. He occasionally teaches "Roman Culture and Hispanic America," a practical course for high-school Latin and Spanish teachers. The author of articles and books on Vergil and Hellenistic poetry, Apollonius Rhodius, and the Latin writings of the Spanish Humanist Juan Luis Vives (1493–1540), he has served as Vice-President of the American Classical League, President of the Texas Classical Association, and Chair of the Texas Council for the Humanities. *ed.george@ttacs1.ttu.edu*

JOHN GRUBER-MILLER is Associate Professor of Classics at Cornell College in Mount Vernon, Iowa. His research interests in Greek and Roman comedy, language instruction, and technology frequently intersect with his teaching: he and his Latin students have regularly staged bi-lingual productions of Plautus and Terence; he has authored *Scriba: Software to Accompany the Oxford Latin Course, Part 1,* is a core faculty member of the "VRoma Project: A Virtual Community for the Teaching of Classics," is editor of *Changing Paradigms: Teaching Beginning Latin and Greek* (forthcoming 1998), a volume that explores ways of teaching Latin and Greek using collaborative and communicative approaches. *grubermiller@cornell-iowa.edu*

JANE H. HALL is founder and Chair of the ACL/NJCL National Latin Exam. She has taught at every level from kindergarten through college. Retiring from Fairfax County Public Schools after 35 years, she has recently taught Latin at Aquinas Montessori and Mary Washington College. She is a recipient of the Virginia Distinguished Foreign Language Teacher Award presented by the Virginia Department of Education. Her publications include the Longman Latin Reader *Selections from Vergil's Aeneid, Books I, IV, VI: Dido and Aeneas* (with Alexander McKay). *jhhall@pen.k12.va.us*

KENNETH F. KITCHELL, JR. taught high-school Latin in Chicago from 1974–76. In 1976 he came to Louisiana State University, where he is Distinguished Alumni Professor and head of the Classics Section. He has published on Catullus, the island of Crete, animals and animal lore in antiquity and the middle ages; his most recent project is *Albertus Magnus De Animalibus* (with I. Resnick, forthcoming from Johns Hopkins). Long active in promoting Classics, he has served as head of the CAMWS Committee for the Promotion of Latin and as a member of the APA Education Committee, the National Committee for Latin and Greek, and the Committee for the Promotion of Greek. An Associate Editor for the *Classical Outlook,* he has written its "Clearing House" column since 1988. *kitchell@homer.forlang.lsu.edu*

GLENN M. KNUDSVIG is Professor of Latin and Director of the elementary Latin program and the Latin teacher certification program at the University of Michigan. Long active in the promotion of Classics, and President of the American Classical League during 1994–98, his publications include *Latin for Reading: A Beginner's Textbook with Exercises* and *Critical Thinking: Building the Basics. knudsvig@umich.edu*

RICHARD A. LAFLEUR is Professor and Head of Classics at the University of Georgia and Editor (since 1979) of the *Classical Outlook.* A past President of the American Classical League (1984–86) and recipient of a CAMWS *Ovatio* and the American Philological Association's Award for Excellence in the Teaching of Classics, his publications include numerous articles and reviews on Latin literature and pedagogy, as well as *The Teaching of Latin in American Schools*, *Latin Poetry for the Beginning Student*, *Love and Transformation: An Ovid Reader*, *Wheelock's Latin* (5th ed.), and *A Workbook for Wheelock's Latin* (with Paul Comeau). *rlafleur@parallel.park.uga.edu*

ROB LATOUSEK is President of Centaur Systems and Chair of the American Classical League's Committee on Educational Computer Applications. While completing an M.A. and teacher certification in Latin at Loyola University of Chicago (1982–85), he taught students aged 7–47 and began his current endeavors in designing and evaluating software and presenting workshops on "classical computing." His semi-annual column on computer-based resources for the Classics, "Random Access," appears in the *Classical Outlook*; and he has recently completed his seventh biennial update of the *Software Directory for the Classics* in both print and electronic formats. *latousek@centaursystems.com*

GILBERT W. LAWALL is Professor and Director of Graduate Studies in the Department of Classics at the University of Massachusetts at Amherst. He has served as President of the American Classical League, Secretary-Treasurer of the Classical Association of New England, and Editor of the *New England Classical Newsletter and Journal*. His research interests are Greek and Latin poetry and Latin pedagogy, and he has published on Theocritus, Apollonius, Plautus, Cicero, Catullus, Petronius, and Seneca. He served as Revision Editor of the *Ecce Romani* Latin course. *glawall@classics.umass.edu*

JAMES M. MAY is Professor of Classics and Associate Dean for Humanities at St. Olaf College, Northfield, Minnesota. He has published extensively on the Roman orator Cicero, and is co-author (with Anne Groton) of a supplemental reader for *Wheelock's Latin*, *Thirty-Eight Latin Stories*. In 1986, May was awarded the American Philological Association's Award for Excellence in the Teaching of the Classics, and in 1991 he won the Sears-Roebuck Foundation's Award for Teaching Excellence and Campus Leadership. He has served as APA Vice-President for Education and as editor of the *Classical Journal*'s "Forum" department. *may@stolaf.edu*

MARK MORFORD taught in secondary schools in Britain and the United States from 1952–63, at Ohio State University from 1964–84, and since 1984 as Professor of Classics at the University of Virginia. He was Kennedy Professor of Renaissance Studies at Smith College in 1995. Recipient of the Alumni Award for Distinguished Teaching at Ohio State University, he has served as Vice-President for Education and a Director of the American

Philological Association and President of the Classical Association of the Middle West and South. He is the author of numerous articles in professional journals, books on Lucan, Persius, and *Stoics and Neostoics*, and several textbooks including (with Robert Lenardon) *Classical Mythology.*   *mpm8b@virginia.edu*

LEAANN A. OSBURN teaches Latin, levels I–V, at Barrington High School in Barrington, Illinois, and is a half-time instructor at Northern Illinois University in DeKalb. She also designed, implemented, and taught in the 6th-through 8th-grade Latin program at Barrington Middle School from 1980–96. A past President of the Illinois Classical Conference and the Illinois Foreign Language Leadership Council, her awards include the ICC Latin Teacher of the Year Award, the Lieutenant Governor's Award for Outstanding Contribution to Foreign Language Education in Illinois, the Illinois State Superintendent's Award of Merit, and the Classical Association of the Middle West and South Good Teacher Award. *ProfLatin@aol.com*

DAVID J. PERRY holds a Bachelor's degree from Williams College and a M.A.T. from the University of Massachusetts, with additional graduate work at Fordham University. He has taught Latin from grade 6 through college level, and currently serves as Latin teacher and Chairman of the Foreign Language Department in the Rye City Schools in New York. He is active in the Classical Association of the Empire State, having served as Newsletter Editor, Publications Chair, and Vice-President, and is the author of several publications, including *Literature* (CAES Latin Teaching Handbooks), and co-author of Book 3 of *Ecce Romani. perryd@ryehs1.lhric.org*

CHARLES PLATTER is Associate Professor of Classics at the University of Georgia, where he served six years as Undergraduate Coordinator. He has published numerous articles on Greek and Latin literature. Most recently, he completed a commentary on Aristophanes' *Acharnians* for the Bryn Mawr Commentary series and co-edited a collection of essays, *Rethinking Sexuality: Foucault and Classical Antiquity* (Princeton 1997). *cplatter@uga.cc.uga.edu*

MARION POLSKY, Ph.D., teaches Latin, Myths and Legends, and Spanish in Scarsdale (New York) High School. She is the author of *First Latin: A Language Discovery Program*, which emerged from her work as Director of the Latin Cornerstone Project, a program funded by the National Endowment for the Humanities to introduce Latin to young students in New York City, under the auspices of Brooklyn College of CUNY. She has taught Latin at Princeton University and linguistics at the New School Graduate Faculty, where her oldest student was 81 years of age. She misses, most of all, the young learners at P.S. 75 in Manhattan. *545 W. 111th St., Apt. 5C, New York, NY 10025*

DEBORAH PENNELL ROSS is Adjunct Assistant Professor in the Department of Classical Studies at the University of Michigan. She has teaching experience in Latin at the high-school as well as at the college level, and is particularly concerned with teaching Latin for reading and other aspects of Latin pedagogy. A linguist by training, her research is in the areas of Indo-European studies, functional grammar, and discourse analysis, and she has published on word order and various discourse issues in Latin. *dpross@umich.edu*

JUDITH LYNN SEBESTA, Professor of Classics at the University of South Dakota, is author of the textbook *Carl Orff Carmina Burana Cantiones Profanae* (Bolchazy-Carducci Publishers) and co-editor of the *World of Roman Costume* (University of Wisconsin Press). Chair of the Methodology Committee of the American Classical League for many years, she is editor of the *Classical World*'s annual survey of Greek and Latin textbooks. *jsebesta@charlie.usd.edu*

KAREN LEE SINGH is Professor of Latin, English, and Greek at the Florida State University School, where she has taught since 1977; she has also taught in the Classics Departments at both Florida State and the University of Wisconsin, where she received her Ph.D. in 1971. The recipient of numerous teaching awards and a past President of the Florida Foreign Language Association, she has worked extensively in Latin language education at all levels and served as a member of the national Task Force on Standards for Classical Language Learning. She has published on Cicero, the national classical language standards, and a variety of pedagogical topics. *singh@mail.firn.edu*

PETER M. SMITH is Associate Professor of Classics at the University of North Carolina, Chapel Hill. He teaches primarily Greek, from the elementary to graduate level; his research is in archaic and classical Greek literature and philosophy, and he has published on Homer, Hesiod, the Homeric Hymns, and Aeschylus. He has recently learned a lot about the third century B.C., wishes he knew more about the Phoenicians, and looks forward to the map of Sicily in R. Talbert's forthcoming *Classical Atlas*. *pmsmith@email.unc.edu*

CYNTHIA WHITE is Assistant Professor of Classics and Director of the Latin program at the University of Arizona, Tucson. She teaches courses in classical, late antique, and medieval Latin literature, as well as New Testament Greek. Her research is in Latin pedagogy, Greek and Latin epithalamia, and medieval Latin literature. She has produced an edition and translation of the Alnwick Bestiary, a 13th-century, gothic-hand manuscript (Brepolis, 1998), and her current research project is a two-volume study of Greek and Latin epithalamia entitled *Felix Hymenaeus*. *ckwhite@ccit.arizona.edu*

Bibliography

This bibliography is primarily a list of works cited and does not aim to be a comprehensive catalog of all textbooks (for which, see the periodic textbook surveys in the Classical World) *or of all pedagogical and other studies of value to Latin teachers; only books, articles, and Web sites are included (for computer software, maps, games, and other classroom resources, see the relevant chapters of the book and the Index, as well as the periodic audiovisuals surveys in the* Classical World *and the* Software Directory for the Classics, *cited in Chapter 23). Journal abbreviations employed include:* CJ (Classical Journal), CO (Classical Outlook), CW (Classical World), *and* FLA (Foreign Language Annals).

TEXTBOOKS

Amery, Heather, and Patricia Vanag. 1993. *Rome and Romans*. London, ENG: Usborne.

Ashley, Clara W., and Austin M. Lashbrook. 1981. *Living Latin: A Contemporary Approach*. Books 1-2. Skokie, IL: National Textbook Co.

Ashworth, Kathryn R., and Elaine S. Robbins. 1995. *Discovering Languages: Latin*. New York, NY: Amsco. Teacher's ed. available.

Ball, Robert J. 1987. *Reading Classical Latin: A Reasonable Approach*. Lawrence, KS: Coronado Press.

Balme, Maurice. 1973. *The Millionaire's Dinner Party: An Adaptation of the Cena Trimalchionis of Petronius*. New York, NY: Oxford Univ. Press.

_____, and James Morwood. 1976. *Cupid and Psyche: An Adaptation from the Golden Ass of Apuleius*. New York, NY: Oxford Univ. Press.

_____. 1996-97. *Oxford Latin Course*. Parts 1-3. 2nd ed. New York, NY: Oxford Univ. Press. The *Oxford Latin Reader*, an anthology designed to follow Part 3, and teacher's manuals available.

Burnell, Dick. 1991. *Vesuvius and Other Latin Plays*. New York, NY: Cambridge Univ. Press.

Campbell, Ann. 1988. *Look and Do Workbook: The Art and Architecture of Ancient Rome*. Boulder, CO: Alarion Press.

A Coloring Book of Rome: Liber Romanus pingendus. N.D. Santa Barbara, CA: Bellerophon Press.

A Coloring Book of the Olympics. N.D. Santa Barbara, CA: Bellerophon Press.

A Coloring Book of the Trojan War. N.D. Santa Barbara, CA: Bellerophon Press.

Comeau, Paul T., and Richard A. LaFleur. 1997. *Workbook for Wheelock's Latin*. 3rd ed. New York, NY: HarperCollins. Answer key available.

D'Aulaire, Ingri, and Edgar Parin D'Aulaire. 1962. *Book of Greek Myths*. Garden City, NY: Doubleday.

DuBose, Gaylan. 1997. *Farrago Latina*. Wauconda, IL: Bolchazy-Carducci/L & L Enterprises.

Edwards, Ann, Susan Hengelsberg, and Elizabeth Hubbard. N.D. *The Mythology Songbook*. Miami, OH: American Classical League.

Esler, Carol Clemeau. N.D. *Roman Voices: Everyday Latin in Ancient Rome*. Amherst, MA: New England Classical Newsletter Publications.

Florian, David. 1990. *Phenomenon of Language*. 2nd ed. Glenview, IL: Scott Foresman-Addison Wesley. Teacher's guide available.

Garieri, Anita. 1995. *How Would You Survive as an Ancient Roman*. Danbury, CT: Franklin Watts.

Geisel, Theodor S. 1994. *O loca tu ibis*. Trans. Leone Roselle. Portland, ME: J. Weston Walch.

Goldman, Norma, and Jacob Nyenhuis. 1982. *Latin via Ovid: A First Course*. 2nd ed. Detroit, MI: Wayne State Univ. Press.

Goldman, Norma, and Ladislas Szymanski. 1993. *English Grammar for Students of Latin*. 2nd ed. Ann Arbor, MI: Olivia and Hill.

Grote, Dale A. 1994. *Comprehensive Study Guide for Wheelock's Latin*. Lanham, MD: Univ. Press of America.

Groton, Anne H., and James M. May. 1995. *Thirty-Eight Latin Stories*. 5th ed. Wauconda, IL: Bolchazy-Carducci.

Hanlin, Jayne, and Beverly Lichtenstein. 1991. *Learning Latin through Mythology*. New York, NY: Cambridge Univ. Press.

Henrich, Jean, and Steve Henrich. 1989. *Story Starters on Ancient Rome*. U.S.A.: Henrich Enterprises.

_____. 1994. *Big Book of Roman Activities*. U.S.A.: Henrich Enterprises.

Hines, Lillian M., and Ruth B. Howard. 1967–81. *Our Latin Heritage*. Books 1–4. 3rd ed. New York, NY: Harcourt Brace Jovanovich.

Jenney, Charles, Jr., et al. 1990. *First Year Latin* and *Second Year Latin*. Englewood Cliffs, NJ: Prentice-Hall. Teacher's guides available. Rev. Peter N. Howard and Linda Sharrard Montross, *CO* 68 (1990–91): 73–74.

Johnston, Patricia A. 1988. *Traditio: An Introduction to the Latin Language and Its Influence*. New York, NY: Macmillan.

Jones, Peter V., and Keith C. Sidwell. 1986. *Reading Latin*. 2 vols. (*Text and Grammar, Vocabulary and Exercises*). New York, NY: Cambridge Univ. Press.

Knudsvig, Glenn M., et al. 1986. *Latin for Reading: A Beginner's Textbook with Exercises*. 2nd ed. Ann Arbor, MI: Univ. of Michigan Press.

Lawall, Gilbert, Ronald B. Palma, and David J. Perry. 1994–95. *Ecce Romani: A Latin Reading Program*. Books 1–3. 2nd ed. Glenview, IL: Scott Foresman-Addison Wesley. Supplements include teacher's guides, language activity books, and test masters. Rev. of Books 1–2 by Gail Polk, *CO* 73 (1995): 34; rev. of Book 3 by Gregory A. Staley, *CO* 73 (1995): 36.

Los Angeles Unified School District. 1989. *Marcus et Julia: Vita et lingua Romana antiqua. Ancient Roman Life and Language. Teacher's Guide*. "A Humanistic Approach to Latin, Level I, for Elementary School Children. Adapted, Expanded and Rewritten from *How the Romans Lived and Spoke* (*Romani viventes et dicentes*)." Los Angeles, CA: Los Angeles Unified School District.

Mateos Muñoz, Agustín. 1990. *Compendio de etimologías grecolatinas del Español*. Naucalpan, MEX: Editorial Esfinge.

McCarthy, Brian C. J. 1992. *Latin Epigraphy for the Classroom*. Amherst, MA: New England Classical Newsletter Publications.

Moreland, Floyd L., and Rita M. Fleischer. 1977. *Latin: An Intensive Course*. Berkeley, CA: Univ. of California Press.

Morford, Mark, and Robert Lenardon. 1995. *Classical Mythology*. 5th ed. White Plains, NY: Longman.

_____. *Companion to Classical Mythology.* 1997. White Plains, NY: Longman.

Morwood, James, and Mark Warman. 1990. *Our Greek and Latin Roots.* New York, NY: Cambridge Univ. Press.

Osburn, LeaAnn A. 1994a. *Meus libellus de animalibus.* Gilberts, IL: L & L Enterprises.

_____. 1994b. *Meus libellus de numeris.* Gilberts, IL: L & L Enterprises.

_____, trans. 1995a. *Tres ursi.* Cincinnati, OH: Another Language Press.

_____. 1995b. *Learning Latin through Song.* Gilberts, IL: L & L Enterprises.

Perry, David J., and Gilbert Lawall. 1993. *Fabulae Romanae.* Glenview, IL: Scott Foresman-Addison Wesley.

Phinney, Ed, and Patricia Bell, eds. 1988-91. *The Cambridge Latin Course.* Units 1-4. North American 3rd ed. New York, NY: Cambridge Univ. Press. Supplements include teacher's guide, workbooks for Units 1-3, worksheet copymasters for Units 1-3, and a cassette for Units 1-2; other materials are available from the North American Cambridge Classics Project.

_____, Mary Catherine Phinney, and Stan Farrow. 1995. *Salvete! A First Course in Latin.* Books 1-2. New York, NY: Cambridge Univ. Press. Rev. Warren Roby and Wesley Callihan, *CO* 74 (1997): 161.

Polsky, Marion. 1998. *First Latin: A Language Discovery Program.* 2nd ed. Glenview, IL: Scott Foresman-Addison Wesley. Rev. of 1st ed., Nancy Mavrogenes, *CO* 65 (1987-88): 71.

Ross, Cynthia. 1993. *A Literature Unit for D'Aulaires' Book of Greek Myths.* Huntington Beach, CA: Teacher Created Materials, Inc.

Royo, Marta. 1983. *Latín 1-2: lengua y civilización.* Buenos Aires, ARG: Ediciones Colihue. With teacher's manuals.

Russell, William F. 1989. *Classic Myths to Read Aloud.* New York, NY: Crown Publications.

Schlosser, Franz, trans. *Latine cantemus: Cantica popularia Latine reddita.* 1996. Wauconda, IL: Bolchazy-Carducci.

Stapleton, Michael. 1986. *The Illustrated Dictionary of Greek and Roman Mythology.* New York, NY: Peter Bedrick Books.

Sweet, Waldo. 1957. *Latin: A Structural Approach.* Ann Arbor, MI: Univ. of Michigan Press.

_____. 1966. *Artes Latinae.* Wauconda, IL: Bolchazy-Carducci Publishers. CD ROM ed. 1996-97 by Jeffrey Lyon; audio tape by Robert Sonkowsky.

_____, R. Craig, and G. Seligson. 1966. *Latin: A Structural Approach.* Rev. ed. Ann Arbor, MI: Univ. of Michigan Press.

Traupman, John C. 1989. *Latin Is Fun, Book 1: Lively Lessons for Beginners.* New York, NY: Amsco. With teacher's manual and key. Rev. Lynne McClendon, *CO* 67 (1990): 98-99.

_____. 1995. *Latin Is Fun, Book 2: Lively Lessons for Advancing Students.* New York, NY: Amsco. With teacher's manual and key. Rev. Ephy Howard, *CO* 74 (1997): 122-23.

_____. 1997. *Conversational Latin for Oral Proficiency.* 2nd ed. Wauconda, IL: Bolchazy-Carducci.

Ullman, B.L., et al. 1997. *Latin for Americans.* Books 1-3. 8th ed. New York, NY: Glencoe/McGraw Hill. Series includes teacher's manuals, tests, crossword puzzles, workbooks, cassettes, and cassette scripts.

Wheelock, Frederic M. 1995. *Wheelock's Latin.* 5th ed. R.A. LaFleur, ed. New York, NY: HarperCollins. Rev. Cecil W. Wooten, III., *CJ* 91 (1996): 185-91.

Wilkes, Angela. 1985. *Latin for Beginners*. Lincolnwood, IL: NTC Publishing Group.

_____. 1987. *Spanish for Beginners*. Lincolnwood, IL: NTC Publishing Group.

Wingate, Philippa. 1995. *The Romans*. Tulsa, OK: Educational Development Corp.

Wohlberg, Joseph. 1964. *201 Latin Verbs Fully Conjugated in All the Tenses*. New York, NY: Barron's Educational Series.

LATIN LANGUAGE, CURRICULUM, AND PEDAGOGY

Abbott, Martha G. 1991. "Critical Instructional Issues in the Classics for American Schools." *FLA* 24: 27–37.

_____. 1992. "The Virginia Governor's Latin Academy." *CJ* 87: 265–73.

_____, et al. 1997. "Standards for Classical Language Learning: A Progress Report." *New England Classical Journal* 24: 131–38.

Abernathy, Faye, et al. 1990. *The Development of Oral Skills in Latin with Visuals: A Supplementary Guide to the Syllabus Latin for Communication*. Draft Copy. Albany, NY: New York State Education Dept.

Advisory Committee of the American Classical League. 1924. *The Classical Investigation, Part One: General Report*. Princeton, NJ: Princeton Univ. Press.

Allen, Thomas. 1996. "On the Air: VSEN Offers Distance Learning to Students across the Country." *Virginia Journal of Education* June: 7–10.

American Classical League. 1997. *Standards for Classical Language Learning*. Oxford, OH: American Classical League.

American Philological Association. 1899. *Report of the Committee of Twelve of the American Philological Association on Courses in Latin and Greek for Secondary Schools*. Boston, MA: Ginn.

_____. 1996. *Guide to Graduate Programs in the Classics in the United States and Canada*. Worcester, MA: American Philological Association.

Ancona, Ronnie. 1982. "Latin and a Dyslexic Student: An Experience in Teaching." *CW* 76: 33–36.

Ashmore, Rhea, and John D. Madden. 1990. "Literacy via Latin: A Case Study." *Journal of College Reading and Learning* 23: 63–70.

Baca, Albert. 1991. "Il Language Transfer Program di Los Angeles: nuovo metodo per l'insegnamento del Latino." *Rinascita della scuola* 6: 403–13.

_____, et al. 1979. "Language Transfer Project of the Los Angeles Unified School District." *CO* 56: 74–80.

Ball, Robert J., and J.D. Ellsworth. 1989. "Against Teaching Composition in Classical Languages." *CJ* 85: 54–62.

_____. 1992. "Flushing Out the Dinosaurs: Against Teaching Composition II." *CJ* 88: 55–65.

Barrett, Conrad. 1982. "Speech before Script." *CO* 60: 41–43.

_____. 1991. "Classics and Global Education." *Prospects* Summer: 1–4.

Bender, Henry V. 1996. "Audio-Visual Materials in the Classics: 1996 Survey." *CW* 89: 313–62. Updated periodically in *CW*.

Boyd, Barbara Weiden. 1997. "Changes in the 1999 Advanced Placement Examinations in Latin: Vergil and Latin Literature." *CO* 74: 93–96.

Braidi, Susan M. 1988–89. "In Ancient Rome: A Computer Game Uses Artificial Intelligence to Instruct Language Students." *Enquiry* (Univ. of Delaware) Winter: 17–21.

Briggs, Ward W., Jr., ed. 1992. *The Selected Papers of Basil Lanneau Gildersleeve*. Atlanta, GA: Scholars Press.

_____, and Herbert Benario, eds. 1985. *Basil Lanneau Gildersleeve: An American Classicist*. Baltimore, MD: Johns Hopkins Univ. Press.

Brucia, Margaret A. 1995a. "Horace and the High-School Latin Student." *CO* 72: 77–78.

_____. 1995b. *Teacher's Guide to Advanced Placement Courses in Latin*. Princeton, NJ: The College Board.

_____, and Kathleen A. Rabiteau. 1992. "An Analysis of Candidate Performance on the Multiple-Choice Section of the Published 1987 AP Latin Examination." *CO* 70: 1–7.

Brunner, Theodore F. 1988. "Overcoming 'Verzettelung': A Humanistic Discipline Meets the Computer." *Humanities* 9.3: 4–7. Rpt. *CO* 66 (1988): 10–13.

Buller, Jeffrey L. 1989. "Historical Novels in the Latin Classroom." *CO* 66: 73–77.

_____. 1991. "Historical Films in the Latin Classroom." *CO* 69: 3–7.

_____. 1994a. "Cicero's *Pro Caelio*: Text and Context." In Robert M. Terry, ed., *Dimension 93–94*. Valdosta, GA: Southern Conference on Language Teaching. 7–27. Rpt. *CO* 71 (1994): 121–28.

_____. 1994b. "Crossing the Rubicon: Bridging the Gap between Grammar and Literature in the Intermediate Latin Course." *CO* 71: 82–89.

Burns, Mary Ann T., and Joseph O'Connor. 1987. *The Classics in American Schools: Teaching the Ancient World*. Atlanta, GA: Scholars Press.

Calboli, G., ed. 1989. *Subordination and Other Topics in Latin*. Philadelphia, PA: John Benjamins.

Calder, William M., III. 1981. "Research Opportunities in the Modern History of Classical Scholarship." *CW* 74: 241–51.

Campbell, Bruce G. 1988. "Reading with Meaning." *CJ* 83: 245–50.

Chapman, James P. 1993. "Using Perseus in the Mythology Classroom." *CO* 71: 1–7.

Christophelsmeier, Carl. 1917. "The Classics and the Citizen." In *The Educational Value of Latin and Greek*. *Univ. of South Dakota Bulletin* ser. 17, 6: 19–22.

Cole, David. 1856. "Classical Education." *American Journal of Education* 1: 67–91.

College Board. 1995. *AP Latin: Free-Response Scoring Guide with Multiple-Choice Section*. Princeton, NJ: The College Board.

_____. 1997a. *Advanced Placement Course Description: Latin*. Princeton, NJ: The College Board.

_____. 1997b. *The Official Guide to the SAT II: Taking the SAT II Subject Tests*. Princeton, NJ: The College Board.

Commission on the Reorganization of Secondary Education. 1918. *Cardinal Principles of Secondary Education*. Washington, DC: USGPO.

Connor, W. Robert. 1971. "The New Classical Profession." *ADFL Bulletin* 2.3: 25–26.

Craib, Carlene. 1992. "Putting the Reading Method into Practice." *CO* 69: 117–19.

Crane, Gregory, and Elli Mylonas. 1991. "Ancient Materials, Modern Media: Shaping the Study of Classics with Hypermedia." In Paul Delany and George Landow, eds., *Hypermedia and Literary Studies*. Cambridge, MA: M.I.T. Press. 205–20.

Crooker, Jill. 1996. "Comparison of AP Part I and SAT II Latin." American Classical League Institute. College Park, MD, June 29.

_____, and Kathleen A. Rabiteau. 1997. "An Analysis of Candidate Performance on the Published SAT II Latin Minitest." *CO* 74: 131–37.

Crown, Rebecca E. 1989. *A Comparison of the Effects of Traditional Instruction, Tutoring, and Software Tutorial in the Latin Classroom*. Ann Arbor, MI: Univ. Microfilms

International.

Culley, Gerald R. 1978. "Computer-Assisted Instruction and Latin: Beyond Flashcards." *CW* 72: 393–401.

_____. 1984–85. "The Delaware Latin Skills Project." *CO* 62: 38–42.

_____, George Mulford, and John Milbury-Steen. 1986. "A Foreign-Language Adventure Game: Progress Report on an Application of AI to Language Instruction." *CALICO Journal* 4: 69–87.

Damrosch, David. 1995. "Can Classics Die?" *Lingua Franca* Sep./Oct.: 61–66.

Davis, Sally. 1991. *Latin in American Schools*. Atlanta GA: Scholars Press.

Deagon, Andrea Webb. 1991. "Learning Process and Exercise Sequencing in Latin Instruction." *CJ* 87: 59–70.

Dee, James H. Forthcoming. *Lexicon of Latin Derivatives*. Hildesheim, GER: Olms.

Dickison, Sheila K. 1992. "The Reasonable Approach to Beginning Greek and Latin." *CJ* 87: 391–96.

_____. 1998. "Seamless Transition from High School to College Latin: An Attainable Goal?" *CW* (forthcoming).

"Distance Learning: A Latin Language Collaborative with Secondary Partners." 1997. www.dartnet.peachnet.edu/Latin.html.

Distler, Paul, S.J. 1969. *Teach the Latin, I Pray You*. Chicago, IL: Loyola Univ. Press.

D'Ooge, Benjamin L. 1928. "A Reorganization of the Latin Curriculum in Secondary Schools." *CJ* 23: 683–92.

Eliot, Charles W. 1884. "What Is a Liberal Education?" *Century Magazine* 28: 203–12.

_____. 1898. "Inaugural Address as President of Harvard College." In *Educational Reform: Essays and Addresses*. New York, NY: The Century Co. 1–46.

_____, ed. 1894. *Report of the Committee of Ten on Secondary School Studies*. New York, NY: American Book Co.

Fromm, Aloysius. 1928. "College Entrance and Graduation Requirements in the Classical Languages." In Felix M. Kirsch, ed., *The Classics: Their History and Present Status in Education Symposium of Essays*. Milwaukee, WI: Bruce Publishing. 186–251.

Froula, V.K., ed. 1904. *National Conference of Secondary Education and its Problems, Held at Northwestern University, October 30 and 31, 1903*. Evanston, IL: Northwestern Univ.

Game, Josiah Bethea. 1916. *Teaching High-School Latin: A Handbook*. Chicago, IL: Univ. of Chicago Press.

Ganss, George E., S.J. 1956. *Saint Ignatius' Idea of a Jesuit University*. Milwaukee, WI: Marquette Univ. Press.

Garmonsway, G.N., ed. 1978. *Aelfric's Colloquy*. Rev. ed. Exeter, ENG: Univ. of Exeter.

Gascoyne, Richard C. 1989. "Latin in the Middle Schools." *Newsletter of the Classical Association of the Empire State* 25.2: 5–8.

Gilleland, Brady B. 1991. "Elitist Professors and the Teaching of Prose Composition." *CW* 84: 215–17.

Glare, P.G.W., ed. 1982. *Oxford Latin Dictionary*. New York, NY: Clarendon Press; Oxford Univ. Press.

Gray, Mason DeWitt. 1929. *The Teaching of Latin*. New York, NY: Appleton.

Grendler, Paul F. 1989. *Schooling in Renaissance Italy: Literacy and Learning, 1300–1600*. Baltimore, MD: Johns Hopkins Univ. Press.

Haase, Wolfgang, and Meyer Reinhold, eds. 1994. *The Classical Tradition in the Americas*. Vol. I: *European Images of the Americas and the Classical Tradition*. Part 1. New York, NY: DeGruyter.

Hale, William G. 1887. *Aims and Methods in Classical Study*. Chicago, IL: Ginn.

Hallett, Judith P. 1990. "Public Programs: Private Initiatives." *CO* 68: 3–8.

Hamilton, Richard. 1992. "Reading Latin." *CJ* 87: 165–74.

Harris, Donalee, and Susan Robertson. 1997a. *SPLAT: Combining Latin and Spanish in the Classroom*. Wolfforth, TX: Texas SPLAT Publications (Box 100, Frenship H.S., Wolfforth, TX 79382).

———. 1997b. "SPLAT: Combining Spanish and Latin." Classical Association of the Middle West and South Convention. Boulder, CO, 4 Apr.

Harwood, Natalie R. 1982. "The Write Way to Teach Latin." *CO* 60: 7–8.

Hill, Barbara, et al. 1995. "Accommodating the Needs of Students with Severe Language Learning Difficulties in Modified Foreign Language Classes." In G. Crouse, ed., *Broadening the Frontiers of Foreign Language Education*. Lincolnwood, IL: National Textbook Co. 46– 56.

Howard, Peter N. 1996. "The Grading of the 1996 Advanced Placement Examinations in Latin: Vergil." *CO* 74: 9–18.

———. 1997. "The Grading of the 1996 Advanced Placement Examinations in Latin: Latin Literature." *CO* 74: 45–55.

Hoyos, B. Dexter. 1993. "Decoding or Sight-reading? Problems with Understanding Latin." *CO* 70: 126–30.

———. 1997. "Translation in the Teaching of Latin: Too Much of a Bad Thing?" *Classicum* 23.1: 15–22.

IJsewijn, Jozef. 1990. *Companion to Neo-Latin Studies*. Leuven, BEL: Leuven Univ. Press.

Imme, G. 1981. "Quid Augustini *Confessiones* ad artem Latine docendi nobis adferant." *Latinitas* 29: 274–77.

Keitel, Elizabeth. "A Model for Latin Teacher Training: The MAT Program at the University of Massachsuetts." In Richard A. LaFleur, ed., *The Teaching of Latin in American Schools: A Profession in Crisis*. Atlanta: Scholars Press, 1987. 63–70.

Kelsey, Francis W. 1911. *Latin and Greek in American Education*. New York, NY: Macmillan.

Kennedy, George A. 1984. "Afterword: An Essay on Classics in America since the Yale Report." In Meyer Reinhold, ed., *Classica Americana: The Greek and Roman Heritage in the United States*. Detroit, MI: Wayne State Univ. Press. 325–51.

———. 1987. "The History of Latin Education." In M. Santirocco, ed., *Latinitas: The Tradition and Teaching of Latin*, Helios 14.2: 7–16.

Kirsch, Felix M., ed. 1928. *The Classics: Their History and Present Status in Education. A Symposium of Essays*. Milwaukee, WI: Bruce Publishing.

Kitchell, Kenneth F., Jr. 1995. "The Challenge of Living In Interesting Times." *CO* 72: 49–53.

———. 1996. "Correspondence Courses in the Classics." weber.u.washington.edu/ ~lwright/ken.html.

Knudsvig, G., D. P. Ross, and G. Seligson. Forthcoming. *Linguistic Perspectives in Reading Latin*. Ann Arbor, MI: Michigan Classics Forum.

Kroon, C. 1995. *Discourse Particles in Latin: A Study of* Nam, Enim, Autem, Vero, *and* At. Amsterdam, NETH: J.C. Gieben.

LaFleur, Richard A. 1981. "Latin Students Score High on SAT and Achievement Tests." *CJ* 77: 254.

———. 1982. "1981 SAT and Latin Achievement Test Results and Enrollment Data." *CJ* 77: 343.

_____. 1987a. *The Teaching of Latin in American Schools: A Profession in Crisis*. Atlanta, GA: Scholars Press.

_____. 1987b. "Perpetuating the Renaissance: A Challenge for Latin in the Coming Decade." In Matthew Santirocco, ed., *Latinitas: The Tradition and Teaching of Latin, Helios* 14.2. 141–46.

_____. 1991. "The Classical Languages and College Admissions." *CO* 68: 124–32.

_____. 1992. "Latin and Classics in the College Curriculum: Something New under the Sun." In Wilga Rivers, ed., *Teaching Languages in College: Curriculum and Content*. Lincolnwood, IL: National Textbook Co. 157–97.

_____. 1997. "*Latina resurgens*: Classical Language Enrollments in American Schools and Colleges." *CO* 74: 125–30.

_____, and James C. Anderson, Jr. 1986–87. "Meeting the Need for Latin Teachers: The American Classical League/University of Georgia NEH Latin Institute." *CO* 64: 42–45.

_____. 1988. "The ACL/UGA/NEH National Latin Institute: Retrospect and Prospect." *CO* 65: 109–16.

Lakoff, R. T. 1968. *Abstract Syntax and Latin Complementation*. Cambridge, MA: M.I.T. Press.

Latousek, Rob. 1989–98. "Random Access." *CO* (spring and fall issues). Archived at www.centaursystems.com/archives.html.

_____. 1997. *Software Directory for the Classics*. Oxford, OH: American Classical League. www.centaursystems.com/soft_dir.html.

Law, Vivian. 1982. *The Insular Latin Grammarians*. Suffolk, ENG: Boydell and Brewer.

Lawall, Gilbert. 1989. *ACTFL Selected List of Instructional Materials for Elementary and Secondary School Programs: Latin*. New York, NY: American Council on the Teaching of Foreign Languages.

Lean, Anne. 1990. "Teaching Two Speeches of Cicero." *CJ* 85: 350–55.

LeBovit, Judith B. 1976. *The Teaching of Latin in the Elementary and Secondary School: A Handbook for Educators and Administrators*. Washington, DC: National Endowment for the Humanities.

Lewis, Charlton T., and Charles Short. 1879. *Latin Dictionary: Founded on Andrews Edition of Freund's Latin Dictionary*. Oxford, ENG: Oxford Univ. Press.

Lewis, Tayler. 1856. "Method of Teaching Greek and Latin." *American Journal of Education* 1: 281–94, 480–94.

Little, Charles Edgar. 1951. *The Institutio oratoria of Marcus Fabius Quintilianus*. 2 vols. Nashville, TN: George Peabody Coll. for Teachers.

Mackail, J.W. 1922. *The Case for Latin in Secondary Schools*. London, ENG: Murray.

Maiken, Peter T. 1991. "Latin as Minority Motivator." *CO* 69: 11–14. Rpt. from *Beloit Magazine*.

Marrou, H.I. 1956. *A History of Education in Antiquity*. Trans. G. Lamb. Madison, WI: Univ. of Wisconsin Press.

Masciantonio, Rudolph. 1972. "The New FLES Latin Program in the School District of Philadelphia." *Modern Language Journal* 56: 167–70.

_____. 1977a. "Tangible Benefits of the Study of Latin." *FLA* 10: 375–82.

_____. 1977b. "A White Paper on Latin and the Classics for Urban Schools." *CO* 55: 26–30.

Mavrogenes, Nancy A. 1977. "The Effect of Elementary Latin Instruction on Language Arts Performance." *Elementary School Journal* 77: 268–73.

_____. 1979. "Latin in the Elementary School: A Help for Reading and Language Arts." *Phi Delta Kappan* 60: 675–77. Rpt. *CO* 57 (1979): 33–35.

_____. 1987. "Latin and Language Arts: An Update." *FLA* 20: 131–37. Rpt. *CO* 66 (1989): 78–83.

May, James M. 1981. "A Syllabus for Intermediate Latin." *CJ* 77: 65–67.

McCartney, Eugene S. 1917. "Was Latin Difficult for a Roman?" *CJ* 23: 163–82.

Moreland, Floyd L., ed. 1981. *Strategies in Teaching Greek and Latin: Two Decades of Experimentation.* American Philological Association Pamphlet 7. Chico, CA: Scholars Press.

Mylonas, Elli. 1989. "Universes to Control: Classics, Computers, and Education." In Phyllis Culham and Lowell Edmunds, eds., *Classics: A Discipline and Profession in Crisis?* Lanham, MD: Univ. Press of America. 133–46.

National Committee for Latin and Greek. 1994. "Private School Enrollments Go Public." *Pro Bono* 2.1: 2.

Newman, J.K. 1990. "Composition: A Reply." *CJ* 85: 344–49.

New York State Education Department. 1986. *Latin for Communication: New York State Syllabus.* Albany, NY: New York State Education Dept.

Nutting, H.C. 1915. "Methods of Teaching Latin." *CJ* 11: 7–24.

Osburn, LeaAnn A. 1992. "Latin in Illinois: *Unde et Quo?*" In Thomas Sienkewicz, ed., *FoxFestschrift.* Monmouth, IL: Monmouth Coll. 102–24.

Owen, Eivion. 1935. "Caesar in American Schools Prior to 1860." *CJ* 31: 212–22.

Panhuis, D. 1980. "Gapping in Latin." *CJ* 75: 229–40.

_____. 1982. *The Communicative Perspective in the Sentence: A Study of Latin Word Order.* Philadelphia, PA: John Benjamins.

Parker, William Riley. 1964. "The Case for Latin." *Publications of the Modern Language Assoc.* 79.4, pt. 2: 3–10.

Pascal, Nannette R. 1988–89. "Integrating the Classics into General Education: The NEH/Richland College Classics Cluster Project." *CO* 66: 38–42.

Paxson, Susan. 1916. *A Handbook for Latin Clubs.* Boston, MA: D.C. Heath.

Perkins, Albert S. 1914. "Latin: A Foundation for English in Commercial Classes." *Boston Teachers Newsletter* 2.9: 3–9.

Phinney, Ed. 1983. "Some Mistakes Latin Student Teachers Make." *CO* 61: 18–21.

_____. 1989. "The Classics in American Education." In Phyllis Culham and Lowell Edmunds, eds., *Classics: A Discipline and Profession in Crisis?* Lanham, MD: Univ. Press of America. 77–87.

_____, ed. 1994. *The History of the American Classical League, 1919–1994.* Oxford, OH: American Classical League.

Pinkster, H. 1990. *Latin Syntax and Semantics.* Trans. H. Mulder. New York, NY: Routledge.

_____, ed. 1983. *Latin Linguistics and Linguistic Theory.* Philadelphia, PA: John Benjamins.

Polsky, Marion. 1986. "The NEH/Brooklyn College Latin Cornerstone Project, 1982–1984: Genesis, Implementation, Evaluation." *CO* 63: 77–83.

_____. 1987. "The New First Latin Program." In Matthew Santirocco, ed., *Latinitas: The Tradition and Teaching of Latin, Helios* 14.2. 147–53.

Porter, David W. 1994. "The Latin Syllabus in Anglo-Saxon Monastic Schools." *Neophilologus* 78: 463–82.

Rabiteau, Kathleen A. 1993. "A Brief History of Horace in the AP Latin Program." Classical Association of the Atlantic States Conference. Philadelphia, PA, Apr.

Ramey, Jack. 1961. "*Quo usque tandem*—How Much Longer Must We Apologize?" *CW* 54: 146–48.

Read, William. 1975. "Aims and Objectives of the Latin Program." *FLA* 8: 118–22.

Reilly, J. F. 1960. "State Education Departments on the Classics I: New York State." *CO* 53: 245–47.

Reinhold, Meyer, ed. 1984. *Classica Americana: The Greek and Roman Heritage in the United States*. Detroit, MI: Wayne State Univ. Press.

_____. 1987. "The Latin Tradition in America." In Matthew Santirocco, ed., *Latinitas: The Tradition and Teaching of Latin, Helios* 14.2. 123–39.

Richard, Carl J. 1994. *The Founders and the Classics: Greece, Rome, and the American Enlightenment*. Cambridge, MA: Harvard Univ. Press.

Ross, D.P. 1987. *The Order of Words in Latin Subordinate Clauses*. Ann Arbor, MI: Univ. Microfilms International.

_____. 1991. "The Role of Displacement in Narrative Prose." In R. Coleman, ed., *New Studies in Latin Linguistics*. Philadelphia, PA: John Benjamins. 453–66.

_____. 1996. "Anaphors and Antecedents in Narrative Text." In H. Rosen, ed., *Aspects of Latin*. Innsbruck, AUS: Innsbrucker Beiträge zur Sprachwissenschaft. 511–23.

Sage, Evan T. 1920. "The Classics for Engineers." *Bulletin of the Society for the Promotion of Engineering Education* 10: 364–70.

Salerno, Dorsey Price. 1985. *Latin in Motion*. Oxford, OH: American Classical League.

Saunders, A. 1993. "The Value of Latin Prose Composition." *CJ* 88: 385–92.

Scanlan, Richard T. 1971. "Computer-Assisted Instruction: PLATO in Latin." *FLA* 5: 84–89.

Seaman, David W. 1996. "Open the Door Wider: Foreign Language Classes for Students at Risk." *Foreign Language Assoc. of Georgia Beacon* 31.1: 15–19.

Searles, George J. 1994. "The Status of Latin Instruction in the Community Colleges." *CO* 71: 117–19.

Sebesta, Judith Lynn. 1996. "Survey of Textbooks in Greek and Latin: 1996 Survey." *CW* 89: 259–312. Updated periodically in *CW*.

Segura Munguia, Santiago. 1985. *Diccionario etimológico Latino-Español*. Madrid, SP: Ediciones Generales Anaya.

Seligson, Gerda. 1992. "Reflections on Latin Textbooks from Great Britain." *CO* 70: 39–41.

_____, and Glenn Knudsvig. 1974. "On Reading Latin." *CO* 51: 52–55.

Sheerin, Daniel. 1987. "In media Latinitate." In M. Santirocco, ed., *Latinitas: The Tradition and Teaching of Latin, Helios* 14.2: 51–67.

Simpson, D. P., ed. 1977. *Cassell's Latin Dictionary: Latin-English, English-Latin*. New York, NY: Macmillan.

_____. 1987. *Cassell's Latin and English Dictionary*. New York, NY: Macmillan.

Smith, William, and John Lockwood, eds. 1992. *Chambers Murray Latin-English Dictionary*. New York, NY: Larousse Kingfisher Chambers.

Sonkowsky, Robert. 1996. "Distance Makes the Heart Grow Fonder." 12th Annual Conference on Distance Education: Designing for Active Learning. Madison, WI, Aug. 7.

Sparks, Richard, et al. 1995. "An Exploratory Study of the Effects of Latin on the Native Language Skills and Foreign Language Aptitude of Students with and without Learning Disabilities." *CJ* 91: 165–84.

Stephens, Stephani. 1990. "Latin and the Learning Disabled Student." *CO* 67: 111–13.

Stevenson, W.H., ed. 1929. *Early Scholastic Colloquies*. Oxford, ENG: Clarendon Press.

Strasheim, Lorraine A. 1984–85. "Latin and Emerging Adolescent Education." *CO* 62: 55–58.

_____. 1987. *Total Physical Response*. Amherst, MA: Classical Association of New England.

_____. 1990. "Latin in the 1990s and Beyond." *NASSP Curriculum Report* 20.1: 1–4.

Sussman, Lewis A. 1978. "The Decline of Basic Skills: A Suggestion So Old that It's New." *CJ* 73: 346–52.

Taylor, D.J., ed. 1987. *The History of Linguistics in the Classical Period*. Philadelphia, PA: John Benjamins.

Tebben, Joseph, ed. 1984–97. *Computing and the Classics*. Newark, OH: Ohio State Univ., Dept. of Classics. Newsletter, online since 1995; available from editor: tebben.1@osu. edu.

Thompson, Peter S. 1983. "Teaching Latin with the Cloze Technique." *CO* 61: 6–8.

Traupman, John C., ed. 1994. *The New College Latin and English Dictionary*. 2nd ed. New York, NY: Amsco.

Waite, Stephen V.F. 1970. "Computer-Supplemented Latin Instruction at Dartmouth College." *Computers and the Humanities* 4: 313–14.

West, Andrew F., ed. 1917. *Value of the Classics*. Princeton, NJ: Princeton Univ. Press.

White, Dorrance S. 1936. "Latin and the Reconstructionists." *CJ* 32: 267–80.

_____. 1941. *The Teaching of Latin*. Chicago, IL: Scott Foresman.

Wigtil, David N. 1982. "Detailed Grammatical Analysis." *CO* 60: 51–52.

Wiley, Patricia Davis. 1984–85. "High School Foreign Language Study and College Academic Performance." *CO* 62: 33–36.

Williams, Mark F. 1991. "Collaborative Learning in the College Latin Classroom." *CJ* 86: 256–61.

Williams, Rose. 1995. *Spanish and Italian through Latin*. Privately published. Available from the author, 2601 S. 38th St., Abilene, TX 79605.

Wills, Garry. 1997. "There's Nothing Conservative about the Classics Revival." *New York Times Magazine* Feb. 16: 38–40, 42.

Wolverton, Robert. 1973. "The Ship of Classics: The Ark, the Titanic, or the Good Ship Lollipop?" *CO* 51: 13–15.

Wooten, Cecil W., III. 1996. "The New Edition of *Wheelock's Latin*." *CJ* 91: 185–91.

GENERAL STUDIES AND REFERENCE

Acosta, José de. 1596. *Iosephi Acosta societatis Iesu De natura novi orbis libri duo, et De promulgatione evangelii apud barbaros, sive De procuranda Indorum salute*. Cologne, GER: Birckmann.

_____. 1984. *De procuranda Indorum salute*. L. Pereña, et al., eds. Madrid, SP: Consejo superior de investigaciones cientificas.

Arnold, J.A. 1988. "Teaching in the Middle Years." *Teaching Education* Spring: 43–46.

Arrowsmith, W.M. 1966. "The Shame of the Graduate Schools." *Harper's Magazine* 232: 51–59.

Asher, James. 1982. *Learning Another Language through Actions: The Complete Teacher's Guide*. Los Gatos, CA: Sky Oak Productions.

Astin, R.E., et al., eds. 1989. *The Cambridge Ancient History*. 2nd. ed. Vol. 7. Cambridge, ENG: Cambridge Univ. Press.

The Atlas of Ancient Worlds. 1994. New York, NY: Dorling Kindersley Publishing.

Azevedo, Milton. 1990. "Professional Development of Teaching Assistants: Training Versus Education." *ADFL Bulletin* 22.1: 24–28.

Bach, E., and R.T. Harms, eds. 1968. *Universals in Linguistic Theory*. New York, NY: Holt, Rinehart and Winston.

Barnett, Marva A. 1989. *More than Meets the Eye: Foreign Language Reading—Theory and Practice*. Englewood Cliffs, NJ: Prentice-Hall.

_____, and Robert Francis Cook. 1992. "The Seamless Web: Developing Teaching Assistants as Professionals." In Joel C. Walz, ed., *Development and Supervision of Teaching Assistants in Foreign Languages*. Boston, MA: Heinle and Heinle. 85–111.

Bethell, Leslie, ed. 1984. *The Cambridge History of Latin America*. Vol. 1. New York, NY: Cambridge Univ. Press.

Bien, Peter, et al. 1982. *Demotic Greek II*. Hanover, NH: Univ. Press of New England.

Block, Lydia, et al. 1995. "Options and Accommodations in Mathematics and Foreign Language for College Students with Learning Disabilities." *HEATH* 14.2-3: 1–5.

Bloomfield, L. 1933. *Language*. New York, NY: Henry Holt.

Boas, F. 1911. *Handbook of American Indian Languages*. Washington, DC: USGPO.

Bonefas, Suzanne, et al. 1996. *The VRoma Project: A Virtual Community for the Teaching of Classics* (NEH Proposal). Available at www.hippocrene.colleges.org/~vroma.

Bowder, Diana, ed. 1982. *Who Was Who in the Greek World*. Ithaca, NY: Cornell Univ. Press.

Bowers, C.A. 1988. *The Cultural Dimensions of Educational Computing*. New York, NY: Teachers Coll. Press.

Boyle, Eloise M. 1993. "Beyond Memorization: Teaching Russian (and Other Languages') Vocabulary." *FLA* 26: 226–32.

Brinckerhoff, L., et al. 1993. *Promoting Postsecondary Education for Students with Learning Disabilities: A Handbook for Practitioners*. Austin, TX: PRO-ED Publishers.

Brown, G., and G. Yule. 1983. *Discourse Analysis*. Cambridge, ENG: Cambridge Univ. Press.

Bunson, Matthew. 1995. *A Dictionary of the Roman Empire*. New York, NY: Oxford Univ. Press.

Canale, Michael. 1983. "From Communicative Competence to Communicative Language Pedagogy." In J. Richards and R. Schmidt, eds., *Language and Communication*. New York, NY: Longman. 2–25.

_____, and Merrill Swain. 1980. "Theoretical Bases of Communicative Approaches to Second Language Teaching and Testing." *Applied Linguistics* 1: 1–47.

Carrell, P. L., and J. Eisterhold. 1983. "Schema Theory and ESL Reading Pedagogy." *TESOL Quarterly* 17: 553–73.

Casas, Bartolomé de las. 1942. *Del unico modo de atraer a todos los pueblos a la verdadera religión*. Mexico City, MEX: Fondo de Cultura Económica.

Celce-Murcia, Marianne, and Sharon Hillis. 1988. *Techniques and Resources in Teaching Grammar*. New York, NY: Oxford Univ. Press.

Cervantes Salazar, Francisco. 1953. *Life in the Imperial and Loyal City of Mexico in New Spain*. Trans. Minnie Lee Barrett Shepherd. Austin, TX: Univ. of Texas Press. Facsimile of 1554 ed.

Chastain, Kenneth. 1976. *Developing Second-Language Skills: Theory to Practice*. 2nd ed. Chicago, IL: Rand-McNally.

Chomsky, Noam. 1957. *Syntactic Structures*. The Hague, NETH: Mouton and Co.

_____. 1965. *Aspects of the Theory of Syntax*. Cambridge, MA: M.I.T. Press.

Cook, G. 1989. *Discourse*. Oxford, ENG: Oxford Univ. Press.

Cook, Vivian. 1996. *Second Language Learning and Language Teaching*. 2nd ed. London, ENG: Edward Arnold.

"Copyright Issues Related to Distance Learning and Multimedia Development." 1997.

www.lib.siu.edu/regional/copyright.html.

Corder, S. Pit. 1988. "Pedagogic Grammars." In William Rutherford and Michael S. Smith, eds., *Grammar and Second Language Teaching: A Book of Readings*. Boston, MA: Heinle and Heinle Publishers. 123–45.

Cornell, Tim, and John Matthews. 1982. *Atlas of the Roman World*. New York, NY: Facts on File.

Corominas, Juan. 1967. *Breve diccionario etimológico de la lengua castellana*. Madrid, SP: Gredos. Biblioteca Románica Hispánica V: Diccionarios.

Crews, Kenneth D. 1995. "Copyright and Distance Education: Lawful Uses of Protected Works." www.ind.net/IPSE/fdhandbook/copyrt.html.

Croft, W. 1990. *Typology and Universals*. Cambridge, ENG: Cambridge Univ. Press.

Cruz, Martín de la. 1996. *Libellus de medicinalis Indorum herbis*. Mexico City, MEX: Fondo de Cultura Económica.

Curchin, Leonard A. 1991. *Roman Spain: Conquest and Assimilation*. New York, NY: Routledge.

Dalby, Andrew, and Sally Grainger. 1996. *The Classical Cookbook*. Los Angeles, CA: J. Paul Getty Museum.

Davison, A., and G.M. Green, eds. 1988. *Linguistic Complexity and Text Comprehension: Readability Issues Reconsidered*. Hillsdale, NJ: Lawrence Erlbaum Associates.

Delany, Paul, and George Landow, eds. 1991. *Hypermedia and Literary Studies*. Cambridge, MA: M.I.T. Press.

Dik, S. 1978. *Functional Grammar*. Amsterdam, NETH: North-Holland.

Diller, Conrad. 1978. *The Language Teaching Controversy*. Rowley, MA: Newbury House.

Donato, R., and R.M. Terry, eds. 1995. *Foreign Language Learning: The Journey of a Lifetime*. Lincolnwood, IL: National Textbook Co.

Downs, Mary, et al. 1995. *Archaeology on Film*. 2nd ed. Dubuque, IA: Kendall/Hunt.

Draper, Jamie B., and June H. Hicks. 1996. "Foreign Language Enrollments in Public Secondary Schools, Fall 1994: Summary Report." *FLA* 29: 305.

Edwards, John. 1986. *Roman Cookery*. Point Roberts, WA: Hartley & Marks, Inc.

Ellis, Rod. 1988. "Investigating Language Teaching: The Case for an Educational Approach." *System* 16: 1–11.

Emmart, Emily W., ed. and trans. 1940. *The Badianus Manuscript (Codex Barberini, Latin 241: Vatican Library): An Aztec Herbal of 1552*. Baltimore, MD: Johns Hopkins Univ. Press.

Epstein, J.L., and D.J. MacIver. 1990. *Education in the Middle Grades: Overview of National Practices and Trends*. Report No. 45. Baltimore, MD: Center for Research on Elementary and Middle Schools, Johns Hopkins Univ.

Fernández-Armesto, Felipe. 1992. "'Aztec' Auguries and Memories of the Conquest of Mexico." *Renaissance Studies* 6: 287–305.

Finley, M.I. 1979. *Ancient Sicily to the Arab Conquest*. 2nd ed. London, ENG: Chatto & Windus.

_____. 1980. *Ancient Slavery and Modern Ideology*. London, ENG: Chatto & Windus.

Flynn, S., and W. O'Neil. 1988. *Linguistic Theory in Second Language Acquisition*. Boston, MA: Kluwer Academic Publishers.

Fodor, J. D. 1977. *Semantics: Theories of Meaning in Generative Grammar*. New York, NY: Thomas Y. Crowell.

Foster, George M. 1960. *Culture and Conquest: America's Spanish Heritage*. Chicago, IL: Quadrangle Books.

Futrell, Mary Hartwood. 1991. "Foreign Language Study: Utilitarian and Moral Imperatives." *FLA* 24: 23–24.

Gairns, Ruth, and Stuart Redman. 1986. *Working with Words: A Guide to Teaching and Learning Vocabulary*. Cambridge, ENG: Cambridge Univ. Press.

Ganschow, Leonore, et al. 1994. "Differences in Language Performance among High-, Average-, and Low-Anxious College Foreign Language Learners." *Modern Language Journal* 78: 41–55.

Gass, S.M., and J. Schachter. 1989. *Linguistic Perspectives on Second Language Acquisition*. Cambridge, ENG: Cambridge Univ. Press.

Giacosa, Ilaria Gozzini. 1992. *A Taste of Ancient Rome*. Chicago, IL: Univ. of Chicago Press.

Gibaldi, Joseph, and James V. Mirollo, eds. 1981. *The Teaching Apprentice Program*. New York, NY: Modern Language Assoc.

Gibson, Charles, ed. 1966. *Spain in America*. New York, NY: Harper.

_____. 1968. *The Spanish Tradition in America*. Columbia, SC: Univ. of South Carolina Press.

Givón, T. 1984. *Syntax: A Functional-Typological Introduction*. Vol. 1. Philadelphia, PA: John Benjamins.

Gleason, H.A., Jr. 1967. *An Introduction to Descriptive Linguistics*. Rev. ed. New York, NY: Holt, Rinehart and Winston.

Goddard, R.E. 1990. *Teacher Certification Requirements in All Fifty States*. 8th ed. Sebring, FL: Teacher Certification Publications.

Gonzalbo, Pilar. 1985. *El humanismo y la educación en la Nueva España*. Mexico City, MEX: Consejo Nacional de Fomento Educativo.

Grafton, Anthony. 1992. *New Worlds, Ancient Texts: The Power of Tradition and the Shock of Discovery*. Cambridge, MA: Harvard Univ. Press.

Grant, Michael. 1995a. *Atlas of Classical History*. New York, NY: Oxford Univ. Press.

_____. 1995b. *Routledge Atlas of Classical History: From 1700 B.C. to A.D. 565*. New York, NY: Routledge.

_____, and John Hazel. 1993. *Who's Who in Classical Mythology*. New York, NY: Oxford Univ. Press.

Grellet, Francoise. 1981. *Developing Reading Skills: A Practical Guide to Reading Comprehension Exercises*. Cambridge, ENG: Cambridge Univ. Press.

Halliday, M.A.K., and R. Hasan. 1976. *Cohesion in English*. New York, NY: Longman.

_____. 1989. *Language, Context, and Text: Aspects of Language in a Social-semiotic Perspective*. Oxford, ENG: Oxford Univ. Press.

Hanke, Lewis. 1949. *The Spanish Struggle for Justice in the Conquest of America*. Philadelphia, PA: Univ. of Pennsylvania Press.

_____. 1959. *Aristotle and the American Indians: A Study of Race Prejudice in the Modern World*. Chicago, IL: Regnery.

_____. 1974. *All Mankind Is One: A Study of the Disputation between Bartolomé de las Casas and Juan Ginés de Sepúlveda in 1550*. De Kalb, IL: Northern Illinois Univ. Press.

Harris, William V. 1989. *Ancient Literacy*. Cambridge, MA: Harvard Univ. Press.

Heath, Shirley B. 1972. *Telling Tongues: Language Policy in Mexico*. New York, NY: Teachers Coll. Press.

Higgs, Theodore V., and Ray Clifford. 1982. "The Push toward Communication." In T.V. Higgs, ed., *Curriculum, Competence, and the Foreign Language Teacher*. Lincolnwood, IL: National Textbook Co. 57–78.

Hockett, C. 1958. *A Course in Modern Linguistics*. New York, NY: Macmillan.

Holloway, R. Ross. 1991. *The Archaeology of Ancient Sicily*. London, ENG: Chatto & Windus.

Hornblower, Simon, and Anthony Spawforth, eds. 1996. *The Oxford Classical Dictionary*. 3rd ed. New York, NY: Oxford Univ. Press.

Howatson, M.C., and Ian Chilvers, eds. 1989. *The Concise Oxford Companion to Classical Literature*. New York, NY: Oxford Univ. Press.

The Independent Study Catalog. 1995. 6th ed. Washington, DC: Peterson's/National Univ. Continuing Education Assoc.

Johnson, David W., Roger T. Holubec, and Edythe J. Holubec. 1990. *Circles of Learning: Cooperation in the Classroom*. Edina, MN: Interaction Books.

Kaster, Robert. 1988. *Guardians of Language: The Grammarian and Society in Late Antiquity*. Berkeley, CA: Univ. of California Press.

Keay, Simon J. 1988. *Roman Spain*. Berkeley, CA: Univ. of California Press.

Kempson, R. 1977. *Semantic Theory*. Cambridge, ENG: Cambridge Univ. Press.

Kendris, Christopher. 1984. *301 Spanish Verbs Fully Conjugated in All the Tenses*. New York, NY: Barron's Educational Series.

Kerman, Sam, and Mary Martin. 1980. *Teacher Expectations and Student Achievement: Teacher Handbook*. Bloomington, IN: Phi Delta Kappa.

Krashen, Stephen. 1982. *Principles and Practice in Second Language Acquisition*. New York, NY: Pergamon Press.

Krause, Suzanne. 1996. "Portfolios in Teacher Education: Effects of Instruction on Preservice Teachers' Early Comprehension of the Portfolio Process." *Journal of Teacher Education* 47: 130–39.

Kubler, George. 1948. *Mexican Architecture of the Sixteenth Century*. 2 vols. New Haven, CT: Yale Univ. Press.

_____, and Martin Soria. 1959. *Art and Architecture in Spain and Portugal and Their American Dominions 1500 to 1800*. Baltimore, MD: Penguin.

Kulik, James A., et al. 1980. "Effectiveness of Computer-based College Teaching: A Meta-analysis of Findings." *Review of Educational Research* 50: 525–44.

Landívar, Rafael. 1948. *Rafael Landívar's Rusticatio Mexicana*. Trans. Graydon Regenos. Philological and Documentary Studies 1.5. New Orleans, LA: Middle American Research Inst.

_____. 1965. *Rusticatio Mexicana*. Spanish trans. Octaviano Valdés. Mexico City, MEX: Editorial Jus.

Larsen-Freeman, Diane. 1991. "Consensus and Divergence in the Content, Role, and Process of Teaching Grammar." In James E. Alatis, ed., *Georgetown University Round Table in Languages and Linguistics 1991: Linguistics and Language Pedagogy The State of the Art*. Washington, DC: Georgetown Univ. Press. 260–72.

Lathrop, Thomas A. 1996. *The Evolution of Spanish*. 3rd ed. Newark, DE: Juan de la Cuesta.

Leaver, Betty Lou, and Stephen B. Stryker. 1989. "Content-Based Instruction for Foreign Language Classrooms." *FLA* 22: 269–73.

Lehmann, W.P. 1993. *Theoretical Bases of Indo-European Linguistics*. New York, NY: Routledge.

Lemprière's Classical Dictionary of Proper Names Mentioned in Ancient Authors. 1986. Boston, MA: Routledge.

Levi, Peter. 1981. *Atlas of the Greek World*. New York, NY: Facts on File.

Levinson, S. 1983. *Pragmatics*. Cambridge, ENG: Cambridge Univ. Press.

Lipton, Gladys C. 1989. *Practical Handbook to Elementary Foreign Language Programs*. Lincolnwood, IL: National Textbook Co.

Littlewood, William T. 1980. "Form and Meaning in Language Teaching Methodology." *Modern Language Journal* 64: 441–45.

Logan, Margaret, 1992. *C.A.T. Caper: A Mystery*. New York, NY: Fawcett Crest.

Loschky, Lester, and Robert Bley-Vroman. 1993. "Grammar and Task-Based Methodology." In Graham Crookes and Susan M. Gass, eds., *Tasks and Language Learning: Integrating Theory and Practice*. Clevedon, ENG: Multilingual Matters. 123–67.

Lowell, James Russell. 1887. *Democracy and Other Addresses*. Boston, MA: Houghton, Mifflin.

Lyons, J. 1977. *Semantics*. 2 vols. Cambridge, ENG: Cambridge Univ. Press.

MacCormack, Sabine. 1991. *Religion in the Andes: Vision and Imagination in Early Colonial Peru*. Princeton, NJ: Princeton Univ. Press.

MacKendrick, Paul. 1969. *The Iberian Stones Speak*. New York, NY: Funk & Wagnalls.

Macwhinney, B., and E. Bates. 1989. *The Crosslinguistic Study of Sentence Processing*. Cambridge, ENG: Cambridge Univ. Press.

Magnan, Sally Sisloff. 1991. "Social Attitudes: The Key to Directing the Evolution of Grammar Teaching." In James E. Alatis, ed., *Georgetown University Round Table in Languages and Linguistics 1991: Linguistics and Language Pedagogy The State of the Art*. Washington, DC: Georgetown Univ. Press. 323–34.

Manley, John. 1991. *The Atlas of Past Worlds*. London, ENG: Cassell.

Marx, Walter, ed. 1981. *Columbus' Letter on His First Voyage*. N.P.: To Phrontisterion.

Mathes, Michael. 1985. *The America's* [sic] *First Academic Library: Santa Cruz de Tlatelolco*. Sacramento, CA: California State Library Foundation.

Matthews, P.H. 1972. *Inflectional Morphology: A Theoretical Study Based on Aspects of Latin Verb Conjugation*. Cambridge, ENG: Cambridge Univ. Press.

Mayer, Jean. 1978. "Education Now." *Saturday Review* Feb. 18: 45.

McCarthy, M. 1991. *Discourse Analysis for Language Teachers*. Cambridge, ENG: Cambridge Univ. Press.

McEwin, C.K., and W.M. Alexander. 1987. *Middle Level Teacher Education Programs: A Second Survey (1986-87)*. Boone, NC: Appalachian State Univ.

McLaughlin, Barry. 1987. *Theories of Second Language Learning*. London, ENG: Edward Arnold.

Merenbloom, Elliot Y. 1988. *Developing Effective Middle Schools through Faculty Participation*. 2nd ed. Columbus, OH: National Middle School Assoc.

Moeller, Alerdine J. 1993. "Making the Match: Middle Level Goals and Foreign Language Instruction." *Schools in the Middle* 3: 35–38.

_____. 1994. "Content-Based Foreign Language Instruction in the Middle Schools: An Experiential Learning Approach." *FLA* 27: 538–44.

Moffitt, John F., and Santiago Sebastián. 1996. *O Brave New People: The European Invention of the American Indian*. Albuquerque, NM: Univ. of New Mexico Press.

Moore, Francis X., III. 1995. "Section 504 and the Americans with Disabilities Act: Accommodating the Learning Disabled Student in the Foreign Language Curriculum." *ADFL Bulletin* 26.2: 59–62.

Muffaletto, Robert, and Nancy Nelson Knupfer, eds. 1993. *Computers in Education: Social, Political, and Historical Perspectives*. Cresskill, NJ: Hampton Press.

Nation, I. S. P. 1990. *Teaching and Learning Vocabulary*. New York, NY: Newbury House.

National Association of Secondary School Principals. 1986. *An Agenda for Excellence at the Middle Level*. Reston, VA: National Assoc. of Secondary School Principals.

National Joint Committee on Learning Disabilities. 1994. *Collective Perspectives on Issues Affecting Learning Disabilities*. Austin, TX: PRO-ED Publishers.

National Middle School Association. 1986. *Professional Certification and Preparation for the Middle Level*. Columbus, OH: National Middle School Assoc.

Newmeyer, F.J., ed. 1988. *Linguistics: The Cambridge Survey*. Cambridge, ENG: Cambridge Univ. Press.

Nyquist, J.D., and D.H. Wulff. 1996. *Working Effectively with Graduate Assistants*. Thousand Oaks, CA: Sage Publications.

O'Brien, Wendy, and Tracey Cullen. 1995. *Archaeology in the Classroom: A Resource Guide for Teachers and Parents*. Boston, MA: Archaeological Inst. of America.

Odlin, Terence. 1989. *Language Transfer*. Cambridge, ENG: Cambridge Univ. Press.

Omaggio (Hadley), Alice. 1993. *Teaching Language in Context*. 2nd ed. Boston, MA: Heinle and Heinle.

Osorio Romero, Ignacio. 1981. "Jano o la literatura neolatina de México." *Humanistica Lovaniensia* 30: 124–55.

Pagden, Anthony. 1990. *Spanish Imperialism and the Political Imagination: Studies in European and Spanish-American Social and Political Theory 1513–1830*. New Haven, CT: Yale Univ. Press.

_____. 1995 . *Lords of All the World: Ideologies of Empire in Spain, Britain and France c. 1500–1800*. New Haven, CT: Yale Univ. Press.

Palencia-Roth, Michael. 1990. "Transformations of Latinity: The New-Old Civilization of Latin America." *Comparative Civilizations Review* 23: 19–39.

Palmer, Robert, ed. 1991. *Historical Atlas of the World*. Chicago, IL: Rand McNally.

Past Worlds: The Times Atlas of Archaeology. 1988. Maplewood, NJ: Hammond.

Patterson, William T. 1982. *The Genealogical Structure of Spanish: A Correlation of Basic Word Properties*. Washington, DC: Univ. Press of America.

Peter Martyr. 1892. *De orbe novo Petri Martyris Anglerii decades octo*. Ed. Joachim Torres Asensio. Madrid, SP: Gomez Fuentenebro.

_____. 1912. *De orbe novo: The Eight Decades of Peter Martyr D'Anghiera*. 2 vols. Trans. Francis A. MacNutt. New York, NY: G.P. Putnam's Sons.

Phillips, June K. 1984. "Practical Implications of Recent Research in Reading." *FLA* 17: 285–96.

Pinker, S. 1994. *The Language Instinct*. New York, NY: William Morrow.

Pinsent, John. 1990. *Greek Mythology*. New York, NY: Peter Bedrick Books.

Radice, Betty. 1973. *Who's Who in the Ancient World*. New York, NY: Viking Penguin.

Ravitch, Diane. 1983. *The Troubled Crusade: American Education, 1945-1980*. New York, NY: Basic Books.

Richards, Jack C. 1990. *The Language Teaching Matrix*. New York, NY: Cambridge Univ. Press.

_____, and Theodore S. Rodgers. 1986. *Approaches and Methods in Language Teaching: A Description and Analysis*. Cambridge, ENG: Cambridge Univ. Press.

_____, and Charles Lockhart. 1994. *Reflective Teaching in Second Language Classrooms*. New York, NY: Cambridge Univ. Press.

Room, Adrian. 1990. *NTC's Classical Dictionary: The Origins of the Names of Characters in Classical Mythology*. Lincolnwood, IL: National Textbook Co.

Ross, J.R. 1970. "Gapping and the Order of Constituents." In M. Bierwisch, et al., eds.,

Progress in Linguistics. The Hague, NETH: Mouton. 249–60.

Rusciolelli, Judith. 1995. "Student Responses to Reading Strategies Instruction." *FLA* 28: 262–73.

Sacks, David. 1995. *Encyclopedia of the Ancient Greek World.* New York, NY: Facts on File.

_____. 1997. *A Dictionary of the Ancient Greek World.* New York, NY: Oxford Univ. Press.

Sapir, E. 1921. *Language.* New York, NY: Harcourt Brace Jovanovich.

Scarre, Chris. 1995. *The Penguin Historical Atlas of Ancient Rome.* New York, NY: Viking Penguin. Rev. Hans Pohlsander, *CO* 73 (1996): 103, 105.

Searle, J. 1969. *Speech Acts: An Essay in the Philosophy of Language.* Cambridge, ENG: Cambridge Univ. Press.

Seed, Patricia. 1995. *Ceremonies of Possession in Europe's Conquest of the New World, 1492–1640.* Cambridge, ENG: Cambridge Univ. Press.

Sherron, Gene T., and Judith V. Boettcher. 1997. *Distance Learning: The Shift to Interactivity.* CAUSE Professional Papers 17. Boulder, CO: CAUSE.

Sherry, Lorraine. 1996. "Issues in Distance Learning." *International Journal of Distance Education* 1: 337–65.

Simon, Paul. 1991. "Priority: Public Relations." *FLA* 24: 13–18.

Sloan, Douglas, ed. 1984. *The Computer in Education: A Critical Perspective.* New York, NY: Teachers Coll. Press.

Smith, F. 1988. *Understanding Reading: A Psycholinguistic Analysis of Reading and Learning to Read.* Hillsdale, NJ: Lawrence Erlbaum Associates.

Solomon, Jon, ed. 1993. *Accessing Antiquity: The Computerization of Classical Studies.* Tucson, AZ: Univ. of Arizona Press.

Sparks, Richard, et al. 1992. "The Effects of Multisensory Structured Language Instruction on Native Language and Foreign Language Aptitude Skills of At-Risk High School Foreign Language Learners." *Annals of Dyslexia* 42: 25–53.

_____, and Leonore Ganschow. 1993. "Identifying and Instructing At-Risk Foreign Language Learners in College." In David P. Benseler, ed., *The Dynamics of Language Program Direction.* Boston: Heinle and Heinle. 173–99.

Standards for Foreign Language Learning: Preparing for the 21st Century. 1996. Lawrence, KS: Allen Press.

Stanislawski, Dan. 1947. "Early Spanish Town Planning in the New World." *Geographical Review* 30: 94–105.

Steck, Francisco Borgia, O.F.M. 1944. *El primero colegio de America: Santa Cruz de Tlalteloco.* Mexico City, MEX: Centro de estudios Franciscanos.

Swaffar, Janet, Katherine Arens, and Heidi Byrnes. 1991. *Reading for Meaning: An Integrated Approach to Language Learning.* Englewood Cliffs, NJ: Prentice-Hall.

Talbert, Richard. 1985. *Atlas of Classical History.* New York, NY: Routledge.

_____. 1992. "Mapping the Classical World: Major Atlases and Map Series 1872–1990." *Journal of Roman Archaeology* 5: 5–38.

Tanner, Marie. 1993. *The Last Descendant of Aeneas: The Hapsburgs and the Mythic Image of the Emperor.* New Haven, CT: Yale Univ. Press.

Taylor, J.R. 1989. *Linguistic Categorization: Prototypes in Linguistic Theory.* Oxford, ENG: Clarendon Press; Oxford Univ. Press.

Taylor, Robert, ed. 1980. *The Computer in the School: Tutor, Tool, Tutee.* New York, NY: Teachers Coll. Press.

Thomas, Russell. 1962. *The Search for a Common Learning: General Education, 1800–*

1960. New York, NY: McGraw Hill.

Todorov, Tzvetan. 1982. *The Conquest of America: The Question of the Other*. Trans. Richard Howard. New York, NY: Harper and Row.

Ur, Penny. 1988. *Grammar Practice Activities: A Practical Guide for Teachers*. Cambridge, ENG: Cambridge Univ. Press.

U.S. Department of Commerce, Bureau of the Census. 1996. *Current Population Reports: Population Projections of the United States by Age, Sex, Race, and Hispanic Origin: 1995-2050*. Document P25-1130. Washington, DC: USGPO.

Vars, Gordon F. 1987. *Interdisciplinary Teaching in the Middle Grades: Why and How*. Columbus, OH: National Middle School Assoc.

Villagrá, Gaspar Pérez de. 1992 . *Historia de la Nueva México, 1610*. Ed. and trans. Miguel Encinias, et al. Albuquerque, NM: Univ. of New Mexico Press.

Volz, Robert. 1969. *The Concept of Empire in Western Europe from the Fifth to the Fourteenth Century*. Trans. Sheila Ann Ogilvie. New York, NY: Harper and Row.

Vygotsky, Lev. 1962. *Thought and Language*. Trans. Myshlenie Rech. Ed. Alex Kozulin. Cambridge, MA: M.I.T. Press.

Walker, Alexis J. 1996. "Cooperative Learning in the College Classroom." *Family Relations* 45: 327-36.

Wallace, C. 1992. *Reading*. Oxford, ENG: Oxford Univ. Press.

Wilson, R.J.A. 1990. *Sicily under the Roman Empire: The Archaeology of a Roman Province, 36 BC-AD 535*. London, ENG: Aris & Phillips.

Winterfeld, Henry. 1971. *Mystery of the Roman Ransom*. New York, NY: Harcourt Brace Jovanovich.

_____. 1984. *Detectives in Togas*. San Diego, CA: Harcourt Brace Jovanovich.

Yates, Frances A. 1975. *Astraea: The Imperial Theme in the Sixteenth Century*. Boston, MA: Routledge and Kegan Paul.

Yule, G. 1996. *A Study of Language*. 2nd ed. Cambridge, ENG: Cambridge Univ. Press.

Zimmerman, J.E. 1964. *Dictionary of Classical Mythology*. New York, NY: Harper and Row.

Index of Topics

Only major topics are indexed; in general, names are included only when appearing as topics discussed, not merely as citations.